Dear Lindsay,

I would love
to have you join our
harmonious haven —

Most fondly,
Stella

FALLING

Author's Note: This work is a memoir and memories are imperfect. With the characters' permission, I took copious notes and did my best under stressful conditions to represent their experiences. The names of the women inmates and staff of the Department of Corrections have been changed to protect their identities.

Falling by Karen Andrea Campbell Published by Karen Campbell Writes Corp.
www.karencampbellwrites.com
P.O. Box 221 N Central Ave. PMB 538, Medford, OR 97501

Cover by Cornelius Matteo

ISBN: 978-1-09834-525-9
Library of Congress Cataloging in Publication data TK
www.cmatteophotography.com

Falling: A Prison Memoir

Hard Lessons and the Redemption of the Woman Next Door

by

Karen Andrea Campbell

karencampbellwrites.com

CONTENTS

PROLOGUE

Fall v. (falling, fallen) – 1. Move downward quickly and without control; 2. To become less or lower; 3. To be captured or defeated in a battle.

Falling also means the day you enter prison. It is a backward collapse through a trapdoor. You become a body without control. Time is meaningless and only exists breath to breath. Cuffed, you are led to transport. It is your first submersion into total obedience—your opinions, your anger, your tears are futile. The self disappears.

JAIL

I am about to step into a jail. It is the first step of my prison sentence. I am leaving my life behind and entering prison for six years and three months. My hands are in cuffs, locked to a waist chain. Deputies are on either side of me, squeezing my arms, showing me who is in charge. I am connected to a rough-looking woman by a chain that jangles along the floor behind me. I glance to each side at the male deputies wearing uniforms with handcuffs dangling from their hips and radios squawking in their hands. The men have thick arms and torsos, their eyes are flat, staring straight ahead.

The metal doors of the jail crash open, my ears ring, my teeth rattle, and the hairs stand up on my arms. The noise screams, *"You are not free, you are here for punishment and this is your life now."* We step into the jail and the doors slam shut behind us. *That's why it's called the **Slammer**.*

"The Tank, Baker. Keep moving," says the deputy, without making eye contact. Our chains clang as we walk down a sloping cement hallway that ends at a metal door. The deputy lets go of my

1

arm, unshackles the chains, and turns the key in the door. I am cold with fear.

The door opened to a concrete 10-x-12-foot room, a room that could easily be hosed down. It was crammed with women. Women standing, women sitting on a concrete bench. Women covering the entire floor, sitting or lying down in the filth.

I stepped over the threshold into the abyss. The door slammed behind me, and I dissolved to liquid. There was nothing to hold on to. The woman who was in chains behind me faded into the room. Women with haunted faces grudgingly yielded me crouch space on the floor against the wall, where I hugged my knees into my chest.

I didn't bother concealing my inspection of the skin now touching me on all sides. Arms and legs quivered and jumped. Frantic chatter rose up around me like a wave—sex, drugs, crews, gangs, pimps. One woman hollered at an overhead camera, "Let me outta the Tank! I want my phone call!"

The Tank was not the drunk tank of the movies, and this was more than alcohol. The toxins were leeching out of their systems. The stale odor was inescapable. One woman's face erupted in blemishes, which she scratched at maniacally. I could not imagine a worse place to come down. I just hoped no one would puke.

I felt no kinship with these women. I wanted personal space. I was wearing a wrist brace from a recent surgery, and I kept a close watch on my body and boundaries. I wanted to scrub my hands with soap but there was none in sight. What did the guards think we would do with it? Swallow it? Make a shiv? Maybe the jailers didn't think we deserved soap. If we got sick and died, it would be one less mouth to feed. *This is my life now.*

I was in the Tank for only an hour when my name was called by a stern-faced female deputy. The women started shouting and complaining. "She just got here. How come Miss High-and-Mighty gets outta here first?"

"She's got a wrist cast," the deputy said, gesturing at my splint. "She's State property now. We don't want anything to happen to our property." She slammed the door to make a point and turned the key. "Let's go, Baker." *I am State property.*

I was led down the hall to the showers. "Strip search goes like this, Baker: Clothes off, one article at a time. Shake out each piece." I was too humiliated to look the deputy in the eye. I just stared at my feet on the cement jail floor. *Those are my forty-seven-year-old feet standing on a cement floor in a jail.* "Get used to skins, Baker. Where you're going, they are not just for your first big day," she said.

I stood fully nude and rotated, thinking the humiliation was over and I could move on to the shower and delousing. But I was wrong. Instead, in a blasé voice, she said, "Turn around, Baker. Now squat down, spread your butt cheeks, and cough." I had no choice. I did as I was told. But it was as if I left my body and floated above myself.

When I was showered and dressed in maroon scrubs with plastic slip-on sandals, we set out for wherever I would be taken.

It had been two years since the car accident, the accident that was my fault, the accident that killed an innocent woman, the accident that killed my husband, Tom. I knew I would be sentenced to prison, and now here I was.

Would I survive the mental anguish of what I'd done? Or would the guilt and shame change me into someone else unrecognizable even to myself? I didn't know. Physically, I was still recuperating from the accident. A few months before sentencing, I'd had my last surgery for a wrist fracture that wouldn't heal, and since the State didn't want its property damaged, I would be placed in solitary confinement.

The deputy turned the key and opened a metal door. She didn't waste words, ordering me inside. I stepped into an 8-x-10 cell with a metal cot and a plastic 1-inch mattress. The door slammed behind me, the keys jangling in the lock.

The walls and bright lights closed in on me, I felt myself being dragged down. My arms reached out and grasped at nothing. My legs buckled and swayed. I drew my arms into the center of my body and closed my eyes, clasping my hands together over my pounding heart. A loud shout by a woman nearby brought me back to the bright room and my jail scrubs. How long had I been standing in place?

I looked around the room. After meeting the women in the Tank, I thought maybe a single cell wouldn't be so bad. It might be a place to collect myself, a place of safety. On the mattress was a heap of unfolded sheets and I wondered if they were clean. Without touching them, I bent over to give it a sniff. *Cheap laundry soap, itchy.* "At least it's clean," I said to the walls. My voice echoed.

"Clean," I said, louder. The walls bounced it back. Was that *my* voice on the walls of a jail cell? I sounded throaty, emotionless. I didn't want to think or feel. I needed to *do* something.

I lifted the sheets. There were a scratchy wool blanket and a piece of foam in the shape of a pizza box: *a pillow?* I got busy and made the bed, tucking the corners like I had done for years in my home with my two daughters. *Don't think of your home, you don't have one anymore.*

I turned in a slow circle and looked at the room. It had an overhead camera and a stainless-steel sink/toilet combo, just like the Tank. But now I had a small bar of what looked like lye soap, a bendable

4

toothbrush, and a tube of cheap toothpaste. The walls were bright white under the lights. The door was metal and had a pass slot with a skinny vertical window.

As I sat on the hard cot, I thought of my husband, Tom, his smile, his exuberance, now extinguished. I thought of the innocent woman I had killed. I thought of my daughters. What were they each doing and thinking at this moment, knowing that their mom was on the way to prison for six years? The sudden pain was crushing. I had to will myself to inhale. I didn't dare think too deeply about any of them. *Keep it together, Karen.* I stood up and paced around the cell. How would I make it through six years like this? I might have slept or passed out. I wouldn't remember those first hours. It would be another blank in my memory, this time from shock. I was falling hard.

It had been a beautiful spring day on Mount Hood in Oregon. I decided to go for one last run—Glade Trail, the 6.3-mile ski trail that starts at Timberline Lodge and winds downhill to the town of Government Camp. My husband, Tom, was tired and told me he would meet me at a bar in the town, so I set off with a seasoned bunch of skiers. We started down a gentle slope, whooping and tucking for speed. It was dusk, the day had been warm. The light grew flat and the going got tough. Our group would be gliding along, then suddenly we would hit a patch of snow that had been in the sun and turned to "peanut butter." My fellow hard-core skiers grunted it out with screaming quadriceps. For me, the weakest in the pack, it was quicksand. I lost count after falling ten times. On my final fall, I lay in the snow and cried with exhaustion. But in the dimming light, I saw the silhouette of my group waiting for me. It would be dark soon and we had to get off the mountain. These were the type of skiers who summit mountains and ski down. They would not leave me behind. I had to get up for their safety.

Finally, the lights of town were ahead. We slid down onto the snowy street, I unclipped my skis, loosened my boots, and slung my skis over my shoulder for the uphill walk to the bar. I didn't know if I could make the hike. I needed food and water.

My memories from here on out come to me in snapshots. I remember entering a steamy, packed bar. I see Tom's beautiful profile, people huddled in his glow as usual. One of my crew from the Glade Trail, Sean, calls out, "Get her a glass of wine, she just did the Glade Trail!" Blank. The second snapshot: a big glass filled with golden wine. Blank again. The third snapshot: Tom and I loading the car. Always a gentleman, Tom opens my door. I am not driving. But from the passenger seat, I watch as Tom weaves around the front of the car, losing his balance several times. It's not the ice. He's drunk. My final snapshot of the day: we are backing out, Tom at the wheel. We hear a loud rap on the driver's-side window. Tom rolls it down. A sweet face peers in, a friend from town. "Damn it, you guys," he says tenderly, "I want what you have. I want someone to love me." Tom chuckles, then rolls up his window. In the light from the bar, our friend stands waving goodbye in the snow.

We didn't know that would be the last time we saw our friend. He would die of an aggressive brain tumor six months later. We didn't know that my husband, Tom, would die on the way home.

Tom backed the car up and turned for the drive down the mountain. After that, my memory is dark. Somewhere on that drive, we must have switched drivers.

In my solitary cell, through the vents, I could hear the other women hollering. Some were swearing and ranting. Others demanded attention. The voices never went quiet and the hallway lights never went dim. There was no clock; I could not tell when one day ended and another began. I tried to gauge the passing of days according to meals and routines. Breakfast started a new day, and unless the guards were trying to mess with me, oatmeal meant morning. After they collected the tray, I would pace five steps, turn, five steps, back and forth until my pulse was 120 beats per minute. Stretch. Read the toothpaste tube. Later, lunch. It had to be, it wasn't oatmeal. Nap. Later, I would pace again, do sit-ups and reread the toothpaste tube, memorizing the ingredients. Wait for dinner—or breakfast? It all started melting together. I kept moving so I wouldn't think.

A loud rap on my cell door shook me from numbness. "Shower time," and keys jangled in the lock. The door opened to a dour, formidable female guard.

Helga of the Birch Boughs led me to a cold, tiled room and stood by as I stripped off my jail scrubs. I wondered whether I was to be naked in front of people for the next six years. I looked down at my body under the stream of tepid water and noticed that some of my scars from the accident were starting to flatten out, looking less angry. My seven surgeries had left my body like a railroad yard: scars crisscrossed my legs, ribs, torso front and back. I had them on my face. I had been shattered to bits and patched together. But the surgery to correct my back and pelvis had failed, and now I was crooked. I had to wear a heel lift in order to stand straight.

The deputy took the lift away during my first strip search, so I stood in the shower, one leg an inch and a half shorter than the other. But I knew the fact I could stand at all was a miracle. After the shower, I dressed in fresh maroon jail scrubs and I kept the wrist splint off just

7

long enough to test my range of motion and give it some semi-fresh air. It felt frail, but I had gotten used to feeling frail. I put the brace back on and tightened it down.

On the return march to my cell, I asked my captor the time and she said it was 8:20 p.m. My guess was off by about five hours. I thought it was midday. I lay down and hoped for sleep of any form under the bright lights. It was not to be. A new yowler had joined the women in the Solitary wing. She had a deep voice and barked out complaints, "Let me outta here, I got rights! When's my phone call?" Then, unimaginative swearing. Eventually, she wore herself out and switched from anger to grief. She cried so hard it sounded like she was choking, then she whimpered and went quiet. I knew I had made people cry like that.

It was the alcohol that turned an accident into a felony. It was March 24, 2003. I read the accident report like anyone else, horrified by the details. It was a complicated T-bone mash of metal and bodies. Tom and the other woman died at the scene. I was life-flighted to the local trauma unit.

My uncle, a doctor, said to my father, "Sam, you need to be prepared; Karen may not make it. The complications from infection and multiple surgeries just might be too much."

My older sister, Christine, told me she got the call from our father in the middle of the night. When she arrived at the hospital, I was hooked up to lights, tubes, and machines. The police wanted to talk to me, but she stayed in the room all night to protect me and keep them out. She told me that I briefly woke and tried to take out my breathing tube. I was asking about Tom.

The next morning my daughters arrived at the hospital. They were thirteen and sixteen years old at the time. A fierce kind of wisdom was forced upon them that day, and they would never be the same. Haley told me years later that it was still hard to think about that day. "It was kind of a blur. When I saw you in the hospital for the first time, I fainted. You were unrecognizable, bruised, bloody, and broken. You couldn't talk. You signed T-O-M. No one had told you that he didn't make it."

Christine told me months later that Dad was the one who told me Tom was dead. I guess she thought there was only so much I could handle. "We were standing around your hospital bed, the four of us— Dad, Nikki, Haley, and me." She stopped talking, struggling with her emotions. The corners of her eyes slanted down and tears leaked over the brim. "The look on your face when you heard the news about Tom… You needed your girls to keep you going." She paused and wept, hands limp in her lap, head down. I wept with her, humbled at her anguish. She went on in a whisper. "There was a light in the room. It was not from the machines." She lifted her head and stared at me, taking ragged breaths. "Everyone saw it. I have never seen a light like this. It was the colors, like an overexposed picture and a little foggy, like you were there and not there." Then, barely audible, "The light was trying to take you away." She dropped her head again. Her long dark hair fell like a curtain over her face.

While drifting in and out of consciousness, I recall two visual snapshots through the bed rails. The first was the tall, thin bodies of my daughters. They were gripping the bed rails, their posture bent in pain. Their stepfather was dead. Their mother might die. I wanted to touch them, but I could not move. *I'm still here.* That was the day I made The Deal. Raised secularly, I had not been a praying woman, but that day I promised wholeheartedly to God that I would endure anything to avoid my daughters losing their mother. I begged.

The second snapshot. It was the same view through the hospital bed rails but on a different day. I could see the torso and feet of two men in expensive suits and quality leather shoes. I cannot recall the conversation but I have an auditory memory of their polished and practical speaking tones. *Lawyers*. I knew they would be back. But all I cared about was staying alive for my daughters; I would endure anything for them.

"Baker, chow!" As the metal slot banged open, the smell of cheap meat and grease slid forward on the slot shelf into my cell. The guard moved along the row—first the keys, then the slot slamming open, followed by a garbled name echoing down the line. I rose from the cot and picked up a beige tray containing a whirly gelatinous square of what appeared to be the main dish, accompanied by a scoop of instant mashed potatoes. Army green beans were in the next compartment, then yellow Jell-O and a half-pint of milk.

At the time, I felt so low, I was grateful to be fed. I drank the milk and ate the instant potatoes and green beans as the cells momentarily quieted. Later, a guard came and collected my tray. I could hear him jangling along the hallway. The slots rattled open and closed but the lights stayed on. Some blind hours later, I decided it must be night and lay down on the cot staring up at the ceiling. I tried to say things to myself like, *It could be worse, this could be some shithole jail in a third world country. I could be sleeping on the ground, I could have had bugs for dinner*. It made the metal cot and mattress less miserable, but still, it was like trying to sleep on a cookie sheet covered with a kindergarten nap mat. I tried to lie as flat as I could to spread out the weight of my body. But it wasn't just the mattress that kept me awake. The fluorescent lights glared down on me and I could hear the shouting of women in cells nearby. One woman was moaning rhythmically; another burst out foul curses, many I had never heard. This was my world now. I lay sleepless. What would my children do without their mother? I was scared—but not angry. The sentencing was fair.

The evening before my sentencing had been quiet. For the previous year, I had been living with my dear friend Gerry, whom I had known for thirteen years. Because prison was certain, I had left my house and pared down my belongings to a few plastic tubs and boxes that would fit in my sister's attic. In the days I was still free, I hugged my daughters, smelled their hair, listened to their quiet whispers at night in the room they shared. I stared at each of them, trying to sear their images into my brain, saving them for the years we would be apart.

We decided that my younger daughter, Haley, should move to California to live with her father. If she left after her freshman year in high school, she could settle in with her dad, be ready for a new school, and try out for the fall volleyball team. It was the only thing to do, the best thing, we thought, for Haley.

When the time came, I packed Haley's life into duffels, childhood toys and teenage makeup all jammed together. It all had to go or get thrown out; there would be no family home in Oregon. Before she left, to console us both, I wrapped her in a blanket on the couch. I cuddled next to her and stroked her glossy brown hair and held her feet, the same way I did when she was a baby. We sat like that until she fell asleep.

Her best friend, her best friend's mother, and I took her to the airport. We walked her as far as security allowed and said goodbye. Helpless, we watched her pass through scanners, leaving behind her house, her sister, her friends, her left-outside hitter position on the volleyball team, and her mother. We watched as she turned and waved, walked down the concourse, turned and waved again, the last time just standing there crying for all to see. She finally turned and we watched until the very last sight of her duffel bag disappeared.

Nikki, who was eighteen and in college, spent the last night with me before sentencing. Just as she had done when she was a little girl, she slept with one hand on my cheek. Even as we shifted in bed during the night, she sought me out. As I lay awake beside her, I memorized her face. In sleep, she was a young angel with tangled curls and rose-bud lips, mumbling every once in a while. She would wake as a grown woman with the weight of the world on her slim shoulders. She will be living under the circumstances of forced emancipation. *What have I done?* I begged silently, *Please, please give me a chance to make this up to you, my first-born child, my child of stuffed seals and blanket capes, of Bobbi Brown makeup and thrift stores.* I had more to teach my girls. I wasn't done yet. Who else was going to explain how to use silverware from the outside to the inside of the plate, or how to walk in New York? Me, their mother. They needed me.

Finally, the night was over. I untangled myself from Nikki and stood before the mirror. *I am going to prison today.* I looked exhausted. I used to be a tall, blue-eyed, vivacious woman. I looked like I had aged twenty years since the accident. My cheekbones poked through parched skin, my eyes were ringed with dark circles. The woman in the mirror may not survive the prison sentence of six years and three months.

I put on the clothes that I had carefully chosen the night before when I stood before my closet and wondered, *What shall I wear to prison tomorrow?* Then, *How can I even be thinking about this?* I settled on a Chico's travel ensemble in basic black. Stretch-wear for comfort, black for the grime. I heard footsteps on the stairs. Gerry was up, and soon the rest of my family would be arriving to go to the courthouse. I slipped out of the room and went downstairs. Gerry was standing in her Great Pondering Pose. She stood with her feet apart, one thin arm wrapped like a vise across her waist, the other hand on her cheek. She looked up at me with grim dread. We didn't speak, there was nothing to say. Gerry pushed a plate toward me. It was my final planned breakfast: a perfectly ripe Hass avocado with cracked black pepper on a Triscuit and dark coffee with cream. I tried to enjoy it, but I could barely swallow.

Nikki came down the stairs, dressed in somber clothing. I held her carefully. I was afraid the grief would snap her bones. One by one my friends and family gathered at the house. My father, Sam, and his wife, Audrey, arrived. Sam, normally energetic, stood with slumped shoulders and none of his usual bounce. Audrey held Nikki. Christine had dark circles around her eyes. She and her son, Shane, had come, to be present for the sentencing. We all hugged and muttered brave affirmations before the drive to the courthouse for sentencing. My family was exhausted; it was time to go.

When we arrived at the courthouse, my close friends Jack, Robin, and Loretta were waiting. They joined our group, and we walked silently to the courtroom. My two defense attorneys were waiting outside the courtroom with grim expressions.

The lead defense attorney stepped forward. "The district attorney has broken the mediated agreement of two counts of concurrent Manslaughter II and a seventy-five-month sentence. He's going for full charges. The D.A. is pressing for two consecutive counts of Manslaughter I, a minimum ten-year sentence, possibly twenty. That way, he might get two consecutive sentences of Manslaughter II, twelve years."

I felt liquid. We had endured so much loss and pain, how is it possible that things could get worse? I had resigned myself to six years. I did the math regarding my daughters' ages, my elderly father's age, my *own* age, and barring illness and catastrophe, imagined life on the other side. How would my children cope? Would my father still be alive? I remember thinking that perhaps the best thing they could do was just to forget about me and get on with their lives.

I entered the courtroom in a daze, my lawyers guiding me to a table before the bench. My heart was racing. My nose and the roof of my mouth tingled.

I peeked over my shoulder to see Christine, Shane, my father, Audrey, and Nikki seated in the first row of benches behind us. I could hear my sister weeping. She was clutching a stuffed green frog that we both had shared as adults in times of sorrow. Nikki cried on my father's shoulder.

The judge entered. "All rise."

I had to push on the table to stand. When he began to speak, it was clear he was furious with the district attorney for throwing out the mediated agreement between the victim's family and me. Would the judge's anger work in my favor? I didn't know. It all came down to the daughter and grandson of the woman I killed in the oncoming lane. The judge asked the victim's family to rise and to state what they thought was a fair sentence. They held my life in their hands. Would they say I should serve longer?

I turned to see them rise; they were shaken. The mother and son faced the judge and tearfully stated that they agreed that six years was long enough for my children to be away from their mother. The gavel went down. I felt my legs go weak with relief. I was to serve six years and three months. Given the choice to punish, they chose compassion. For my children and the entire family.

I turned to see my daughter, sister, nephew, father, and friends embracing and crying with this family. I witnessed this family's grace and forgiveness. At that moment I felt a shift deep in my being, down to my cells. It was a sense of rising up. There was no other direction to go except toward a life worthy of their grace. It was the moment where everything stopped sliding downhill. Instead, there was a chance for all of us to move in another direction. The victim's family and my family would go home and try to pick up the pieces of their lives, and I would go to prison.

A female bailiff stood before me with a grim expression on her face. She was holding heavy chains and handcuffs. She had been in the courtroom and witnessed the tension and emotion of the sentencing. As she brought the chains to me, her eyes were moist, which surprised me. She fastened the chains around my waist and cuffed my wrists. The sliding links sounded like a door closing between the free world and imprisonment. She stood back and spoke with her eyes: *You got lucky.*

She pointed the way to a hallway that led to a room where another woman was shackled at the waist, just as I was. She looked rough, with yesterday's hair and tear-smeared mascara. The bailiff ordered us to stand in line and linked the two of us together on a single chain. I had seen this in prison movies like *Shawshank Redemption*. Now it was me. I was chained to a woman I never would have met in my ordinary life. I was cold with fear.

We shuffled awkwardly toward the large, unmarked white van that would take us from the courthouse directly to jail, my first stop on the way to prison. My lawyer explained that the paperwork had to catch up to me so I would do jail time anywhere from two days to two weeks before going to prison. What did it matter? It was all captivity. As we entered the van, we were released from the chain that bound us together. Hands still cuffed at the waist, we carefully loaded ourselves onto the bench seats behind a cage that separated felons from free people. The van rolled up and over a hill and traveled away from shops and homes, away from what used to be my life.

Each day in Solitary, a nurse visited me in my cell. I looked forward to the visits; they offered a break in the boredom. Each nurse weighed about two hundred and fifty pounds, some of them looked as ragged as me. None of them seemed to have the energy to care whether I was ill or in pain. *Is that what working in a jail or prison does to a person?*

The life-saving event was the book cart, which appeared the second or third day. It meant I could read something besides the toothpaste tube. The book cart choices were the Bible, addiction recovery guides, and tawdry romance novels. I chose the tawdry novel and the Bible, sin and repentance. At least with the Bible, I would never have to read the toothpaste tube again.

After what must have been three or four days, I no longer slept in long stretches, only in short periods when the women in the nearby cells stopped ranting and screaming. I guessed that the guards kept watch from the overhead cameras and showed up at the door only if the woman was hurting their property or herself. Surveillance had to be the reason the lights stayed on. I tried to imagine the poor schmuck guard whose job it was to watch the loonies on the monitors in the Solitary wing. I'll bet he or she counted the hours until it was time to go home. But at least they got to go home.

In Solitary, my brain just kept circling like a buzzard. I went over and over the story of the accident. I wondered about different endings. What would have happened if I had eaten something before we drove? What if I had not skied that last run? Had it just been that one big glass of wine? What if I hadn't switched places with Tom behind the wheel? Would we both be dead? Or would we have somehow avoided the accident? I sat down on the cot and looked at my narrow body, lost in the folds of scrub fabric. The skin on my exposed arms was mottled under the lights. I pulled them into my scrub top so I didn't have to look.

I am a living miracle. I broke over twenty bones in the accident, including my face and teeth. I lacerated my spleen, GI tract, and bladder, and punctured a lung. I was put back together in a trauma hospital. The surgeries began on the night I arrived at the hospital and continued for days afterward. My medical file was Bible thick.

The next series of surgeries were performed by the orthopedists. They reconstructed my back and pelvis and placed an external fixation device into and around my hips. This hip halo was gigantic. It held my broken bones in place in hopes that I would fuse.

A team from Rehab, from my own profession, came several days later to get me out of bed. It took three of them. They lowered the bed rail, and inch by inch, like a glacier, I swiveled toward the edge. I did my best to push through my elbows to keep my upper body lined up with my legs.

"Wait! Please, go slow," I begged, trying to steady my breathing. But it was hard with broken ribs, a feeding tube, a catheter, and a bag hanging out of my lung; every inch was hard-won. The attempts out of bed continued, all were excruciating. *This is what it will feel like to walk.* But I kept trying, I knew I had to. I shut out the pain and kept going. I started with two steps, then worked my way to the door.

Once I was discharged home from the Rehab unit, my medical care was transferred to an orthopedist at the hospital where I worked. Like me, he was a skier and had heard about my accident. He walked into the exam room and took in the spectacle of me: an emaciated woman at 5-feet, 9-inches, 115 pounds, in a hip halo using a platform walker for a casted wrist. He grunted, shook his head sympathetically.

When he turned to the X-rays on the light board, he recoiled and then tried to compose himself. I heard him exhale in huffs as he just kept looking at the images, leaning in or pulling away, saying nothing. Finally he turned, his face grim. "I'll be right back."

He returned with another orthopedist and they muttered in front of the X-rays for several minutes. I heard phrases like, "...totally displaced...painful ambulation...pubic bone dislodged...is it poking into the bladder? A fall would be lethal." At last, they turned to me. The second surgeon averted his eyes. He looked at his colleague and put a hand on his shoulder, his lips in a thin line, and walked out of the room.

My orthopedist sat down on a small black stool in the corner of the room. He placed his head in his hands for several seconds. When he looked up, his eyes were red and shiny. "It's ruined. The surgery is ruined. Your right side is an inch and a half higher than your left, there is torsion at your spine, your pubic bones are out of place." He paused, his face set in purpose. "There are only two of us in the United

States who would ever go back into your pelvis. The outcomes could be worse." He stared into my eyes. "You are going to live with a great deal of discomfort. Your life will be limited. You can *never* fall. No one will fix you." *I may not make it through my prison sentence. These final days of freedom might be all I will have left.* We sat in silence. Then he continued, "Did you fall in the hospital? Do you remember twisting somehow?"

I nodded, suddenly remembering the day in the hospital that the rehab team came to get me out of bed. "We were almost to the edge of the bed," I said. "My legs were diagonal and not yet squared up to a sitting position. One of the therapists got impatient and grabbed the bed pad and yanked. I felt my lower body twisting in one direction, my torso in the other. I screamed in pain, almost blacking out."

Still seated on the stool, he bent his head and raked his nails through his scalp, then he sat up suddenly, angry. "They destroyed the surgery." He waved his long arm at my hip halo. "That's not doing you any good." He stood up and walked over to the exam table. "I can schedule a surgery, give you a little sedation, and pull those rods out."

"How much will it hurt to take them out?"

"What kind of pain are you in right now?"

I shrugged. "I don't think that pain scale really applies to me anymore. If it did, I'd never be up walking."

"I can take them out right here, right now."

"Do it."

I lay back on the table. He dismantled the crossbars, then met my eyes, "I'll start on your so-called good side." With a few turns, he unscrewed the first of four. It felt like he was pulling out my bone marrow. It made a squishy sucking sound.

"OK?"

I nodded.

He quickly removed the next three 7-inch rods. It felt like part of my soul was clinging to the rods as they left my body. I lay panting, looking at the ceiling tile.

The doctor walked back to the stool, rolled to the desk, and got out a prescription pad. "I want you to see one of your fellow PTs for a while." He turned and looked at me. "There is nothing else I can do."

I might be diminished but I am alive.

I left the orthopedist's office and limped my way out of the building to the car where Christine was waiting. I saw myself in the reflection of the glass door. My shoulder bones poked through my skin. My legs were lost in sweat pants. I looked ancient.

Four months after the accident, I was still in an arm cast. I had begun walking slowly on my own around the house and using the walker for short trips out of the house. Then two things happened that moved life forward very quickly. First, I received a letter stating that my medical insurance would be canceled if I did not return to work in thirty days. Second, my lawyers informed me that in Oregon, a mandatory minimum prison sentence was inevitable. It was just a matter of how long I would serve. Like the scene from Forrest Gump where he runs out of his leg braces, I ditched the walker and ramped up my rehab. I got busy training for prison.

In Solitary, I was physically safe, but mentally I was in a steep decline. I no longer knew what day it was. I was done with meal trays delivered through a slot. My legs ached from the lack of taking a full stride. The women's screams up and down the hallway were making me want to scream alongside them. The last straw was the woman next door, who had begun slamming something—her meal tray?—repeatedly into the metal cot, shouting and cursing with each blow. Living with other female inmates was inevitable; it was time to go.

I removed the brace and rolled my wrist around. I tried using my toothbrush, I lifted the Bible with one hand. Good enough. I decided to tell the jail nurse I no longer needed the wrist brace and was ready to join the general population. I practiced a speech with a fib or two about the surgeon's orders—that I should be fully recovered by now. It sounded pretty good in the empty room. If there was a way out of Solitary, I knew I had to find it.

Keys were coming. Here was my chance. A tray with grits and canned peaches slid through the slot on the door. My clue another day had begun, day four? Five? Shortly after, the nurse rolled into the unit with the medication cart. Speech time.

"The doctor said I could remove the brace once I had range of motion." I rolled my wrist and tried not to gasp.

She looked at me through the thin window and said, "OK." All that prep and she couldn't have cared less. "Here, sign this waiver." One less person on her beat. Not long after breakfast, I was collected by a guard, unshackled, and walked toward the women's general population unit.

The screams and moans of solitary confinement receded behind me, and I entered a long, windowless rectangular room with cement walls and noise. It was crowded. Women in maroon scrubs were sitting at tables or pacing in the open space. Some of the women at the tables stopped talking and stared; the walkers just kept walking. I was ordered to turn toward a long line of cells that ran the length of the rectangular room. The guard pointed to a cell midway down the line. "That's you." She turned and took off. *Don't leave me with these women.* I did not make eye contact. I was focused on making it across the room to the cell. I waited at the pacing area then dashed across to the other side. The cell was empty. It was dingy and smelled like a moldy basement. There were twin bunk beds, one metal table, a cheap plastic wall mirror above the toilet/sink combo and, of course, an overhead camera. The mattress was the same bone crusher of Solitary with the pizza-box foam pillow.

A woman entered. Her skin was pale and she smiled with neglected teeth.

"Hi, I'm Holly. I'm here for drugs." She just came right out with it. "Been here for two months, I got eighteen months to go. Heroin." She shrugged then dropped her eyes. "This is my third time in jail."

I had never met a heroin addict. I assumed they'd be monstrous. So far, so good.

"How 'bout you?" she asked.

"I'm Karen. I was in a car accident. I was driving. I had a blood alcohol of .08, right on the line. My husband died. So did another woman. It was bad, I was life-flighted. I am lucky to be alive." My story was a tragedy. She just shrugged her shoulders without offering any sort of sympathy. Then she climbed up and sat on the top bunk. I was relieved. The standing area of the cell afforded little room—we only had about one foot between us.

"This is me," she said and patted the bunk. "Yours is the bottom. See that mirror?" she asked, pointing to the wall. "It's two-way. There's an inner hallway that runs behind the cells. The guard walks up and down and looks through the mirror into our cells. It could be a man or it could be a woman, you never know. They like to sneak up on you. Sometimes you can hear them coming and sometimes you hear that they have already passed by. Freaks me out."

Would this happen in prison too? Would I have creepy cops staring into my cell whenever they wanted to? Was this utter disregard of dignity something that was even legal? It occurred to me that no one cared. Many probably thought that the fact that I was fed and clothed was more than I deserved. How would I survive this? How would I make it to the other side of six years?

My family understood that I would be in the jail for up to two weeks before being moved to the prison. I decided before my sentencing that I would not call from jail, but wait until I arrived in prison. This meant that for the first time since the accident I did not have their daily support. But I wanted to let them go on, heal, and resume their own schedules for the first time in years. I was in a different world now, and they couldn't help me if they wanted to.

A stack of bedding was on the bunk. I was glad I had something to do. I felt fear in my gut, just under the surface. But it wasn't a time for tears; I would save them up for a time when it was safe to shed them all. In the crush of female bodies, would there ever be such a time?

Holly and I chatted about safe topics like the lousy food and the boredom. I knew I was going away soon and I would never see her again, so we did not pretend to be friends. I slept in fits and starts, ate *chow,* and was allowed a daily shower. The shower setup was open-stall–style, with a curtain that separated the stalls from the unit. A daily shower wasn't enough for the women in drug withdrawal. They needed one every hour. I have never smelled such gamy, rank malodor from a human being's pores and genitalia. The stench was a crime.

I began to pick up a little jail slang. The next morning while I was taking a shower, a new woman entered the curtained-off area. The women on my unit would say she was "tore-up." Her face had abscessed pimples. Her hair looked like it had been cut in chunks without a mirror. I saw it all in a moment and looked away, concentrating on washing my feet. In the corner of my eye, I saw the woman was squatting. *What is she… Oh my god. She is shitting on the cement floor!* Maybe that part of her didn't work anymore? But then she did something unthinkable. She began to dig through her poop. She was muttering.

"Where's the fuckin' stash? It's gotta to be here. I need a fix!"

I turned away, frozen in place. Then my body took over. My hands turned off the water and swiped the towel over my torso. I yanked on my scrubs, picked up my plastic sandals, and made an awkward launch into the shower curtain, moving away from the butt smuggler still crouched on the floor. I found an opening in the curtain and dove through.

I clung to routine and made it my new way of life in jail. Every day, I paced with my limp and listened to the chatter, keeping my ears open. I learned by listening that most of the women at the jail were there for drug-related crimes: parole violations, distribution, and theft to fund the habit. I was the woman next door who ironically was about to do more time than most of them put together. That is, except for an unforgettable trio: Silver, Tizzy, and Buzz Cut. I sat with them at breakfast on my third day in the general population unit.

These three women were my fairy godmothers, although Buzz Cut would have preferred to be aligned with something a little more masculine. All of them had served time in prison. Each one began telling the story of what brought her back. Tizzy was a big-sister sort. If you were picking teams on the playground, she would be chosen first—she had that kind of body type. She was back on new drug-related charges. Silver was a different sort of big sister. She had the wisdom that comes with silver hair and was more understated, like the power behind the throne. She had already been serving time in prison, but she was brought back to court for additional charges, and now was heading back to prison. Buzz Cut was an adorable lesbian pixie. She intentionally planned and committed a crime, just to return to prison to be with the girlfriend she left behind. This made no sense, but nothing made sense and I dared not ask questions.

"I fell five days ago. When are we gonna go to prison?" asked Tizzy, slapping a hand on the metal table.

"We're not in charge of the clock anymore." Buzz Cut laughed. "I fell a week ago." She looked at me and tipped her head. "You fell a couple days ago, right?"

I looked at the floor for something I could trip over but all I saw was concrete. "Fall?" I was confused.

Buzz Cut laughed and shook her head, smirking. She leaned back and crossed her muscled arms and looked me over top to bottom. "Fall, it means the first day you go to prison or jail."

"My god, that is exactly what my first day felt like. I almost collapsed on the floor. The day I fell," I said trying the word out, "was a complete and utter disconnect with my life." I shook my head. "I was in Solitary. I lost track of time and days, it was like a vacuum. The day I was sentenced, my wrist was in a splint. But I took it off because I thought I would lose my mind back there." I rolled my wrist around, wondering if I had made a mistake.

Silver sighed, world-weary. "The day you fall is the first day in a long string of the worst days in your life."

The trio surprised me by being pleasant and sympathetic. To these women, I was still Karen, not Baker. During my first days out of Solitary, they began to school me in prison survival: no snitching, no stealing, shower every day, don't turn your back to the room, and keep your mouth shut. Compared to the living conditions in jail, the way Silver, Tizzy, and Buzz Cut described prison sounded like a major improvement.

"Everyone is clean, not like these women puking though withdrawal. They make you shower. You get a job. The food still sucks but at least you won't die from it." They talked about Intake, the unit where you begin your sentence. They warned me that I would be locked up in a cell nearly all day, but unlike Solitary, I could come out for meals, and church services. They asked me about my crime, the whole backstory. Silver was in for something similar. "There is no mercy about it," she said. "There's quite a few of us in prison with similar crimes."

"Look, Karen," said Tizzy, "don't think you're cleaner than the rest of us. You killed people, straight and simple. The women in there have been in and out of prison, taken every drug and stole or hooked for her habit, but they will look straight at you and say, 'Well at least I didn't kill anybody.' The sooner you get over yourself, the better you will get along in there."

"Yeah," said Buzz Cut. "You gotta own it. Introduce yourself by time and crime. No one wants to hear a sad story of innocence. They just want to make sure you're not locked up for committing a crime against children. Here's your speech: 'I'm Karen, I'm here for a Man II/DUI car accident. I got six years, no good time, no programs.'"

26

All along I called it an accident, never Man-*slaughter*. But these women held a mirror to my face and their harsh words stung. It would take time and practice to admit to that speech. But I was a sponge, and I soaked up their advice, grateful that they had taken me under their wings.

On my fourteenth day in jail, I got word that the next day I would go to prison. The van would take me, Tizzy, Silver, and Buzz Cut together. These were the women I would literally be bound to on my first days. I found Holly reading on her bunk and told her I would be leaving and said, "It is the oddest thing to be looking forward to prison."

"Yeah," she said, "that's how bad jail is."

That night after dinner, as we celled in for the night, Tizzy called out from down the row of cells, "You'll survive, Karen. We'll keep an eye on you, but if you fuck up, you're on your own."

I didn't sleep at all my last night in jail. I vowed I would never come back. I would never put myself and my family through this sense-less harm again. How did my life get away from me? I was a mother; I needed to be at home. I wasn't done teaching my daughters the value of a good education or that life existed in the world outside the suburbs. I would miss their volleyball games, their graduations and important rites of passage. Would they grow into confident women or would my huge mistake change the course of their lives? The day I met Tom on the mountain, I realized I changed my focus. I split myself into mother and mate. On the days my daughters were with their father, in the last boom of my youth, I took up the chase of Tom's adventurous lifestyle. I thought I could handle it. Instead, I drowned in it, and I dragged my daughters, my family, my closest friends down with me.

When our paperwork was in order, Tizzy, Silver, Buzz Cut, and I were chained just as I was in the courthouse. Buzz Cut said, "We're on the chain together." When I asked what that meant, she explained that it gave others a reference to see what kind of person I was. They could ask Silver, for example, "Hey, what's her story? I heard you came in on the chain with her." Silver could make or break my entrance by saying I didn't shower, or worse, that I was a snitch, a reputation I would learn could stick for years.

The chained march to the van with recidivists was more orderly than my stutter steps out of the courthouse. Once the door was shut, the three women began talking spiritedly, like they were taking a road trip. I was astonished. I expected at least a few moments of wretchedness and tears. After all, as opposed to jail time, prison means doing time, a stretch, a grip of time.

The driver turned on the radio and blasted the van with Latin polka music. It was deafening. The women laughed maniacally. I suspected false bravado. We had to holler back and forth across the bench seats. I couldn't hear myself think, which was just as well.

As the women shouted back and forth over the music, our breath fogged up the windows, obscuring the trees and passing cars. The longer we rode, the thicker the fog. I rubbed a peephole out the window and looked down into the cars of commuters off to work and moms shuttling kids to school. Those workers and mothers used to be me, but no longer; I was damaged goods. I sat with my hands in my lap and watched as the peephole slowly filled in. It was as if I were leaving this world.

That is how it feels to fall.

As the van began to slow down, the women got quiet. The music was turned off. Looking out the front window I could see we were entering a series of fence lines. Then the van stopped, the door opened, this was it. It was foggy both inside and outside the van. It was surreal, like stepping out into a cloud. I could see dim outlines of gravel, fence, and cement buildings—no green anywhere. On our way to a windowless door, pebbles crunched under my feet, my shoulders hunched. I was cold.

In those twenty steps to the door, I disconnected from my former life and began to fall into my new one. It was the day I entered prison, the beginning of my new calendar, my incarciversary. For the next six years and three months, I would mark an X on each day. I would X off six birthdays, six Christmases, six incarciversaries.

We were led into a large room similar to the Tank, without the press of humanity. Silver and Buzz Cut flopped down on the cement benches, Tizzy made use of the stainless-steel potty/sink combo without any effort at modesty toward us or the overhead camera. After a short wait in the prison holding cell, I was called out for delousing.

"Baker!"

I later learned that I drew the toughest cop in the prison. She was angular and brittle, with elbows so sharp they could be lethal weapons. Her black eyes had seen it all, no love there. Her commands were terse: come, walk this way, stand here, save your questions. I wondered if she practiced her stare in the bathroom mirror. Still, I accepted it. I assumed all the guards were this hard-boiled. I walked ahead of her to a large shower stall and she pulled the curtain behind us.

"Baker! Take off your clothes, all of them! One at a time, shake each piece out."

Off went my jail scrubs, my worn-out underpants and bra, and plastic sandals. "Turn around, squat! Spread your cheeks and cough." It was my second strip search. I wondered how many "skins" I would be subjected to; I couldn't imagine getting used to them. I was humiliated all over again. Fully nude, I was ordered to wash myself with what appeared to be another form of lye-based soap, body and hair. It burned on my skin, and I knew my hair would be as dry as straw. I overheard another guard, behind the curtain next door, tell a woman to lift her belly fat. I stole a glance at my captor. She sure had a miserable job, but she *chose* to come here, day after day. *This must be hell*, I thought as I stood there ashamed and raw.

The prison guards ordered Tizzy, Buzz Cut, and me into scrubs and toe-gripping tan plastic sandals that slowed us to a shuffle. Our Intake scrubs were blue and identified us as New To Prison! I no longer had the armor of clothing—jeans and boots or a nice leather handbag to separate myself from other women. I was a number.

Silver was dressed in jeans, a T-shirt, and sweatshirt because she was continuing with a sentence already underway. She had tennis shoes. I envied her. She didn't look quite so vulnerable. "See ya, Karen. Keep your chin up." She separated from us and went through a clanging door back to wherever she had been housed. I looked at the remaining three of us dressed in our identical Intake scrubs. Buzz Cut had an adrenaline-crazy look, Tizzy looked like she just woke up with a monster hangover, and I must have been a wild-haired hag. It was a comradeship of misery in a brand-new world.

Once dressed, we were fingerprinted and swabbed for DNA. I was officially entered in the Naughty column of the worldwide data bank. My genetics would be traceable alongside global terrorists. The last order of business was to create an ID card with my Pitiful Pearl photo, my in date, my out date, and my State ID number, or SID number. Your ID hangs around your neck and is a grim reminder of each and every day you will be locked up. The mug shot is the meanest part of the day. I wish someone had told me: Take a decent mug shot. It will follow you all the days of your life. While you're in prison, it is your only thingy. It is your knife for food, your screwdriver, and, of course, your new identity. Here is the lowdown: They put the camera above your head. Looking up only turns down the corners of your mouth like a reptile. You will not feel like smiling but it is better than looking like Kermit.

Finally, I was given two clear bags. One contained my bedding: a scratchy wool blanket, a nubby towel, and a set of twin sheets with a thin piece of square foam for a pillow. The other bag contained my intake scrubs, a tatty sports bra, grannie panties, gray socks, a nightshirt, a jean jacket with a wool liner, a navy beanie cap, and well-worn Keds. With my lanyard around my neck and one twenty-pound bag in each hand, I was directed by the stern black-eyed cop to the hallway as she said, "Remember, Baker, your worst day in prison can always be worse."

The doors clanged open and before me lay a long fluorescent hallway. I was unmoored. I took the first steps guard rail to guard rail. *Just move.* I marveled at my feet moving forward, my hands gripping plastic bags. I heard my breath and the sound of plastic dragging over linoleum, down the longest tunnel of my life.

INTAKE

I was alone in the corridor. I could just drop my bags and run. *Run to where? I am locked in.* The severity of jail and iron hand of prison intake had left me drained of my personal power. In my previous life, obedience used to mean submission and faint-heartedness. Now obedience meant survival. I was to do what I was told. I marched forward. The hiss of the bags was the only sound in the corridor. I began to lose my grip with the hand not yet healed. I stopped and rolled my wrist around. Somewhere above me thundered: "Keep movin'!" I jumped and looked up at the ceiling. "Next unit on the left," spoke God. I gathered my bags and hissed into the Intake Unit and stood before a guard at a podium. He turned his head toward me but did not make eye contact; instead he stared at my ID card hanging from the lanyard around my neck. He sighed wearily, like I was unworthy of his time.

"Name."

"Karen," I said, innocently. He referenced his list.

"You are Baker."

I decided on that very day to change my name back to my maiden name immediately upon release. As if I would someday be able to leave all this behind me.

The room I entered was a large dayroom with high ceilings. There was no one in the room, and I would later learn that everyone was locked in their cell, or "celled in." Had I looked, I would have seen the faces behind the glass watching the new girl coming in. They would have seen a raw middle-age lady with frizzy lye-soap hair, who was far from her element.

The room held fixed circular metal tables, an officer's podium, and two tiers of cells with metal doors. Each cell was numbered and had a thin vertical window. There were two televisions placed high on the walls at each end of the room. At one end of the room was a set of showers and laundry machines, the other end held three exercise bikes in front of a blessed window. It was the first window facing outdoors that I had seen in two weeks. It looked out on a lifeless patio, the yard. I had been imagining the grime and ghosts of Alcatraz, and instead I got a granite-hard, dull-but-tidy environment. The color of the walls, floor, and podium were shades of gray and beige. Mint green tables, doors, and staircases were the accent color. The only break in the wall was a bulletin board.

Officer Frosty pointed to it and said, "There is the call-out list. It is your responsibility to read it and be where you are supposed to be. Miss a call-out and you are bunked in. Here are your envelopes and paper, and the Rule Book. Read it." He still had not looked at me and kept his gaze just below my eyes. He was young, in the prime of his male life. He might have been handsome but he was just too bitter. He placed a toothbrush, lye soap, and a small envelope on the podium. "Baking soda. Toothpaste. You're in 204B." He pointed to the top tier and finally stared at me with dull eyes. What he didn't say was,

"Scram!" or "Good luck." Nothing. I might have been broken, but as with the jail nurse, I could see that the people who worked for the Department of Corrections (DOC) could be damaged too.

I dragged my bags—*hiss*—across the floor to the mint-colored staircase and thudded my way to 204. Bags, step, step. Bags, step, step.

"Hey! Karen!" I heard.

Who the heck? I looked in the direction of the voice. It was Buzz Cut calling from behind the glass of her cell door, about four doors down from me on the same upper tier. "I'll kick ya down some shampoo, and maybe a cup of coffee at lunch." Her voice was garbled behind the door, but she had a huge grin on her face. This was the gal who came back on purpose to be with her girlfriend. She actually looked happy. *What we do for love.* But I was grateful for her attention.

As I passed down the tier, I could see the faces at the windows, checking me out, just inches away, separated by the metal mint green doors and wired glass. Who would be behind my door? Would she be violent or crazy? I stopped in front of 204. The door clanged open and there stood a pretty thirty-year-old Latina woman. I was relieved. At least she looked approachable. I stepped into the cell and the door slammed shut behind me. The cell was about six feet by twelve feet and contained mint green bunk beds, a mint green table, shelves, a stainless-steel sink/toilet combo, and hooks for clothing and a towel. The amenities were a small wavy plastic mirror and a reading light. The cell door had a narrow window. If I looked through it, I could see the left side of the dayroom and the officer's podium.

From Tizzy, Buzz Cut, and Silver, I learned that when you are on Intake, you are celled in most of the day. The only exceptions were meals, call-outs, perhaps a job, and one hour of dayroom/yard. It would be more togetherness than I had shared with even Tom.

The pretty Latina—I'll call her Lupita—and I made a quick introduction. She had been on Intake for three weeks and seemed seasoned. She introduced herself as I was taught to do, by crime and time. She was in prison for two years on a drug-related crime. She wasted no time in telling me she was a mother and was broken-hearted and angry at herself for her mistake. Now it was my turn to share my history, my first time to give The Speech. "My name is Karen. The cop down there said it was Baker. I'm here for Man II/DUI. I will be here for seventy-five months, no good time." *I really did that, I got a DUI. I manslaughtered.* I felt sick. I would have to say it over and over. Lupita nodded. She didn't act sympathetic or ask questions about the accident. As Buzz Cut said, no one wants to hear your sad story. Every inmate has her own.

My haunted days before prison were filled with questions: Who would I be at release? Would my children survive, would they still want me to be their mom? Will I still have a sense of humor? Will I be old and fat? I didn't know these answers, but I thought if I could somehow prepare for life on the inside, perhaps I could survive this mess I made of my life and others' lives and go on to pick up the pieces instead of becoming a burden to everyone I loved. Awaiting trial, I had been consumed with researching life in a women's prison. I was desperate for information. I looked in the bookstores and on the Internet. I scoured newspapers. I found a few interviews with Heidi Fleiss, the Hollywood Madam, and Martha Stewart, but they contained very little detail of prison life. *Orange Is the New Black* by Piper Kerman had not yet been written. Most of what I found was vivid and depressing material on men's prisons, gang rapes, shivs, and fecal boomerangs. A women's guide to the Slammer did not exist.

Besides personal and family concerns, I wanted to know things like: Will I get a bra? What do I use for menstrual products? How will I survive on prison food and will I get regular exercise? I was born in Minnesota. If I could endure the frozen tundra and mosquitos, I could certainly survive bunk beds and lousy food. The looming question about prison life was, who were the women? What did they do to get in there, and how did the prison staff determine who would be your cellmate? Would we be grouped by crime or level of violence, or perhaps by age? Would they beat me up? Will I survive?

Once inside, I learned that prison was organized by the level of custody for each inmate. It was not how dangerous you were or how evil your crime was; custody was determined by how long you were locked up. The prison where I was serving was officially called a Medium/Minimum facility but it was the only one in the state so it held women with life sentences, even one on death row. That seemed Maximum to me.

Everyone started on Intake in the Medium/Maximum facility, then was housed according to the time they would serve. The women who were given approximately three years or less were classified as "Minimum Custody" and moved "across the street" to a set of buildings in the Minimum facility. Anyone like me who had more than three years was housed in the Medium facility, which resembled a traditional concrete block. Once I had served three years, I would be Minimum custody and transferred to the Minimum facility.

There was no separate grouping for types of crime. The woman who killed and burned her parents and the woman with ID theft could be cellmates. The DOC tosses the sharks and the seals into the waves and lets them work out survival on their own.

I had never been a person who read the manual first, but that day I cracked open the Rule Book and read every word. I learned that no one is allowed on another's bunk. I learned that you must always be dressed. The Rule Book was dense with action-consequence instruction that I didn't understand. My brain was mush. I would need to read it again.

"Lupita, what about the girls who can't read? How do they learn all the rules?"

She smirked down at me from her bunk. "It's pretty much the school of hard knocks for all of us. That's why we look out for each other. The cops don't cut you slack, they figure you can read the Rule Book on your cell-in. That asshole down there will bust your chops for the slightest mistake." She gestured past our locked cell door to the podium. "He's training sheep. That fucker probably stands in the mirror in the morning and says, 'I'm gonna write up some bitches to-*day!*' You might be one of those SUV soccer moms out there, but in here, it's us against them. We're the ones who teach you the rules and have your back. They have seen hundreds of women come and go. They just want to go home at the end of the day. We are your people now."

I began to understand why Buzz Cut, Tizzy, and Silver were so nice to me. It was us against them. It was a lot to take in. Part of me wanted to resist it. Because I *did* have more in common with the guards: I worked, had a family, volunteered, and voted. But I understood that that life was gone and my job now was to learn the ropes.

Lupita told me it was almost lunchtime. She tried to comb her long thick hair with a cheap comb, but instead made a quick braid and put on her plastic sandals. My hair was a mess, so to keep with her rhythm and so I wouldn't look like I had just been electrocuted, I wet and scrunched it. Who knew you had to groom yourself in prison? She stood at the door like a race horse in the gate. I flashed back momentarily to my early twenties when I lived in San Diego and attended the opening day at the Del Mar race track. We wore dresses and hats and even chipped in for a limo. How free and hopeful I was. How would I ever relate to these women? I gave myself a mental shake, thinking of Lupita's words: "We are your people now." I was about to learn how to relate to a whole unit of them.

If one metal door is thunderous, fifty in unison is the sound of ear damage. The doors run on line movements and open one tier at a time. For this meal, the doors slammed open on the bottom first. Looking over Lupita's shoulder, I could see that the women stampeded into a line before a metal food cart. The trays were slapped onto a plastic table positioned in front of the cart. The women snatched them up and found a table. The smell rose up to our tier, and it smelled predictably bad.

The line went down and it was our turn. I was big eyes, big ears, and beating heart. The cafeteria scenarios of my imagination ran wild. I pictured a bloodthirsty room with leering butchies reaching for my meatloaf with husky, tattooed arms. I saw myself standing with my dorky tray and looking for a place to sit. I dreaded this moment.

I was in no hurry to go downstairs, but like a rioting crowd, you had to keep pace or be trampled. I went down the stairs faster than was safe, my worn-out sports bra not up to the task. Here I was, in the thick of felons with my boobs hanging out. Did I attempt to tuck or cover? I decided against digging into my shirt. I had to prioritize my actions, like finding a seat. In the free-for-all I had lost my cellmate. Across the room, I saw Buzz Cut. She was sitting with women wearing jeans and T-shirts instead of Intake scrubs. It looked like there was an open seat, thank god, so I approached.

"Hey, Buzz Cut, can I sit here?"

The women in jeans and T-shirts heads' swiveled, talking ceased. "Hell no," said the woman to her right, "This table ain't for Nobodies, go sit somewhere else."

They looked at me with the mean prison faces of my imagination.

"Naw, she's OK. We came in on the chain together." Buzz Cut tried, but it did not have any effect. Then, looking at the harsh woman on her right, she said proudly, "This is my girl!"

I will call her Scarlett O'Hara for her thick Southern accent. She had long brown hair and could have been pretty if not for her cruel expression, lips curled like she'd bitten a lemon. The table was dead silent. As I slunk off to find another seat, my face hot with shame. I could feel Scarlett O'Hara's fierce eyes bore into my back. I had clearly tried to climb the totem pole out of order.

Later, I recalled the incident to my cellmate, and she laughed. "Those girls are badass. They like to live on this unit because when all the Intake women are celled in, they have the place to themselves." I didn't realize inmates had a choice in this; there was so much to learn.

"Scarlett moved over to this unit to be here when Buzz Cut got here," Lupita continued. "That way they can eat together and have yard together until Buzz Cut is off Intake. Scarlett is a jealous one, so watch your back and don't be too friendly to her girlfriend."

Right, I thought. But even if I did swing that way, who would want me? I was a limping middle-age white woman with Einstein hair at the beginning of six long years of downhill aging. I had killed two people. I wasn't worthy of anyone's love.

Somehow the day progressed. I made it through the dinner meal by avoiding Buzz Cut's table and sitting near women who didn't look crazy. I tried to find some sort of nutrition on the plastic tray, even if it was canned or reconstituted. In those early days, it was hard to gather an appetite when all my body wanted to do was *run away!*

Lupita told me the cell doors ran from about five a.m. to nine p.m., which meant that at ten minutes to every hour, the doors would open. We would have ten minutes in the dayroom to check call-outs or ask questions. We had to be in front of our door at the top of the hour to get back in. Finally, at nine p.m. it was lights out, or rather dimmed. I had survived my first day in the Slammer. Tomorrow I would have yard time. I would be able to step outside and breathe real air. Would it smell different? Would it be safe? I was so desperate for fresh air, I was willing to take that chance.

No one was coming to rescue me. No one I loved could see I was upstairs in an Intake Unit, standing in scrubs looking out a skinny window. My family knew I was locked up in a great big cinderblock, but had no idea where I was inside the gray walls. I stood close to the cell window and huffed my breath, creating a small circle of fog on the glass. I made a fist and imprinted the pinky side of my hand to make a baby foot and dotted the toes, just like I had done as a child, riding in the backseat of the red Chevy station wagon rolling over the Minnesota prairies. The foggy footprint on the cell glass was evidence that I still existed, but like the footprint, we were both fading away. If I pressed my cheek against the narrow glass window, I could see a sliver of the dayroom window that stood between the unit and the yard. I cupped my hands close to my face and could see the moon of my childhood, the same moon looking down on my children, still there waiting in the January sky.

One of the benefits of sentencing postponements was to arrange to have money available for an account when I landed in prison. That meant I could call home. What I began to learn—even in those first days in prison—was that nothing happened quickly on the Inside and rarely did your bright ideas make sense to the people in charge. In other words, my account was not activated yet. It had been over two weeks since I had spoken to my girls and I was desperate to hear their voices.

Listening to Lupita or the other women around the meal table, I learned I wasn't alone in my worries about my girls. Many of the women were mothers, single parents with absent fathers. Many of them didn't even know where their children were. Some actually hoped their kids were in foster care. A weepy brunette at the lunch table suspected that her teenage daughter was living on the streets and using drugs, doing whatever she had to for money. Nikki and Haley had family, they were lucky, but still, I felt uneasy. When I looked out of my cell window, straining to see the sky, I imagined my daughters were like birds, just circling, groundless.

I knew my family was worried about me, so on my second day of Intake, I decided to make a very expensive collect call to my sister. She was the point person for the family and the closest person in my life. We agreed that she would take the first call so she could filter out my agony instead of letting that fall to my children. So late in the afternoon, as the free hour approached, I stood at the door awaiting line movement. As soon as it rumbled open, I hustled down the stairs to grab one of the four available phones. I dialed her number and clung to the cord, trying to crawl through the receiver. *Be there, be there.*

"Hello?" Then came a recording stating that the call was coming from a correctional facility.

"Karen!" she said in a rush, "I've been so worried. I cry all day."

I couldn't answer because a sob was forcing its way up my throat. If I let it go, it would have sounded like some wild animal. So I stuffed my emotions and curled into the kiosk.

"Be strong, Sis. If you're OK, I'll be OK," she said.

She cried freely. My throat felt like it was going to burst, but I swallowed my tears—I was afraid to cry in prison, afraid I would be cut out of the herd and cannibalized. I thought of all the things I could tell her, but I didn't know where to start; my life was unrelatable. I apologized for the collect call and asked her please to let the girls know I would call them when my account was established. She told me the girls were surviving. Both were healthy and going to school. She told me both Sam and Audrey had checked in. She asked if my cellmate was OK and I said I had been lucky so far. Then we joked about bad food for a while, listening closely for the tone of voice that would indicate if the other was going to make it or not.

Christine had always been my loyal champion. She was everyone's sweetheart. She not only allowed me to tag along with the older kids in the neighborhood, but she *insisted* I come along. Her friends would roll their eyes at my attempts to be cool. In the guitar circle, I had sung the Dylan folk songs all wrong, too flashy. I whiffed in kickball. I read their diaries. I don't know how she put up with me.

Now I was calling her from a prison phone. I was guilt-ridden, but an apology seemed limp. *Sorry I destroyed our family. Sorry you and the others have to take over my parenting duties. Sorry you have to manage the details of my mistake.*

Christine asked a few questions about the bunks and the other women. I chose to edit the details of prison life. I didn't want to scare her. In the back of my mind, I knew the calls were recorded and that someone was listening. That did two things: it made me cautious with the words I chose to say, and it made the call very expensive. But for a few brief moments, I was connected to my former life.

"Please tell the girls I'm OK and I will call them when my account is set up. Tell them to save their money for themselves. Remind them, I promised to live through this." "I know you will." She was crying again. "We want you home."

Huddled into the phone, I thought of the life I had lost. I imagined standing in the doorway of my daughters' bedroom, watching them sleep. But now, neither one of them was home. No more burnt toast mornings or quarrels over messy bedrooms. There was no family home. In her voice, I could hear that Christine was beginning to pick up the pieces from the wreckage, and I was relieved. I wanted her to live a normal life: wake up, go to work, walk the dog, eat ice cream.

After hanging up the phone, I had time for a shower. The yard could wait. Buzz Cut, true to her word, had kicked me down some shampoo, pressing it into my hand at a line movement. I was looking forward to a good cry under the spray. The showers were semi-private tile stalls arranged side by side with a curtain separating the showers from the dayroom. I was tall so the tile division between the stalls rose as only as high as my ribs. Anyone in a stall alongside me could see the whole show, but I didn't have it in me to care.

I turned on the faucet, waited for the water to heat up, and settled on a degree above lukewarm. I backed into the spray and closed my eyes, hoping I could cry unnoticed as I thought of my sister's choked voice.

Then I heard, "Them are nice."

I opened my eyes to find a small blond woman staring at my chest. She smiled and turned away, finishing her shower. "*Them are nice."* *Was this a pass?* I quickly finished showering, went back to the cell, and put my game face back on.

I made it through dinner on my second day without breaking a rule or breaking prison code. I sat where I was supposed to for meals and stood where I was supposed to for the final line movement. When the doors slammed shut on cell number 204, I was in for the night.

Second to the doors, the most obnoxious feature of prison is the 24-hour fluorescent lighting. The intensity ranges from murky to living on the sun. The lights dimmed at nine p.m. and returned to max at five a.m. The hallways and common rooms were bright twenty-four hours a day. You could see a bread crumb from thirty feet away.

Emotionally exhausted, I just wanted to sleep. I crawled into my nubby sheets and pulled up the wool blanket. The pizza box foam pillow was no comfort at all. In jail, I was still on the move. In prison, I had begun a lifetime of days that seemed endless. I knew I would wake up in prison. I knew it was not a dream. I killed two people. I pulled the wool blanket over my head, my eyes filling with tears. *I killed you, Tom. I killed you. You trusted me to get you home. It was my fault. How could you leave me? How could you leave me to do this alone?* Tears threatened to fall. I missed him.

Everyone he knew missed him, all those bad jokes, all that charisma—gone. It had been almost two years since he died. I missed the simple things: his soft rumbly voice, his silver and turquoise man-jewelry. Most of all, I missed coming home after work, my final trudge up the steps to the porch, and within seconds, the sound of his recliner slamming to upright, the running footsteps and the dog toenails across the wooden floor, the door flung open, man and dog, his wingspan, his smile: "Honey! You're home!" He never got tired of it. If Tom had his way, he would like to be remembered as the best skier, kayaker, a mountain rescue agent, and the greatest Grateful Dead fan that ever lived. He loved his pals and his golden retriever. He loved me.

Tom was a twin to a shining star brother. He told me as a little boy, he had been the shy twin. He hid in the closet when a baby sitter came and stayed there until she left. "Otherwise, we were hellions, my twin, my little brother and me. My poor mother." He laughed at the memory and shook his head. "I was a little *funny*. I was smart but I had a hard time concentrating." Tom had a high IQ but didn't fit into formal education and got offtrack as a teenager. He told me he began experimenting with recreational drugs and decided to sign up for the navy to get straightened out.

One day, after we had been married a couple of years, I went looking for him out in his toy trailer. I found him behind motorcycles, boats, skis, and camping equipment, digging through some old boxes. He was chuckling and shaking his head, holding an old photo album.

"Gee, I don't know if you wanna see this, but here I am as a navy cadet." He shyly passed the album open to a picture of a skinny young man with a sharp Adam's apple and Coke bottle glasses. *Ichabod Crane, oh sweetheart.*

The navy quickly discovered his genius for electronics and made him an engineer on an aircraft carrier. His duty was to go up in a navigation plane, equipped with an early GPS system, and keep track of the fighter pilots. After the navy, he became a whiz for companies like Intel installing enormous computer systems.

When Tom was in his late thirties he had laser eye surgery, ditched his thick glasses, and swanned into a beautiful man. He was quick to laugh and quick to brag good-naturedly: "Enough about me, what do you think of me?" On anyone else, it would be tedious, but he was tickled with himself. People couldn't help but like him, I couldn't help but love him.

Intake lasts four to six weeks. During those first days, Lupita would stand in front of the window and give me the lowdown about the cop at the podium or the nutjob at the microwave. I expected a rough crowd, and they were. I could hear their chatter about guns, drugs, crimes, and men. I told Lupita about a comment at lunch that really disturbed me. As we were watching television coverage of the devastation of the tsunami that killed hundreds of thousands of people in Southeast Asia some fried-out woman with a swastika tattoo said, "Wipe 'em all out, fuckin' slant eyes, polluting our planet, I hope those waves get every last one of them."

Lupita rolled her eyes. "She's a skinhead. She doesn't like me either." She shrugged. "We have women who have committed every crime you can imagine: theft, arson, manslaughter, child abuse, ID theft, and every possible drug crime. Over half of these women are crazy and about a third of them have been a hooker in one way or another. There are a lot of women here for assault. That's why all the stools in the unit are screwed to the ground, so we don't use them as weapons against each other."

I had never met such women, yet now they stood right next to me in meal lines and walked behind me at yard. None of them would be invited to the family BBQ at my house and yet, *these were my people?* So far I wasn't buying it. I missed my family. I missed my girls. Alone on my bunk in the dim lights at night was the only time I dared to think of them.

The accident crushed my daughters' lives. They became the girls everyone whispered about. After Haley moved to California, she was able to make a fresh start but was isolated and not able to talk about her loss with her trusted friends. Nikki, who was still living with me, bore the brunt of social humiliation after the accident. She spared me the sloppy details of how the kids at school treated her, but I knew it was bad. She became serious and withdrawn. What she endured was incomprehensible to both the kids and their parents, as they went about planning shoes and purses for the prom. Nikki was terrified about what life would be without me, but she was also terrified of what would happen to me in prison. She turned eighteen seven months before I entered prison. She was accepted at the University of Oregon and began packing. I envied the other mothers at IKEA as we shopped for laundry bags and storage items. Unlike them, I would not be at home waiting for my daughter over semester breaks. I imagined her difficulties trying to relate to excitable freshmen. She would be on her own.

At the time of sentencing, Haley had been living in California with her father for about seven months. Initially, she and her father shared a section of a house near the beach where her father worked doing construction projects. In our first phone calls, I gushed about the beach and she agreed but her voice was flat.

A few weeks later when school began, I tried to imagine her first day in a new school I had never seen, perhaps alone at lunchtime, the kids whispering about the new girl. She would be an outsider in a school where the kids had all grown up together. At fifteen, she would have to invent a new identity. With so many changes in her life, our family tried to shield Haley from some of the details of the accident and impending prison. Now she was isolated by both distance and details. I hoped she would be able to make a new friend.

As an inmate, I felt like motherhood was water through my hands, no longer mine to hold. My children were downstream. I could not see them. I looked around the cell in the semi-dim lights. My ears picked up sounds of the prison at night: squawking radios, a single door opening and slamming shut in the corridor. I felt the pull of despair, so dark and tempting.

Intake was a waiting game. Wait for the door to open. Wait for our free hour to shower, wait to go outside or do laundry, and wait for meals. A job meant something to do. In my state, prisoners worked full-time. There was no freeloading. Since we knew that work was inevitable, our goal was to avoid the kitchen. Each night before bed, we would check our call-outs, waiting for the call to duty. Buzz Cut with her connections and know-how, breezed into a janitor job; the rest of us were thrown kitchen whites and a cheap pair of worn-out Keds.

On my first day in the kitchen, I woke up at five a.m. and joined the women sitting in the dayroom waiting to be called.

"Intake Unit, kitchen workers!"

We entered a large set of rooms midway down the central corridor. This was the origin of an odor that loosely smelled like food. Women in white scrubs bustled around and guards watched their progress. The women from my unit who were already dressed in white scrubs went directly to work. I was called over by an officer with a clipboard.

"Name!"

"Baker," I managed.

"Jones! Get Baker outfitted in kitchen whites. *Rápido!*"

I followed a woman inmate I had never seen to a short hallway with heaps of unorganized tops and bottoms. I was handed a hair net and white scrubs and went to change in a toilet stall. Like the showers, the toilet stalls in prison are built for short women. They reminded me of visiting my kids' open house in grade school where I towered over everything.

I conjured up the days of my daughters' elementary school. I tried to remember the smell of their grade school, the polish on the wooden hallways, chalk and sweaty kids. I loved taking the girls shopping for school supplies, lunch boxes, and new backpacks in August. I remembered my lousy attempts at packing lunches with odd bits of leftovers in recycled produce bags instead of Ziplocs. They never had the cool food; it was more like their lunches were packed by an impoverished hippie. My throat swelled. *Nikki, Haley, my innocent girls.* The weight of guilt pressed me down. But I had to get a grip. *Karen! Not now, keep your wits, don't think, just move.* I left the toilet stall in my new uniform to find the cop with the clipboard.

My first kitchen job was as a server. It didn't take a Rhodes scholar to understand it was an entry-level position. Before we started in with serving duty, we were fed, a quick fifteen minutes, then it was battle stations: "Tray up! Let's go!" Time to feed the prisoners.

We were called to line up at metal serving lines. At one end was a set of trays, at the other was a rolling cart that carried the trays to the units. The work was frantic and impressive. The trays barrel down the chute at a rate of about a thousand in about twenty minutes. It was a serving rodeo, hard and fast. The cart door slammed shut, locked by the guards so no one would swipe a stale cookie en route. The carts rolled out the kitchen doors and into the units. It was a mad dash to clean the serving line, in order to be ready to clean out the carts as they rolled back into the kitchen. When they did, I would stand by a trash can, open the cart door, grab a tray, and smack it into the trash can. Pull, smack, smack again. We kept slapping the trays into garbage cans until they were done. Food and liquid were everywhere, and I slipped all over the floor in my cheap tennis shoes. Finishing the job meant hosing down the floor. It was the most inelegant thing I had done in my working career. But I tried to do a good job because maintaining a work ethic meant maintaining a part of myself over which I still had control.

The morning shift ended with a pat-down. This meant an over-the-clothing search on my way out the door. The inmate stands in a crucifixion pose, the guard sweeps the arms, the legs, back, and the cross-your-heart mid-bra line. What are they looking for? Stolen spices, knives, pens, Ziplocs? When you have nothing, everything has a potential use. Some women steal just to steal. One woman hid two saucer-sized cookies in her underwear to bring back to her new girl-friend. I worked alongside this girl. She was uncouth. She stared just a little too long, smiling all the while, revealing yellow teeth and a puffy gum line. She was busted during the pat-out.

New to prison, I did not understand there could be punishment for smuggling, but I did notice that after that she was no longer around. Tongues waggled all the way back to the unit and swept through the entire prison by evening. The retelling went wild. "Did you hear about Breezy? Girl shoved a whole batch of cookies up her cranny to bring back to her nasty-ass girlfriend. They gonna take her *down* for that." I wondered if there was a basement. I was so innocent then.

The servers worked three split shifts, 5 a.m. to 8 a.m., 10:30 to 1:30 p.m. and 4:30 to 6:30 p.m. In between shifts we napped or took a shower before we stank up the entire tier. The split shifts were intolerable. After a few days of work, I no longer scanned the menu for taste, I scanned for the splatter factor. The beans and oatmeal were the worst and took at least five whacks on the edge of the garbage can. Given the lack of sleep from overhead lights, the noise, and the wretchedness, I was a mess. I needed to call my daughters but first I needed to pull myself together. I had to get a straight shift.

When I returned the next day to the kitchen, I asked the cop with the clipboard this question: "Do you promote by seniority or merit?" He paused and stared, then he barked an incredulous laugh. I wondered if he understood the concepts. I waited.

"Name!"

"Baker," I replied.

Mr. Clipboard studied his list. "Baker, you've been promoted," he said. "Tomorrow you start on sanitation."

I understood what that was—I would clean the kitchen floors, sinks, deep fryers, cooking vents, and toilets. The duties were worse, but it meant a straight shift, 6 a.m. to 1 p.m., five days a week. I created a calendar with a piece of paper and my bendable Intake pen, a pen that could not be used to make a tattoo or a shiv. Looking ahead, I marked the date I would get my first month's pay. It would be about thirty dollars. I could finally call my girls without burdening them with the expense of a collect call. I began to understand the importance of small gratitudes: clean sheets, warmish showers, socks, breath, and therefore hope.

One day during my second week in prison, I had two new call-outs. The call-out list looked like this:

204	Baker	SID # 15197720	Kitchen	06:00
			Counselor	09:30
			Medical	13:00

The call-outs would provide a break from the monotony and I was going to get some necessary medical attention and see a counselor! Thus far I had been ordered to wake up, go to sleep, stand where I was supposed to stand, walk on the right side of the hallway, eat when served, avoid physical contact, do not share, do not ask unnecessary questions, *and* obey the laws of the jungle. But I was finally going to get an opportunity in a safe environment to offload the weight of my experience to someone other than a friend or family member. The timing was right. I had been holding on so hard for so long.

I left my shift in the kitchen at nine-thirty to search the hallway for the counselor. She was waiting for me in an interrogation room. My file was open on the table, including my reptilian mug shot.

"Sit." No eye contact.

I began blabbering away at how happy I was to see her as she shuffled through the papers in my file. That's when I saw the criminal history worksheet. My heart sank. Not again. That worksheet almost ruined me and would have sentenced me to ten or twenty years instead of six.

"That woman is not me," I said, pointing to the criminal worksheet, feeling desperate all over again. "We have the same name, but I assure you, that's not me. I had to go through a psychiatric eval just to prove it."

The counselor looked up from the file with the face of another exhausted justice worker. She wore heavy makeup that caked in the creases under her eyes. "Look, Baker, it really doesn't matter, this is not a counseling session. I am an intake counselor. My job is to look over your file, make sure your paperwork matches your seventy-five-month sentence, and house you in the correct unit. I am not a psychotherapist; I'm a clerk. You will have to contact mental health services for anything else. Are you suicidal?"

"No," I answered.

I was dismissed.

I lingered in the hallway taking it all in. First my damned criminal history worksheet again, then the disappointment about the session. It was quiet in the hall, an empty quiet, like I was standing in an abandoned warehouse at the end of the world.

The Karen Baker identity error followed me everywhere. After the accident, the court ordered a presentencing investigation. From the beginning, the Oregon district attorney had me confused with another Karen Baker. Another Karen Baker who was nefarious. You would think in the digital age, the fact finders might have investigated our photos or Social Security numbers and realized the criminal worksheet belonged to someone else. But they didn't, and the D.A. leaped on the chance for an impressive conviction, a reassurance of voter confidence and job security. Every time the district attorney's office changed prosecutors, my lawyers would have to prove again that the other Karen Baker was not me. There are hundreds of Karen Bakers. While in prison I would receive mail for a Karen Baker who evidently had a robust love life prior to lockup. That day in the prison counseling office, the worksheet resurfaced again.

The other Karen Baker's criminal history worksheet contained:

Disorderly conduct/Prostitution

Fraud w/intent to obtain aid

UUMV (auto theft)

PCS (conspiracy)

Possession of driver's license to commit forgery

A key part of the investigation to prove I was not a car thief, forger, or prostitute included a four-hour test and an interview with a psychologist. The psychologist had read the D.A.'s report and believed that I was the wrong Karen Baker. In the interview, he was relentless. I explained the mistake, but he kept at me like an interrogator. He tried to sneak the other Karen Baker's crimes in, manipulating the conversation to see if I would stumble. He referred to my days as a prostitute or when I was a car thief. I had to deny committing those crimes, over and over. I tried to explain that I was a professional and a mother and that I was devastated by the accident. If that weren't enough, I was accused of someone else's crimes on top of my own. After the interview, when I spoke to my lawyers, I learned that from the beginning of the case, while I lay in the hospital, this is who the prosecuting team thought I was. What is worse, they told the family of the woman I killed in the oncoming lane that that was who I was.

At each sentencing postponement, we were no closer to settling out of court. The judge referred us to mediation to work out the differences. Separately, the victim's family and I went to court to clarify the issues. If we reached a mutually negotiated agreement, we would avoid a trial and have a single day in court for sentencing.

I met first with the Clackamas County mediator. Despite my appointment with the psychologist, there was the rap sheet of the wrong Karen Baker open in the file. I gave her the information to prove my identity and, although dubious, she made the proper notes.

She shuffled some papers around and brought forth Tom's accident report. Tom had had a prior car accident that took out power lines.

"It says here that Thomas Baker's truck had marijuana and two pipes. The sheriff counted over three hundred beer bottles and cans. The report says the cans and bottles were bagged, but a third of them were in the cab, behind the seat, and in the toolboxes."

I was horrified. Over three hundred beer bottles and cans? He never told me the details and I never saw an accident report. *This is the kind of person the victims thought we were.* I knew my only chance to avoid incarceration for ten or twenty years was to reveal everything to the mediator that day. I thought hard about my life leading up to the accident and began:

"I feel like my life just got away from me. I fell in love with a charismatic, beautiful man." I nodded to the accident report. "But before that first accident, his drinking and the party atmosphere in our home was out of control. I fooled myself by telling Tom's friends to smoke their pot outside, but who was I kidding? In essence, I was saying to my daughters, *This is acceptable behavior.* I was raised by a traditional mother and grew up believing that good wives and mothers don't rock the boat. So I juggled two roles, mother and playmate. I was not doing a good job of either one. My role as mother won out."

I met her eyes. "I have never told anyone this." I needed a moment to wrestle with the disloyalty I felt toward Tom, tears stung in my eyes; but I knew I must stay steady and reliable. "I went to a lawyer at St. Andrew Legal Clinic and started divorce proceedings. Tom had no idea. Neither did my girls. I should have told them. They needed to know that this behavior wasn't right."

The mediator had stopped writing and was leaning forward, just listening.

"After the first accident, things turned around," I said. "Tom went through Diversion, he stopped drinking and cleaned up his act. He had more energy and was cognizant. He began helping out in the kitchen. He found recipes, shopped for ingredients, and cooked. On the days I had the girls, we had dinner and watched movies. He paid his fines. I didn't have to say a word; it was all his doing."

I paused and the mediator nodded that I continue.

"A second change occurred. My daughter, Nikki, came to me and said, 'Just once before the end of my childhood, I would like to live in a normal house in a normal neighborhood.' I had to make that happen and Tom agreed, so we moved out of the farmhouse that served as a clubhouse for all his ski and boating buddies and found a house walking distance to town and closer to school. I closed my case at the legal clinic. I had hope.

"But little by little he starting drinking again, just a beer here and there. He never stopped smoking pot. A beer here and there became a drunk here and there. I would come home from work, never knowing what I would find, a sober husband, or a rip-roaring drunk husband. The day he died was one of those days.

"On the day of the accident, I do remember having a glass of wine. When we left, he was behind the wheel. I took over somewhere down the mountain highway, before that fatal spot. I have no memory of the accident. I was tired and that glass of wine certainly had something to do with it. I wonder sometimes, did a deer jump out onto the road? Was it slippery? I ask myself, Why didn't we eat some sort of lousy bar food, or wait? We will never know, I am the only survivor and I cannot remember."

The mediator nodded again.

"I was life-flighted from the scene. I broke over twenty bones, I ruptured my insides." I wasn't looking for pity, but I wanted this woman, this decider of futures, to know everything. "It took my entire family to put me back together again using a great deal of their time and their money."

She stared back at me, her face was open. I felt no judgment. "I nearly died three times and will hurt the rest of my life." I leaned forward, looking into her eyes. "My physical pain will be the easy part. The hard part will be living with the fact that I have destroyed lives. My children will be split apart. One will stay here and try to put herself through college, the other will have to move to Southern California. Her dad will be a single parent with no financial support from me. I took another daughter's mother away. She was completely innocent. I killed my husband." The words were heavy in my mouth and though I knew it was true, I never imagined that this would be my story. I paused to collect myself.

"I know I will go to prison. At times when I am scared, I blame Tom. I am not proud of that. I just don't want my children to lose their mother again. They have suffered so much." What I didn't say was that I was terrified—for myself. I was afraid after all my injuries, I would get sick and my parts and plumbing wouldn't work, or that some brute would break my bones. I was afraid I would lose my role as a primary parent. I was afraid I would lose myself and not survive prison for over six years.

The mediator shuffled the pages of the file and found her legal pad underneath. "I will make some notes and present this to the family." I nodded, gathered my jacket and purse, and left the courthouse.

A few weeks passed and my lawyers call me in for the results. "The family agreed to a six-year and three months sentence, seventy-five months, the mandatory minimum sentence for Manslaughter II." *Six years, I could do that*. I could muster the courage for that amount of time. I would be released while the girls were still young women and, perhaps, they would give me a chance to have a meaningful role in their lives. The victims showed mercy.

I walked out of my lawyers' building. It was an elegant high-rise in downtown Portland. Every time I came to their office, I had to pass a man sitting on a blanket leaning up against the brick wall, just under the roofline. He was a vet and had lost both legs in Vietnam. In the early days after the accident, I shuffled past him in my walker, consumed by my own troubles. As the weeks turned to months and then almost two years, I learned his name and brought him food or slipped a few bucks into his hat. I was the lucky one.

"Hey!" said a voice from a microphone overhead.

I jumped.

"Get back to the kitchen!"

I looked up and this time, I saw the overhead camera. There was actually a long series of them. The ceiling had ears and a voice. I was never alone, though I certainly felt I was.

At one p.m., I left the kitchen again, this time for the Medical Unit. *This has got to go better than the last call-out*, I thought. This was my damned health. I had written my lawyers and requested a package that would contain my medical records, a heel lift, and a second wrist splint. So far, I had toughed it out without the lift in my shoe because my mobility was limited, but now that I was standing and working in the kitchen, I needed that heel lift. My limp was obvious. My back, where it had been pinned together, was killing me.

The only thing I learned on the Intake Unit about the medical services was in the form of criticism. I arrived at the Medical Unit and sat in the waiting room with ten other women. Eight of them were in jeans, one was in Intake scrubs like me. The woman wearing the Intake scrubs was talking.

"My leg is messed up bad," she said. The seated group didn't take the bait. "I kicked my shin into the concrete seat so I could get out of kitchen duty."

The women groaned.

"Listen, you dumb shit," said a woman with a threatening stare. The others smiled and snickered, satisfied that she was the speaker to deliver the lesson. A pip-squeak seated next to her started wiggling in anticipation.

"You probably broke it." The woman leaned forward, one hand on her wide-spread thighs. "But how ya gonna find out, huh?" She cocked an ear to listen.

The Intake girl glanced around the room.

"There ain't no X-ray machine back there." She gestured with her thumb. "Hell, most times there ain't even a doctor. You fuck your leg up in here, you're still gonna have to walk on it." The woman sat back and crossed her arms.

"You might have just signed your death sentence," said a woman in jeans, who looked unflustered by the situation. She nodded to the Intake girl's leg. "Most likely you will get an infection, then they'll have to chain you to a hospital bed." She paused and shrugged. "Won't stop the infection. They just leave you back there. They might have to cut off your leg."

The Intake girl's cheeks flushed scarlet and her eyes were saucers.

"Damned right," said the first woman, nodding. "If you *live*, you'll still have to go back to the kitchen!" The eight howled.

"Jones," said a tiny woman in a medical smock with runny mascara. The Intake woman pushed off her chair and limped forward. The women snickered and swore at the girl's stupidity. Then the leader turned her glare toward me.

"How 'bout you, cupcake?"

My heart convulsed. "First appointment," I managed.

"Run, grasshopper, run far away," she said, staring just a few seconds too long, like a serpent.

Still, I was hopeful as my name was called and I walked into the exam room. The DOC medical staff doctor was a portly fellow who wore round wire-rim glasses. He rolled his chair back and forth on the linoleum as we talked. There was no record of my medical chart nor had my heel lift or wrist splint arrived. I tried my best to list my physical complications. I pleaded that I needed the heel lift to correct my crooked pelvis. Denied. I told him I should be in a wrist splint. Also denied. His hands were tied, he said. According to DOC, any accessory could be used as a weapon or could conceal contraband.

I asked him about mental health counseling.

"Ha! You're too well." He shook his head at me. "Baker, if you haven't noticed, about seventy percent of the women in here have a mental illness. They have been self-medicating with street drugs, not psych meds. Mental health workers have to get them to baseline so they can live communally without hearing voices. Their first duty is to segregate the inmates who are a danger to themselves and others. Second, they attend to legitimate diagnoses such as schizophrenia or bipolar disorder. There isn't funding or staff for much else. Everyone has PTSD. Everyone is depressed. You may not be religious, but some of the inmates use religious services for help. The only thing I can offer you is depression medication."

My heart sank for the second time that day. I agreed to the meds. Why not?

Limping unevenly down the hallway, I decided to think of DOC medicine as M*A*S*H without Klinger in high heels: no technology, no X-ray machine, and instead of soldiers from the battlefield, the patients were drug addicts and women who had never had access to regular medical care. When I got back to the Intake Unit, I went to the toilet, opened a box with a maxi-pad, and shoved it in my right worn-out Keds shoe. I crossed off that rotten day on my calendar.

One morning when I got to the kitchen, I had a surprise. Tizzy was standing on a stool over an enormous cauldron of oatmeal. She had been a cook on her first go-round, and when she returned to prison, they ordered her back. I was happy to see her. She was trying to get the oatmeal finished for the serving line, at the same time she was complaining about a coworker: "She makes me want to keep my teeth in just so I can cuss her out." Her grumpiness was good-natured. What I didn't know then was that she and I would be linked by experiences and jobs my entire stay. Beginning in jail, she taught me hard lessons with a humorous ruler.

My lesson that day was the No Tell Speech. At a "coffee break," the coffee made of mostly chicory and decaf, she told me, "Never be a teller. Even if the cops pressure you, never tell on another inmate." The rough justice served by women inmates was far worse. "Here's your speech," she said. "One, state where you were. Two, what you were doing, and three, what you did (not) see."

I nodded my head, trying to memorize the guidelines. I didn't realize I'd have the chance to test my recall just days later.

A planned fight was set on the Intake Unit to punish a thief. The thief was a penny-ante, sloppy-looking woman. She stole from her cellmate and her neighbors during cell sanitation, when, for about fifteen minutes, all the cell doors on the tier are open. Many of the women inmates were serving time for theft, usually to fund a drug habit, but stealing in prison is strictly taboo. When you have next to nothing, theft is intolerable and answered with swift, violent prison justice. Sloppy Thief was caught after she ducked into a room and swiped a bottle of shampoo from one of the women dressed in jeans and a T-shirt. She was one of the women who scared me to death on my first day when I tried to sit at their table as a Nobody.

The day of reckoning was set, and Buzz Cut and the women in jeans and T-shirts and prison blues gathered at the metal tables to watch. The fighter was the Enforcer. She was six feet tall and carried herself like a queen. When she walked at yard, she held her head high, her long blond curls waving behind her. The women stared, so did the cops. She was a rare thing of beauty in our harsh environment.

"She's a goddess but don't fuck with her," Buzz Cut had told me. "Now me? I love to fight but not with her. Oh *hell* no. She'd beat my guts out. She's fast and powerful. Look at her arms!" Buzz Cut held out one of her own and motioned how much longer the Enforcer's wingspan would be. "I'd never get close to her." She chuckled wickedly and shook her head. "Sloppy Thief is goin' *down!*"

That afternoon, Sloppy Thief was at the microwave and had just finished heating a cup of ramen soup. I was in line behind her to heat some hot water. I should have known to keep my distance, but I knew nothing then. Suddenly, out of nowhere, the Enforcer was there. She connected to Slops with a right hook, left hook, and a right jab—and was *gone*. Sloppy Thief's ramen soup took to the air and landed all over me. Then she took off, as well. I looked down at my clothes to see curly noodles and broth all down the front of my shirt, pants, pooling in my plastic sandals. There, toe-to-toe with me, appeared a pair of polished black boots. I looked up to a pair of primate eyebrows of the PO-lice, a big galoot of a man.

"What happened here?" he shouted in my face.

I smelled Starbucks on his breath. "I, I..." I stammered and looked beyond him at the metal table to see the faces of Buzz Cut, Scarlett, the Enforcer, and the whole Badass gang, holding their breath, waiting to see what the new girl was going to say, the same girl they humiliated at the lunch table on my first day in prison. In a sweeping moment, I connected to my lessons from Tizzy: state your crime and time, do not steal, do not snitch, and the most important lesson: *these are your people.*

I looked up at him, gulped. *One, state where you were:* "I was here. Standing in line." I pointed to the floor. *Two, what you were doing:* "I was waiting to heat my water." *Three, what you didn't see:* "I was looking at my cup and the next thing I knew, I was covered in soup. I didn't see a thing!" My heart was hammering.

The cop was disgusted with me. He knew I'd learned the drill. He stomped off, not willing to waste his time.

The women at the table were jubilant: "You da savior o' da fight club!"

"You might make it after all, Mary Tyler Moore."

"Welcome to the Big House, you passed your first lesson."

If we could have touched each other, it would have been with hugs and high fives, but of course, there was no touching in prison. I was dizzy with relief. My life got a little easier that day. Buzz Cut talked to me like a pal and Scarlett was no longer hostile. The Enforcer looked me in the eye but never struck up a conversation. She was a lone wolf. Is it possible? Could these badass women really be my people?

Shortly after my visit to the doctor, I began to take the drug he prescribed for depression. DOC handed out antidepressants liberally; it was crowd control. No ifs, ands, or buts, I was depressed. But at the same time, my adrenaline was flowing. The hairs on my arms were standing on end in anticipation of danger. What I needed was a decent night's sleep and I thought maybe the meds would help. But soon after I started taking them, I got stuck in the cycle of sleep, carbs, and weight gain. If I kept this up, I would look like the rest of the herd in Med Line.

Med Line ran three times a day after meals. Women sat at the metal tables closest to the door doing the half-cheek sneak on metal stools, knees bobbing, itching to make the mad dash out the door and down the hallway to get those meds! For some, it was their only form of regular exercise. The unit was called, and off we went like the running of the bulls in Pamplona, lard on the hoof, elbows flying, pockets swishing. It was the same every time—hurry up to wait in line. Some poor stooge cop had to stand at the end of the line and visually inspect each inmate's mouth for pills they did not swallow, cheeking medication to sell or store. One day I heard the guard on duty say, "I deserve hazard pay for this, ladies. Just open your mouth, don't huff your meth breath all over me."

I used the time in line to observe the women from other units. I studied the different shades of denim, noting that the more confident they were, the more faded and fitted their pants. They stood and moved like women who had been in prison for a while. In contrast, Intake women started out slumped over and sucked up from street drugs or stress and soon turned into belugas from the starchy diet and depression medication. An Intake inmate's skin was pale and parched from overexposure to fluorescent lights. Intake hair is chaos: half-heads of box-dye hair with zebra-stripe grow-out. Fingernails were chewed to nubbins.

I was feeling flabby from the lack of mobility. I was not lifting groceries, running errands, or raking leaves. Everything in my cell was an arm's-length away. The cleaning cart rolled to my cell door, the carb wagon rolled to my unit. The work commute was forty-five seconds. I had to admit I was consoling myself with fish sticks and instant mashed potatoes. I needed exercise. I needed to take a long, decent stride and pump my arms. Women moved out of Intake every day. Soon it would be my turn, and I would be able to leave my cell and have access to more yard hours.

The yard was like Death Valley. It was set up like an urban track. There was a cement sidewalk along the fence line. The center of the track was mostly blacktop with a grimy stretch of sand, a weight pile, and heavy cement tables that you could not pick up and throw. Jails and prisons enforce a walking pattern. It made it easier to spot any transgressions. We were ordered to walk counterclockwise. I wouldn't call it walking, it was more of a shuffle in our plastic sandals. The flat sneakers weren't much of an upgrade.

Yard was the only site in the prison that women were allowed to stand in place. Anywhere else in the prison block, you have to be sitting or walking somewhere. It was a form of crowd control. Most of the women inmates sat on the benches or stood in groups, sniffing out gossip.

Looking out the chain-link fence across a patch of grass and dirt, I could see the neighboring yard of the Honor Unit. The women looked healthier, less desperate. They had decent haircuts and fitted clothing. They wore good tennis shoes and walked at all paces, some even jogging. It appeared to me that there were friendships, even romantic pairs. I was too far away to hear their conversations but I could see them smile and even laugh. I felt like a freshman in high school and they were the cool seniors. Best of all, a few of the women had dogs. I learned there was a Canine Companion program at the prison and the inmates were the trainers. The dogs I saw through the fence looked young. The inmate handlers appeared dedicated and knowledgeable. I had always had dogs in my life, but they were always someone else's, never my own. I wondered what it would take to have that opportunity myself? I could survive six years in prison if I had a dog to train and love. As I watched their wiggly butts and their devoted expressions, I felt a little hope, perhaps even a little joy. I made a mental note of the feeling—it would give me something positive to say to my daughters when we talked.

At the end of week three, my call-outs listed Church. I signed up as the doctor suggested. At the dinner table that evening, I mentioned that I was attending my first church service. I was sitting with the wild and bawdy Lala from the kitchen; Rainy, whose name was her mood; Hippie Chick, whom I met in the kitchen; and another middle-age woman, Birdie, who drank, drove, and killed people, just like me. When I asked the table, "What is the allure of church, why do so many women go, besides the chance to get out of the cell?" It seemed like everyone had something to say.

"I'm still not sure about the whole church thing," said Lala, laughing. "But I'm pretty sure the Creator of the Universe can handle a little doubt and a few questions."

"I check in at the door of the chapel and go straight for the hankies before choosing a seat," said Hippie Chick, tears already brimming in her dark brown eyes. "I've tried to plan a good cry in the shower only to stand under the trickle making crying faces. Nothing comes out. I turn off the water and keep going."

Birdie, with her sharp nose and small mouth, said, "I was brought up in the Catholic Church. I went to parochial school and sang in the choir. It's good for my mom to know I am going to services; it's like we're together going to Mass."

"I just can't go to church," said Rainy. "It brings up all my crap. I about lost it the last time I went to church. Then what? Mental health can't help me. I don't want their drugs. I tried it and I gained forty-five pounds."

This gave me pause—not her feelings about church, but the meds and weight gain. In my midnight heart, I knew those meds were no good and I was getting rounder and rounder.

They all agreed it was also a social activity, a chance for gossip, and to check out the women who lived on other units. "They play music! It is loud and they let you stand and dance."

Standing and dancing were a draw in and of itself. I left the table moved by their honest words. I wondered if Lala's comment about religion was one of the wisest I heard. I shuffled up the metal steps back to the cell. The church call-out was for seven-thirty p.m. In the time after dinner and before church, in the safe zone of my bunk, I dared to think of my family.

I thought of Haley at the airport, alone on the concourse, duffel bag over her shoulder, walking herself to a new life. I thought of Nikki, back to college after winter break. Was she alone? Did she have enough money to put gas in her car or buy cold medicine? Even though I was granted twenty-one months of freedom from the accident to my incarceration, it was not enough time to set things right. During that time, I went through physical therapy, participated in my legal defense, went back to work, gave away belongings. There would never be enough time for loved ones before the collapse of life as we knew it.

I thought of my father, Sam. "When you were in the hospital," he told me, "I knew there were matters to attend to. I learned who I could trust. We bit off as much as we could to ease your life afterward, including your defense. It was a call to arms. I asked relatives, including friends dating back to college roommates. I never felt resentful about helping." Audrey gathered e-mails, phone numbers, addresses. She took on the task of connecting the community to the facts about my health.

Just before my sentencing, my dear friend Gerry opened her home to me. She was a gourmet cook and while she prepared my "last meals," I sat at the counter watching her measured movements from chopping board to the stove as we talked. Our discussions examined my situation from all sides. One night she stopped stirring the red sauce. I knew that look, Gerry never backed down from a discussion.

Gerry was college writing instructor. I attended a writing class just to watch her provoke her Writing 101 students to work up some emotions. She picked hot-button subjects and would take the controversial side just to light a fire under their slouched rear ends. She spun an emotional web until the students woke up and began asserting their views. . In the heat of the exchange, she slapped her hand on the desk and shouted, "There! Write." They stared at her stunned. "Write, right now!" She stabbed her finger on a student's blank page. The students paused one long moment and obeyed.

That night at her house, her conjurer's gaze zeroed in on me. She stood, hands on fly-weight New Jersey girl hips, leaning her intense blue eyes toward me.

"Don't you want to get this over with and go in? How many sentencing postponements have there been? The accident was a year and a half ago."

It was a crazy question. A good question. I thought about the scraps of time I got with my daughters before they were adults. I thought about my broken-down body, now healing. "Would you want to hurry into prison? What if I die in there? Your chili Colorado might be my last best meal."

That night she offered me ten thousand dollars to leave the country. A similar discussion happened between my father and my cousin, Drew, who was more like a brother than cousin to Christine and me. Drew suggested the same thing to my dad. He me called one day. "Sam and I have schemed a way to get you out of the country, to a non-extradition country. Brazil popped up."

But I never considered it. Running wouldn't bring back Tom or that innocent woman. And I'd get caught anyway. I had read about a couple from the Pacific Northwest who had knocked over a couple of ATMs and were caught far away in South Africa. There was no hiding. After all, what was worse? Six years in prison or a life on the run without my family?

At seven-thirty that night, the evening officer called out, "Intake, chapel service." I stood. *What did I have to lose?* I was willing to try God. I stepped across the threshold of the chapel, and the rafters didn't fall. The recorded music was loud, women were standing and singing the lyrics projected on the wall. The pews were filled with women in prison blues and Intake scrubs. The women had their heads down or hands in the air, many of them in tears. I don't know what it is about a place of worship, but just walking through the doors seemed to release emotions. Maybe because it's safe. Maybe because it's a place you can't lie to yourself. I had been afraid to cry in prison, afraid I would be seen as prey. But I was so tired of being brave. I went to the pews near the front, where most of the Intake women were standing.

The women in Intake scrubs were a shipwrecked group of human beings. We were at our worst and we knew it. I spotted Hippie Chick and went to the seat beside her. Through her tears, she looked at me and laughed, then sobbed, then laughed again. She cried tidal waves of tears and used her hands as a squeegee. She was the first woman I met in prison that didn't scare me. We sang and listened to the service, and she just kept on crying, her tissues in shreds. I appreciated the pastor's complete sentences of proper English instead of prison slang. I loved sitting on a padded chair, and there was short-pile carpeting under my feet. It was amazing how these small things softened me.

Sitting in the collective misery, singing and listening to the preacher, I dared to open the door, just a slit, of my locked-down heart. And in that sliver of space, this nonspiritual woman felt the breath of something greater. It was purer and bigger than my mortal being. All trying ceased. I simply sang and breathed. I inhaled a whiff of forgiveness. And as quickly as it overtook me, I shut it down. I wasn't ready for it. I slammed the door. The warm feelings in my heart rocketed upward to mixed-up thoughts in my head. I hadn't beaten myself up enough yet; I didn't deserve forgiveness. Mercy frightened me. If I chose to let that in, I would have to look all the way down into my blackness. I did not want to remember the accident; I still had no memories of it.

I want to be clear: I felt something during that first church service. A very small part of me opened up. I could feel it as I walked back to my cell; I was woozy. My heart ached, and my hands hung like anvils. Brushing my teeth in the plastic mirror later that night took effort. A stranger's face stared back at me. The face was heartbroken, doped up and puffy from the depression medication. After all I had been through, I was truly at my lifetime worst. Enough. No more depression medication. I'd rather take on the crushing emotions of guilt and loneliness with courage than walk around like a fat coward. What good would I do my daughters like this? The person my family was afraid of losing was a fighter, an adventurer, an obnoxious morning person. I needed to find her again—Karen, the dorky kid, the wild teen, the pleaser, the wife. That night was the night I decided to start writing. It would be a way for this new life to make sense. Writing just might give me purpose, help me find a way back to myself.

While I awaited sentencing, I had made an appointment with a hypnotist, thinking it would help me remember the accident. I rode two buses and the MAX train to the appointment. I walked up to a remodeled Victorian house where the office was located, and started up the steep staircase. I looked at the door and stopped. *No.* Why would I want to remember? I had imagined the mangled cars, the blood, my body being loaded on a life-flight stretcher and Tom's body under a sheet. I clamped both hands onto the banister. *If the memories returned now, I might have a breakdown and not be able to recover. I have to stay strong to survive a prison sentence for my girls, my father, my sister, and all the loved ones who patched me back together.* I stood still, panting until I could see. I looked at my hands and could not make them let go. I had to mentally pry my hands off the railing. I felt like my body was made of glass. I turned on fragile knees and went home to Gerry's house.

Both Lupita and I were nearing the end of our time on the Intake Unit. Pacing or sitting in the mint green cell, we talked about our children, our former lives, our guilt, and even though we were just beginning our sentences, we talked about our dreams of release. Lupita would be home four years ahead of me. When we imagined our future, the difference in our sentences was night and day. She could realistically imagine her future. She had a home. Her clothes might still be in fashion. Her children would still be children and not teenagers. She could snuggle up with her arms around them and watch Disney movies.

In comparison, my life would be redefined. Haley would have lived in California for nearly seven years and, nothing short of a miracle, she would be graduating from college. I would miss milestones like her learning to drive, proms, and first loves. Would Nikki have finished college? How will she be supporting herself? Would they be safe? Would there be room for me in their lives?

Lupita's sentence was only two years, so she would be moved directly to Minimum after Intake. She heard from recidivists on our unit that Minimum was set up more like a campus of dormitories, with classrooms and a cafeteria. I would remain in Medium/Maximum for at least three years before I was eligible for Minimum. I was hoping to be housed in the safety one of the two Honor Units. The women housed on those units were intimidating but did not seem violent. I had no priors to my Big Mistake. I was teachable. I was looking forward to a consistent routine, including regular phone calls home and a visit from family. Perhaps I could talk to someone about the dog program. Those were the innocent days.

Meanwhile, I woke up, ate gruel, trudged off to the kitchen, and waited for my account to be set up so I could call my daughters. I wrote a letter to each of them and saved the last two pieces of paper for my journal. I wrote about my first day of prison and my teachers, Tizzy, Silver, and Buzz Cut. I wrote about the wretchedness and hope of church. I began a glossary of my new language. I became an observer with a mission. There was no end of material. I would have to ask for more paper.

The women housed on the Intake Unit were restless. Day in and day out, the 108 women on my unit spent hours talking and digging for gossip. Repulsed at first, I came to understand that gossip provided the lessons of how to do time and stay under the DOC radar. Every day someone was getting written up for misbehavior, mild to wild: hoarding extra fruit, not wearing a bra, fighting, or sex. It seemed to me that gossip was less about describing how smelly another woman was than it was about the woman's ability to dig up shit and sound like a big shot.

Sex was the ubiquitous topic of conversation at meals, yard, and in the kitchen. There they talked about sex as much as the food we were told to prepare. Lala couldn't hold a carrot without some raunchy phallic comparison: "Dudes! This looks just like my last boyfriend, thick at the bottom and fuckin' worthless at the tip."

There was a lady at the head of the serving line whose job it was to send the trays down the chute. She was a horny old goat and had a keen eye for the new girls. I overheard her propositioning some poor young woman in the shower. She let the Billy Goat have a quick fondle over the tile partition for a cup of coffee. I was learning that sex in prison is not regular sex.

My first initiation of sex in prison was a metal table. Ten of us, including Lala and Tizzy and I, were sitting around the table on a break in the kitchen. Talk turned, of course, to sex and then to appliances. "Oh my god, you guys," said Lala, "I had the bomb washer. My floor was crooked and it went like this, *baBUM, baBUM, baBUM.*" She began to pound with her fists and the whole metal table took to the tribal drums—*baBUM, baBUM*—we pounded together. I was nervous about the noise and the cameras, but this group was not action-consequence driven. They pounded savagely.

Enter Hippie Chick.

"Sit on the table!" yelled Lala.

Hippie Chick sat near the edge and tipped forward on her girl parts. The pounding was a

deranged pent-up event. She started blinking, her neck sank into her shoulders, her backbone

began undulating as she became undone. We shook with laughter as Hippie Chick coasted to a stop with a sloppy smile. I was embarrassed; she wasn't. I wondered if I would ever loosen up. Fast-forward about a year later, when Hippie Chick and I had moved on from the kitchen and were housed on the same tier, four cells apart, and she was leaning fanny first on a railing outside her cell. I had a devilish thought and began pounding on the metal rail. The vibration perked her up.

"Hey," I called. "Remember?"

She gave me the same sloppy smile, "Oh *yeah*, dude."

We laughed about it all the days we were incarcerated together.

New to prison, I couldn't imagine those days ahead, but I was determined to learn how to hang on, and eventually go home. Intake would be over when I had a call-out to the clothing room. It was a yeah-boo: *Yeah!* I was no longer branded as an Intake woman, and *boo*, it meant I was at the beginning of a long stretch of time as an incarcerated individual. Each night I would check the call-outs hoping for a sign. By then I had learned how to synchronize my bladder to the doors opening and closing. I learned how to take a quick shower by dashing out the door, leaping into the shower, to be back in front of my cell door by the top of the hour. Occasionally, I slept. I was diligent in the kitchen and used a written communication form called a "kite" for another promotion to chop vegetables instead of cleaning toilets.

Finally, after about six weeks, it was my turn to go. I had a clothing room call-out in the morning. Lupita had left a day or two earlier. She came back to the unit dressed in blues and looked all grown up. That same day they took her across the street to Minimum. She was one step closer to going home. We said good luck and goodbye, not making any false promises to stay in touch. I watched her walk out the door, dragging her plastic bags. She was smiling.

From what I could see, prison clothing was the least of my worries. The DOC chooses clothing with a wide-body design meant to cover as much skin as possible. That morning I gathered up my scrubs, slid on those miserable, worthless, beige plastic sandals, and did the Intake shuffle to the clothing room. I was assigned to an inmate worker who would fit me for jeans and T-shirts. I was to be issued a brassiere, one that actually had two compartments. I stood behind a curtain and was handed the items. The State-issued bra was not a big improvement. I looked like Ma Joad in *The Grapes of Wrath*. The underwear were grannie panties and came up to my bra line. I was hoping for jeans of faded denim that I saw on the Old Timers, but clearly I didn't have the right connection yet. I was handed a pair of dark blue jeans with little tiny pockets and a pair of thick double-knit red shorts for exercise. I kept my mouth shut. I could hear other women getting dressed out. One woman complained, "I never believed I'd be thirty-six years old and in prison, I am losing my best years, I am over the hill!"

The woman helping her said, "Girl, you ain't even *on* the hill."

Dressed in my new set of clothing, I looked like I was dressed to clean out the garage with one distinct difference. I had a large orange stamp on my back and thigh. It was the State seal. "Is this for decoration?" I asked.

"Hey, girls! She thinks the stamp is for decoration!"

Wails of laughter, even the DOC supervising sergeant was amused. "That, Baker," said the sergeant, "is a rifle target. The stamp on your thigh will slow you down. The stamp in the middle of your back will kill you." I never forgot where I was, but now I was wearing a rifle target. I could die here.

The next day, my door rolled open alone, out of time. Frosty called out from the podium, "Baker! Roll up. Come get your bags." That meant to pack my belongings into clear plastic bags, I was moving on. I smiled at him.

"You're going to G Unit."

I deflated.

"G Unit? Are you sure? That's the Discipline Unit." I felt sick to my stomach. I was being moved to the unit that had the most fights, searches, sex, busts, and noise. How could this be? Was it the mistaken criminal worksheet again? "I'll be eaten alive over there!"

"You're an inmate, Baker. You got nothing coming. Now get. G 111."

All the days of lethargy were gone in an instant, and like on my day of sentencing, I was in fight or flight mode again. G Unit was off the hook, off the chain, and I would be housed with the hardest, most violent women in prison. That day as I packed my simple belongings, I was afraid for my life.

As I bumped my bags down the tier, I held out hope that Frosty would see a mistake. I passed his desk as I walked toward the door, eyes pleading, but he just looked at me like he couldn't care less. So I squared my shoulders and hoped the wheel of karma would hit him square in the eyes. Perhaps he or someone in his perfect life would make a mistake. I hoped I wouldn't see him for a long time.

The hiss of my plastic bags followed me across the floor as I walked away from Intake to my new housing unit. I walked toward a new pecking order in a hostile environment. I would have to work, sleep, find a place to sit for meals, and obey DOC and the laws of the badlands.

I was still Falling.

G UNIT

I took a deep breath and, bags in hand, stepped forward, out of the Intake Unit. Scared as I was, I wanted to leave behind the place of my initial Fall. Those first weeks in prison left me skinned raw. Maybe that is exactly how DOC wanted me to feel. The hiss of my bags across the floor was a familiar sound, but it was soon replaced by a buzzing noise, like the sound of a hive. It was coming from G Unit.

Approaching the unit I could hear women's voices at all decibels, a radio squawking, a loud male voice calling out a name. As I stepped into the unit, I could see the room was exactly the same layout with one clear distinction. It was filled with women. Women sitting at tables, doing laundry, walking through the dayroom, reading the call-out list, or standing at the podium. A line movement occurred and the unit was in full swing. More women moved from their cells with purpose, their faces set for battle. Some rushed to claim territory at a table, others jockeyed for a place in line at the microwave. I was afraid to step in their path. I had been told by Tizzy and Buzz Cut that G Unit was the wild, wild West, so I guessed it was among outlaws that I would learn how to live in a women's prison.

I checked in with the officer on duty. I had seen him before. He was the same galoot cop I met on the Intake Unit who tried to get me to tattle about the fight between the Enforcer and Sloppy Thief. I dragged my bags to the podium, Galoot leaned his primitive forehead with bristly eyebrows toward me and stared hard. At least he looked me in the eye, even if it was with suspicion. While he did the paperwork, I noticed the stares of the women living on the unit, sizing me up. Not one face was friendly. I felt like I had walked onto a full airplane with a screaming toddler, no one wanted me in their space. I would come to understand the constant influx of women represented a threat to the pecking order. None of them wanted to lose rank.

"Baker, 111B," said Galoot, as he motioned with his heavy eyebrow in the direction of the cell. I dragged my bags to the door, the cell door rolled open, and I stepped into an empty cell. I took a deep breath—momentary relief—but I knew the prison was bursting at the seams, so it would be minutes, not hours, until a new cellmate would be at the door.

With so few belongings, I took just five minutes to unpack. I was relieved to be assigned a lower bunk. I was surprised that the medical order of a lower bunk was still in place. A fall from the lower bunk would only be about thirty inches. A fall from the top bunk was a five-foot drop and might put me in a wheelchair.

Under my bunk, I placed my clothing in the first tank box. In my second tank box, I placed my plastic mug, my instant coffee and creamer, my newsprint Intake paper and envelopes, and my bendable pen. As I slid home the second tank box, my coffee cup and creamer rolled around with a hollow sound. It had come to this. All my former possessions of the houses I'd lived in were condensed to cheap coffee and powdered creamer. I placed my toothbrush and toothpaste on my assigned shelf by the sink. Alongside it, I placed my deodorant with a ghastly teen spirit scent, a 'fro pick for my Marge Simpson curls, and my shampoo that doubled as soap. I had finally gathered the basics of hygiene and I was grateful to have them. *Imagine no possessions. Well, I tell you, John Lennon, it's harder than you would have imagined.*

I went to the window to look out at the women in the day-room, a living cliché: *rode hard put away wet.* I wondered what sort of demented criminal would be dragging her bags to the cell door. I didn't bother to settle in or read; I paced. Even in my State-issued gray socks I noticed the cement was hard and slick. My thoughts wandered to varicose veins. Walk, breathe, turn. Then, my cell door crashed open.

A young woman was at the podium looking toward my cell. *This must be her.* She looked to be in her early twenties, a strong body and glossy black hair. She turned and began to make her way to the cell. I stepped back, away from the door. I was afraid she saw me staring at her and I was eager to make a good impression. As she got closer, I could see that she had tattoos on her neck and a teardrop tattoo by her eye. She walked in, bumping her bags through the door.

"Hello, Celly," she said in a soft voice.

In that moment she didn't frighten me, and I was relieved.

She sighed and chuckled. "I'm not surprised they put me across from the podium, on Front Street. They like to keep an eye on me. Sometimes I don't follow the rules." She looked me over, still smiling. "You look like a nice lady. They probably put you in here with me to keep me from misbehaving."

I wondered what kind of trouble she had caused—fighting? riot-ing? I didn't dare ask. I did a quick check toward the red panic button on the wall. I learned in my first days that if I pressed that button, the cops would come, but there better be blood. I scooted onto the back of my bunk and pulled my knees into my chest. She had four bags compared to my two, and nearly everything on the canteen list: shampoo, lotion, CDs, white socks, and a canteen brassiere with two separate cups instead of the faded State uni-boob sports bra. She also had one bag of art supplies and books. *How long had she been here?*

She began unpacking, humming to herself. She wore the status symbol of a faded T-shirt and jeans instead of my drop-pocket jeans and shiny blue shirt that smelled like petroleum. I watched her line up her toiletries on her shelf like she had done it before.

"Nice system," I said.

"Yep, I got this down. I have been in for about two years. Before that, I spent some time in a psych facility. I caused some trouble there." Again, the shy smile.

She looked so innocent that I couldn't help myself, I smiled right back. I lifted an eyebrow of encouragement for her to continue.

She paused from her unpacking. "I led an escape out the window of an upper floor of the building. I remember looking down and thinking it wasn't that far but I guess it was. Some of the ones who followed me out didn't do so well. My legs took a hit."

She led an escape from a psych ward? My head filled with questions: *Did they catch you? Why were you there? How bad were the others hurt? Did they die?* But I kept my mouth shut. She finished unpacking and made her bed. She put a tablet and a drawing pen on the mattress and climbed up the ladder. I stayed seated, leaning on the wall listening to the scratch of her pen. She sang softly in a clear voice like she was soothing herself. Should I be afraid of this girl? What did she do to get locked up?

"I like the little blue tattoo by your eye. It looks like a teardrop."

She stopped singing immediately and peeked her head over the edge of the bunk, grinning. "You are really green, Celly. You don't know what that means, do you?"

I shook my head.

"A teardrop tattoo is a gang thing. It means you have been to prison or you were ordered to do a hit and you succeeded. It can mean you were raped." She withdrew and didn't offer an explanation for her tattoo.

Oh hell no. And then my mother instinct kicked in: *Such tragedy, so young.*

She lowered her tablet over the edge of her bunk. "This is a drawing for a tattoo some girl wants me to do."

I had never seen pen and ink like this. It was intricate and dark. "You have real talent, Celly." I liked calling her that back. "Do they sell tattoo supplies on the canteen list?"

She laughed out loud.

"Oh, Celly. No. You use the ink from pens and take apart a disposable razor blade. If DOC catches you, you're in big trouble."

Trouble seemed to nip at her heels. *Who are you?*

Later when she left the cell, I watched her walk through the day-room. She moved like the Alpha of the unit. Inmates turned toward her, leaning in, hoping to catch her eye, a word, or approval. She was dignified and soft-spoken, not like the rest of the crude voices that carried through the cell door. She drifted across the room with ease, not hurrying or looking like she had something to prove. I was fascinated.

That evening I was doing a load of laundry. I had seen women sitting in front of the dryers to make sure no one would steal their clothes. But my clothes were not worthy of theft, even among thieves, so I went outside for a walk. When I went to collect my laundry from the dryers, the area was abnormally quiet. I felt observed. When I opened my dryer, I pulled out my dark blue jeans and my puffy red shorts and shiny shirts, but there were no pajamas. I reached in and ran my hand around the drum. I looked in the washer I'd used. No pajamas. *Someone stole them!* I was indignant for about six seconds. And then, reality check. *Look where you are, Karen.* My pajamas were the only decent thing in my prison wardrobe.

Use your brains, Karen. Time to be brave.

I turned around. "Hmm," I said loudly to no one in particular. "My Celly is not going to be happy when she hears *her* pajamas are missing." Then I walked across the room to my cell and waited for the door to open near the top of the hour.

Celly was sitting on the top bunk, lost in a drawing. When I entered she brightened. "Hi, Celly!"

I was all puffed up. "Celly, let me try to get the slang right: I think I've been punked. Someone jacked my jammies."

She looked at me, still peaceful, then eased down the ladder of her bunk. The cell door was still open for the final minute of the line movement. She exited and walked over to the laundry area. I could not hear what she said, but it could only have been a sentence or two. And then she was back, only gone twenty seconds. She took up her pens and paper again, humming. The cell door closed.

I rubbernecked at the cell door window like a yokel and could see a mad dash of activity in the laundry area.

Knock, knock. Standing before the cell door was a girl-woman with a few important teeth and a fawning smile. In her hands was a folded stack that looked like my pajamas. "Tell your celly we found her pajamas. They must have fallen behind the dryer." (Nervous giggle.) "Tell her we are sorry." (Blink.) "Don't forget to tell her!"

The girl-woman placed the pajamas on the floor outside the cell and slid them under the door. I took the pajamas and walked over to the bunk. I stood before my celly. I was quiet and waited for her to look up. When she did, I had the courage to ask, "Who are you?"

I would never forget that smirk. She lifted her chin with a backward nod I'd seen between Buzz Cut and the Enforcer. As in, *We cool? Yeah, we cool.* I nodded backward to Celly, trying it out. She beamed her approval.

One on one, late into the night, she told me the details of who she was. She was the stepdaughter of a Los Angeles gang chief. In her twenty-two years, she had lived through experiences that no young woman should. She told her story in her soft voice, a voice that did not match the razors of her world. Sometimes she laughed, acting out the expression of the scene: the swagger of a thug or an evil cop. Sometimes she cried when she talked about her injuries from knife fights. Other times she would just stop midsentence. I suspect she decided the details might have been too much for me, or maybe they were too much for her. Although she was old enough to be a mother herself, I felt a mother's love for this Alpha, this gang member. She was not what I expected. It's true, I expected murderers, thieves, and hookers. Buzz Cut, Silver, and Tizzy warned me of that. I did not expect to like them. I certainly didn't expect them to like me. My celly was a woman whose criminal past, both on and off record, would have had me running from the room. But she wasn't like that. She was vulnerable. I wanted to protect *her.* She might have sensed that from me, so, lucky for me, from that day of the laundry incident, I was looked after. In return, out of respect for her, I vowed never to give up the details of her life.

There are a handful of good sounds in prison. One is the *hiss*—not of plastic bags across the floor, but of a letter, sliding under your cell door. Mail became a time of day. We could hear the keys jangling as the strides approached our door. But so far, the footsteps kept a steady pace as the officer continued past. Maybe my kids didn't want to write?

Every day, we listened for the halt at our cell. Finally, "Baker!" *Hiss, hiss, hiss.* Three letters—a jackpot! Nikki, Haley, and Christine. The postmarks on the envelopes were two to three weeks prior. A letter would have been a godsend in my early days on Intake. I had asked Celly why it took so long for mail to come in.

"DOC is looking for drugs," she said. "They've found drugs in glue, tape, glitter, and crayons. DOC sends a lot of letters back—my family gets so frustrated. There's a lot of moms in here. The kid wants to send his mom a drawing, and while he is drawing it, he talks to her, thinks about her the whole time. Later he finds out that she never even saw it. It's a miracle they write at all."

I took the letters to my bunk. I was bitter imagining their letters on the shelf for the last two weeks. But I had them now. I held my daughters' letters to my cheek, inhaling the paper, hoping for their scent. I was holding something my daughters had touched. I brought them to my heart; I had tangible proof that I had family, my *true* people. I felt connected to myself again.

I studied the handwriting and could see that all of them—even my sister—took their time forming the letters, like it really meant something to them. I could imagine my sister's contorted left hand, and my daughters, sitting before the blank page, *I am writing my mother in prison.*

I took my time and opened my sister's first. She told me that the package from jail arrived containing my Chico's travel clothes, shoes, underwear, and heel lift. *My god, burn them.* She gave me a boost of encouragement and signed off with love, insisting I remain safe.

Next, on to my daughters' letters. They were worried about my health: Are you eating? How is your wrist? Are the women scary? Is there anyone you can talk to? They offered a smattering of personal details but did not burden me with their struggles, which I could only imagine. Both girls wrote that I was a good mother and that I was loved. They encouraged me to be strong and come home. Nikki signed off with elongated hearts that reminded me of her tall slender body. Haley sketched herself and me standing heart to heart, arms flung backward, with silly love-you grins.

Under Celly's bunk, in her safety, for the first time since I was sentenced to prison I finally cried without fear. I cried ragged tears that scraped my insides, clawed at my throat, and covered my sheets. I cried for their struggles. I cried for the *years* ahead. I would miss Haley's teenage rites of passage. I cried for Nikki's struggle as a woman—no money, no family home. I placed the letters over my face, tented, and let the tears fall.

I began to pace my breathing, willing myself to stop before I thought of Tom. The cell doors would open soon. I had to be ready to go out to the dayroom for dinner. Above me, Celly was quiet. I could not hear the sound of her pen and paper. Perhaps my grief reminded her of her own. I put the letters in my pillowcase. I willed the scars to form, and the power to persevere.

The cell doors banged open. "Chow!"

Forward march.

Every morning, bright lights, cell sanitation.

"Let's go, ladies! Roll out of those racks!" I looked out my cell door at the cop barking orders. He was a real Barney Fife, with little-man's syndrome. He paced up and down, thumbs in the gun belt.

"You girls need to learn how to make a living! Just like us, you gotta get up in the morning, take a shower, eat breakfast, clean your cell, and head off to work. A little struggle to get what you want is part of the real world, ladies. Most of you girls never had a job and don't know what it means to go to the same place, day after day. Here's your chance. Now get up and clean those cells, I'm coming around to see if your floor has been swept and mopped." He scanned the rows, sniffed Fife-like through big nostrils, and stood a little taller. "Chop chop!"

The job experience of the women on G Unit was probably more hustle, less nine to five, but I resented him nonetheless. Celly and I cleaned the cell then downed our breakfast of turds and whey. It was my "weekend" and I needed yard time. My cell door clanged open and I stood just inside the cell door gripping the door frame as the women charged out of their cells. *It's like taking your life in your hands.* When the tables were secure and the line at the microwave established, I threaded my way through the voices in the dayroom.

The hive was in full swing: "Hey! Who's gonna front me a cup of coffee?... Go tell that fat-assed snitch to get her laundry out the dryer right now or I'll shove it in the toilet... Look, they got a new Little Debbies on the canteen list, I gotta write Baby Daddy and get some money on my books...yak, yak, yak." Every set of lips in the dayroom was moving at once. Not one woman listening to another. I planned to walk until their voices in my brain went quiet.

I made it to the yard door and waited for the female cop to saunter over to open it up. The door opened, and I was first on the yard. The yard air was cold and dusty; a light wind blew

across the dirty patch of sand, which collected along the border of the building. I stretched my legs out in front of me, walking as fast as I could. After about twenty steps, the sound of the wind replaced the voices and I slowed my steps. I could see the sway of the Oregon pine trees in the distance, high on the hillside beyond the fence lines. The prison was down in a sinkhole. The trees provided an organic barrier that separated the good folks from the bad.

Just beyond the chain-link were some weeds and tufts of grass, and a brave, early season dandelion. *Yellow.* I began to love yellow that day, to pay attention to each dandelion. I turned the far corner and headed back to the building, picking up the pace. I kept my eyes on the ground, about seven feet in front of me, sweeping left and right, to stay safe from attack and to give the impression that I did not want to engage. I was walking.

In those early days, I walked myself back to health. It took an effort to lose the weight I gained from the depression medication. My pants were still tight from repulsive and odious food. Breakfast: Styrofoam scrabbled eggs in cheap shimmering oil, aging testicular prunes swaying in a milky liquid, and cold toast, served with fake butter that would not melt under scalding water.

That day, during the yard hour, I saw Hippie Chick. I walked over, hoping she would remember me.

"Dude!" she said, smiling. We circled and talked about the shock of arriving on G Unit and discovered we were just a few cells away from each other. I learned we would serve sentences of the same length. Like me, every inmate's crime is a matter of public record.

In keeping "the code," to protect her privacy, I can say only that she meant to punish her creep boyfriend for actions toward her daughter. She had a few skirmishes with the law but had never been to prison.

I told her about Nikki and Haley, how they were mucking along, motherless. That hit home. A gut-wrenching sob escaped her throat and tears gushed down her cheeks. Her daughter was stranded as well. We walked and talked, and in her safety, I shed a cautious tear.

"Sorry, I cry all the time." Then she laughed and cried again, using her squeegee hands to wipe her tears as she had in church.

"Aren't you afraid these thugs will see you as weak?" I gestured to my twiggy arms. "I got nothin' to defend myself."

Hippie Chick rolled up her sweatshirt sleeves and curled her bicep.

"My god!" I said and tried out some slang. "Girrrl, I hope we can be friends, I need a bouncer up in here." *I sounded ridiculous.* I could just imagine my daughters' revulsion: "Mother. *Please!*" But my daughters were far away from me. Hippie Chick was pleased with my compliment and flexed her arms and laughed. She had a wide smile and held nothing back. I was shocked at how unconcerned she was at what the other women would think.

"Yeah, dude. I got guns!" She threw her head back and howled. She just kept laughing. She laughed too long; it was awkward and that made me laugh.

We circled the yard and stopped in front of the window that looked into the unit. It rose from ground level to about ten feet. From the inside, it was a godsend and provided a view of the sky and, in that portion of the room, some natural light. From the outside, with the sun reflecting on the green glass, it was a mirror. Our only other mirror was a wavy plastic 8-x-10 above the sink. The window was the only way to look at your body below the neck.

"Oh my god, is that me?" I stammered. "I have never had skinnier arms and legs and a rounder middle. I look like a squeezed toothpaste tube, from the arms and leg in. Gross."

She laughed and bent forward slapping her legs. "Dude! That's not OK."

"Why do I care?" I asked her. "I shouldn't care, I am *incarcerated*." I waved my arm around the yard. "Why do these girls even bother with the cheap eye shadow and all that hair braiding?"

"For a lot of these girls, their looks are all they have," Hippie Chick said, suddenly serious. "I'd say at least half of the women on G Unit have turned a trick, danced, or used their looks to con someone out of money. They need the money to feed their kids or get a fix. Now they're stuck in here, young and horny, hittin' on each other, gay for the stay, straight at the gate, yee-op." She looked at herself in the window. She had the enviable kind of hair that comes with a mix of Native blood. She had one of those bodies that could have been honed into an Olympian. She turned side to side. "How come no one's hittin' on this? Huh? I'm not gay, but I'd like to be asked to the dance."

We looked at ourselves in the green window, side by side, the athlete and the hausfrau. It felt so good to laugh, really laugh.

"I gotta write this down. Is that OK?" I asked. "I have been writing quotes and stories of the women. I don't know what I'm gonna do with all these scraps of paper, but for now, it's a way for me to make sense of this…" I paused, word searching and looking around at the yard and settled on "…life."

"Are you gonna write a book or something?"

"Who knows? I edit the stories for the letters home. I don't want to burden them with the realities of this pit." I turned to her. "I think they'd like you, and I know they'd like to know I had someone I could laugh with."

Tears welled up again and she looked at me, unashamed. "I heard one of the Old Timers in the kitchen say that there are no friends in prison. But I would really like a friend."

"I would like that," I said, now letting a few tears leak over the brim. We both laughed. I felt a little stronger. "I'm countin' on those guns."

That evening after dinner, I saw Hippie Chick sitting at a table in the dayroom with another woman. I asked if I could join them. The new woman was round and adorable and had the gift of gab. I'll call her Teddy Bear. She had a way of talking about our common predicament that was both humorous and tragic at the same time. She was sentenced to five years for a drug-related crime. A fourth woman joined us and sat down.

"Hey ladies." The woman turned to me. "I'm Pearl." Pearl had a long swishy braid and lustrous pearly skin under round John Denver glasses. She had us giggling from her pithy comments, and I appreciated her proper English. She had a crime similar to mine. By the time we went in for the night, the four of us had figured out that none of us had been in prison before, we had fallen around the same time, had similar outdates: at least five years, no good time. And we all worked in the kitchen.

Teddy Bear cried, "We all have five years and we're livin' through it! We're Five Alive!" And our little gang was formed. Already Five Alive was a circle of safety.

"Baker!" *Hiss.* This was the DOC notice I was waiting for. My account was set up with the money I saved while awaiting sentencing and my first thirty-dollar paycheck at about ninety cents an hour. That night after dinner when the dayroom opened, I would call my daughters. I was at the door when it opened and I rushed together with the other women fighting for prime territory. I chose the far side of the circular kiosk so that my back would be to the doorway instead of facing the activity of the dayroom, just like a veteran. I composed myself for a moment willing my heartbeat to slow down. I started with Nikki, in order of birth. It was ringing. Nikki's hello was followed by the announcement of a call from prison. "To accept press one, to decline..."

"Hello, Mom?" It was her voice. I choked back a sob.

"Nik, yeah, it's me. Hi, sweetheart." I struggled for steadiness.

"I've been waiting for your call." Then, *crash!* Line movement. "What was that? Did a bomb go off?" She was serious.

I chuckle-snorted. "That is the sound of about forty-four doors slamming shut at the same time. I figured out that's why prisons are called 'slammers.'"

I heard her huff.

"I am learning things I never would have imagined." To reassure her I added, "But I'm all right. How are you?"

Nikki sighed and evaded any details, mumbling brave assurances as I did, both of us trying to save each other from the truth. The second set of doors crashed shut.

"What are the women like?" she asked.

"Very different from anyone I've met but there are a few who might just make this experience livable." I told her about Celly and the laundry story. I told her I felt safe in my cell. I told her about my Five Alive group. I tried to describe Hippie Chick posing in the window during yard. I told her I laughed and how good it felt. "I think I might have made a real friend." Nikki was relieved. I asked her about her dorm and the women she was living with.

She sighed. "It's hard to relate to them. I mean, I don't blame them for acting like college freshmen who have never been on their own before. It's just that their priorities don't line up with mine." She talked about her roommate, a friend from high school. She knew Nikki's ugly story but she and her family treated her with kindness. "Her parents always ask if there is anything they can do, or if I need help."

"They are good people," I said, relieved but still crushed by guilt.

"We get along fine. It's just me, I can't wait to get out of this dorm." She spoke so softly I had to plug my other ear. I pictured her bowed lips barely moving, as if she could keep from releasing emotion. "Nate comes here on weekends or I go to his house."

"I am so glad you are still together." *Thank you, Nate.* Nikki told me she talked to Haley regularly and called Christine and Audrey whenever she needed family support. She didn't fool me. It sounded like she was held together with filament. But I didn't pry. She couldn't fall apart, any more than I could.

"I need to go now, Nik. I want to save the money to call again."

"OK, Mama. Love you."

"Love you too, so much. I miss you."

"Miss you. Glad you've got someone to talk to."

We said our final goodbyes. The sound of her voice was curative. I hoped she felt the same. I waited for her to hang up, not wanting to let go, and then I sat with the phone to my ear, not wanting to separate from my daughter. I pictured Nikki in her dorm room, alone with confusing emotions while the swirl of female voices was just outside the door, gossiping or shouting about boys and parties. We were both alone in environments beyond our control. I glanced at the other women curled into the concave silver partitions of the circular kiosk. Each huddled protectively in her private conversation. Before I lost the chance to call Haley, I dialed.

"Mama!" She was already crying. "Are you OK?"

"I'm OK. I'm learning the ways of the jungle."

She laughed a little, but it was more like a groan. I asked her the basics about school and living with her dad. Her answers were brief. She wanted to know more about my life in prison. I had to protect my children so I kept the details close to the surface and groused about the bad food and a lousy pillow.

"Your mom met the Alpha inmate. She is powerful but soft and kind. She is an amazing artist and sings like an angel." I told her the laundry story as well. "I underestimated the women in here, Haley. They are not all bad. I am still scared of some of them, but now thanks to Celly, I have someone who looks out for me. How about you? Do you like your new school? Have you made any friends?"

Haley sounded motivated in her classes, and although money was tight, she and her dad were OK. She had begun to make a few friends, but Nikki was her primary confidante and they talked every day.

"It will be spring soon," I said. "You lucky-duck down there in Southern California."

"I don't feel lucky. I miss you." She was crying softly. "I miss Nikki and my friends." She cried until we said goodbye. She was too young to bear such grief. I kept the phone to my ear and shaded my eyes with my hand until I could blink away the tears.

When I hung up, I took a deep breath. I heard love in their voices. A phone call was worth the sharp, delicate knife.

The doctor was right; the only available salve for the inmate soul was the chapel. I signed up for everything. One evening, on my way to a save-a-sinner Baptist church service, I passed a window and, looking through the wired glass, I saw inmates in a room, sitting on cushions. There were also women in Buddhist robes. The monks or priests or whatever they called themselves looked peaceful. But what was more intriguing was the serene expressions on the faces of the inmates. Gone was the ruffled agitation and the bravado. They were listening to one another. They all sat cross-legged on round, thick pillows. They sat up tall. What it would be like to sit on something soft again? I wanted that softness and that peace. I wanted in.

I wrote a kite, and a week later, I got my wish to attend the weekly Zen service. That evening, I entered the room, found a cushion, and, using the example set by the teachers, I sat as they did. We did a check-in. It was our moment for each to be listened to without interruption. I told them that in college, I took world religion classes to learn the culture and customs of places to which I'd like to travel. I had toured churches and temples but never sat in formal meditation.

The teachers were a pair of women. One was white-haired with intense blue eyes and spoke with a Scandinavian accent. I recognized it from growing up in Minnesota. The other teacher was a brunette with a playful smile. They instructed us to count breaths.

"Notice in the body, where you feel the sensation of the breath. If you start to think, notice that those thoughts are like clouds moving across the sky—they come, they go. Return to the breath."

We sat for twenty minutes. I spent the first ten minutes trying to ignore the thick seams in my jeans and my crooked hip. I could hear a few of the other women shifting and resettling. I peeked through my lashes. Most were in seated repose, the tension was out of their brows, their jaws were slack. The less I struggled, the easier it became, and somewhere between breaths, I found spaces of time when my hamster wheel mind was still. It was the first silence I had experienced since my sentencing.

The woman with blue eyes was called Getshushin (Get-chin). The other, Keisei (Kee-say), rang the bell to end meditation. The sermon or teaching was called a "Dharma talk." They were discussing the book *Radical Acceptance* by Tara Brach. The topic of the evening was the sacred pause. Slow down. Pause before you speak or react, pause before you spin the story and cast judgment. Pause, feel the reaction in your body. Just observe, be nonreactive. *I never had time to pause. What would have happened if I did? I was the breadwinner, the insurance provider. I had kids and a husband. If I slowed down, the momentum of my crazy life would have come to a grinding halt. And then what?*

I paused and stopped my usual diatribe, just like I was supposed to, then thought, *Maybe I would have made better decisions. Maybe I would have had time to listen to someone other than myself, like my own kids.*

I went back to the cell that night and told Celly about my experience. "Celly, I know the taxpayer wants me to be locked away so I can think about what I did. Until tonight, I don't know if I knew *how* to think about it." I decided I liked the women in robes.

After another month in prison Keds, scrubbing sinks and toilets, taking out trash and degreasing deep fryers, I finally had enough money on my account to buy tennis shoes. I would finally be able to walk at an athletic pace without my shoes falling off. Celly and I were talking about setting up supplies. "The canteen prices remind me of buying a cheeseburger at a ski lodge. They charge you twenty bucks because they know you'll pay it."

"I couldn't afford a plastic razor for three months," Celly said. "I went to a visit, and my brother got a look up my sleeve and said, 'Whoa, Sister, you look like you got Don King in a headlock.'"

We both cracked up.

Later, I sat in the dayroom with Hippie Chick, who had also got paid and was looking over the canteen list. "I can't believe what they charge us for this shit," she said. "We gotta buy our own toothpaste fer fuck sake. It will take me a year to get set up with shoes and shampoo. How do they expect me to call my daughter? Phone calls are a total rip-off." She was circling items for her wish list: tampons, a radio with headphones to watch the unit television, a plastic cup, coffee, a toenail clipper, a real toothbrush and toothpaste. She sighed. "This stuff is crap, but at least it will be my crap."

"Before I got in here, I spent a lot of time researching women's prisons," I said. "Heidi Fleiss, the Hollywood Madam, said her only beauty aids were a comb and bar of soap. After reading that, I had figured at parole, my face would be a prune. I just cried when I learned I could buy lotion and shampoo. I'll pay whatever they ask."

"My celly bought vitamins," said Hippie Chick. "Guess what? They expired two years ago. Same with some of the cookies and stuff. This is where food comes to die." She started to laugh.

I learned that, in the early days of my incarceration, the man who brokered all the canteen items was arrested. He bought damaged and expired goods by the truckful. He and his wife lived the high life. DOC caught him in the act. He was indicted, but he fled the country with the loot and left his wife holding the bag. The good news was that after that, we no longer had expired items on our list.

Canteen pick-up was once a week. When our unit was called, I ran with the bulls to get those shoes. The women in line were chattering, bouncing foot to foot, and picking at ragged patches of skin.

"Baker." I approached the window, and there they were, my precious shoes in the canteen window. It felt like Christmas morning. I hustled back to the unit and stood outside my cell waiting for line movement. I wanted to try them on alone.

In the dayroom, bags of sugar-plunder were emptied onto tables. Women fidgeted in line at the microwave. Voices reverberated off the floor, the walls and tables in that cold, hard room. The hive began to spin like cotton candy. The cop paced behind the podium, hand on the hilt, ear cocked to his radio. I watched in revulsion as women ate like they'd been tied up for a week, trading one addiction for another.

I overheard the conversation of a group of young women sitting at a table in front of my cell. There was an empty box of Little Debbie's Honey Buns on the table. A black girl with well-built arms leaned back and said to her tablemates, "Little Debbie snack cakes are crack canteen. Little Debbie be an evil bitch. She be sittin' there smilin', all the time she know what she doin'."

I tried not to bark out a laugh and turned my eyes in another direction but kept my ears toward the table.

"Oh fuck me, I feel sick, I ate too much," said another girl in the group. "I think I'll go make myself barf so I can keep eating."

"That reminds me of workin' in the clubs. I used to barf every time I drank too much so I could keep makin' money." It was the girl with the arms. I stole a glance, pretending to look past them.

"I stuck to the watered-down drinks so I could dance and keep picking up those large bills," she said. "Other girls be barfin', all drunk and shit. I would just go home with my pockets full. Me? I'd rather smoke me a blunt and get it over with." It was hard to imagine that young girl in a G string and spangles. My head was spinning trying to imagine their lives. Then I heard the cheerful voice of Teddy Bear from the other side of the room.

"Here's how you make a prison tamale: first, you take a snack bag of Doritos or Flaming Hot Cheetos, crush them up, and cover the chips with reconstituted beans and rice, then chop up a Slim Jim, drizzle squeeze cheese all over the top, pop it in the microwave. I've been waiting all week!"

She won't shit for three days. I added up the cost of a prison tamale in my head: $4.75. I wasn't that desperate yet.

The doors clanged open and I went inside cradling my bright, white New Balance tennis shoes. I sat down on my bunk, dug into my tank box and found my best pair of gray State socks. I shoved a maxi pad into the right shoe, under the insole, and placed the tennis shoes on my feet. Angels sang, my bones settled. The shoes were a lifeline, eclipsing everything else on the canteen list. I paid thirty-five dollars for them. The best money I ever spent.

Later that night, when Celly staggered in after the canteen day bacchanal, I asked her why people go wild on the junk food.

"It isn't the food itself. It's the opportunity to have control over what you eat, a break from the same institutional food, day after day. I buy it too. I can eat as slow as I want. I can eat it in my cell, any time of day. No offense, Celly, you just don't get it. A lot of these girls have gone hungry. Canteen food, hell, even the food in the carts is good eatin' to most of them. The worst junk food is still safer than shoving a needle in your arm." I was shocked at the ugly truth. "Just wait. You'll buy it too. You're gonna find something on that list that makes you happy, even if it's just for the moment. A Snickers is a damned good candy bar, inside or out, Celly."

I was completely out of touch with the women I had met in prison. I had never been hungry. I've always had shelter. It never would have occurred to me to stick a needle in my arm.

When I was thirty-five years old, my marriage to the girls' father was over. We had married when I was twenty-seven, before I had finished college. I had always regretted that. It was time to go back and finish my college degree so I could get a reliable job that could support my children. I took interest tests and researched employment trends. The results pointed me in the direction of physical therapy. I knew I couldn't afford a doctorate, so I opted for a lesser degree of a licensed physical therapist assistant. The starting pay was more than I had ever made and came with full benefits. I would be able to provide for my children and help people.

When I met Tom, I was thirty-nine years old, he was forty-four. We married three years later. With our combined incomes, we were able to rent a nice home. His parents passed away and we filled the house with his family's classic furniture. Outside was Man-land: motorcycles, kayaks, canoes, and rafts. I bought him a used race car trailer and he filled it with skis, camping equipment, and all the accessories and tools for their upkeep. At the far end, he stored a mishmash of boxes and bins from his former lives.

After I was out of the hospital and knew I was going to prison, I began downsizing. I began storing things in the race car trailer. I kept it at the home of Tom's ski buddy, Ricky. Ricky loved Tom. They were the most beautiful skiers on the mountain. After Tom died, Ricky stepped up and helped my father sort the mountain of legalities and divestment. Sam and Ricky were a godsend.

With all my rugs, furniture, kitchen supplies, clothing, and the rest of a three-bedroom house safely stowed in the trailer, I could imagine one day starting over. But the best-laid plans often come to naught. Oregon moisture and mold invaded the trailer.

I remember looking into the trailer at rugs, a dining room table, couches, and boxes. It was a houseful of my precious belongings. But it all had to go. I stood by and watched as Sam, my cousin Drew, and Ricky chopped up my furniture, sawing it into chunks for the dump. All those meals at that table, Tom's big blue TV chair, Fergie's dog rug. I just let it go. I watched a small table get sawed apart so it would fit into the truck. It wouldn't have meant anything to anyone else, but I'd bought it for Nikki on a border trip from San Diego to Mexico. As a toddler, she used to stand on it and sing and dance. Nikki, when she was an innocent, happy child in a halo of blond curls, singing unself-consciously. I loved to tickle a soft pouch of chubby skin under her neck and she would peal in laughter. Sam tossed the table into the truck and stomped it into the heap and I realized how long it had been since I heard Nikki laugh anywhere near like that—years?

Finally, I pared down to a few things in my sister's attic: photos, a starter wardrobe, my kids' baby clothes, and stuffed animals in mold-free plastic tubs. I kept a few boxes of kitchen stuff, I figured that pottery had survived Pompeii so I might as well save what I could in the way of dishes and saucepans. A houseful of memories was like sand through my open fingers.

The conversation with Celly about simple canteen purchases brought me back to the reality that I may not be rehired in my former career. I would be starting over with a box of clothes and a few pots and pans. But that was more than many of the women in prison. I was grateful that my daughters' stuffed otter and seals were safe and dry. It meant I was a good mother.

One thing that I knew would help me get through the days and years was a book. Now that I was off Intake, I could check out books from the prison library and read myself to sleep. As a child, I had started with A. A. Milne and *Winnie-the-Pooh*, grew up with Ponyboy from *The Outsiders*, diversified as a curious young adult with Anaïs Nin, and later fell in love with David Sedaris and Garrison Keillor.

Waiting for the library call-out after dinner, I thought back to the rolling cart "library" in jail. It held about thirty books and looked as though the women had chewed on the pages during drug withdrawal. In Solitary, I read that damn toothpaste tube over and over, playing memory games to keep my brain from turning to mush. The prison library had to be better. I walked the long shiny corridor toward the library door and turned the handle.

I entered a large room with about a thousand worn spines on the shelves and I was flooded with relief. It smelled like a library. The women spoke in unexpected whispers. *I'm gonna make it.*

Romance novels took up an entire wall, floor to ceiling. The second largest category was crime novels, no surprise. There was a fiction shelf above a dusty section of classics. I bent down to investigate the titles of all the books I was *supposed* to read and love: *Moby-Dick, War and Peace*. I picked up *Don Quixote*. I certainly had the time.

A woman shuffled past, observing my search. "I know I am supposed to read that stuff, but I am locked up and miserable enough."

Touché. I put *Don Quixote* back.

I turned the corner along the chest-high shelves in the center of the room and saw the nonfiction area. First, craft books, Martha Stewart—our home girl, with her holiday entertainment books. There was a long low shelf of ancient encyclopedias. There was an ample supply of self-help books. *Well, here ya go, Karen.* AA, NA, parenting, domestic violence, and depression, all a reflection of incarcerated women.

The most popular shelf in the library was the magazine shelf. The women crowded around what looked like tattered editions of *People*, *Glamour*, and other women's magazines.

I circled the room and ended up in the mystery/crime section. Smack dab at eye level was my friend Janet Evanovich. I read her while awaiting trial so I could run away into a book. I liked the sexual intrigue between her hunky boyfriend, Morelli, and the dark and brooding Ranger. A woman was standing next to me, looking at the same section. She was talking to herself.

"Sandra Brown, score! Here's a new one!" She looked over at me with a wild, crooked grin. Her eyes were slightly off, one drifting to the side. The Moe haircut of *The Three Stooges* was just plain overkill. One of her eyes looked at the shelves, "None of these are about bank robbin'. That's what I did."

"Wow." I thought of Butch Cassidy and the Sundance Kid. "Can I ask how you did it?"

"I used a note." She was still looking at me that wild grin.

"A note!" I said. "What else? A gun? A knife?"

"No. Just a note." She deflated.

"You just walked in with a note?"

"Yeah."

"Must've been a helluva note," I offered.

She looked up, her roaming eyes flattened. "It just said, 'This is a robbery. Give me your money.'" She paused a moment. "I must have really been high. I guess that's why I'm here."

"Well," I said, "you're in the right section—crime novels. Maybe you could learn a trick or two?"

She grunted, took her book, and made her way to the clerk's table.

"Five minutes!" the library cop shouted.

I took just one of Janet Evanovich's books, saving the others for another day. On my way out, I looked around for Garrison Keillor or David Sedaris. No luck. I asked the inmate clerk how to get books from my family.

"Your family has to use an outside book source like Amazon," said the inmate library clerk, Wise Owl. "They can't send books in directly because DOC is afraid they would hide a hacksaw, drugs, and cell phones in the pages." She looked at me with an expression that said, *Our life has come to this. What the hell happened?*

I reluctantly left the library and walked as slowly as I could without drawing the attention of the hallway sergeant or the overhead cameras. Hacksaws indeed.

The hacksaw reminded me of the party that Gerry threw on my final day of freedom. It was a "Going into the Clink" party. Sam and Audrey, Christine, Shane, Nikki, Gerry, Jack, Loretta, Ricky, and a few work friends were there. My former secretary brought a carrot cake and slid a hacksaw in the middle. Prior to that we were making the most of a grim situation. The hacksaw prank loosened things up to the surreal. At the height of distraction and strained laughter, we set up a human tableau of the Last Supper: I was Christ. We had goblets of the blood and baskets of the body. Gerry found a photo of Leonardo da Vinci's *Last Supper* and we recreated the scene. It was irreverent, desperate entertainment. We took pictures. When I'd see the photos years later, I'd realize how vacant and disconnected I looked, as if I'd already left that world. I wouldn't think the photo was funny at all.

Back in our cell, I told Celly that I'd gotten a book.

"What did you get?" Celly was putting on eyeliner. She made the line perfectly with the cat-eye finish, something I was never able to do.

"A Janet Evanovich, *Stephanie Plum*. One of the early ones I had missed."

Celly smiled, distracted by her prison toilette.

"You look great," I said.

"Visit with the family." That sweet smile.

The visiting room was open Wednesday through Sunday from 1:30 to 4:00 and 6:00 to 9:00 pm. I tried not to stare as she got ready. She styled her hair like many of the Latinas did: long hair slicked back with a flip at the ends. She teased the front into a three-inch bump and swept the bangs to one side.

"I met a kinda wild-eyed lady in the crime section of the library. She told me she robbed a bank with a note. No gun, no knife, just a note! She said she was high."

Celly laughed. "You're in the land of cluster fuck, unplanned crimes. *Most* of these girls were totally fucked up or Jonesin' to get that way when they committed their crime. There are some bad drugs out there. They make you loca, Celly."

"Damn, I was hoping to learn some sophisticated criminal skills, like tunneling, or safe cracking. I want to learn how to heist jewels and slink around in a Catwoman outfit," I joked. "Too bad. I guess when I parole, I'll have to work for a living."

"If you can get a job."

I sighed and slouched against the wall of my bunk. I wasn't in the mood to think about that. I was clinging to the happiness I felt in the library.

"What's the big deal with the magazines?" I asked. "It was like a clothing sale, women grabbing them up as quick as they could."

Now Celly was lining her lips and putting on glossy lipstick. "Magazines are the link to the outside world," she said. "We learn about movies and popular culture, look at hot guys. Or girls. I try to style my hair to match the movie stars just so I don't look out-of-date. Magazines are pictures of the life we are missing." She looked over her shoulder to the dayroom and gestured to the cell door with her chin, "Look out the window, Celly."

I got up and stood by the narrow window.

"That girl sitting by the microwave with the magazine? She is twenty years old. She's doing hard time, she may never get out of here. She fell when she was fifteen. She killed her mother, lost her mind. We don't know what hell that mom put her through. There are two sides, you know. There she is, staring at the photos in a magazine of a life that's passing her by. She will never be tangled in the grass with the Calvin Klein boyfriend or attend a Gap hot tub party. I can't imagine what goes on in her head."

She killed her mother and maybe she is not the monster. My mind
went blank. I stared at the wall across from my bunk, mint green. I
was really beginning to hate that color. I noticed Celly's shelf. She had
a cheap photo album standing open like a picture frame. In it were
images cut from magazines of tropical islands, Latin men and women,
chocolate, and words like *Pizzaz! Flirt!*

"Is this what happens to the magazines, Celly? Do women cut
them up for collages?" I asked, pointing to her shelf.

"Yeah, I use them for drawing models. We don't have scissors
so we have to fold and tear with a straight edge and then use toothpaste for glue." The cell door clanged open. "See ya!" Celly left for her
visit. Her family was loyal, the code of the gangs, and came regularly.
I stayed on my bunk for the rest of the night with my book. I hoped
that books would help me through the years ahead. I settled into the
nubby cotton sheets, folded my foam square pillow, cracked open
Janet Evanovich's book, ready to read. Now that I had seen the library,
I knew I would be able to preserve a sacred nighttime ritual from my
former life. I would seek escapist literature and get a new book every
week. If I ran out of choices, I would read a bodice ripper or an old
encyclopedia. At Christmas, I could blubber over the glossy family
scenes in the books of Martha Stewart. At the end of the day, there was
always *Don Quixote.*

Cautiously, I began to check out my neighbors on G Unit. I
noticed a tiny older lady in the next cell. Every morning she pushed
her walker out to the nearest table. I watched her juggle the walker and
a plastic cup, sloshing a trail of acrid instant coffee. Under her arm was
a daily newspaper. She spread the pages out on the table and sipped.
I imagined the smell of that paper, I longed to run my hand across it.

The newspaper brought her the world. I was curious how it was delivered so I struck up a conversation.

"Hi, I am your next-door neighbor. I just moved over here from Intake."

She looked up from her paper and took in my new-to-prison clothing, my grown-out hair color, and gave a little grunt. "I can see that." But she smiled. "Have a seat, honey."

I slithered onto a stool and tried not to covet her newspaper.

"I didn't know we could get a paper in here," I said.

"You can order it if you can afford it. Whatcha in for?"

"Man II car accident."

She just shrugged her shoulders.

"You can read my paper when I am done with it. I read it for routine. Helps pass the time." She folded the paper and passed it to me. I stammered something but could not find the words to properly thank her. "It's tough in here, honey, but you'll survive." She smiled and shuffled back to her cell.

She passed the paper for a couple weeks. The newspaper made morning in prison something to get up and look forward to. I felt connected with the world and my city again. I even read the advertisements. The prices at the stores were the same. Of course they were. I had only been gone for three months, but it felt like a lifetime.

A few more of the women on the unit were curious about the news. They came over to the table and asked if they could have a look. Most wanted to read Dear Abby and the horoscopes. One woman, Amiga, would stride up to my table and, in an efficient athletic move, sit down uninvited.

"All right, let's see who's comin' in." She'd find the local section and turn to the arrest report. She took it upon herself to inform the unit not only of who was coming in but why. "Thief, thief. Everybody's a thief because they're a damned drug addict." Her face went dark and her fists wrinkled the pages. "A baby killer is on her way in here. I bet she's P.C.'d up for months. Solitary time for protective custody is gonna be the easiest time she does in here." She looked up at me, her dark eyes fierce. "They'll turn her out onto the unit someday with the rest of us. She's gonna do some hard time and die in here. At least I hope so. She ain't sittin' at my table."

I was just too scared to ask her what she was talking about. I knew it involved children.

The next day, I woke up and, with Folgers in hand, went to the table outside my cell to wait for the paper. The lady next door didn't come out. Maybe she was sick? A few days passed. She no longer came out in the morning. One evening around the table with Five Alive, I asked Teddy Bear what happened to her.

"She went home! I guess she was here a pretty long time." Teddy Bear grinned.

"Well, good for her! What was she in here for?" I asked, halo over my head.

Teddy Bear could hardly contain herself. "Did you see *Fargo*?" She paused and looked around the table, leaning in. "Remember the wood chipper?" Teddy Bear waited, looking at each of us, then in a stage whisper: "That's what she did to her boyfriend." Pearl blanched. Hippie Chick roared.

"Where the hell are we?" I said. We all laughed so hard Galoot had to holler at us to keep it down.

One morning, on my trudge to the kitchen with a group of kitchen workers, I heard a voice behind me: "I remember the misery of working in the kitchen." I turned around, looking for a rare source of compassion. It was Wise Owl, the inmate clerk in the library. She took a longer stride and caught up with me. "We are all one slip away from wearing kitchen whites again. DOC doesn't care—an inmate might be pregnant, ill, or a Fulbright scholar, but until you have six months clear conduct, you have to accept your fate at the oars and slap food onto trays."

I smiled at her. "I didn't think I'd meet anyone in here who knew what a Fulbright scholar was."

"There are few," she said.

When I entered the kitchen, I picked up my scrub bucket and began cleaning windows. I started with the veggie room. The room was under lock and key because they used knives to prepare the food. I slowly wiped the window sill as I scoped out the layout of the room. I saw Lala, the black girl with the strong arms, and about four other women behind the glass. The kitchen officer was issuing knives. Each knife was attached to a chain that was secured to the stainless-steel tables. *They can murder each other but no one else outside the door.* The women brought out carrots and peeled them into garbage cans, others chopped cabbage. Beyond that door were all the bio-available vitamins my trashed-out body craved.

At the break, I approached the officer I saw behind the glass and asked for a job in the veggie room. She looked at the ID hanging around my neck. "Baker?"

"Yes, I'm Karen Baker."

"Noted." I noticed her talking to Mr. Clipboard, and not long after, I was hired. I walked into the room and was greeted by the moisture and smell of a produce department. I filled my lungs with the humidity from running water. I picked up the scent of fresh dirt from the potatoes. The room was alive.

The kitchen officer in the veggie room was my first introduction to a decent badge-wearing human being. She looked us in the eye. She laughed with us. She put up with the hormonal raunchy talk. Every so often she would have to leave the room and things got a little wild. One woman, desperate for a bath, hopped into the utility sink fully clothed. Another time, I caught a glimpse of a woman flashing one bare buttock. Women went off in pairs into the cold storage for a quick bam-bam-biggity-bam. I was older than them by about twenty years. I remembered that drive. I kept my eyes down and chopped the cauliflower until I disappeared into the flowerets like a stoner—chop, chop, chop—and time passed.

One day, I had radish duty. I popped one in my mouth. I hadn't eaten a radish in years. It reminded me of my mother. She used to chop them into roses, like so many other housewives of the Sixties. To honor her, I chopped all the radishes into roses for the prison. As I did, I pictured her in her apron, singing Broadway show tunes to Taffy, our cocker spaniel. Singing show tunes to myself became a coping mechanism throughout my sentence. I silently sang *West Side Story*, *Camelot*, *My Fair Lady*, and *The Sound of Music*, overture to reprise. It took at least two hours to sing the score, and two hours of my seventy-five-month sentence were gone. It lifted me up and connected me to my mother.

My little veggie room crew was there for me the day I went into menopause. Perhaps "the change" was brought on to balance out the young women's hormones. One day, quite suddenly, I felt warm and loose, my body juices circulating. My chest, nostrils, and the roof of my mouth were tingling. I knew this sensation; I used to feel this way at the beginning of an orgasm. It was building like a sneeze for the entire body. The girls could see I was moving into a state of arousal. They stopped their work.

Unable to speak, I remember their faces, some horrified, some lascivious. I grabbed the cool metal table with both hands, I opened my nostrils and breathed the words, "I think I am having a hot flash." It was almost there, it was coming, not like so many orgasms that tease and fall away; this was for sure. "Oh yes, ladies! Wow!" I was *hot* all right. Did I sweat? Who cares? I was in a full-body charging, whoa Nelly, OK! When it was over, I stood slack-jawed, stunned stupid, and so did they for about three long seconds, then it was a riot. We howled. We wept tears of laughter.

"Oh, do it again!" they cried. "Wow, I wanna be old!"

Recovering, I said, "I have always been cold, I grew up in Minnesota. It felt so *good*." It happened again a few days later. This time the girls were prepared. They had saved a large piece of cardboard and wrote on it: *Gettin' it done while you're down.* When the sensation began, one of the girls grabbed the cardboard sign and fanned me. Even the kitchen cop laughed. After it passed I said, "Ladies, this might be all the sex I need in here."

In my new life charged with survival, time played tricks on me. It had been perhaps four months since Intake. In the moments between sleep and awareness, my first thoughts were still those of a free woman: What do we need from the grocery store? Did I remember to put Nikki's volleyball kneepads in the dryer?

Then the full light of five a.m. glared through closed eyes and the hollow sounds of metal and concrete, voices filtered in, and I knew before I opened my eyes where I was. This all happened in an instant.

I am in prison. I am a mother, I cannot be in here. I have responsibilities. Am I still alive? No one knew me in here; my very existence could be living in another plane. If I had disappeared, would anyone have noticed?

But then I got my first visit. It was afternoon and our cell doors rolled open.

"Baker! Visit!"

My people. I wondered who it could be. No one wrote to tell me they were coming. Could it be Nikki? I wanted to see her and Haley but I was also scared. How does a mother, now inmate, console her free daughter? I spun around in my cell like a pinball, drawer to shelf, shelf to sink. Whoever it was might change their mind and go back to their comfortable home and social life. *Brush teeth, tame hair, suck in gut, damned those instant mashed potatoes!* I took one final check in the cheap plastic mirror. I saw my stricken face, my mother's face, staring back from a place she would not have survived.

My heart hammered down the corridor to join the lineup to the visiting room. The women were trussed up as best they could in canteen makeup. Their cheap glossy-pink mouths chatted expectantly. *Who is here to see me? Who sacrificed their sunshine and entered this hell?* I listened to the blood rush into my ears. In the holding area outside the visiting room, I counted the ceiling tiles and waited my turn in the pat-out line. The holding area was the last stop before exiting through the heavy metal door into the visiting room. The pleasure of anticipation was almost unbearable. *Pat me down, Frau Blucher, I have real people in there and I will do anything you ask to get into that room.*

One by one, the inmates stood in the star position, endured the frisk, and exited through the visiting room door. It was finally my turn. I stepped forward into a bright large room filled with plastic tables and chairs. It was my moment in the searchlights, warts and all. I stood alone, in prison blues, before the colorful citizens of the world. I scanned the rows of tables, hoping for a familiar face. Then I saw her. My dear, true-hearted friend Gerry. We quickly clasped and snuffled, then took our seats.

She gave me the once-over, staring into my eyes and searching my face for claw marks. She took in my prison blues and leaned back, satisfied by my bland denim. "I was expecting *O Brother, Where Art Thou?* striped pajamas. T-shirt and jeans, not so bad."

I was relieved that she spoke to me with her usual direct approach, using the same sort of pithy comment she was famous for. Sitting on the plastic chair across from her, I remembered when I first met Gerry ten years ago. Her bold East Coast delivery was foreign to my apologetic Minnesota speak. She possessed a wit and clear seeing. Over the years we became the best of friends and I learned that her direct honesty was valuable. I always knew where I stood with her. She loved me fiercely and delivered a fitting dope slap in the air above my head when I deserved it. Now here she was, in prison, the first to show up, my dear constant connection. I wanted to tell her to run and leave this underworld, and at the same time I was desperate for her to stay. She held my gaze, her large blue eyes were shiny. She pulled her body close, her arms tight across her chest, one hand on her cheek. Her thin legs weaved together like vines, crossing at the thighs and again at the ankle, a body on red alert. What kind of hot coals had she walked over to enter this room?

Between us, on the table, was a Ziploc bag with her driver's license, her car key, and about six bucks' worth of quarters for the vending machines. As close as we had been for all those years, neither one of us wanted to be the first to speak. What would I tell her? What could she handle? To break the tension she suggested, "Let's go get some crap from the machines."

"Yes! I love crap now! It's variety!" I was told by the escort cop that I was not allowed to touch the vending machines. I supposed some idiot felon tried to break into a machine in years past or perhaps the cops didn't want our cooties all over the buttons *they* used. I remember standing and looking through the glass like the Little Match Girl, taking in the abundance of cookies, candy, and salty chips. I finally chose Red Vines and a Diet Dr Pepper. Gerry, who had not had Cheetos in years, loaded up on guilty pleasure: "What the hell, I'm in the joint." Her childhood New Jersey twang made it all the more wicked.

We walked slowly back to the low table and chairs, and I watched her trying not to stare at the other women in blues. After she sat, her questions came out in a rush.

"Who is that?"

I looked over to where she had glanced. "Hey, that's my Celly! I really like her." *Who'd a thunk?*

"What did she do to get in here? What's with the teardrop tattoo on her face?"

"I am not sure what she did, her family are big-time gang members so I don't ask. The teardrop usually means a hit completed." You think that would have made her pause but she was in sensory overload and kept the questions going rapid-fire.

"Over there"—she nodded to the back of the room—"why are those women behind glass in orange jumpsuits? What the hell did they do? Are they the ones who committed murder or something?"

I peeked over my shoulder pretending I was looking at the clock. "I'm not sure. I have never seen them before. While we were waiting in the corridor, I saw one of them come out of a different hallway. She was cuffed to a waist chain with a cop on each arm. Maybe they're death row people!"

Gerry still had not opened her Cheetos. Coiled in caution and curious, she turned toward the side of the room. "Look at that one to my left, she looks like you, a soccer mom."

The woman did look tame and out of place. I had not seen her before.

"There seems to be a lot of moms in here," I said. "I have seen pregnant girls in here. Unbelievable."

"What's the deal with the guards in the waiting room? One guy was a real prick. Some poor lady couldn't pass the metal detector. He pointed to her chest and said, 'Is that an underwire bra?' The lady nodded. He handed her a scissor and told her to go in the restroom and cut it out. She was humiliated." Gerry shook her head and uncrossed her legs. She turned carefully to look around the room to see if she could find the lady with the underwire bra. Giving up quickly, she resettled into her defensive posture, switching her crossed legs. Gerry was the best-dressed woman in the room. She wore black professional slacks and a black and taupe sweater. Her blond bob had not a hair out of place.

"The waiting area was filled with families," she said. "It took so long, I wondered if they knew where you were. How are you surviving this mess?"

"I don't know where to begin. I moved off Intake and I have been housed in the roughest, most dangerous unit in the prison, it's called G Unit. DOC doesn't care whether I taught school or stole cars; crime is crime. DOC assigns housing based on the length of our sentences, not murderers with murderers and thieves with thieves." And then I told her about the sweet old gal who gave me her morning newspaper. "Yep, just like *Fargo*."

"Oh my god." Gerry put her forehead in her hand.

"That's my new neighborhood." I nodded toward my Celly. "My Celly has led a very hard adult life and, my guess, an even worse childhood."

I told her what I could about Celly, but I explained that since she had confided in me, I could only talk about general details. "It's the code in here. You can be a murderer or an arsonist but you better not be a snitch." I told her the laundry story and how Celly looked out for me. "Evening time in our cell is bearable. She draws and sings and tells me stories of her wild past or we gossip about the other inmates. She has a girlfriend and we talk about her. I don't think she has always been gay. Boundaries are all over the place in here. She's clever and funny. I actually laugh. And, for the first time in her safety, I finally cried. I cried my heart out."

Gerry sat up tall, legs apart, hands on knees. "You got a lot to cry about. You have always held it all in and it's not good for you. You're human, just like the rest of us."

We caught up as best we could on her life and the goings-on around town. She seemed to settle in. She broke the seal of her Cheetos and nibbled on a few. "Damn, I like these."

I told her that Cheetos were a step up from my instant potatoes and dry scrambled eggs. I asked her to describe what she cooked that week, in detail.

"I made my chili Colorado. I like to make a batch of it and eat it all week."

I moaned. "Walk me through the whole process, grocery list to freezer storage." I made her slow down as though it was cooking class, asking what size she chopped the vegetables and what brand of tomato paste she used. I could picture my tiny friend working at her counter, singing along with Sting or Talking Heads. In the gaps of simmering the chili, I imagined her petting her cats, or flipping through a *Bon Appétit*.

"Five minutes!"

The visit was over. I must have thanked her to the point of embarrassment. For two hours, I was Karen. I was not Baker, not Bunk 111B, not the new felony car accident. We fell quiet, Gerry gathered up the empty bags of junk food, and went to throw them in the trash. She moved cautiously, protecting her personal space at the trash can, just as I did on the unit. She came back to our chairs and remained standing. I gave her the allowed hug described in the Handbook.

"I'll be back," she said.

"You don't have to."

"Hey, I get to eat Cheetos." She paused, took one last look around the room. Celly was saying goodbye to a large group of visitors that looked like family. "I am glad you have that girl for your celly. Tell her thanks from me." Her face was pained.

I tried to put on a brave face. "I'll be OK. I have a lot of cheap entertainment to keep me busy." I tried to laugh.

"What a waste to have you in here. You could be put to work or give speeches." She was heated. "This is stupid." We both stood and stared at each other not knowing how to say goodbye. "I'll see you next week or the week after that." She flapped her wrist and turned to go. *Thank you, my friend.*

The inmates were ordered to remain seated until the visitors left. The visitors were ushered in clumps into a sally port, a purgatory, where we saw each other silently through the glass. This is where it really hits you. You aren't going out that door for a long time. The middle of my body felt so heavy, like my guts were going to hit the floor. *Keep eye contact, keep that smile, Karen.* I was looking at a glass room of miserable souls with survivor guilt. I watched them waving with forced happiness, the inmates waving back with the same brave faces. A door opened on the other side and they shuffled through the final door, back to the real world.

Once the free people were gone, the guarded emotions were free. A young woman wailed. The excited mood on the way over was now deflated. The pink lipstick was smeared, most women were quiet, each of us clinging to our memories and our past identities.

"Let's go, ladies!" the sergeant shouted. When the room had been filled with visitors, the guards seemed less dour. One had wandered among the rows stopping to chat or greet a child. I wished them away from Gerry and me. I did not want to waste a moment of my visit playing false. Once the visitors were gone, it was business as usual. They put their grim expressions back on and ordered us through the door from whence we came. We were given a pat-out or, if your name was called, a full strip search. I wondered how they chose those women. Was it random or were these women on the radar? What were they looking for? Cans of soda pop? We listened to the strip searches from behind the curtain: "Shirt, shake out your pants, underwear, squat, and cough." The seasoned inmates strode out from the curtain like it was just another day. This life was my penalty.

The next morning, I was up at five-thirty and off to work in the kitchen. During our lunch break at ten-thirty a.m., I was sitting on a milk cart next to Tizzy. With a fishy grin, she passed me a cup of lemonade. I shrugged, hoped I had a strong immune system, and took a sip. I felt that familiar warm sensation in my chest and tasted the fermentation of fruit. Alcohol? "Pruno?" I whispered.

"They have been brewing it in cold storage, behind a bunch of plastic tubs," she said.

I had heard the word "pruno" when I was still on the serving line. I learned that prison booze is brewed in makeshift containers, plastic buckets, or even toilets, and kept in hiding places under bunks, closets, or the kitchen.

I felt the gleeful allure of misbehavior. *I'm in prison, what could happen?* I looked at her, she was smiling mischievously. I looked into the cup. It was Grateful Dead yellow. I took another taste. It tasted like a monster headache with a steep decline into psychedelic vomit. I'd be sizzled by noon. Not worth giving up a jog in the sunshine. I heaved a sigh and passed the cup back to Tizzy. *This is what got me here in the first place.*

The party raged on. The secret stash splashed freely in the break room of the kitchen. The voices got louder and louder. A chunky woman who looked like a roller derby queen was sitting under the break table, outside the view of the overhead cameras. She lifted her top and took off her bra. "Check out these babies, I have the pinkest nipples!" Two women crawled under the table to have a closer look. A crash came from the toilets beyond the table. All heads swiveled to the window between the break room and the toilets.

"The Amazon went down!" slurred a dark-haired woman. "She smacked her head on the toilet! Whoa, she's out cold." I looked around for the kitchen cops but they were busy in the main room supervising the set up of lunch service. Meanwhile, the noise level rose as the booze loosened tongues and inhibitions. I stayed on my milk crate, wide-eyed and listening. I learned scandalous tricks from hookers. It was shocking to learn what men will pay for and what these women were willing to do.

Tempers rose in a group toward the back of the room. One coffee-skinned woman with a grating voice was drilling a scowling blonde with insults. "I got a list of all kinds of bitches to call you. Bitch just be the start of it." It was thrilling. Love trysts of twos and threes sneaked off to the bathroom stalls. You could see the heads over the top and know exactly who was doing whom and how. Moods changed rapid-fire, laughter to tears. The pruno bash hit a crescendo in about fifteen minutes. I hadn't been inside for long but I knew this about criminals: They know how to do the deed and be gone, wham, bam, thank you ma'am.

A guard appeared at the break room door and shouted, "Break's over. Let's go." In the activity, it would have been difficult to notice if a woman was walking a straight line to the serving area. The assembly line was chaos. Spoonsful of mashed potatoes slapped into trays like modern art. The woman across from me on coleslaw stopped serving and leaned forward to talk and gesture like Lucille Ball in the Vitameatavegamin scene. When a gal went face down in the Jell-O, the guards caught on. The whistles started blowing and the lunch service shut down. The kitchen cops looked shocked and angry, jaws set for punishment. I could not believe it took them so long. And yet, we were a crazy group to begin with. What is normal crazy in prison? I hadn't had a "normal" predictable day since sentencing.

The entire prison was in lockdown. Who knew you could still get in trouble once you were in prison? That was the day I learned about the Hole, Segregation. Fear rippled through the inmates of the kitchen. The atmosphere turned grim. Women were powering down chicory coffee and cola. One woman sat on a milk crate and rocked back and forth holding her stomach. Another was trying to pace, but staggered in jagged lines. "Damn it! I just got out of the Hole," she said. "My family will be so pissed, need more coffee. Fuckin' chicory, I need some damned caffeine!" The girls who were drinking in the back before they brought it to the break room at ten-thirty were a lost cause. They looked drunk-sick and could barely sit straight. The rest of us acted like whipped dogs, expecting punishment.

The doors of the kitchen slid open and in walked the top brass of DOC: the Captain, her lieutenants, sergeants, corporals, and assorted minions. They were loaded for bear with radios and cuffs and started by hauling out the obvious drunks. They wheeled out the Amazon; it took three cops to load her onto a wheelchair. The one mouthy gal with the grating voice, somehow still upright, was led away by the Captain herself. The girl's head was bobbing forward then suddenly jerked back, her swirling vision came to rest on top of the Captain's head. "Whoa," she slurred, "you need to get some Rogaine." Then the head dropped down again.

The rest of the kitchen crew was ordered to undergo a breath test as we exited the kitchen. We were ordered to huff a breath into a double line of frowning guards. It was pass or fail. One line to the left held the doomed revelers, one line to the right, the relieved. I was nervous about the taste I took earlier. I kept testing my breath in my hand. One by one we stepped forward. When it was my turn, I exhaled into the face of a mean little woman. It was the closest I had ever been to a guard; I could see the pores on her nose. She scowled at me and pointed to the right. Walking away, I began to shake. I looked back toward the faces of the condemned lineup. One woman was vomiting. Others were just sick with their predicament. Every woman in prison knows that same wretched feeling. There is no greater shame than the shame of arrest. My heart went out to the line to the left.

The DOC was humiliated, they were furious. How the hell did so many women get plastered under supervision and cameras? How was the stash not discovered? The girls in the line to the left would be punished. Given my crime, I cannot say how I would have lived with myself to be arrested and cuffed again. How would I have explained it to my family? I thought about the sacrifices they endured as a direct result of that glass of wine I drank. What was I thinking even tasting the pruno? *Selfish, stupid.*

Shaken, I returned to my cell. The gossip had already reached Celly. She knew about the bust and who had been taken to the Hole. What a gossip mill. Celly wanted to hear firsthand what happened. I told her the story of the debauchery. "What happens to the girl they hauled off to the Hole? I figured we were already in prison; I didn't know you could get in more trouble. What rocket to hell is this?"

"Falling is just the beginning," Celly said, looking down from her bunk. "Not only can you get written up and bunked in, but you can get more charges. One of those girls that got busted for pruno just got out of the Hole for hitting some redhead snitch with a tray. The girl she beat up was taken away by medical with her eyeball hanging on her cheek."

Celly outlined the progressive discipline protocol and I listened carefully.

"First, know this: you cannot finesse yourself out of trouble. They have heard it all. Your sad, sad story has been told a hundred times. Nothing works—no whining, no tears, no grinding your hips at the podium. Your anger, your innocence? They just shrug their shoulders and write you up." She shook her head and sat back on her bunk.

"Get out that damned handbook. It's all in there, but no one reads it. A lot of these girls can't read."

I dug into my tank box and pulled out the handbook I received on Intake. I had skimmed over the discipline section thinking I wouldn't need it. That was for real criminals.

"OK, here it is, 'The Stages of Progressive Discipline.'"

Celly hung her head over the edge briefly. "That's it." I couldn't help but giggle, her face was like a brown moon in the cell sky. The list went like this:

1. Documented verbal warning

2. 4-hour cell-in

3. 8-hour cell-in

4. Disciplinary Report (DR). The result is Loss of Privileges status (LOP). Includes loss of a job, program failure that effects release date and loss of housing on the Honor Unit and cell-in. The inmate is required to wear a lime green shirt for easy surveillance.

5. Segregation (The Hole, Seg). Housed in Solitary. A prison trial between the inmate and the top brass of DOC to determine length of stay.

Celly climbed down the ladder and stood before me, all business. "A DR and Seg are lifestyle changes. A DR is for someone who has taken something like a pen from work or smuggled out some spices from the kitchen. There is a girl down the row in a lime green shirt."

"Oh yeah, I saw that. Dirty blond hair?" I asked.

"They all have dirty blond hair." She laughed. "Anyway, her cellmate had a pair of tennis shoes that she didn't wear, gave her blisters. They're just sittin' there, under her bunk. So Dirty Blonde tries them on, they fit perfectly. She took a chance and made just a few turns around the yard. The cop in the bubble caught her.

"The bubble cop just sits on her ass all day in a glass room between the units and watches the cameras, day after day. Can you imagine anything more boring than watching us? The cop probably noticed she was wearing different shoes and looked up her property list. No shoes. Later that same day, two cops were at her door with plastic bags. When they come to your door with plastic bags, it is never a good sign. They order you to sit at the table outside your cell. Everyone in the dayroom is watching as your cell gets tossed. They open every drawer, rifle through your books and toss them on the floor. They rip up your bed, go through your pockets. That day, they came out of her cell with the shoes in a plastic bag."

"That's so stupid, those shoes were just sitting there!" I said.

"You can't share your property. I guess they're worried about people running scams, like the Mafia."

"Seems like a waste. What happened next?"

"She got celled in. The cops with the plastic bags go off to the Captain or whatever cop is in charge and come back with the paper-work for a DR. They send her to the clothing room for a lime green LOP shirt."

"As if the mint green isn't bad enough."

"Yeah, I know." Celly laughed, breaking out of teacher mode. "God, I hate that color!" She looked out at the dayroom of ubiquitous mint green. "It's supposed to *soothe* us. Anyway"—she waved her hand dismissing the lightheartedness—"if Dirty Blonde lived in an Honor Unit, she would have been kicked back down here to G Unit. If you get a DR and have a job in the library, or something decent, that's gone. You're back to the serving line, slapping out trays into garbage cans in split shifts three times a day. No yard, no free time out of the cell. You can come out for meals and one church service a week."

I groaned. "Over comfortable feet?"

"Wait until your family sees you in the visiting room. Now you have to explain to them why you are in trouble again."

"My kids would disown me." I thought of their faces, conjured their betrayed expressions. "We can't share shoes or anything else without sneaking around. We can't hug or touch, what kind of people do they turn out of here?"

"Fucked-up people who don't even know how to hug someone anymore." Her face was dark. She turned toward the window and looked at the officer at the podium. "Touching? They will give you a sexual misconduct and send you to the Hole." Then she said quietly, "Sometimes it's worth the risk."

I wondered about her and the slim woman at yard. She didn't offer anything else about the relationship so I changed the subject back to the pruno bust.

"What happens next to the girls they hauled out of the kitchen in cuffs?"

"They will be housed in the Hole—it's like Solitary."

"For how long?"

"Oh, they're gonna punish. This has never happened before in the women's prison. DOC will be on it. They will never want it to happen again. My guess at least four to six months."

"Months?" I thought of my four days in Solitary. I would be mentally damaged after all that time.

"Wait, it gets worse. You might get a visit," said Celly. "Normally a visit is great, right? But in Seg it is the worst. We could hear the guards coming down the Seg hallway with the chains. I would think to myself, 'Not me, please, not me.' Then they get closer and stop in front of your cell. Fuck! No, no, no! You're plucked like a carrot with bad hair, shackled in chains, promenaded through the prison with a cop on each arm. That's the easy part.

"They take you into the visiting building and lock you in a room behind the glass. Your family sees you on the other side, and they start crying. It breaks their hearts."

"My kids would disown me," I said again, imagining my shame.

"There you are, in an orange jumpsuit. You're still shackled, wrists together. The phone is on the wall so you have to crook your neck to talk and try to look at them all crouched over. They can't hug you. They can't help you. A visit in the Hole is the absolute worst."

"Look, I don't mean to pry, but how do you know all this?" I dared.

"I told you about the trouble I got into at the psych hospital."

I nodded.

"Well, I've been back there for sexuals. And fighting."

I shook my head. *Fighting?* I couldn't see it. Maybe I didn't want to.

"The Hole is for major rules breakers: fighters, thieves, anyone who gets caught with sexual misconduct. There are quite a few women back there on suicide watch. They call it 'a danger to themselves.' That person is DOC property. They don't care about them; they just don't want a suicide on their watch. Then, some women are a danger to others. They get thrown back there for fighting and as soon as they are out, they do it again. Some of them are really nice, you would never think they would hurt a soul. Others are just crazy and uncontrollable.

DOC will also put people back there for protective custody, they're P.C.'d up. These are the people that the inmates will harm. Most of them are Chomos. That's a child molester or anyone who has harmed a kid in any way. In men's prisons, if you are a Chomo, the inmates might kill you or make your life miserable. A lot of men inside are fathers. Guys will commit a crime just to get inside to make a hit on a Chomo or a snitch. They'll throw pee on their beds, or worse. You can always spot a Cho."

Looking out the cell window, she pointed to the two women at the puzzle table. "See those two right there? Chomos." I saw her eyes harden in a way I had not seen before. "They band together and sit there because it is the only table for two. No one else will let them sit at their table. They are the lowest of the low. Stay away from them."

I nodded. I told her about Amiga reading the arrest report in the newspaper. "She meant to do that woman harm."

Celly laughed. "That woman is a fighter, she'd beat the shit out of them." She turned back to the narrow window, crossed her arms, and leaned on the cell door so she could see more of the dayroom.

She stared outward but didn't seem to be tracking anyone, her body was still. Her eyes narrowed. "Most of the women in the Hole are there for fucking or fighting. I've been there for both." She paused. "It's hard in here," she said wearily. "There are layers and layers of hell. Sometimes you just gotta do what you want."

The days following the pruno bust were filled with gossip. One evening, Celly was getting ready for another visit. "Someone saw the Amazon," she said, applying her signature eyeliner. "She was outside for her one hour of yard a week. You can see them through the fence lines." She turned to me. "Seg yard is a chain-link cage like a dog kennel with four sides and a top." She finished her makeup and moved on to her hair.

I thought back on that day and all the women in the break room. "I think a lot more women could have been caught. It scared the shit out of me."

"Humiliation is DOC's strategy." She turned back to the mirror and finished brushing her hair into a Sixties flip. She looked so pretty.

"Oh, Celly," I said. "I just can't see you back there."

She smiled sadly, looking at her reflection. Then she turned away from the mirror and went to the window to wait for her visit. "I heard that the Hole is almost full. The cops are still *pissed* that the bust went down in the first place. I guess the hangover was wicked; they were sick for days."

The door rolled open. "This must be my visit," she said.

"Baker. Visit."

"What?" *Oh my gosh, who?* Celly smiled and moved to her bunk so I could throw myself together. I put on a clean sweatshirt and brushed my hair and teeth. That was all I could do. "I'll see you down there!" Just like the visit with Gerry, I felt I had to hurry in case they changed their mind. I worried that it was the wrong Baker. Again.

I had butterflies in my stomach, but this time I knew the logistics and could pay attention to the walk over to the visiting room. We waited at a bench in the middle of the corridor until a group of about six or seven inmates was gathered. We walked past the kitchen, the library, the chapel, and the Medical Unit. We exited at the end of the corridor to a no-man's-land between the main prison block and the visiting building. Everywhere I looked was menacing razor wire. This was not the wire of ordinary cow pastures, this was wire that meant to slice deep into the tendons of the hand and quadriceps. I counted seven lines of fencing. We entered through the back door of the visiting building and waited our turn in the pat-down area. Each disconnecting with each other, lost in desire to see our people on the other side of the door.

I stepped forward into the visiting room. The colors of the clothing and chaos of new faces were paralyzing. Then, in the swirl, a beautiful golden head of curls rose tall. It was Nikki. She was standing very still, her hands folded in front of her as though she was protecting herself from touching anyone or anything. She had a tiny smile on her lips. She held my gaze from door to chair. I was torn between telling her to stay and to run away as fast as she could. I fell into her arms, my one-second allowed hug. I squeezed her narrow bones, bones that should break from responsibility and burden. I breathed deeply trying to capture the scent of her hair and that neck I used to kiss as a baby. She was trembling.

We stared at each other. She was the cherub who danced on the table, the gawky adolescent who learned to connect with a volleyball. She was the young woman who completed childhood by herself. But there was no anger in her eyes. She held my gaze.

"Mama."

I almost collapsed. Then after an eternity or a moment, I came back to myself. "We'd better sit."

She looked around politely. There was a lot for her to take in. She looked toward the officers at the desk. She narrowed her eyes. "How do they treat you?"

"I just do what they say, Nik. That way, I stay off the radar so they leave me alone." *Who was protecting whom?* I tried to lighten the mood. "The guards remind me of that scene in *Jurassic Park*. Remember when the two kids are trapped in the car and the *T. rex* is staring in with his beady red eye? That's me. If I stand very still, the guards don't notice me and move along to juicier prey." I smile awkwardly. "Luckily, my kitchen boss is all right. She looks us in the eye. She laughs at our jokes. The worst are the ones who don't make eye contact, like we're infectious. But the majority just do their jobs and keep their distance. I can't imagine *choosing* to come to work at a prison."

I wanted to change the subject. I was her mother, not her responsibility. I looked around the room.

"Do you remember our phone call when I told you about my cell mate, Celly? She rescued me when my pajamas got stolen? She just walked in." I pointed her out.

Celly walked over to a group of four. There was hugging and laughter after a few phrases in Spanglish. They had done this before. There was not the heaviness of Nikki and me. Right away before sitting, Celly walked over to the vending machines, escorted by her entourage. She looked over at us, and I mouthed, *My daughter, Nikki.*

She smiled and waved, a big warm gesture that was against the rules: no fraternizing with other families in the visiting room! My heart swelled.

"Wow, Mom, she seems great." Nikki smiled back, a full smile this time. "I am glad you have her to talk to."

"Me too, Olive. More than you know." Nikki got her nickname, Olive, by being an early speaker as a toddler. "All-of-the-day" she liked things or did things: "Olive the day I eat 'cados, (avocados) and "Olive the day I eat ha-hogs (hot dogs)." She used the phrase inaccurately, but to proud parents, we thought she was genius and the name Olive stuck.

I asked her about Haley Rose and what was going on in Southern California. The two girls, despite their geographical distance, were closer to each other than anyone else. It had been that way for them as children. Sometimes they would fight like alley cats but no one else could criticize or come between them. Nikki said they talked nearly every day.

"The college dorm life is not for me. It helps to know someone understands you. I am hoping Nate will come and take classes next year. We could rent something and I could get out of the dorm." She smiled, tucking her chin with a memory. "I don't know if he could leave Chester though, he loves that cat."

"I am so grateful you have him, Nik." I felt a wave of gratitude for Nate and his father. They were becoming her primary local support. I wondered who suffered more, Haley in Southern California, transplanted to a new life, or Nikki, who bore the brunt of public humiliation and pennilessness. But unlike Haley, Nikki had Nate, Christine, Sam, and Audrey, and she had access to me.

The details of the rest of that visit are a blur. But the ending I will never forget. Just before the end of the visit, Nikki reached for my hand. I hardly recognized my red kitchen skin and raw knuckles in her delicate hands.

She stared at my hands in hers for several moments and then she focused on me. "I forgive you," she said slowly, never looking away.

I did not see that coming. I took a breath before my heart would burst.

"It is inconvenient having you here, but I can still get to you. Money is tight, like, I don't have money for shampoo, but I will be OK." She didn't cry.

How could she forgive me? How could she forgive me so quickly? Then a deeper question: *Did she want me that much?*

At a time she could have felt intensely sorry for herself, she reached out to me. I could feel my body vibrating, as though my cells were reorganizing and growing. *If she can rise, so must I.* There were no words, no promises, or tears. We just sat there holding hands and staring into each other's eyes. It was like sitting in a vortex of purity and simplicity. The other women and sounds were gone. It was just mother and daughter, daughter leading.

"Five minutes!"

We did not say goodbye. We both stood, one final hug, and she slipped from my arms to the exit. Nikki stood behind the silent glass chamber of the sally port. She was jammed into the space alongside grandparents and screaming children. And as she had done as a child, she pointed at her heart and pointed to me, back and forth, our silent signal of connection and love. I sat as tall as I could and smiled bravely until she was gone. My heart walked out that door. But now, I knew, she would be back.

I looked around the room, and again, I was not alone in my grief. I noticed the tender transformation on the most hardened and bitter-hearted women. In profile, I saw the Enforcer. She melted after her visitor left. Her broad shoulders shook, her jaw working as she swallowed lumps of tears.

We were a resigned group, herded through strip searches and pat-downs. The Enforcer sat at an angle on the waiting bench, away from the rest of the group, her hand on her thigh, elbow jutting out toward the seat next to her to give her some privacy. She kept her eyes on the tile floor. I had not credited her with such vulnerability. *I hurt, she hurts, everybody hurts.* She and I were the last to walk out, she looked up and we locked eyes. *Ouch.* That day I became less afraid to walk the tier.

Returning from my visit, I checked my call-outs for the next day. Church? Yes. I could think about my visit with Nikki in a safe place.

The next day after dinner, Celly was getting dressed and groomed at the sink.

"Do you have another visit?" I asked.

"Nope, going to church tonight. I am meeting my girl. We have a date in the chapel. If there was another place to meet my girl, trust me, I'd go."

My parents hadn't been religious, but as a family, we occasionally attended the United Methodist church in town. The minister was animated and used his low voice like a wave, building his message to draw in his congregants. In my father's case, it lulled him to sleep. Then suddenly, the minister shouted out a blast from hell. "Transgressions!" He stabbed the air with his billowing black sleeve and my dad's head snapped up with a snort. I used to stare at my father waiting for the spectacle and then go back to drawing pictures of Winnie-the-Pooh on the offertory envelopes. I don't think my parents gave a hoot about church. I think they were just trying to keep up appearances. I can still conjure the smell of the fusty old women—wool-coat closets soaked in snow and Avon perfume. Afterward was the purgatory of the church basement. You could smell the Folgers during the benediction. I couldn't wait to rush home and strip off my confining church clothes of tights and velveteen jumpers and put on some stretch pants and sit on the floor with my trolls.

Once I was in prison, church was becoming more than an excuse to get out of my cell. Turning out of the unit, I could hear the worship music in the main corridor, our church bell. The chapel was full, the women were standing and singing. We waited in line and filed in. The Intake girls were down in front, up close to God. Even from a distance, they looked as though they were yanked by the hair and pulled out of the ground, their skin translucent and posture broken. As the rows went backward, the prayers changed. The middle group swayed with eyes closed or stared at the ground seeking answers and wrestling with demons.

The back rows held those who were there for entertainment and distraction. I was surprised to see how dressed up these women were. One tough young blonde looked as though she was trying out all four colors of the canteen eye shadow at once, working church like a meat market. I thought I caught a glimpse of Celly sitting down next to her short-haired girlfriend in the rear seats.

The music was loud, meant to fill your soul. I found my Five Alive group and sat in the middle. I tried to release my thoughts and just listen to the words about Jesus. I wanted the music to soak into my dark hard places. But I was self-conscious. I wish I'd known that no one looked at me, no one cared.

I was singing along to the music and did not hear the jangling cuffs and radios. It didn't take long to notice the stir of attention toward the back of the room. The singing went on, but the congregants were no longer in the pull of the Lord. Women started to turn and talk. "They're takin' 'em to the Hole! Her and her girlfriend were in the back row, I saw them! They're gonna get a Sexual." *Oh no, Celly!* I pushed my way out of the pew just in time to see my very own Celly and her girlfriend surrounded by cops. Her face was detached. They cuffed her hands behind her back and pushed her toward the door, one cop on each arm. Then, her girlfriend. Celly didn't fight it. She was composed and just let them push her forward. *On no, not her, oh please, she has suffered enough!*

Church finally ended. I hustled down the hall and turned into my cell. Her lotion and makeup were gone. Her bunk was stripped. I opened her tank boxes to find a few crumbs from her dried foods. The cell was hollow, no humming or singing. Her shampoo scent was still in the air. I pictured her in a single cell and remembered my days in the medical solitary unit in jail and the 24-hour lights. *Celly!* Her gentle protection had rescued me. Now, she was like a leaf in the river, swirling, swirling, then gone. There was nothing I could do. I was helpless to help.

I first learned about prison overcrowding from my lawyers. Oregon is one of twenty states in the U.S. with mandatory minimum sentencing. Sentencing is set by the state legislature, not judges, and requires automatic minimum prison terms for certain crimes. The judges just follow the recipe and bang the gavel. There is no consideration for community service or creative sentencing that might keep a mother and child together. Women were dropped off at the prison gate in a constant flow. I knew I would never get another cellmate like Celly. I wondered about her night in the Hole, I doubt she sang to herself.

First thing in the morning, Galoot banged on the door and yelled, "Roll up, Baker, you're movin' to 113B."

I was nervous as I packed my plastic bags, *Who will it be? Will I be in danger?* I dragged my bags to a new cell, the familiar hiss following me down the row. I stopped two doors down, in front of cell 113 and waited for Galoot to call the bubble and order the cell door open.

All eyes in the dayroom were on me. I didn't know which was worse, staring out at the crowd or turning to see just who was in that cell.

The door rolled open. A young black woman was pacing inside. I apologized for coming into her space.

"Sorry. I'm your new celly."

She turned toward me and shrugged her shoulders.

"Ain't no extra beds, prison's full."

I recognized this woman. It was the girl with the strong arms from canteen day who was talking about being an exotic dancer. She and I worked in the veggie room but neither of us had attempted to get to know one another. I was at least twenty years older. It was the first time I had been this close to a woman who made her living by taking off her clothes.

She walked past me to the window and looked out at the dayroom, allowing me space to unpack. The lower bunk was mine, the medical order was still in place. It did not take long to unpack. Clothes in one tank box, coffee and creamer in the next, toothbrush on the shelf and my wonderful tennis shoes under the bunk. I quickly made the bed and climbed into my bunk and slumped against the wall. My new celly resumed her pacing.

"What you in for?" she asked.

I gave her the speech: Man II/DUI car accident. Seventy-five months, no good time. She nodded her head and seemed satisfied. None of the women I had met in prison felt sorry for me. No one said, "Geez, that could have been me!" Or, "Wow, that seems harsh." People who have never been in trouble are the only ones who think like that. She volunteered the information about her crime.

"I'm here for fighting." She held up her fists. "I got mittens." She moved quickly to a staggered stance. Her arm muscles bulged into defined biceps and triceps. She held one fist in front of her face and the other, ready to strike. Mittens looked down at her balled up hands and tucked them under her armpits like she had to place them in a safe, locked place. Then she turned away and leaned on the wall, gazing out the cell window. "I been down about a year. Crimes up in here be all over the place. A lot of cluster-fuck robberies for drugs, lots of ID theft and murder. As long as you ain't in here for a child crime, we'll get along OK."

I took in her frame as she faced outward. Mittens was short and curvy. Her waist was tiny, like a corset, which blossomed into a round rump. *My God, you could set a teacup on that thing. I bet she can kick too.* I just kept staring at those arms. I could feel my heart pounding.

"What's your name?"

"Karen."

"You ain't never been in prison before, have you, Ka-a-ren?" She drew out my name.

"No." I hoped that was the right answer.

"Uh-huh."

She didn't tell me her name. We could all see the last name on our IDs. They were on the lanyards around our neck, but the last name was what the cops called us.

She resumed pacing. She stopped at the mirror and turned her head side to side to check her face and hair. She was exotic, like her profession. She had large black eyes and a pouty bottom lip.

"Livin' in a cell means you gotta take care of yourself, not let yourself go. If you look a hot mess, all the nasty stank of a women's prison is gonna be blamed on you." She did not make eye contact but went back to pacing, like a schoolteacher. "Make an attempt. You gotta shower every day, change your shirt and underwear, wear deodorant, brush your teeth. Don't be sneezin' and coughin' all over the cell. Pick up after yourself. Don't put wet clothes in your laundry bag."

"OK," I said meekly, like a child, taking orders from a child. I peered up at her, she looked about nineteen, twenty at the most. I wondered who taught her this stuff. Did she learn from other inmates or did she have a mother who taught her the basics of personal care?

"Never, never touch my stuff. I will share if you need it, but if you be touchin' and taking peoples' property, you gonna do some hard time. Ain't nobody gonna wanna live with a thief." She went back to the window. She said all this matter-of-factly. Not mean, not threatening. I was relieved. At least we had some ground rules and I knew she would tell me what I needed to learn. I did not want to meet those mittens. I planned on walking out through the fences of prison with all my teeth.

"One last thing, Ka-a-ren, anyone taught you a courtesy flush?"

"Nope."

"When you gotta take a crap, you gotta sit all the way back on that cold-ass toilet seat and make a booty seal with yo' ass. Then you flush. It be cold, uh-huh. You might have to flush more than once. You do what it takes cuz no one wants to be smelling your shit."

"OK!" I'm sure my eyes were the size of dinner plates. *My god, I just met this person and she's telling me how to have a bowel movement.* Then, *How had I not learned this yet?*

The doors of the cell opened for line movement and she went out into the dayroom, no goodbye, no backward glance. The lecture was over. I watched her round black bottom moving through the tables in a staccato beat: bumpity BOOM, bumpity BOOM, *the boo-ty-seal queen.*

While Mittens was gone I brushed my teeth, sniffed my pits, and gave myself a little birdbath. Now for the booty seal. My legs were returning to their regular shape from walking the yard. I had a long body with a rack on top and a white woman's rear end. I would have to work harder than my cellmate for a proper seal. I sat all the way back on the seat and used my legs to fill the gaps. The prison spent good money on a powerful plumbing system. A backup would be unthinkable. The stainless-steel toilets were connected to an enormous cavern of plumbing tunnels so when you flushed, the noise was like the call of the dinosaurs. *Here goes.* "Jeeeeeheeesus Christ! Wow." It was a wet blast from the arctic tundra. I stood and checked, I had a tender butt hickey but everything went down: matter, tissue, and odor. A small price to pay for peace.

During the confinement of count time or lights dim, Mittens and I began to share our personal histories. It was like chess. Each of us placed a fact on the table and slowly watched the other's reaction. She talked about her childhood—violence in the home and in her relationships. There was drug addiction and poverty. "My little brother and I used to put water on our cereal. Sometimes it was the only food in the house."

I pictured her as a little girl, teaching her brother how to pour water into the bowl of breakfast cereal. Did anyone hit her? Who took the drugs in her home?

We continued the chess game of sharing the bits and pieces of our past over the days and weeks we lived together. I told her about the accident and Tom. She wasn't overly sympathetic. Despite the killing of my husband and another woman in the car accident, her reaction to my crime was just the same old story.

It didn't feel that way to me. "I loved him," I told her, "but he was a risk taker. He was a pretty man, a dead ringer for Sam Elliott, dimples and all. I have a favorite memory of him skiing.

"He was at the top of a mountain." I stood, assuming the pose of a skier. Mittens sat on the desk stool so I could act it out. "On the edge of a cornice, sizing up his line." I gestured the shape of the snow. "Then he leans forward, until gravity took him over the edge." I pretended I was falling forward. "He skied the steeps in a fragile balance between falling and flying. It was breathtaking."

Mittens released her fists from under her crossed elbows and leaned back against the desk.

"Recreational drugs went part and parcel, either fueling him up or calming him down. Over the four years Tom and I were together, he began feeling the aches and pains of his adrenaline-fueled stunts. I laughed at a memory. "He whined like a baby when he climbed the stairs of our old rambling farmhouse. One day he paused on the landing with a faraway look in his eyes and told me, 'Honey, I've used up my nine lives. I won't live to see fifty.'"

"'Bah!' I told him. 'You are larger than life.' I didn't want it to be true." I sat back down on my bunk. "Maybe it was a prophecy."

"Or a death wise, Ka-a-ren." We were quiet for a bit. I dared to think a little harder about my part in all this. Tom never twisted my arm. He would have just adventured on.

"I began taking risks to keep up."

Mittens raised an eyebrow.

"On the days my daughters were with their dad, I waded into whatever extreme sport came up—boating, skiing, mountain climbing. I was the chick who hung out with the dudes. I got something out of that. There was a lot of tailgating. All the guys smoked weed. I drank might-as-well chardonnay. My life was out of control. I was hungering for adventure and willingly boarded a roller coaster."

She sighed and shook her head, just like Celly, underwhelmed. I thought about her bland reaction for the rest of the day and tried to see it through her eyes. My crime was a self-made blunder, a suburban mom crime, a luxury crime of selfishness, not stealing to eat or hooking to buy milk for your little brother's cereal.

In that first week, Mittens continued to pace and "teach" about life in prison. She was an entertainer and I wanted the material. It was like a full immersion prison school. My next lesson was hookers.

She shrugged her shoulders, "I take the money both on and off the stage." Then she walked to the window and turned her attention to another woman. "See that one by the call-out board? Girl ain't got no game. She thinks she's all that, but she ain't nothing but a flat backer." She stayed at the window and kept looking at her. "I know God don't like that blue eyeliner. Umph." Then she walked back to my bunk and turned her pretty peepers at me. "Girl's a mess, Ka-a-ren."

I laughed. My new celly was cute all right, but she worked it. "OK, I'll bite, what's a flat backer?"

"Flat backer is a hooker who actually has to lay down to get paid. Their last known address is the backseat of a Coupe DeVille behind the Waffle House. They do a quick PTA—that's pussy, tits, and ass—in the sink at the Shell gas station between clients. They hit the top of the skank-o-meter. There are girls like me that dance. Sometimes I just go with someone to let them do what they do. No sex." She shrugged. "One man pays me to watch him dress up in his wife's clothes."

I laughed and leaned forward. "Oh, do tell."

She struck a commanding pose, hand on hips. "I had to tell him, 'Oh no! Those shoes are all wrong with that dress, you gotta start over, and wear the right bra and panty set.' I say it soft and sweet so he will keep playing dress-up for hours."

"Tell me more," I begged.

"There's all kinds of workin' girls. A lady your age might be a golf cart ho."

"What?" I laughed.

"Golf cart hos ride around in golf carts working the men playin' golf." She shrugged. "Blow job behind a tree? They make good money with those rich old guys.

"The primo hooker is the call girl, a top dolla' ho. Call girls look down on corner girls. We have a call girl in here. They call her Helen of Troy. One of her Johns was murdered, she was in the room, so she went down. She's prime pussy, even stays pretty in prison. I'll point her out at yard. Just watch her walk, all ladylike. Girl can raise a jealous ruckus all right, make straight girls go gay and fighters see red."

"Do you make a lot of money dancing and, you know, the other stuff?" I asked.

"Listen, not everyone's meant for the game. Why should I wear some paper hat and stand in grease all day? I can make a whole day's wages in ten minutes. Ka-a-ren, your Tom? Girl, you ain't falling in love with the right things. I know I'm gonna fall in love with a Bentley and a trip to the Poconos, and a pink diamond. Eat your heart out

J.Lo. Do you understand Visa Platinum?" She resumed pacing, but this time with a little more catwalk.

"I'm gonna have men buy me a dress so tight it would shame a priest for lookin'. I don't care if that man is Arabian, white, Native. If he's got no teeth, I'd bake him a cake and put it in the blender. I'll just keep my jewelry and the Land Rover with the leather interior. That's the truth. Ain't no shame in the game." She stopped talking and stood before me. "When you grow up eating breakfast cereal with water, whatcha gonna do?"

"You had to have been a pretty strong kid."

"I'm a survivor, Ka-a-ren."

"I have never heard a story like yours, except on *Oprah* or in a book."

"Humph."

"You're a natural-born storyteller." She liked that. She looked at herself in the mirror, cocking her head side to side, liking what she saw. "You have a lot to teach a woman like me."

"You sho nuff got a lot to learn, umph."

I just laughed. She was right. "I'd like to write down some of the things you just said. Is that OK? I think I might write a book someday, and let me tell you, you would be a star."

"A book? Somebody gotta do that, OK?"

I reached for a sheet of paper. "OK, let's go back to the beginning, the hookers, then you said something like 'Why should I wear a paper hat and stand around in grease all day?'"

"For real, Ka-a-ren." Her hard life stories and lessons continued into the days and nights. She encouraged me to write. She would even slow down and repeat things so I could get the direct quotes.

She did a good job of telling a lively story, but I could hear the hurt and disappointment in her voice when she talked about her family or fighting and I began to recognize how pride covered up the damage. I felt the stirring of tenderness for this girl, but I kept a watchful eye on those mittens.

Rain or shine I walked the yard. Every so often, I could see one of the pruno girls out in the Seg yard. I kept watch for Celly. No one had seen her since her date night in church.

The Seg "yard" was as Celly described: a locked cage with four sides and a roof, like a dog kennel. It sat close to a rear door of the prison block, across two fence lines and a no-man's-land of parched grass and dandelions. The women from Seg stepped out of the prison in orange jumpsuits with wrist shackles and waist chains. The escorting officer was dressed in S.W.A.T. black. He or she placed the inmate in the cage, unshackled their wrist shackles from the waist chain and locked the woman in the cage. Once outside, they had to stay, rain or shine, until their weekly hour was up. The women from the Hole would face our yard and wave. If we responded, we would be punished. It was heartbreaking. Even from a distance, they looked diminished and pale, like ghosts. They looked incapable of exercise and drastically lost weight. The jumpsuits hung on their bones after only one week. They just stood, facing our direction, calling out our names, waiting for a wave. *I am not an animal.*

The telephone was the best way to stay in touch with Haley in Southern California. Her letters were sweet, I used them for bookmarks and then filed them away to reread on a lonely day. But it was her voice that exposed her heart and revealed if it still held a place for me.

Like Nikki, she had matured rapidly. Our conversations began with safe, warm-up questions: How was her school, did she have friends? I asked cautiously if she was still seeing the same boy. I felt like I had jeopardized my right to ask.

"Yeah," she said sweetly. "Same guy." She changed the subject. "Are you getting enough to eat? Do mean women steal your food?"

"Not yet. But for some, food is worth fighting for. No one misses a meal. It's something to do out of your cell and our only guaranteed source of variety. You're given about ten minutes to spork it in. You have no idea if you are full or not. You just chew as fast as you can."

"I worry about you all the time, Mama. What are the guards like? Do they treat you OK? Are they mean to you?"

"I obey and they seem to leave me alone. I think they have the worst job in the world. Yesterday, one of the guards was wandering around the breakfast tables making a big show out of sucking down his Jamba Juice smoothie. He'd make all these smacking noises and say things like, 'This sure is good ladies. Too bad you screwed up and you can't have one.' A lady at my table said, 'I'll get him back. I'm gonna give him a drive-by while he's stuck at the podium.'"

Haley groaned.

"When the dayroom opened she gave us the high sign and strolled past the podium. She paused like she was reading a posted message and then kept going. After about five seconds he shouts, 'Hey! Who did the crop duster?' He started fanning his arms and cursing. The girl circled back to our table, smug as hell, and says, 'Take that asshole!'"

"That is disgusting and hilarious," and yet she didn't laugh. I meant to entertain her with distracting stories but I failed to keep her from worrying about me.

Haley remained quiet; I waited. It seemed like she was working up to saying something. She said in a small stretched voice, "It's so hard to think of you in there. I really miss you, Mama."

I blinked back tears and curled into the kiosk. "I miss you, too." I was struggling for self-control.

"I'm going to get my driver's permit. I can't believe you're not here, or I am not there." *I am missing this!* "I want to be next to you wrapped in a blanket and fall asleep. I miss you too much."

"I wish we could bottle that feeling, Hales." We had run out of words and I listened to her weep.

"Goodbye, Mama."

"Goodbye, Haley Rose." I sat at the kiosk with the phone to my ear, waiting until she hung up. For a few moments, I was suspended in between worlds. Then the sounds of 108 women, metal doors, keys, the microwave, pulled me away from my daughter. I pictured her lying on a bed in a room I had never seen, perhaps holding one of the stuffed animals she packed into the duffel, the same duffel she took to the airport when I watched her walk away to a new life. *I can't soothe you or save you from here.*

After the phone call with Haley, I went out to the yard. I wanted to wallow in guilt but it was not meant to be. Spring had arrived, the yard was full. That meant I had to concentrate on safe personal boundaries. Women were walking, standing, and sitting at tables. Mittens was sitting at a yard table with her face in the sun as another woman braided her hair. As I passed, she called my name.

"Ka-a-ren, come 'ere." She crooked her finger, I leaned down to her. "That fancy call girl, Helen of Troy, is over there." She rolled her eyes to the back fence. "Blonde."

"Oh, yeah. I see her." I watched her walk. She took small steps in a toe-heel gait instead of heel-toe. It slowed her down and made her hips sway. "She's pretty all right," I said.

Mittens grunted in agreement, closed her eyes, and gave herself over to sun and the rare allowed human touch.

Hippie Chick came out, caught up with me, and as always, we circled the yard counterclockwise.

"My bunkie told me that that girl over by the fence, the blonde, is a high-class call girl," I said.

"Dude, I know. The girl with her is my cellmate. They're girl-friends," said Hippie Chick waving quote fingers. "My cellmate is one angry motherfucker. If she don't like you, you gotta worry about it, and she don't like me." Hippie Chick shivered. "I am only in that cell when I have to be. She's jealous of anyone who talks to Helen of Troy. Those two argue constantly, then she bitches about it to me. Sounds like she has had some pretty fucked-up relationships, lots of domestic violence. She's just too far gone to fix."

She was quiet for a full turn around the yard. Then she stopped walking and turned to me. "I used to fight. I see red when I fight. I black out and keep fighting." Hippie Chick looked away and went into her thoughts. *Does everyone fight in here?* We circled in silence. Then she turned to me again, tears at the brim, "I used to love it. Fuckin' scares me, I don't want to ever do that again." She used the heels of her hands to swipe her eyes.

From a distance, we could hear Angry Girlfriend shouting at Helen of Troy. Helen of Troy's head was down. She was walking close to the fence line, her shoulders were hunched. Angry Girlfriend was getting loud.

We circled closer to the argument. Angry Girlfriend's voice was escalating. Hippie Chick slowed her walk and said low and even, "Oh shit, Karen. I don't like it." We were about ten feet away. A third girl was involved. The girl was puffing out her chest at Angry Girlfriend. It looked like a lover's triangle.

"You stay away from my girl, bitch," Angry Girlfriend shouted.

"I guess I'll talk to whoever I want." The third girl scowled.

"If you're lookin' for trouble, you done found it," said Angry Girlfriend.

Suddenly, right in front of us, Angry Girlfriend started to swing. We froze in our tracks. This wasn't bitch-slapping and hair-pulling. It was pummeling. The third girl fell on the second punch. We tried to scoot back but were blocked by the instant crowd of spectators gathering in sick fascination. The loser on her back, Angry Girlfriend kneeled over her and just kept on swinging. The only sound was fist and face. The blood flew through the air in chunks, not droplets, maybe it held some teeth or a bit of flesh. It seemed like an eternity, someone beside me puked. Finally the alarm, *whoop, whoop, whoop.* The cops dragged Angry Girlfriend off the unconscious woman, her face sweating with rage. They cuffed Angry Girlfriend and Helen of Troy and led them away. Then they loaded the wounded woman into a wheelchair and wheeled her off the yard.

I was shaken. I never knew women were capable of fighting like that, like a scene in a Tarantino movie, but this happened right in front of me, not on a movie screen. I was horrified, my heart pounding in my ears.

Hippie Chick was shaking. "I can't see that kind of fighting."

"Why are they taking the girl on the ground? She never took a swing," I screeched. "Helen of Troy was just standing there!"

"They take 'em all," said a voice in the crowd. "They figure if you're playin' with fire, you're burnt."

"Whoa, dude," said Hippie Chick. "I'm just glad it wasn't me." Then she brightened, "Hey, looks like I get a new cellmate!"

The crowd broke up. Hippie Chick and I circled the yard for the rest of the hour, trying to recover from the violence. We sidestepped the patch of cement where the fight had taken place, the bloodstains turning brown in the sun. I hoped rain was in the forecast.

Before I was sentenced, awaiting my day in court, I continued to research prison life. Fighting was a topic in every book. I stood before in the mirror, *C'mon Karen, get mad.* I made fists and scowled. My hands were wee brittle claws, and my face was more freak show than fight club. I needed to learn the basics of fighting. I called my dad and he recommended self-defense lessons.

"I'll pay for it," he said.

I made an appointment at a local martial arts studio near Gerry's house. The instructor looked all of seventeen with a face full of acne and peach fuzz.

"I'm going to prison," I told this child. "It's just a matter of time before I go in. I need to know how to protect myself."

He was shocked. A smile tugged at his lips, *You're kidding, right?* But my eyes said I was dead serious.

"Oh, um, OK," he stammered. "Let's start with some padding." He dressed me in a padded helmet, vest, and boxing gloves. I stood before the gym mirror. *There's no pads in prison.*

"First," he says, all puffed up with authority. "Women don't fight like men. I think the most you'll ever see would be a little pushing and slapping. The best thing you can do is just get away." He taught me how to talk someone down, roll in a ball, and cover my head. Lesson over.

I went to Gerry's house after my lesson. "How'd it go?" she asked.

"What a joke. The teacher was a patronizing choirboy," I complained.

Gerry offered a solution. Her son, Michael, was a martial artist, and lucky for me, a med student on his way to becoming an ER doc. Michael was a strong, capable man. He came to the house one day and we went upstairs to Gerry's large bedroom. We pushed back the furniture and rolled up the rugs.

My lesson started with the basics: Keep your thumbs outside your fists. Keep one hand in front of your face, the other in a fist. Stand in a staggered stance.

"Try to avoid a fight," he said, "but be prepared." Then he made an intense angry face and roared, lunging at me with his hands. I crumpled.

"At least you covered your head." He was trying not to laugh. "Get up, let's go!"

I scrambled to my feet and he attacked. "Block! Kick!" he commanded. "Keep that hand in front of your face." He pulled back and came again. "That's it, nice protection. Keep your teeth." He lunged and jabbed over and over. It was a workout. I tried to bob and weave but I was slow and clumsy. "You dropped your hand!"

I looked at my hand like it didn't belong to me.

He laughed, put up his hands, and shook his head. "OK. Let's keep it simple. You're not gonna get this in one lesson. But you can yell. Yell for help!" He charged at me.

"Help." I kept one hand in front of my face, the other in a fist.

"*Yell!*" he shouted.

"*Help!*" I shouted, hunkering in my pose, "*HELP!*"

"Yes, just like that. Let's call it a day." He looked worried. "Just stay out of trouble."

We headed for the stairs. Michael bounced down and began to dig into the fridge. Gerry looked up as I hobbled down, leaning on the banister.

"Looks like you had a tough lesson," she said, hands on hips. "You two have been crashing around for about an hour. I was afraid the neighbors would call the cops."

"Oh, Michael's got the information," I said. "Too bad his student is past her prime."

Michael grinned and tore into his sandwich.

After witnessing the fighting skills of Angry Girlfriend, I knew I was incapable of protecting myself. I made a new plan: scream, run, and hide. That evening before the lights dimmed, I brought up the fight with Mittens.

"It just came out of nowhere. Hippie Chick and I were right there."

"There will always be fights when people live on top of each other in here. For some of us, fighting is a way of life." She was matter-of-fact, like it was just another day. I stayed quiet, hoping she would continue. Mittens was trying out hairdos in the tiny mirror. "Yep," she drawled as she applied oil to her hair and wrestled it into a high ponytail. She stopped and stared into her reflection. "These women in here have had the shit beaten out of them. Most of them have had to learn how to fight from their own family. Our mamas fought, we fight." She paused. "I learned to fight from men."

Mittens put down the comb and turned to me. "One day I got in trouble in school. The principal called me down to the office. He chewed me out and said, 'I'm gonna call your mother.' I laughed." She shook her head. "I told him, you can lecture me as much as you want. I'll listen. But, you do *not* want to mess with my mother. She gets mad. It ain't safe." She began to pace, she didn't look at me. When she continued, it was in a soft voice. "My dad didn't trust women. One time he got so mad, he took it out on me, held me down by the back of my neck and made me eat food out of a dog dish. He yellin' at me, 'All you women are bitches.'" Mittens stopped pacing and looked in the mirror. She picked up her comb and just stared at it in her hand. She squeezed her fingers around the comb.

I was quiet and kept my eyes down to give her privacy. I imagined that scene with her young head over a dog dish, kneeling on the floor. *How old was she? How did she get through it?* Mittens went back to pacing, this time with purpose, as if to shake off the memory. She stopped in front of my bunk and held up her fists, grinning, in an abrupt mental shift.

"I was taught to square off and box. I'm fast." She feinted a fast fury of fist work. "I use my hands, legs, and any object I need." She was still grinning, then the smile slid away and she went to her perch at the window. She crossed her arms and hid her fists, tight against her ribs. "Fightin's gotten me in a lot of trouble, I've broken legs." I waited. She spoke to the window, "I rebroke the same leg. That's why I am here.

I can't ever fight again." She stood still, staring out the window. Her breath came in huffs as though she was silently sobbing. Then, almost inaudibly, "I can't come back here."

Our cell was quiet for the rest of the night. I held back my questions and let the violence rest. How could this young girl ever learn to trust anyone?

The following evening, she wanted to talk about fighting again. I was surprised. I knew how deeply it affected her the night before.

"When it comes to fighting, men will kill each other, break both legs, maybe throw boiling water in someone's face." She resumed pacing as the sassy schoolteacher, her vulnerability stuffed away. "Women are smarter than men. You can settle a score without ever taking a swing." She looked at her hygiene shelf. "Weapons be sittin' right here."

I looked at her shelf. Like Celly, she had been down longer than me and had accumulated not only the basics but also cheap canteen makeup, a banana hair clip, and a disposable razor.

"Would you mind if I wrote?" I asked.

"Oh yeah, get this down, Ka-a-ren. They don't teach this in your neighborhood." She struck a pose, arms crossed, one hip jutting out. "I heard your girl Hippie Chick got a new roommate." She laughed and shook her head. "She went from the angriest bitch in prison to the most obnoxious." She sighed and lowered her eyes. "I can't talk down about her new celly, Ka-a-ren. Her story is about the saddest one you'll ever hear. She got pregnant at nine, had a baby at ten. By someone in her family. She just ain't right, you know. But man, her voice! You can hear her baby talk all over the dayroom. She gets on my last nerve. But then I have to think—poor girl."

Mittens was rearranging some of the items on her shelf, sniffing her hair products and looking at me. "Some low-down dirty sneak got fed up with her talking all the time and put Nair in her shampoo. All her hair fell out in clumps." She turned to me, lifting her chin. "That's how most women fight, Ka-a-ren. Women use tricks and gossip before they throw down. They can say you're a thief or a snitch. The rap'll fuck you up, even if it's not true. It's tough to shake."

"Most of the fights in here are between cellies."

My head jerked up, but she did not notice my alarm. I stopped writing, all ears.

"You don't have to get all Clint Eastwood and pull a publicity stunt"—she waved her hands—"yellin' at your roommate. That's punk-ass shit. Just put a lock in sock and get it over with, uh-huh."

I was rigid, blood rushed from my head to my limbs. I watched her powerful body pace back and forth and I looked at her arms. It was like being in a cage with a beautiful tiger.

Nearly every night, I put on my pajamas and read in my cell. Even though I had not saved enough money for a radio or headphones to watch the TVs, I preferred to read, I always had. I would read until the dayroom closed and wait for Mittens to return with new gossip, stories of her past, or lessons for prison life. One night, Mittens strolled in looking bored. "What you readin'?"

"David Sedaris. He's one of my favorites, very funny." I was thrilled when I found Sedaris in the library. I read her a few lines about his job as an elf at a department store.

"First book I read was in this cell," she said.

"Really?" I was shocked.

"Yep. Now I'm reading every Sandra Brown book in the library. She's my girl, all full of twists and turns, you never know who done it until the last page. What else you got there?"

"I picked up a children's book. It's one I used to read to my kids. It's called *Where the Wild Things Are*." I handed it to her and she climbed up on her bunk. "The illustrations are great. My kids liked the way the monsters roared their terrible roars and gnashed their terrible teeth." I stared up at the bottom of her bunk hoping she would give it a try and I heard her turning to the final page..

"Ah. It was still hot." *Yes.* I wondered if anyone ever read to her as a child. Then as if she read my mind, she said,

"My grandma used to read to me. She taught me a song. 'Baby Moon.'" Mittens began to sing about a tiny moon in the sky. I leaned out of my bunk to see her sing. She was on her back and was pointing her neat little feet into the corner like a moon.

She looked so young and innocent. I missed my girls.

"Teach me that song."

And so she began: *Baby moon, keep shining....*

Mittens was a fighter, an erotic dancer, and perhaps a hooker of sorts, but she was also just a young girl. When I spoke to her, my voice had an eager tone, a motherly tone. I might have redirected my desire to mother my children to this girl. But she didn't seem to mind. For those days we celled together, she filled the hole in my heart.

The following weekend, Gerry came for another visit. I saw her immediately—black jeans and a black top. Three-quarters of her closet was black: black shoes, black dresses, black jackets, black purses. Her running joke was, "What black outfit shall I wear today?" I missed that color.

I was less emotional this time as I approached her. I gave her a quick allowed squeeze and we sat down. She did not look around the room wild-eyed, as she had on the first visit. She smiled at me, her posture less entwined, both hands on her knees, giving them a slap.

"So. What's up?"

When I told her about Celly going to the Hole, she seemed genuinely upset.

"Damn. She was good for you. Somehow you came in here and right away, you found a badass babe to watch out for you. I was impressed. You stay out of trouble, I better not come here and find you behind a glass window dressed in orange."

"Trust me, these blue clothes are bad enough. I don't think I will ever wear this color again. The very next day, I had a new celly. She's an exotic dancer." Gerry snorted, shrugged a shoulder like it was no surprise to her, a woman of the world. "She's also a fighter, she's locked up for assault."

Gerry sat back, resumed her pose of vine-wrapped legs, one arm around her ribs, now forehead in hand. She looked up, concerned.

"I'm glad you had the self-defense lesson from Michael. I hope you don't have to use it."

I filled her in about Mittens. "I can't help but like her. She gave me the rules of cell life on the first day—and trust me, I walk the line. I think she had a pretty rough childhood and had to make her own way. She's street-smart, got her eyes on livin' large—you know, a Bentley, vacations, and an unlimited credit card. I think she'd do about anything to get it.

"I told Mittens a few things about Tom, his wild friends, his exploits, his charm. She said I fell in love with the wrong things."

Gerry smiled sadly. "Tom and his friends were fun. Cute guys, like playing with matches." Gerry sat back in the chair. "You have always been a stunning woman and loved to have fun. I think it's what got you into trouble in the first place." She paused and thought. "I dunno. In many ways, Tom was perfect for you and a disaster for you. A stunning man and woman. His motto, 'We're not here for a long time, we're here for a good time,' was a fucked-up way of life. And yet he was a loveable guy. I was genuinely fond of him."

"People who met him never forgot him. But unlike me, you liked him from a distance. Did I ever tell you that my cousin, Drew, met Tom, many years ago in Snowbird, Utah? One of Drew's buddies had taken a nasty fall, broke his leg, and they had to go for help. It was Tom and his mountain rescue crew that brought him out."

"What are the odds?" said Gerry.

"Drew told me he was very young then, maybe eighteen or twenty, and Tom left a lasting impression on him. After he heard about the accident, he and his buddies had a private remembrance for Tom during a bow-hunting trip. They listened to 'Touch of Gray' by the Grateful Dead, smoked a little something, and then tied a cloth soaked in booze to an arrow. He told me how he notched it in the bow, brought it all the way back, his friend lit it, and they let it sail off into the darkness down a huge ravine, a thousand feet below into the rocks."

"Tom would have liked that. He was a free spirit," said Gerry, nodding.

That night on my bunk, I was able to conjure up some of Tom's memories, his shtick, and his laugh. I thought again about coming home at the end of my workday, that final trudge up the steps to the porch, and, within seconds, the sound of his recliner slamming upright, the running footsteps and the dog toenails across the wooden floor of the farmhouse, the door flung open, man and dog, his wing-span, his smile, "Honey! You're home!" Who could not love such a greeting? *I was not wrong to love him.*

G Unit meant harsh lessons in prison survival. I learned to avoid the fighters and the mentally unstable women. I learned a little street slang to sound like I knew what was goin' down. I learned how to swipe extra fruit in the chow line. Incarcerated people learn all the wrong things.

In the first days on G Unit, I watched the more experienced felons pick up their food tray and walk to the fruit crate at the end of the line. They would take a look at the cop by the cart and, if the coast was clear, they made a quick snag for an extra mushy apple or dry orange. The quick double grab was an art form: the hand opens wide, grabs two pieces of fruit, and as the hand closes, one of the oranges is tucked up the sleeve of the sweatshirt. To keep the extra orange hidden, the cuff is pinched together with the pinky and ring finger. The thumb, pointer, and tall man hold the visible fruit. That way, the cop sees her walk away with just one piece of fruit.

We hid all kinds of things up our sweatshirt sleeves. On chilly mornings at yard, we broke the rules and wore socks on our hands for mittens and tucked them in our sleeves just to stay warm. From our sleeves we exchanged stamped envelopes, a serving of coffee, or any other form of prison currency. Some women stowed extra bags of potato chips, or even a frosted piece of cake.

We were creative with our few possessions; everything had an alternative purpose. I jammed a large library book under my mattress, a narrow edge sticking out for a bedside shelf. I used my beanie cap as a purse. Every item that came in through the canteen was repurposed. We washed out plastic bags until they were sieves. Hippie Chick said to me one day, "Dude! Are you gonna throw out your twist tie? Do you know what you can do with that? You can make a paper clip for your letters or use it for a hair tie."

Inmates are the ultimate MacGyvers. The wildest example was a homemade dildo. About five months into my time, the Po-Po came squawking and jangling into my unit. They headed directly to the cell four doors down the row. Everyone knew they were a "couple," and apparently the cops did too. Mittens pressed her face to the window. I stood behind her as we watched the women get cuffed and hauled off to the Hole. The gossip started in the vents.

"I bet they came for the dildo!" one woman shouted.

"What? Dildo? I ain't seen that on the canteen list, how they get ahold of one of those?"

"Hey! I want one!"

Everyone seemed to talk at once. You could hear voices in the cells above and on either side of us. One voice spoke up with the low-down: "They made a dildo out of those Tupperware dishes they used to have on canteen. Only the Old Timers have them. Those two must have gotten ahold of a dish when someone paroled. They melted it in the microwave and molded it. I've seen them bring it out in a sweat-shirt sleeve and reform it."

"They made a drilldo!" someone shouted.

Mittens shouted into the vent near the ceiling from her upper bunk, "They loose-lipped. They be bragging about how they use it on each other. I hear the gay one from the streets saying, 'We can certainly throw together a decent strap-on if that's what my girl wants.' I saw it. It looked like it would hurt your poonanny. It wasn't very big, kinda like a little white-guy dick, not like those big black or purple rubber ones at the porno store."

Jesus wept. I heated tea water in that microwave!

The talk went on for the rest of the day. I was uncomfortable talking about sex with Mittens. I felt like nasty old lady. I saved sex talk for the women my age.

That night, a blue-eyed woman from the Honor Unit brought it up during the Zen group check-in. "I can't believe they don't offer a vibrator on canteen," said Blue Eyes. "It would be a much better source of crowd control. It would calm women down and get people off all the depression medications they dole out." She looked around, heads nodded in agreement. "I am not going to become gay, even if it is temporary. All we have is Brawny." She looked around at our blank faces. "That's our name for the bullet shower nozzle on the top tier of J Unit," she explained. "He's the resident stud."

There was laughter all around the circle, even the teachers.

"Right?" she said, holding her palms up and shrugging her shoulders in the *duh* pose.

"Brawny, huh?" said a woman I recognized from G Unit. "One more reason to stay out of trouble and move to the Honor Unit."

The Honor Unit—that's where I hoped I'd be soon.

Eventually, Celly got out after her sexual charge. They placed her with a different cellmate, again near the podium. She had to wear the lime green LOP shirt for about two weeks. When she was allowed out of the cell, she would see me and cry out, "Celly!" and I would answer the same. The experience didn't seem to affect her at all, though by now I knew that it probably had.

"Keys comin'," Mittens said one morning. I was just about to change out of my pajamas and into my exercise clothes of red shorts and a T-shirt. I waited until the sound of boots and keys had passed the cell. Even clothing had rules, namely, you had to be in them and properly dressed around the clock. We had to change quickly and not stand around in our birthday suits and underwear or we would be punished for sexual behavior, a threat to both inmates and staff.

Mittens looked at my exercise clothes. "You just too nice a lady to be wearin' those rape-o status shorts clear up to your titties."

"Rape-o status?"

"Shorts make you look like you don't know shit, like someone could *rape* you. For real." She yanked them down to below my belly button and made a face. "Ka-a-ren, those puffy shorts smell like a new car, all plastic and shit. You gotta get rid of your jeans too, they all shiny blue with the drop pockets, make your flat white ass look as wide as a garage door. People look at you and think they can treat you like a punk."

"A punk? Like *West Side Story*?" I was hopeful. "It's my favorite musical. I sing it in my head!"

"Lord, Lord. You didn't grow up in my neighborhood, did you?" She looked at me hard and long. Then she took a breath and spoke slowly, "A 'punk' means you somebody's bitch." She took her finger and swiped it across her chin. "That's the sign for a punk. It means you have to wipe the cum off your chin."

I laughed. "I'm going to thank you now for the day I run into a particular holier-than-thou lady of my old neighborhood. What a bully. She embarrassed my kids. I didn't mind that she looked down on me. But that bitch messed with my kids." I felt powerful just saying the words. I tried the chin swipe in the mirror. I could see Mittens smiling proudly behind me in the mirror. "I'll just smile at her and swipe my finger across my chin, like this. She won't have a clue."

"You startin' to get it, you startin' to sound like you ain't some Nobody." She shook her head. "But you still look a mess, Ka-a-ren." She walked to the window. "See that big blue recycle bin over by the call-outs? That's for clothing going back to the clothing room. We call it the 'Con Marché.' Clothes in the bin are the nasty ones like yours. The good clothes, like faded jeans and T-shirts and thin cotton shorts, are placed on top. You're not supposed to trade clothes that way. They catch you, you get a cell-in. You gotta be fast. That's why you never see clothes on top for very long. Just keep your eyes peeled. Just make sure you get rid of your old stuff. You can get a cell-in for having extra clothes. Trade up piece by piece."

"I know my clothes suck. The Lifers see me and just look through me."

"Careful not to get the Lifer jeans of the women who sit on the metal stools and watch TV all day. Ya see 'em walk down the hall with a faded circle on their ass. Shape of the metal stool, Ka-a-ren. It's a damned shame."

"Clothes are like a status symbol in here, aren't they?" I asked, knowing I still had so much to learn.

"Clothes all look the same to an outsider, but to an inmate, it's a symbol of where you are in the pecking order. Took me about two months to get the right stuff." She twisted her body back and forth. "I'm going to have all new clothes when I get out. I am going to buy myself a set of double-Ds too, balance out this booty." She went to the mirror. The face-height 8-x-10-inch plastic didn't allow a boob to booty view. She stood back and jumped a couple of times. Then she stood on the toilet seat and turned backward and forward.

"I think you're perfect the just way you are," I said. "I tell my kids on the phone all about you and how much you teach me. They wish they could thank you."

She liked that and swayed her head side to side, satisfied.

"I try out the slang you've taught me and they say 'Eeew, Mom. You can't talk like that.' Maybe they're afraid I'll change."

"Maybe cuz you can't say it right."

I just threw my head back and laughed. Who was I kidding?

In the evenings at our Five Alive table, we would talk about our cellies. So far I had been luckier than the rest of the group. Hippie Chick wanted to puncture her eardrums.

"She never stops talking. It's the same loud buzzing baby talk day after day. 'Mama—' That's what she calls everybody—'Mama, I needs some coooffee. You got coooffee? I want coooffee. Sho could use some coooffee, you got any coooffee?' It just goes on and on. She just keeps those jaws flappin' like George Thorogood, ya know, that song? 'You Talk Too Much.'" She started singing.

Hippie Chick was getting louder, women turned to stare. She lifted off the stool an inch or two and played a mean air guitar, face melt, and everything. *Bwaaaa waaaaaa...* She sat back down and laughed long and loud with her huge smile.

It was infectious, we all started laughing. She kept on laughing like she always did, long after everyone else. Women had turned from their tables to watch the crazy girl laugh. The cop at the podium was staring our way, his head cocked to the radio near his shoulder. Hippie Chick finished her performance and settled onto her stool, still grinning. Most women at the other tables turned away and went back to their own conversations, but a few still stared and scowled. To hell with 'em; she was great. How can you get mad at someone for laughing? In prison? The girl was pure entertainment.

"Hey, Teddy Bear, what do you know about the new woman who came in a couple of days ago?" I nodded subtly to the woman across the dayroom by the call-out board.

"I haven't talked to her. But damn. There she is, New Girl, already getting her hair braided by the black mamas. She got a place to sit at meals right away. We white folk just don't show the love." Teddy Bear crinkled up her nose and shook her head. "I'm kinda jealous."

I had noticed how easily the races fell into each other. Natives sought out Natives. Latinas spoke Spanglish together and called the elders "Auntie," and the young girls "Mi'ja." It seemed like white people were more competitive with one another. I asked Mittens about it that evening.

"Yeah, we watch each other's back. It goes back in history, Ka-a-ren, but not very far. The movie *Roots* wasn't that long ago." She looked out the window. "I'll tell you what I hate. Look at that one. The one by the microwave. Girl gets on my last nerve, trying to be black. I hate it when white women from the suburbs start talkin' like they raised in the ghetto. Wavin' they hands, like Joe Cocker. Pull up your pants, Miss Tiffany. Girl looks like SpongeBob, for real."

"Why do people wear their pants so low anyway?"

"Comes from the men's prison. The cops used to make them wear their pants low so they couldn't run or move fast. All the ghetto boys wanna look like they badass too. Now all you white people do it and you don't even know why. Me? I can't wait to wear a dress."

I asked her how much longer she had before she went to Minimum.

"Maybe next month. I just gotta get out of here. It's so hard for me to keep my temper with all these damned women. I can't get more time, Ka-a-ren." She tucked her fists into her armpits again and stared out the window. When the door opened up, she went out.

In the days leading up to Mitten's exit to Minimum, she became agitated. She had a girlfriend for a spell. They took showers at the same time, long showers. The two of them watched TV together, walked at yard, and ate evil Little Debbie's snack cakes together. At times, they would argue. It was not good for Mittens. One day, our cell door slid open. The sound of a single cell door opening and closing meant something was out of order. Mittens burst through the threshold in a thunderstorm, crying and shaking, fists locked under her arms. "I want to hit her so had. Give her the fuckin' Exorcist. Make her head spin around." She shook and she paced, barely under control. "I can't. I can't. I can't get new charges. I gotta get out of here."

"Do you need some space?"

"No! No! Don't! Don't leave. I need someone to talk to." Tears ran down her cheeks. She tried to spit out her story, but her words were tangled. I just let her rant and pace until she was done. She finally lay down on her bunk and slept, her breath rising and falling unevenly. She shivered and moaned. Her life before prison left her in a raw state of hypersensitivity. The more she bragged about being tough, the more I could see that her walls of survival were faulty. But that night, she didn't swing. "One in a row, Mittens," I whispered. "Let's hope it's the first of many."

She left a few days later for Minimum. The door rolled open, Galoot yowled, "One-thirteen A, roll up, you're going to Minimum." It was my first experience watching someone leave and move across the street to the set of buildings that had an exit to the free world. Mittens danced to the podium and picked up her plastic bags, her feet barely touching the ground. She returned, lit from within. She took one plastic bag to her toiletry shelf and in one motion swept everything in. She did the same with her drawers. She was chattering excitedly, talking to herself, as if I weren't there. "I'm outta here. I'm going, I'm really going, this is all going to end one day."

After all the primping I'd witnessed, I was surprised that she just swept her hair back in her clip and was ready to go. The door was still open, and she stopped in the doorway and turned to look at me.

"This is goodbye, Ka-a-ren. My people wouldn't get us bein' friends," she said, pointing back and forth between us. "My mother *for sure* wouldn't get this."

I nodded, a bubble of tears in my throat; she was disconnecting. And then she grabbed her bags and started across the dayroom. She looked briefly at the woman who was her girlfriend and kept right on going. I memorized the sight of her sweet little head, her round rump, and the plastic bags hissing across the dayroom. She was headed to the hallway that led to her freedom, and eventually to mine. *Goodbye, Mittens. Stay safe. I'll never forget you.*

She never turned back. I hoped it would stay that way.

Over the six years I was incarcerated, I had nine cellmates, some just for a day or two. My next significant cellmate was not just the Alpha of G Unit, but the Alpha of the prison. A lieutenant came to the veggie room one day and told my supervisor to send me out to the corridor. My first thought was that something happened to my family. We walked out of the kitchen and he pointed to a bench. I was surprised as he sat down next to me. It was the first time I had shared a surface with my captors; usually, they stood above me, at arm's length. *This must be very bad news.*

"We are thinking of moving you, Baker. You are not yet six months clear conduct, but one of the dog rooms on J Unit needs a new cellmate."

Dog room? The Honor Unit? My heart leaped. A dog meant love, affection, essential things that I went without.

"You will have to talk with that inmate. She is the head of the dog program, it's up to her. You've had clear conduct and stayed out of trouble but you understand this is a privilege, Baker. Do you know what privilege means?"

You condescending turd, let's get on with this. "Yes."

"We will be watching your behavior. I'll call her down." He squawked his radio command and we waited in silence. Within an uncomfortable space of time, a woman entered the hallway and approached. She was trim with short brown hair and intense dark eyes.

"Is this the one?" she asked the lieutenant. She looked me up and down. She sighed, a little deflated. "How much longer does she have to work in the kitchen? I hate that smell."

I felt like I was on the auction block.

"She's not six months clear conduct," he answered. "She's got four more weeks." He turned to me. "You're going to have to be on the top bunk, Baker. She needs access to the dog."

I wanted to be near a dog so badly, I was willing to risk my safety and agreed to the top bunk. "I'll do it." I had been lucky with my last two cellmates. If I stayed on G Unit, the mathematical probabilities that my next celly would be violent, a predator, or a woman who just never shuts up was about 100 percent. I went back to the kitchen and told Hippie Chick my news. I got the waterworks, the rubbery chin, and the hand swipes across the eyes.

"Hey, it's only a month and then you can move over!" I said.

"'K," she hiccupped.

Looking around the kitchen, my best source of information about my new celly was Tizzy.

"She's a bitch," she said straight away and went back to mixing a cauldron of macaroni salad. "It's her way or the highway. Good luck, no one lasts in that cell for more than about a month. Women who used to be in the dog program quit because of her. She doesn't care about anyone but herself."

"Is she gay or straight?" I asked.

"Like it matters in here." She looked at me and grinned. "She's gay but she fell when she was really young, wasn't even legal drinking age. She's got a life sentence; someone died in her crime. She might be up for parole when she's about your age. Good luck, you're gonna need it."

Despite all the warning signs, I hustled down the hall with a shiny heart. I was blinded by the opportunity to be near a dog. A dog would not judge me. I couldn't wait to sink to my knees and bury my face in fur.

On the short walk back to my unit, I was dreaming of becoming a handler myself. I walked back to G Unit and thought, *This is it, I will never have to live on this violent unit again.* My character had been recognized and I was granted a move upward in the pecking order. *Yes! This is how you do it, ladies.* How naïve I still was.

I stripped my bed, loaded up my plastic bags, and hissed down the corridor away from the voices of the hive. I walked further down the corridor than I had been before and turned into J Unit, the Honor Unit. The room layout was the same but I was struck by how quiet it was. A few women were sitting at the tables and they looked up, but went right back to their TV shows or artwork. In hindsight, they probably averted their eyes in pity and muttered to each other, "Here comes another poor schmuck. I wonder how long this one will last."

It was about five minutes before the first line movement. I found the proper door. Looking inside, I saw a dog crate at the back of the cell. The dog was inside. It looked like a golden lab. Top Dog was standing inside, a few steps away from the door. She put up her hand in a stop signal. "You're not coming in here with those work boots. Take them off and leave them by the door. I'm going out for ten minutes and you need to change out of those kitchen clothes, you can't bring that smell in here. You'll have to do laundry every day." The doors rolled open and she looked me, emotionless. "Don't bother the dog."

The room had a slight odor that brought back memories of the dogs in my life—my sister's cocker spaniel, and the three golden retrievers brought to me via relationships. I went into action. I undressed and dressed as quickly as I could. I placed my clothes in the tank boxes. The dog remained crated and quiet. My palms were itching to pet it.

The next task was to make my bed. I tossed my bedding up on the bare mattress of the top bunk. The ladder was precarious. I had just enough room on top to crawl on my hands and knees. Making the bed on the top bunk with no ceiling clearance was like wrestling an alligator. There was no kiddie rail on the bunk, one turn and you were on a five-foot fall to the concrete floor. I carefully made my way down the ladder, clinging tightly so that if my foot slipped, I could hang by my arms.

My remaining personal belongings were few: a handful of books and simple toiletries. A small narrow shelf for my shampoo, toothbrush, and toothpaste was open near the toilet. The area of the desk that was designated for me was filled with dog supplies, a CD player, and a case. The two stools were filled with folders and books, there was no place to sit and I did not want to risk another climb to the upper bunk so I just stood in the only clear space near the door. I assumed she had not made the time to clear her things from my desk area and bookshelf, but you know what they say about assumptions.

The doors rolled open and Top Dog strode in. She continued on with her orders about living in a dog room. The room was too crowded for both of us to stand and talk so I receded to my bunk. I could not sit up straight. I gargoyled, Snoopy in the tree. It hurt to sit like that. I asked her polite questions about the dog and what type of service they perform.

"They are Canine Companions, service dogs for people who have sight. We train every day. The doors will open for me and the other handlers, but that doesn't mean you can come out unless it's a regular line movement."

"Can I say hello? What is its name?"

"Thor. You can't touch the dog unless I say so." *So close and yet so far.*

Things never got better. Over the first two weeks, our time in the cell during count or in the evenings consisted of me confined to my upper bunk and her talking about herself or complaining about someone's bad behavior and how that person better "check themselves." She had all the ghetto lingo down, but to her credit, she said it like a white girl instead of a SpongeBob poser. After about a week, she cleared a stool but not my allowed bookshelf. "When I'm not in the room, you can sit at the corner of the desk and use the top if you want to write, just don't touch my stuff.

I was a fool. Why did I have the delusion that no one before had offered these hard people a chance, and that by sheer will and determination, I would be the person to break through?

A submarine's warning sounds *pinged* in my head all day. My so-called move up was miserable, and to make matters worse, I was taking chances with life and limb, sleeping on the top bunk. I could hear my orthopedist's voice every time I climbed up the ladder. *You cannot fall. No one is going back into that pelvis to fix you.*

Each day I went to work, changed out of my kitchen whites, and showered immediately. In the evenings and my two days off, I left the cell and stayed out all day. I suppose that is just what she wanted. I was so mad at myself and so disappointed.

From my early days of incarceration, I had asked questions about the Honor Unit. The residents had a reputation for being inflexible and boring. But I liked it fine. It was quiet. The tables in the dayroom were filled with women reading books, doing crafts, or talking quietly to each other. No one stole your laundry or conned you for a cup of coffee. The yard was orderly, the exercise room was not just a place for hasty sex. Best of all, a set of middle-age women who seemed to stay off the radar offered a regular seat for meals.

Whenever I returned to the cell and looked at the dog, it just made me sad. I got to pet the dog a few times. But I could not lie on the floor and snuggle or jostle its slobbery jowls. It was a tease. Top Dog showed me one kindness. When she got a magazine, she ripped out the men's cologne samples for herself and gave the women's perfume samples to me.

I lasted exactly two weeks in the dog room. Top Dog got back together with a girlfriend and together they requested a room change. Top Dog swiftly moved me out. *How did she do that? What kind of power does she have?*

I would learn later that because she was the head of the Canine Companion Dog Program, and it was a feather in the cap of DOC, they allowed her to have a few extra privileges, such as a choice of a cellmate.

That cell was a prison within a prison. I was subjected to domination by one of my own "people." But at least I had graduated to the Honor Unit. I was just two weeks short of the six months' clear conduct. Surely I could stay in the Honor Unit since my good behavior had been recognized. They wouldn't move me back now, would they? Could I count on Top Dog to do the right thing and use her leverage to help me out?

When the officer on duty approached the cell holding a set of clear plastic bags, my heart fell. "Baker, roll up. You're going back to G Unit." I was so humiliated I felt feverish. I did not look at Top Dog. I grabbed the set of plastic bags and began to pack. I threw my belongings into the bags as fast as I could. Top Dog was quiet, she did not apologize; it was just another day inside the joint for her.

"Don't think they give a shit about you," she said. "You're an inmate, you got nothing comin."

I was growing to hate that phrase. I looked up at her standing in front of the dog kennel, her feet apart and arms folded casually across her chest. She was pulling on an invisible piece of lint on her sweatshirt sleeve. Her face was impassive; she had no heart. This must be what happens to institutionalized people. *You go ahead and be the queen of a prison unit. At least I have an out date.*

I felt rotten the minute I thought it. What would it be like, spending most of your life as an inmate, year after year, watching the Intake turnstile churn out women like me who have out dates? Her dogs were safe to love, just a little, but then they left too.

You are going to struggle, woman. No one will recognize you as Queen of the Dog Program or queen of anything. You will argue with the checkout girl at the grocery store. You will get fired. You will assert your rules and opinions, and guess what? People will walk away because they can. By the time you get out, it will be a whole new world, and it won't be your world.

I muttered that speech on the long walk back to G Unit, cosseted in self-righteousness. I think of myself that day, dragging those bags along the corridor, looking as rough as I felt. My colored hair had six months' worth of grow-out—a four-inch skunk line of gray hair at the center part, brown hair on the sides. My skin was fluorescent pale, my posture folded forward in defeat. I trudged toward the sound of the hive. I could hear Hippie Chick's celly clear out in the corridor.

"Mama! I needs some cooooffee. Somebody got some cooooffee?"

"Who's in dryer number two? Get your shit out right now!"

Turning into the unit, I did not want to meet the eyes of the women sitting at the tables. I *was* just an inmate after all. I was falling, again.

As I started to hiss my way across G Unit, stinging with embarrassment, a husky woman seated with another bruiser in front of the TV was screaming at WWE, "This is my show! Look at that guy, I'd like to ram him good." The other hollered, "Whoa, slam down!" She slapped the metal table with an open palm. "I'm gonna try that out on my asshole boyfriend!" The unit was the decibel of a rock polisher.

Galoot was behind the podium. "Did they kick you out, Baker?"

I did not take the bait; I just tried to look appropriately humble to end the conversation. He was quiet. I was forced to look up and I expected a smirk. Instead, he wore the face of *What a world!*—not sympathy, exactly, but not cruel. "You're in 117B."

A woman stood in the center of the dark cell. She had the outline of a princess. Her hair hung in ringlets like in the painting *The Lady of Shalott* by James William Waterhouse. The doors rolled open. I stepped inside and saw that the ringlets were a frame for tragic scars all over her face and arms. I made a conscious effort to focus on her blue eyes.

We made the routine crime introductions: "I'm Karen, I'm here for a Man II car accident, got six years."

She shrugged. "I'm Snow, I was a meth cook." She touched the scars on her face and her arms. "Got stuck in a bad meth fire. I got burned really bad. You had better know, I have to wear this." She lifted her shirt to show me a colostomy bag. "Burned my insides."

I sat down on my bunk at a loss for words. Any form of torture or death would be better than a fire. She must have endured excruciating pain.

"Now I'm stuck with DOC medicine. It's the worst." Her face was resigned. "They never fix anything. They do just enough so that you survive your time and send you out the door. Then they'll pass me onto welfare."

I nodded to her stomach. "Is surgery an option?"

"Yeah, someday. I'll have to wait until I get out and somehow figure out a way to pay for it. Until then, I'll have to carry this bag around." She turned slowly, and carefully stepped to the cell door window. The light exposed angry tissue on the right side of her face, which traced down her neck and reappeared as raised welts crisscrossing her arms. A narrow swath on the left side of her face was spared. She had been so pretty.

I unpacked my bags and settled on my bunk. I thought about my own family tree. I had a grandfather who was a doctor and died from self-medicating with pills and drinking. My mother and father's generation invented the martini lunch. My generation had the typical experimentation, a Pabst at the lake, pot and a little whiff, but nothing like what Snow had lived through.

"Snow? The meth, is it really that good?"

"The first high is, then you chase it for the rest of your life. Commit almost any crime to get it. First come theft and prostitution. If you got a kid, you can get charged with child abandonment or endangerment. Then when things really go wrong, murder. Meth takes over your life."

"What does it feel like, how would I know if someone was high on meth?"

She turned to me, her scarred face rapturous. "It's like being in the stars. You can do anything. You are wild with ideas. The next high, you're just wild. You have to touch everything, that's why so many women pick at their skin. Look at Hippie Chick's arms."

I hadn't thought of Hippy Chick that way, but I'd noticed her arms.

"You can't stop moving. It's like this—" Snow proceeded to act out a meth high, rearranging her toiletry shelf, knocking it over, doing it again, and then changing focus: lining up her shoes under the bunks, then pulling at her face in the mirror. It was forty-five seconds of hell. *How could that be good?* I made me sick to my stomach to watch. "Doesn't take long before your teeth fall out and your skin is covered in sores."

Snow went back to the window. "See that woman by the podium?"

I peeked over her shoulder. She was pointing with her chin to an emaciated blonde. "How old do you think she is?" She looked a year or two younger than me.

"Thirty-nine, forty?"

"She's twenty-three."

"My god. Meth?"

"Meth and heroin, crack. Everything." Snow sighed. "Once you're hooked on drugs, you'll do anything to get them."

I had unpacked by now and settled into my lower bunk to hear the stories of other drug addicts.

"What's the difference between a heroin high and a meth high?" I asked.

"Heroin feels like you are on a fluffy cloud and then it just goes to oblivion." She sat on the stainless-steel toilet seat and leaned back, eyes half-open. "On heroin, I would be talking to you just like this and"—she nodded her head forward and hung there for about three very slow breaths then lifted it back up—"then I would pick up where ever I left off, maybe nod out a little longer."

Then came the shocking revelation that topped it all. "I can't wait to get out and get high. First thing I'm gonna do, even before I get laid." She swiped her hand through the air. "Love it."

The space just underneath my heart caved in. I couldn't breathe. I looked at this once beautiful girl. *She will die and there's nothing anyone can do. It's pure evil. Please, God, if you're there, keep my daughters safe.*

Two weeks with Snow passed quickly. Finally, I was six months' clear conduct. I would trade the fighters and con artists of G Unit for the murderers, kidnappers, and Lifers of J. I started asking around for openings on J Unit and was approached by Rainy, a woman I had met on Intake.

"I heard you were looking for a move to J Unit. I need a cellmate." I remembered her from Intake talking about gaining weight from depression medication. She inspired me to stop taking the meds and hit the yard instead.

"Oh yes. Please," I answered. "I could send in the kite request today."

"Good." She half smiled and turned away. She had a can-do sort of walk, like a gunslinger. A woman of few words: a boon as a celly.

I was about to take the next step on my way toward freedom. First, it was the crush of Jail and Intake, then the rough discipline of G Unit; now hopefully, the steadiness and perhaps boredom of the Honor Unit. I could stay there for the next two and a half years until it was time to go across the street to finish my last three years in Minimum. Each rung got me closer to sitting on the couch with my arms around my daughters.

I hoped that in a safer, quieter environment, I might be able to hear myself think.

I could begin the inner work that sent me running from the hypnotist. It wouldn't be easy. I'd have to take an honest, hard look at myself. I would need help. I would keep going to church and my Zen group. I would read, exercise, and listen to NPR. I would write. I'd start with Celly, then Mittens, while they were still fresh in my mind.

Within a week I was summoned to the G Unit podium.

"Pack up, Baker. You're movin' to J Unit." Galoot stared at me with one raised weary brow. "Again."

I packed up my two plastic bags quickly. I did say not goodbye. Like a rocket shedding its thrusters, I left the turbulence behind.

J UNIT

I *hissed* my way to J Unit and checked in, bright and breathless. The officer on duty at the podium was Grim. I had seen him in the corridor. He struck me as a bitter man who was resigned to work out his retirement until he paroled. Emboldened, I used both my names: "I'm Karen Baker." He looked at me with contempt. Without shifting his stare from me, he verbally pounced on a woman digging in the bottom drawer of the podium.

"Johnson! You are in an unauthorized area."

"I'm just getting a kite," grumbled the woman from below. She stood up and scowled at Grim. "I'm here for murder not theft."

I hiccup-laughed. She had the pale skin of a woman on a Lifer unit and severely parted black hair like Wednesday from *The Addams Family*. She ambled away, not in any particular hurry.

Grim continued to stare at me. "Two-ten B."

I would need to be very careful around this man. I turned to the dayroom and found 210 on the upper tier. Since Intake, I had been on the ground level. I was excited to feel a change in elevation. I self-consciously passed through the quiet dayroom and stood at the bottom of the mint-green, woven metal steps. I thought nothing of the climb. I still believed I was the badass who skied like a dude. I hoisted my two bags and lifted my foot to the first step and could barely transfer the weight forward. I had thirteen more to go. It must have been a fluke; I attempted the second stair and gave up on the third. I had to back down and reconnoiter. Disgusted with myself, I ended up breaking the trips in two so that I could use one flabby arm to haul my carcass up the stairs and the other to drag the bag. I was even weaker on the way down; it was terrifying. I could see the ground floor through the open metal. The height made me dizzy, my legs were shaking, my knees felt like they were made of glass. *I'm a jellyfish!*

Finally, at the top with both bags, the cop rolled open the door and I went in. Rainy was not in the cell. In one glance, I could tell that she was tidy. Her upper bunk had tight corners, her toiletry shelf was organized. Unlike Top Dog, I could see that she had made room at the desk for me and left my allotted shelves clean. I made quick work of setting up my bunk and lined up my growing set of personal items: shampoo, conditioner, a hairbrush, and lotion. I was learning to fold my clothes into condensed shapes that would fit into the tank drawer and stay reasonably organized. My canteen essentials were coffee, powdered creamer, dry oatmeal, and the staff of life: peanut butter. I slammed that tank box home and got ready for yard. I needed to reclaim my strength and vitality.

Dressed and ready to go for the next line movement, I stood at the window, checking out my new surroundings. The view provided a very different perspective. The second tier was about fifteen feet above the ground floor. I could see that the officer on duty had a small bald spot on the back of his head that would grow into a Friar Tuck one day. I looked down at the women sitting at the tables and could see some were reading, some were eating, and one woman was drawing. This woman was talented. She was drawing a beautiful fairy, and though I couldn't make out the details of the face, colors were well chosen in a palette of the Caribbean Sea. Across the dayroom, the view out the window included a horizontal sliver of sky. I would be able to check the weather.

The doors crashed open for a line movement. I headed for the stairs, hugging the rail on the way down. As I crossed through the dayroom, a few women looked up, but I was not accosted for a cup of coffee or an envelope. I stepped outside for my second physical wake-up call of the day.

For six months, I had walked the yard circling counterclockwise. J Unit alternated walking patterns, a hidden privilege. Today we were going clockwise. I made one lap and could feel a hitch in my stride. I slowed my pace and scolded myself. By the time yard ended, I felt like I had sprained my ankle from walking a different direction. I hobbled to the foot of the stairs and lugged myself to the top.

Rainy worked at the DMV call center. At the end of her workday, she strolled into the cell with that cowboy swagger, sighed, and said hello. She seemed exhausted, weary, or maybe just sad. I was waiting for her, ready to tell my story of crime and time. "I was in a Man II/DUI car accident."

"I got the same sentence," she said. "I screwed up. I hate myself." Her face was numb, a mask of grief beyond tears. She crossed her arms, squeezing her trunk as if she were holding back a sickness inside her chest, and if she let go, her heart would fall out. She turned toward the cell door. "I have three boys," she said to the window, and that was all she shared about her past that day.

Celly, Mittens, and the others shared their pain as Rainy did, facing outward, toward the window. Perhaps it was a way for the words to project out of the cell so our mistakes wouldn't linger in the air or settle onto our bunks and towels or seep into a stranger's body. The glass in the window had two views. Looking through the glass we could see the dayroom but not be in it, like a veil that protected us. Looking at the glass was like a confessional. We could see a shadow image of our face as we spoke our words. Cell after cell, tier upon tier, Honor Unit to the Hole, it was the windows that heard the truth.

Rainy began pacing, willing to talk about the cop at the podium. She stopped and returned to the window. "I wake up in the morning to see who is on duty. This guy, Grim, hates us. Hates his job. Some days when he is here I don't even come out."

I didn't comment. It took too much energy to agree and try to hate. Instead, I told her about my feeble climb up the staircase and the effects of walking in a different direction. I reminded her about an early conversation we had about depression medication and weight gain. "You look good," I told her.

"We don't move enough in here. You gotta work hard to not look like a blimp," she said. "There is a group of us who work out in the exercise room." She pointed at the small utility room next to the podium. "We have a couple step videos that might help you climb the stairs. We aren't allowed to use hand weights so we roll up magazines and bind them with rubber bands. We MacGyvered our heaviest weight by filling our water pitchers. We're not supposed to use things for anything besides their intended purpose, but we're learning to be pretty good criminals in here."

"Ha!" I laughed. "I know. I've become pretty good at sneaking an extra apple up my sweatshirt sleeve." I nodded to the cell window and shuddered. "I wouldn't want to get caught by Grim."

"I can't get caught," Rainy answered. "I'd lose my job at the DMV. I need the money. No one is going to help me when I get out." I knew she was thinking of her boys.

"I've heard that the DMV pays the most money," I said. "One lady in the library said that she made almost ninety dollars a month. That would be incredible, I could call my kids more often, maybe even send them a little money."

"The days are long, you sit on your butt all day," Rainy said. "I would never do it if I was free. I used to work at a lumber mill. I worked as hard as the men." I looked at her athletic build and that made sense to me. Maybe that's where she got her swagger.

I went out at the next line movement to review the setup in the dayroom. I saw Top Dog at the far end. She was sitting with her girl-friend and eating some sort of prison tamale, and I vowed to avoid her. I checked out the exercise room and my call-outs. I approached the podium and asked Grim for a blank kite. He never raised his eyes. He just slid the paper as far as he could on his outstretched arm. I took the kite to a table and wrote a request to work at the DMV and dropped it into the kite box, another step up and out.

That evening Rainy climbed up on her bunk and put orange foam earplugs in her ears.

"Wow! Do they sell those on canteen?" I asked.

Impatiently she took them out. "I got these by trading coffee to one of the girls on the maintenance crew." She put them back in and turned over to sleep. She was a woman of few words indeed. I'd prob-ably drive her crazy. I walked to the window and looked toward the yard. I put my forehead on the glass and cupped my hands around my eyes. I was hoping to see the night sky, a star or the moon. All I could see were the bright security lights of the yard, shining on the cement. I pulled away and saw my reflection. It was the reflection of a female inmate. *Is that me?* My skin was parched. I had the beginnings of cords in my neck.

I climbed into my bunk, pulled out a tattered paperback, and tried to read myself to sleep. Some nights I slept. Some nights I lay awake and took inventory, rummaging around in my past trying to figure out how things got away from me. Other nights I went through the simple details of my former life: I ran a bath and read a magazine in the bubbles. I made a fresh bed with flannel sheets, I stood in front of the fridge and ate ice cream out of the carton, swiping a spoon around the rim as it melted, one, two, maybe three bites, then I'd put it back.

I spent a lot of time in the dim light thinking about food. I made a mental grocery list for tortilla soup and imagined preparing it start to finish. Taste and smell were hard to conjure so I relied on visual images: a heaped ladle of tortilla soup in my Franciscan Apple bowl, warm avocado chunks on top of a flotilla of chips with melted pepper jack cheese and the healthy clump of cilantro. The simple details were all too beautiful and caused a lump in my throat. My tortilla soup used to be a favorite of Nikki and Haley's. What were the girls eating now? Did I teach them all I could about buying healthy food?

After Tom died, as I awaited sentencing, I made meals an event. From the recipe and shopping, to cooking and eating. On the nights my girls were with their father, before he moved to Southern California, I would soak up the loneliness by cooking. I would research and prepare complicated recipes that would take up the entire evening. I put on music, lit candles, and ate at a table that was properly set.

During one of my one-woman dinner parties, I came up with the idea of a dinner party for my daughters. I wanted to teach them all I could about table etiquette before I went away. I called my best friend from childhood, Patty, and we hatched a plan for our daughters to learn the art of fine dining. Patty guessed I was low on funds and airmailed a dinner box from the Omaha Steaks company. Then, Patty and her daughter Melissa flew out from Arizona to take part.

I set the table for six; I was the waiter. My daughters each invited a friend, Patty and Melissa were the other pair. The invitation requested formal dress, and instruction began with seating. The date or attendant stands to the left and pulls out the chair. The lady scoops the skirt and lowers the body gracefully to the table. They giggled and waxed theatrical. Then the food courses began. I served on the left and removed on the right. The girls learned how to use the silverware outside in, and top down. In between courses, I came around with a crumb catcher and replaced napkins that fell to the floor. After dinner and before dessert, Melissa filled in as the event speaker and read her school report on Sacagawea. The girls were instructed to hold their posture, keep their elbows off the table, and wear a small smile of interest. They had a strong case of the giggles but maintained self-control. Dessert was served, then the girls stood from the table and practiced saying thank you to the hostess. The final instruction was a follow-up thank you card.

By the end of the dinner party, the girls were giddy and stir-crazy. They loosened their zippers and draped over the couches in unladylike positions, laughing and carrying on like girls again.

Was the evening frivolous? A little. Was it necessary? Not in the big scheme of things to come. But it was one less regret for me and a tender memory for all of us.

The bright lights came on at five a.m. and the day began. I would lie for a few moments, glorifying the possibilities of breakfast before the doors rolled open. Maybe the oatmeal would be warm. Maybe there would there be peanut butter, they can't screw up peanut butter, can they? When I heard the carts roll into J Unit that morning, I was already dressed, the tier doors clanged open, and I gripped the rail to the first floor.

"Hey!" called Teddy Bear. "You finally made it over! Now our Five Alive is just waiting for Hippie Chick!"

Normally I would hug this woman, but I'd learned to just stand at arm's length and smile. Pearl was already in line for her meal tray. I saw Tizzy. She was dressed in kitchen whites, choosing to stay in the kitchen as a cook. I saw Blue Eyes from my Zen group and Wise Owl from the library. I wasn't scared of any of them. They spoke full sentences in indoor voices. I joined the serving line without worrying about getting my hair pulled by some violent felon behind me.

"Karen, do you have a place to sit?" It was Wise Owl.

"No."

"We have space at our table. You seem a little more balanced than some of these other girls. You don't eat with your mouth open, do you?" asked Wise Owl bluntly.

"God no! I have seen more rotten teeth in half-chewed food than anyone ever needs to. I swear it was like some of these girls were brought up in a barn," I snarked.

"A barn might be a step up for them, at least they'd have a roof." It was Pearl, the voice of empathy, and immediately I felt snobbish.

"No offense," said Blue Eyes, "but it's a scramble to get good people at your table. Sometimes you're stuck with an obnoxious person, no one else will take them, that's why we jumped on you."

We sat together and shared a few comments about the prison food. As always the chatter at mealtime was minimal; we concentrated on chewing and swallowing until the cops shouted: "Tray up!" "We work out every day. It's a good group. Rainy comes," said Pearl.

"Count me in," I said.

"Baker! Visit!" It was Saturday night. Rainy was in the cell as I was getting ready. I babbled on excitedly—who could it be this time? Rainy ignored me. She gathered up her radio and headphones and put on her tennis shoes. When the cell door rolled open, she couldn't get out soon enough. Looking back, I can see how difficult it must have been to live with someone who gets regular visits. I could have toned it down a bit.

My pulsed raced in anticipation on the walk over. My visitor turned out to be Nikki. She had driven the hour and a half from college to see me and would have to turn around at nine o'clock at night and drive back. She stood to hug me and gave me her signature cupid's-bow smile. Even as a young woman, she presented herself with composure and elegance, despite the hard times. We talked in the usual pleasantries, I scooped her with some prison gossip and asked her if she had eaten any avocados for me.

"We don't have them in our cafeteria and I can't afford to go grocery shopping." *Ouch.* Nikki then told me that she had hit the financial wall and reached out to an elder family member for help. She described how she wrote the letter, evidently putting a great deal of energy into the plea.

"Sorry, Mom, I don't know how to say this without hurting your feelings. I know you can't help me." The tears began to brim at her lashes. It was heartbreaking to see her in pain.

"In my letter, I pointed out that I am going it alone. Dad is down in San Diego with Haley. You are in here. I got a letter back and I was given the money but it came with sermons about fiscal matters, including a payment plan. The crowning insult was a lecture about you, how you had absolutely no remorse." Her tears were replaced with anger, her lips pressed together, her hands in fists. "Yeah."

"Let them say whatever they want," I answered. "I'm already flattened. How much more damage can they do? Take the money, Nicolette."

"Nope. No way." She was having none of it. We talked about her finances and I learned that she needed very simple things: tampons, shampoo, Band-Aids, just like me. She needed gas money, decent tires, and an oil change. I needed that DMV job.

The next afternoon I went outside to walk the yard.

"Baker!" the yard officer called. "Visit!"

I didn't expect another visit. My heart fluttered. Something was wrong. I hustled out of the unit and joined the lineup. I walked through the door and stood in place, scanning the faces at the tables and chairs. Then I saw her; it was Nikki again. I rushed over.

"What's this? Are you OK?"

She was beaming impishly and shrugged. "I came because I could. I can still get to you."

We just grinned at each other. I was locked up, I couldn't help her financially, but I still had worth, my child needed me.

Not long after my move to J Unit, I applied and got the job at the DMV. I turned in my veggie room kitchen scrubs and began a day job similar to people on the outside, except I got searched, counted, and watched by overhead cameras. On my first day, I met my new civilian supervisors and would return on Monday to begin orientation and training. That night, I ate my dinner off a meal tray that I did not chop, serve, or whack into a garbage can. Someone lower on the pecking order was doing that now.

The pay at DMV started at ninety dollars a month and could go as high as a hundred and twenty. I worked out a budget and planned to send money to Nikki as often as I could. I called Haley and told her what I hoped was good news. "I can only afford to help one of you, but I will be able to call you more often. It means so much to me to help her out, even a little bit."

"This is good news, Mama. I've been so worried about her. I knew something needed to be done." The two of them still talked on the phone nearly every day. Haley had her learner's permit now and was getting ready to try out for the volleyball team at her new school.

"I miss you so much," she sniffed quietly. "I don't have any friends. I don't have anyone to celebrate my fifteenth birthday, just Dad." She grunted a laugh.

I felt frustrated and helpless. I would miss all her birthdays until she was twenty years old.

Later that week, at my Zen group, I brought up the phone call to Haley and the visit with Nikki. "The guilt is killing me."

"Do you know the literal meaning of remorse?" asked the teacher, Keisei. She looked at me unblinking. She was sitting, hands in her lap, composed. "It means to bite again." She paused, gathering her thoughts. "Conscience is as important as remorse. Together, it leads you to a new life instead of drowning in guilt." She turned her palms upward. "If we are humble, contrite, and atone for our errors, we can begin again. When our thinking is corrected, then so is our world."

I knew I was hearing something important, something healing. I scrambled to keep up with her words in my notebook. She paused until I looked up. I was surprised by her eyes, which were playful yet challenging. She spoke slowly and enunciated her next words:

"Guilt is the ultimate arrogance."

"Whaaaa…?" I bleated. Then it hit me. *My guilt. It's all about me.* The truth of her words resonated, but the meaning was just out of my grasp. I babbled aloud, looking at the ground as I found my way. *My fault, oh, see how I suffer! First, I did this, then I did that. My guilt. Me, me, me.* I lifted my eyes and stared back at her.

She was waiting for me, the corners of her mouth turned up.

For about three long seconds, I was mad at her. Guilt had become my way of life. *I would have to make changes.* I took a purposeful breath and exhaled. Then, I just *knew.* I barked out an incredulous laugh.

"I get it. I won't do my daughters any good if I am stuck in guilt."

Keisei nodded encouragingly.

"I won't do *anyone* any good."

Sinful, a wise and formidable woman from J Unit, added, "When you fall, you blame the world for being here. That's where the women get stuck. We have mandatory Minimum crimes. We'll never be eligible for good time and an early release. For many women here, there's no incentive to act one way or the other. Where's the motivation for behavior change?" Sinful leaned forward with piercing eyes. "Keisei just told you to stop sucking your thumb and get to work on yourself." Sinful threw back her head and laughed. Then she leaned forward and smiled at me, good-naturedly.

I spent the next few days hunting the beast of guilt. It made sense to me, what Keisei had said, but I wasn't ready to let it go. I didn't deserve to. I hadn't suffered enough. I decided I would ask my favorite pastor, Pastor Alida, about guilt at our next Sunday service. Pastor Alida was powerful and thrilling. She spoke with a pronounced Aussie accent. I listened to the service and waited for a sign. Finally, I was the last woman there. I approached her at the door.

"I carry a lot of guilt. I want to go in a better direction and heal my relationships with my family but I just can't see the way. Will I ever get it right?" I asked.

She threw open her arms and smiled broadly. "We will *neva* get it rioght! Isn't it maavelous?" She was lit from within. "We are forgiven!"

I wept instantly. I felt it. Tears of relief gushed down my cheeks. "Even me?"

"Awl of us." She held my gaze. She reached out and pulled me into an embrace. "*Awl* of us, Karen," she whispered. It was almost too much.

Monday morning and off to work. I was looking forward to listening to someone else's thoughts besides my own. My commute from J Unit to the hallway of the DMV was about forty-five seconds. We waited in line to pass through a metal detector one at a time. We assumed the spread-eagle pose for the pat-in and pat-out by the DOC guard on duty. At the end of each day, the guard snapped on a pair of latex gloves and barked out a name or two for a strip search.

"What are they looking for?" I asked Rainy, who was behind me.

"Pens, markers, or anything worth stealing," she said. "Some people steal just to steal, but not that many back here. No one wants to lose the highest paying job in the prison."

"I have been nude before more strangers than a stripper," someone spoke up.

The training room at the DMV had short-pile carpet and an upholstered swivel chair. I wiggled my rear on the soft seat and spun around. I took off my shoes and indulged in the simple joy of running my feet back and forth on the carpet.

DMV hired and trained in groups. We were eight. The trainers were civilians in regular dress and the inmate trainer was none other than Top Dog. *You're in charge here too?* She greeted me in same bland forgettable way. I was still intimidated by her. She was purposeful with our group and slightly impatient. The training was intense, the subject matter was specific and tedious, but it felt good to use my brain. After two weeks, we had our final test. It was difficult and gave me a new respect for the DMV worker. Top Dog surprised us and hinted at a few answers. We all passed.

In the days that followed, if I approached Top Dog's desk with a question, she would sigh like I was a dumb shit and then help. Over time, I could see she meant no harm and that her wry verbal cuts were a weird sign of endearment. "Oh come on, Karen, what's really goin' on here?" She was good at her job and had the information. I had to wonder. How did she do it, day after day, year after year? How did she not give up?

Each DMV worker had her own glass cubical. I had my own desk and swivel chair, my own pens and paper clips. I had personal space the size of my wingspan. The work was intense and the days were long. "Another day down," was the mantra in the pat-out line at the end of the day. I answered my phone the same way day after day, never knowing who would be on the line. "DMV, this is Karen." Joe Public had no idea he was talking to a felon. Sometimes, I was called "ma'am."

I will never forget my first call. A man called with questions about licensing his trailer. "I'm going huntin'. Me and the pooch." I could hear a dog in the background, snarfeling into the man's hand as he went through his wallet for his driver's license. "Jake! Let me get this out. I know, I know, buddy. Yes, yes we're going," he said to the dog. "I'm sorry it's taking so long." He laughed.

"Oh, don't be, I am a dog person. What kind of dog is he?" I hoped I wouldn't get in trouble for chatting up the customer.

"Oh, he's a mutt, a big lab and something else. He's a knucklehead."

"That's the best kind." He gave me his license number and I asked for the number on the trailer plate.

"I'll have to go outside to get that." I could hear the door swing open, the crunch of big shoes on gravel, the dog barking happily. I was there with him. I closed my eyes and pictured trees and a hillside.

"How's the weather?" I asked, wanting more details.

"Not a cloud in the sky, ma'am. Gonna be warm but not hot. Too bad you're inside." If he only knew. I teared up at the images in my mind, the simple sounds of the outdoors, the dog. He was a free man going on an adventure.

"Thanks, that was pretty painless," he said, laughing.

"Thank *you*."

Most of the calls at the DMV were mundane. Some people got testy with the fees. One man was an anarchist and called to argue with the establishment. About once a week I would schedule a driver's license test for a kid turning sixteen. Each day, the outside world came to me over the telephone.

Back at J Unit, the news came to us on the television sets mounted in the dayroom. By now I could afford a small transistor radio and sync to the television. That year, while I was on Intake, Hurricane Katrina slammed into New Orleans. Like the people of the free world, we watched the televisions in horror. Lives were lost or destroyed. The survivors would have to face the daunting task of rebuilding their lives. When it was my time to rebuild, I hoped I would have the same courage.

I received a phone call at DMV from a man who had visited New Orleans after Katrina. He was a musician and traveled from Oregon with a trailer filled with instruments and the supplies to repair them.

"I have to renew my registration before I go back," he said.

"You're going back?" I asked.

"I have to. They lost everything. They need their music as much as food and shelter. I grew up listening to them. I fell in love with that New Orleans sound. I've made friends down there now. They're still playing, trying to rebuild their lives. I'm doing a fundraiser to get more supplies and instruments. Sold my music shop and this is what I'm doing." He paused. "Just before the storm, my son died, he was fifteen. I am doing it in his name."

I took my hands off the keyboard and sat back in my chair. "I can't imagine."

The man sniffed, he told me about his son's illness. "I had to do something that made sense," he said.

I was awed by his purpose. I wanted to know more about this man and his journey. I was willing to risk a reprimand. I wanted to see the devastation through this good man's eyes.

"What did you see?" I asked.

"I drove through neighborhoods that were completely wiped out. At night, I drove block after block. There was no power of any kind, just darkness. I would stop the truck in an intersection and look in all directions. There were no people, no movement of any kind, just darkness for as far as the eye can see. There was nothing left to loot, nothing left for dogs or rodents to eat." His descriptions went beyond the news. I felt the dark emptiness.

"Quite a drive from Oregon," I said.

"Well, I got a little bit of a head start. I live at the bottom of the state in a small town called Talent. Ha! Great name for a town for someone with a music shop." *Sam and Audrey live there. I've probably walked by the shop. What's happening?* I had more questions but he was a free man and had a trailer to pack.

"Well, godspeed, sir. We're behind you all the way."

"Thanks."

He probably thought when I said *we*, I was referring to the DMV. I wished I could have told him that it meant an unusual circle of people. I spoke for the women in prison, my family in his town, musicians, parents who lost a child, and all those who wanted to help in some way.

I admired his drive. I considered what it would be like to lose a child. He did not fall apart. Here was a man who sold his business, loaded a trailer with musical supplies, and drove across the country to help. And he was doing it again.

That evening, I returned to a dayroom filled with slow-moving women doing laundry, writing letters, snacking on junk food, watching TV. It was a room full of warm bodies, an underutilized human resource. I saw our criminal justice system for what it was, a senseless warehouse. *Put us to work.*

That night, I journaled the man's words while they were fresh. I thought of my father living in the same small Oregon town. I wrote him a letter to see if he knew the shop. I wrote about this man's mission and how inspired I was. I wrote down the name of the man driving on the front inside cover of my journal. I promised myself to thank him someday.

The next morning I did "a Rainy." I looked out the window to see who was on duty, the barometer du jour.

"Hey, it's the guy they call Sarge. I've seen him in the hallways talking, even laughing with the women." Rainy just scowled. I wondered if she saw the humanity in any of them. Something happened to her that was very bad. I didn't know how to help her. But since none of us were leaving together, we concentrated on saving ourselves.

The doors crashed open and I went down the green stairs. I clung a little less desperately to the rail but I still watched my steps. I wandered over to the podium and took a better look at the guard that had a reputation for being approachable.

He was close to my age, a tad stout around the middle with a dollop of cotton candy hair and a limp. He was standing in front of the podium, unprotected and looking amused. I crab-scuttled closer, feigning a look at the laundry sign-up list. He glanced quickly toward me, a safety move for his own protection. He did a quick look at my

ID lanyard and took in my name. He raised his eyes to mine and wore an amused grin.

"Oh, so you're the one who was bumped out of the dog room?" His eyes were twinkling with amusement. I shriveled. "Fear not, I know the story. It's been told before."

"I was a fool," I blurted out.

"Naw, just the next fool. Maybe you dodged a bullet." He chuckled. I could not believe his candor. I smiled and quickly tucked my chin.

"Hold on, Baker, I gotta do my job and yell at these dillydalliers." He assumed a stern expression. "Hey! Smith! That's not your cell. Get away from there." He sighed and turned to me. "Baker, this is how the world works. We all gotta work; I do too."

"What about all the women who have a mental illness?" I asked. "Seems to me like almost half the women on G Unit are unemployable."

"This is where they live, Baker. There is nowhere else for them to go. First, they get a misdemeanor, then their record begins. One woman commits a crime every winter just to have three hots and a cot."

I couldn't imagine. "It's gonna be tough finding a job with a felony on your record," he continued. "If you're lucky enough to get a job, you will have to work harder to prove yourself. That's why we make you work in here. Routine, Baker. Work and wait for the weekend just like everybody else."

I crossed the hall to the DMV and did just that.

The next weekend I got a visit from my sister, Christine. Christine was my angel overseer after the accident and provided the gaps in my memory of those early days when I was still in the hospital, hooked up to tubes and machines. No one thought I would survive, so she planned on helping to raise Nikki and Haley alongside her two teenage sons. Three years later, when I entered prison, she continued her commitment to my daughters by making regular calls to Haley and visiting Nikki at college. To spare me, my loved ones only told me partial truths about what happened after the accident. The day she visited me in prison, she filled in the details of my hospitalization.

"I remember the green tube," she started.

I looked at her, confused.

"You don't remember the green tube disaster." She started laughing, a social laugh. "You were intubated. You broke seven ribs and punctured your lung. Do you remember the tube going in your nose, down your throat and coming out between your ribs? The tube went into a bag that hung on your side. Oh my god, that bag was disgusting. It was filled with this bilious, puke-colored liquid that was coming out of your lungs."

"Was I in a hallway?" I asked with a faint recollection.

"Yeah," she said, holding back a giggle.

"I couldn't breathe." The memory was coming back. I could not see the scene but I could feel the panic of that moment.

"You were on a gurney in the hospital hallway. The tube was backed up and you couldn't breathe." As dire as this sounded to me, she was still giggling. "You just knew what you had to do. You started ripping the tube out of your throat and out your nose, making this gargling sound." Now she took a break and laughed. It was so good to see someone laugh, even at this. "I tried to stop you. But there was no going back."

Her laugh intensified. "Once the tube was free, it sprayed all over the gurney, the walls, the blinds, the floor." She let out another bark of laughter. "It soaked the lobby furniture and the potted plants."

I began to look around. The cops were staring.

In sputters and hiccups she continued, "It was like *The Exorcist*, green and pink slime *everywhere*." She laughed so hard no sound came out. She laughed so hard I thought they'd take her away for a drug test. But when people laugh like that, it is infectious. For the first time since I had been incarcerated, I didn't care what the cops thought. I laughed tears, I laughed until my sight went dark. I could hear the cameras whirring. I knew *they* were watching.

They would have said something like,

"Get me the name and bio on that visitor! Roll back the tape, I want to know if she put something in that Dr Pepper!"

I knew there would be a strip search waiting for me. *What the hell*, I thought. *You wanna look? Have at it.* I was laughing, really laughing this time, not with Hippie Chick but someone from my own family.

My prediction was right. After the visit, my name was called for a skin. I stood up and marched to the curtain. Cushioned in the afterglow of a visit, I did not bother to grovel. This turned out to have a surprising effect. The female cop was congenial, chatty.

I knew the drill, I remained quiet, undressed, and gave the squat-cough as required. I quickly dressed and we were off to the dark block.

"You gotta hate this part of your job, Darcy," I said, addressing her by her last name as she did to me.

We both laughed. "Once you've seen what I have, you are scarred for life. I had to give a skin to Fontaine."

"How long did that take you?" I cracked.

"I think I used some overtime on that one. She had folds like the Michelin Man. It took both her hands to lift just one of her breasts. Her belly hung down so far she had to lift it in portions. It was dark in there. The squat and cough? I will never get over it. She turned her big butt to me, oh god, I can still see it. She was too big to squat, so she bent forward with her ass in the air." Darcy jerked her thumb up.

I was horrified and laughing.

"But wait, it gets worse. When she went to cough, she had a piece of toilet paper stuck to her rectum that tweeted like a New Year's Eve paper horn." Darcy put her hand to her mouth and coughed, fluttering her fingers, *cough-flutter, cough-flutter*. "I tell you, Baker, I wanted to poke my eyes out. I was traumatized, like a war veteran. I hear all the talk from the inmates about PTSD... Well, let me tell you, I got some of my own."

She told the story good-naturedly but I could see she was still reeling from her experience. Now I was too. We entered the Medium facility and the levity faded. We both went back to our roles.

I saw Darcy for years and never brought it up, but there was an ease between us that lasted. I went back to my cell and wrote down the details of her story. I would wait until Hippie Chick moved over to J and read her the story at yard so she could laugh as loud as she wanted without anyone staring at her or commanding her to do a strip search.

In the days and weeks that followed, I learned that the majority of women on J were locked up for a large portion of their lives, and for some, the rest of their lives. That room, that staircase, those showers, that lonely yard, would be the place they would eat, do laundry, and watch TV. The cell might be the place they die.

Like the rest of the gray-haired women on J, I began an ordered routine: up before breakfast to work out, eat, clean my cell, go to my day job, and wait for the weekend.

Rainy and I joined three or four other women in the mornings for exercise. The morning group was Blue Eyes, Wise Owl, Pearl, Rainy and a mix of others. In between the crunches, we had a chance to gossip or vent. It felt safe.

"J Unit is the only place a woman who shot two guys on a gang initiation can live alongside a spoiled rotten embezzler, all in a small space," said Wise Owl. "Somehow we all get along and form a little society."

"Hey! I lived next to that wood chipper woman," I said. "She gave me her newspaper every day. She seemed really nice, I guess you never know."

"J Unit may appear calm in comparison to G, but it's never restful. There are no secrets in here. We all know what these women did to get locked up for so long. You still have to watch your back. Remember, they have nothing to lose," said Wise Owl as she huffed along to Kathy Smith and her repeater knees. "There is a very dangerous current at all times."

"Some of these slow movers did some horrible things," added Pearl. "They've burned their victims, chopped them up. Some have starved children to death. In most cases, somebody died."

We fell quiet and focused on the workout. *My god*, I thought again, *is this where I fit in?*

One morning I walked in on a couple having sex in the exercise room. A young woman was leaning against the wall on the same side of the door, just to my left. I saw it all in an instant. The woman on the wall had her red shorts down around her ankles, her palms were flat on the wall. Her eyes were closed, her face strained in pleasure. Lala, my former coworker from the kitchen, was kneeling on the floor in front of her, her face partially hidden by the woman's thighs. *Sex, they're having sex!* My tennis shoe squeaked as I spun around. I bumbled the exit, banging my water pitcher on the door jam. I glanced back at Lala, who looked amused.

I bolted off to a corner of the dayroom, like a bee looking for an exit. *Sorry, ladies!* I was prickly hot and felt the rush of adrenaline. I knew it went on. I just didn't know where. I thought of those two girls. Both mentioned men in their lives, one was a mother. Are they gay now?

Later that day, I decided I should say something, apologize. After all, we shared the same living room. Lala was by herself at a dayroom table, so I walked over. I was embarrassed that I witnessed their tryst but certainly not judgmental. I thought about how sterile our lives were inside: no hugging, no touching, not even a soothing circle or pat on the back.

"Hey, Lala, sorry about the cunnilingus interruptus."

"Dude, you totally fucked that up." But she laughed rather than seeming mad about it. "You should have seen your face."

"I'll look next time before I go in."

"You can't see that wall from the outside but don't go blabbin' it around. That wall is my secret spot. It's hard enough to get the deal done in here."

I was breaking a rule by standing in place in the dayroom so I sat down. Three other women joined us, one was the girl leaning on the wall, the other two were a known couple they called the Twins. The Twins were very attractive, both with long hair. They took their time to style it like the movie stars in the torn-up magazines from the library. They made an attempt with canteen makeup. They were always together.

"Hey, sorry I walked in on you guys," I said to the girl who had been leaning on the wall.

"At least it wasn't a cop," she answered.

"Oh, did you guys get caught?" giggled Twin One. "Where were you?"

I looked at Lala, who was giving me "keep your trap shut" eyes.

"Oh, same ol' place." Lala shrugged. "We were hoping for a quickie." Lala made teasing eyes at Leaning Girl.

"You gotta be quick, no foreplay. It takes all the spontaneity out of it," said Twin One. "You can't just fuck for as long as you want, you know? We always have to plan it out. It used to be really hot, wondering if we were gonna get caught. Then I stopped coming." She turned to Twin Two. "No offense." Twin Two just shrugged and made a little nod, agreeing.

"So," I leaned forward and whispered, "where do you do this?" I was curious but also sounded like a tabloid reporter. I covered with, "How can I avoid walking in on you guys?"

"Where? Let's see," said Lala. "The showers, janitor closet, toilet stalls, all over the kitchen."

"Cell sanitation," said Twin Two. "We got it down, in and out of a cell in five minutes."

"If I have sex in the shower, I see it as a two-fer, clean up and get laid." Lala slapped her hand on the table and laughed.

"There's always church," said Leaning Girl. They all laughed but I didn't. It reminded me of Celly, caught fondling in the back pews months ago.

"So why do they care? You're not hurting anyone," I said.

"It ends up being a reason for fighting. Most of the worst fighting in here is because of jealousy," said Twin One. I remembered the brutality and carnage of a fight involving Helen of Troy.

"Look, I'm only twenty-four, I got a lot of time," said Twin Two. "I just want to have sex while I still look good doing it." Both twins laughed, but the laughter was cut short, perhaps from raw emotion. *How old would she be when she got out? As old as I am now?*

"I do it to feel sexy." She turned and looked at Twin One, "I want to have someone to put lipstick on for."

"My family won't have anything to do with me," Twin One said. "If I have someone in here, I can make it." She looked at Twin Two. "We do everything together. It feels like I am not alone." These women were refreshingly honest and I began to understand it was far more than sex.

"The only way to have a decent booty call is for someone to count jigs," said Twin Two.

"Count jiggs?" I asked.

"It's kind of a three-way," Lala said. "Someone stands watch outside the shower or the broom closet while we knock it out. She might be pretending to wash the outside of the shower or load supplies on the janitor cart outside the broom closet. You know they're gonna watch."

The Twins smirked. Maybe that was a part of the play.

"It's obvious to anyone in the room what's goin' on behind that door. Sometimes I think the cops know but they just don't want to hassle with the paperwork," said Leaning Girl. "Sex in prison is just sex." She shrugged. "The varieties are all over the map. You got your lipstick lesbians to full-blown dykes. Gay for the stay, straight at the gate, queer for a year, playin' house in the Big House, you never know who's jumpin' in."

They shared their stories and bantered back and forth light-heartedly. But underneath the bravado, I knew they were lonely and craved touch and comfort. I admired them. It took courage to hold on to the joys of the human experience and the willingness to love in return.

"Everybody I know from the outside wants the scoop," said Lala. "They ask if there is a lot of girl-girl action, with the wiggly eyebrows. They want the raunchy facts, but mostly, they want to know if I have started playing for the other team."

Line movement occurred, the doors slammed open, and just as abruptly as the conversation began, it ended. We quickly gathered ourselves up, meeting adjourned. I went to the cell and wrote down our conversation. Later, when I told them I was writing, that I was trying to make sense of our prison lifestyle and all the layers of punishment, Lala said, "Fine with me, someone's got to make sense of this."

The following Saturday afternoon, I had a call-out to the clothing room. I could hear laughter out in the hallway before I arrived. Good Cop sat at her desk behind a wire cage but kept the door open. She raised a hand in the air, "Baker! Stop in when you're done."

The crew was busy with a couple of wretches from Intake. The Intake girls were turning in their scrubs and graduating into rape-o status jeans and puffy red shorts. I had been trading up piece by piece at the Con Marché recycle bins as Mittens had taught me. I had a few soft, faded T-shirts but I still had the puffy red shorts and dark, shiny jeans.

"Hi, Good Cop," I said in the doorway of her office.

"Did you bring any of your writing?"

I pulled out some sheets of paper. I had hoped to share my character sketches of Celly and Mittens.

She read them and smiled. "These are good. I'm not sure who these women are but I can see them in my imagination." Over the following months, I requested a clothing room call-out when I had written something. I shared stories about swiping apples, fights, and the things I was missing. To her credit, she plowed through those early works and encouraged me to sign up for the Write Around Portland workshop that came into the prison. "I think you're onto something, Baker. Your daughters would be proud of this."

I had a chance to tell Gerry about Good Cop at her next visit. She was relieved but not surprised.

"She's a human being just like you. If you were to give up on her humanity, you'd have to give up on your own," Gerry said. "I'm proud of you. You are figuring it out. You've stayed away from petty intrigues and still managed to get a badass bitch like Celly on your side. That girl was awesome."

"She really was. If I knew her history before I met her, I would have had preconceived notions. Knowing nothing helped. So many of these girls have had hard lives but they are still loveable. Take that girl over there." I looked with my eyes and Gerry peeked over her shoulder. "She has short red hair."

"Thin?"

"Yeah, she runs. Runs like a goddess. Had a track scholarship once."

"What's her story?"

"Well, she got in trouble for a bungled robbery, drugs were a part of it, seems like they always are. She's funny and clever but has a short attention span, needs a lot of stimulation. She went to the Hole not too long ago for masturbating with a shampoo bottle. She planned it for count time when the cops come around and look into the cell."

"A shampoo bottle?"

"Yeah, she came and talked to me about it after she got out. She said, 'I suppose you heard the rumors about why I went to the Hole.' I told her I did. She laughed and told me it was true. Then she said, 'You're a nice lady and I don't want you to think bad of me. I'm just a woman who still likes sex, you know?'"

I told Gerry how she went on to tell me about this guy on the outside that she has been writing. "I guess he has some money, sends her a little bit for new running shoes. A lot of the girls work that angle; they get a little money and a lonely man gets a prison babe."

"They probably can't get laid in the real world," said Gerry.

"Yeah." I laughed. "He's right over there." I nodded to the man sitting opposite the redhead. He was rather nondescript, Caucasian, medium build, looked like he bathed regularly.

"So how do they find each other?"

I explained that we could purchase photo tickets on canteen. "Every so often it's photo day, and the girls trowel on the cheap makeup and pose for the inmate photographer. They send it out to friends who pass the picture around or post it on the Internet. One girl stuffed a towel in the back of her jeans, her friend helped her bunch it up so it looked like two big butt cheeks. I overheard her say, 'I gotta get my grind on and send some letters out. I need me a visitor daddy to buy me some new shoes. A little gyrating on the stool oughta do the trick. I've worked harder for the money, ya know?'"

"The oldest profession is a prison enterprise," quipped Gerry.

I was one row back and one table to the left of the redhead and her prey. I had a clear view of the man, who now seemed to be fiddling with the crotch of his pants, sort of arranging things. To his side was a family of visitors, kids of all ages. There was a little girl with long black curly hair about a foot away from his elbow. He was leering at the redhead. Her face was in profile but clearly locked into his action. They were not talking, just staring and then it happened.

"Gerry!" I hissed. "That man is unzipping his pants!" Gerry stiffened, and ever so slowly she swiveled around, stole a glance and snapped back.

"Jeeeesus! What's he doing now?" she whispered.

"He's putting his hands on his thighs and pulling the fabric apart," I whimpered. "Now he's spreading his knees! Oh god! I can't look!" But of course, I did. "There is a family of kids right next to him," I hissed. Gerry did another nimble turn to peek. Suddenly cops came from everywhere. Radios, jangling cuffs, and heavy boots converged on the genital exposer and the girl. He snapped his legs shut and tried for the zipper, but it was too late. The cops grabbed the redhead, hauled her up on her feet, and snapped her into the cuffs. The man was treated no less brusquely. Clearly, he had never been cuffed and was still trying to zip his fly. The cops surrounded him, turning their backs to the family as a shield. In the time it took for him to open his pants to the visiting room, his life made an abrupt turn. He was escorted out of the visiting room into the sally port and out the front door. The redhead was herded in the opposite direction, out the inmate door, and straight to the Hole.

Most of the people in the visiting room were clueless. The family at the next table seemed bewildered and huddled their children together. Gerry and I looked around the room for witnesses, but it was hard to tell who had seen anything. These women were experts at clamming up and looking the other way.

"Well," I said simply. Our junk food just sat on the plastic table between us untouched as we stared at each other. Then we starting laughing, a pitiful "what a world" sort of laugh.

"What's gonna happen to them?" Gerry finally asked.

"Well, she'll go back to the Hole. He might get charges, he should. Imagine flashing, in prison, next to a family with small children. What an idiot."

I never heard how that story ended, or if that man got charges. After she got out of the Hole, I saw the redhead across the fence lines, on the G Unit yard, running laps. Unlike her wild personality, she ran with precision and purpose. *Tramps like her, baby, she was born to run.*

It was fall, and I welcomed each season as proof that time was passing. Haley was coming for a visit. She would be starting in a new school in a new town as a sophomore. Money was tight for her and she wanted to start out right. I remember those vulnerable days. Even wearing the wrong clothes was a social blunder that might set you back years. As an act of love, my friend Patty flew to California to take

Haley back-to-school shopping. Patty deflected my gratitude and said the Lord whispered in her ear.

When Haley came to town, she would do marathons in the visiting room. Instead of connecting with her friends and doing things that young women should do, she chose to visit the prison and spend every possible moment with me. She would come twice a day and sit for hours, first, 1:30 to 4:00 p.m., then take a break, eat, and come back again from 6:00 to 9:00 p.m.

"Baker! Visit!" *She's here.* I couldn't get to her fast enough.

She stood as I entered the visiting room, looking all ages at once, my baby and a young woman, too beautiful to be in that comfortless room. It was hard not to weep and gather her into my arms. I hugged her as long as I was allowed, she still smelled like my child. I held her with outstretched arms: "You look so good!" We sat. "I love your boots, oh, and look at your earrings!" I could tell she dressed up, to let me see she was doing OK.

"I wore it for you. I know you like to keep up with the trends." The trivial talk broke the ice of those miserable, wonderful visits. Haley told me about her shopping trip with Patty. We talked about her school and where she is living, her volleyball tryouts. The details of our conversation are lost to me now but what I remember was the feeling between us. We still had a close mother-daughter connection. I still held my place in her heart.

"I just started a parenting class," I said.

"What?" She looked across the room at the mishmash of families: frazzled grandparents with babies, children of all ages bolting away from parents, single dads with kids who looked as if they'd been dressed in the dark, and a lone gentleman nervously pulling down the pressed cuff of his laundered shirt to cover up a large gold watch. "You could teach the class, Mom."

"If that were true, you and I wouldn't be here."

She just groaned and leaned back in the chair.

"Anyone with a kid under eighteen has to take parenting. I got a funny story about it. You know those health classes that teach the birds and the bees, right? They usually have a lesson where you have to carry around an uncooked egg. It's a reality check about being a teenage parent."

Haley twisted her mouth and looked to the side. "I haven't had that class, but I get it." She was embarrassed to be talking about sex with her mother in any way, shape, or form.

"Well, yours truly flunked the lesson. I sat through the first class thinking, my god, I know all this." I shrugged. "So, I got my egg. I drew a face that looked like a cross between you and Nik. I carried it back to the cell, took it to work the next day and did all the normal things an egg parent would do."

Haley smiled.

"Then I was sitting in our dayroom at a table holding my egg and somehow I just lost my grip. I dropped the egg about four inches. It hit the metal table and made this tiny little hollow sound: *tick! Oh no*, I thought. I picked it up and turned it over. There was a tiny crack as narrow as the curve of a pinky fingernail. I couldn't tell if it had gone into the membrane. I kept hearing that sickening sound in my head, *tick!* Later that day, the crack got bigger, and by the time I went to bed, it looked like a spiderweb. I checked for ooze and found a sort of filmy matter. In the morning, it started to smell. I was the only one who broke my egg. The other girls, who said things like, 'Wow, I never knew you should set a regular bedtime for your kids,' they still had their egg."

"Oh, Mama," Haley said.

"If you take good care of your egg, you get first pick for your stuffed animal baby. Anyone who breaks their egg goes last. I was the only one of twenty-four women."

Haley was laughing quietly and shaking her head.

I describe the pile of ugly stuffed animals from which we could choose. "There were Day-Glo green bears filled with sawdust or scary blue cats, and rainbow elephants. From my chair at the back, I could see a small dog peeking out of the bottom of the pile, a golden retriever-ish-looking mutt. Something went wrong with the stitching on its mouth. It looked like the face was smeared around the side of the muzzle, which made the eyes look a little nutty. But I wanted it."

"What happened? Did you get it?"

"I did. I sweated it out. A couple of other girls picked it up, looked at the mouth, and set it back down. No one seemed to want an irregular dog." Haley was smiling a genuinely happy smile. "I picked her up, and I hugged her so tight I almost cried in class. I haven't held something that no one could take away from me for so long. I love that dog. It sounds so dumb. I just pour my emotions into that scrap of fur. I named her Tulip."

"Tulip! It's not dumb," Haley said with tears in her eyes. "You need something to love. I still sleep with my stuffed animals and my blankie."

From Tulip we segued into memories of the girls playing with various stuffed animals and American Girl dolls. We talked about the dollhouse we made out of a storage cabinet. Each shelf was a floor in the house. The top shelf was a bedroom, the middle shelf a kitchen, and the bottom was a schoolroom. We decorated the cabinet with carpet scraps, furniture, and even chalkboard paint in the schoolroom. Talking about the good times made me feel like I might have done a few things right.

"You must be so lonely, Mama." It would do her no good to know that I wasn't just lonely, I was marooned. And how about her? She moved away from all her childhood friends and her sister. Who did she confide in?

While Haley was still in town, a DOC shift change occurred. Good Cop was now in charge of the visiting room. Her presence created an environment that was kind and steady at the helm. She came over to the table to say hello. I told Haley that Good Cop had been reading some of my attempts at writing. Haley seemed to take comfort in that.

By Haley's final visit, she'd cast aside the trendy clothes and wore a plain gray hoodie. Her eyes were rimmed in dark circles and she slumped on the table between us. We had run out of easy stories; all that remained was raw emotion, the unspoken hurt that was inconsolable. Haley started to cry at the beginning of the visit and cried all the way through. We leaned forward as far as we could across the table. I ached to hold her and stroke her shiny brown hair. At one point she put the hood over her head and wept.

Good Cop came over with her officer. "Sorry, Baker, she can't wear the hoodie." She actually looked sorry for saying it. Near the end of our visit, I looked over at Good Cop. She and her attending female officer were staring at our table, their heads leaning together.

Haley felt so frail as I hugged her goodbye. As she moved into the sally port, I gave her a tight smile, holding back so her final sight of me would not be her mother falling apart. She pulled the hoodie back up, over her head, but I could see she was crying openly. The exit door opened, she turned, and I watched the back of that crumpled gray hoodie until it was out of sight, just like the final day at the airport.

The pat-out/skin area was, as always, more muted after a visit than before. I walked in silence out of the visiting building, toward the cell block. Good Cop fell back to talk to me.

"Is your daughter coming back?"

"Not for a few months, she lives in California."

"Oh. That's hard." She was silent for a few steps and then she started to chuckle sadly. "I don't think I could take another visit, Baker. My god, she just cried and cried. We let her keep her hoodie on for a while; she's not supposed to wear a hat of any kind but we felt so sorry for her, and with her hood up, we couldn't see her cry. She killed me. We were a mess."

We both laughed a little, humor our salvation. We entered the block and each went our own way. I kept walking toward J unit, but I turned to see Good Cop walking down the corridor in the opposite direction. Her arms hung at her sides, her shoulders slumped. *She sees me. She sees my child.*

The best thing that happened in parenting class, besides Tulip—Tules, Toodles—was meeting Blondie. Blondie was about my age, incarcerated for a similar crime, and a parent of two boys. When she spoke, people listened. She told the tragic truth in a way that made you laugh. I sought her out after my visit with Haley. We sat down at a dayroom table and I vomited my wretchedness all over her. "She is so worried about me. She acts like she has to be the parent."

"Yeah, we fucked up." She was grinning and nodding, leading into her spiel. "It is like we're not the parent anymore. We're more like the crazy aunt they come to visit at the prison."

"I definitely do not feel like the primary parent anymore."

"Listen, primary parenting from prison is a joke. I used to yell at my kids through the phone. It's like yelling at a jet airplane. 'I told you not to go...' Where's that gonna get you? They know exactly where you are. You're a hundred miles away and locked up. At best, they're polite, listen, and then hang up. Then, they laugh and do whatever they want. I knew I had to let it go so when they come for a visit, we still have our special time. I never get mad, even when I think they're fucking up. I just keep it simple and stay calm." She shook her head and laughed with a big smile, her shoulders rose up and down like a cartoon character.

"How do we keep our foot in the door?" I asked.

"I try to stay informed. I read the newspaper; it keeps me out of the gossip. I read about climate change and check on who's running the country. I don't want my kids to think their mom is Rip Van Winkle. I still want to be head of the household someday."

Blondie pointed her finger at me, grinning.

"Tell your daughter that you're not so easy to pick off. Tell her you are not the standard poop butt. You tell her: This is *my* house. When I wanna see who's running things in here, I just look in the mirror."

"That's right!" I scowled, trying to look hard. She laughed at me and shook her head.

"You're gonna have to work on your mean mug." I laughed easily with Blondie, everyone did.

"What do you miss the most in here?" I asked.

"What do I miss? The fridge," she said without hesitation. "Just standing in front of it with the door open. A bite of this, a sneaky slurp of that, walking away and then coming back because I can. Yeah, huh?" She laughed her laugh.

"Hey, Blondie, I have been doing some writing in here. Writing about us, our kids, the cops. Do you mind if I write down what you just said?" I asked.

"Oh boy, you just opened a can of worms." She leaned in and squinted her eyes. "I will follow you around and tell you *everything* I know." Someone called her name, she got up from the table, still smiling at me. She stood in place, made fists and wiggled her butt, and was gone. I wrote pages about her.

It took time to heal after Haley's visit. Tulip was my comfort. No one had to remind me to bring her with me everywhere I went. Like Blondie, I read the paper and listened to NPR on my radio, and after being on the wait list for weeks, I was eligible for the Living Yoga class, which was twice a week.

At first, it was hard to be peaceful in my poses. But with the teachers' guidance, I began to concentrate on my breath and not the chatter in my head. I imitated the teacher sitting on the mat, eyes closed, her hands resting on her knees.

"Relax your shoulders and let the quiet come into your heart. Let go of where you came from today or where you would rather be. Let quiet settle over you." *Can I really let go? Will I be OK?*

The teachers from Living Yoga went into the darkest places to teach: prisons, rehab centers, jails, and juvenile detention centers.

hey were physical examples of good living. They radiated light from the inside out. Each teacher brought a fresh perspective. The young athletic teachers calmly kicked our ass and the middle-age women gave us hope that we too could move with beauty at any age.

They shared stories of the outside world. One teacher was grieving the recent death of her mother. She brought a recording of the Dalai Lama chanting as he sat beside a dying friend. "I have been waiting to grieve with you," she said. "More than anyone in my family, you understand indescribable loss." As the Dalai Lama chanted, we sat vigil as she wept. We felt honored and felt useful. It had been years since I had felt that way.

My favorite teacher was Anna. At the beginning of our practice, she greeted us by calling out, "Hello, beautiful women!"

In the weeks to follow, I began to learn self-acceptance and compassion for myself through the poses. If I fell out of tree pose, Anna would say, "We all fall out of things; we simply return to the pose with compassion for ourselves." As the classes went by, my effort on the mat was replaced by ease. I began to feel compassion not just for myself, but for the woman on the next mat straining to press her heels down in dog pose. The yoga teachers encouraged us to bring that compassion from the classroom back to the other women in the prison, the hard, bitter women, the lost women, and the staff of DOC.

Each baby step forward I was learning they are *just like me*. The mother crying after a visit with her young child, the cop who limped along the concrete hallways in orthopedic shoes was *just like me*. We all struggle. I felt different. Gerry noticed the change.

"Somehow, despite your desperate surroundings, you are undergoing a rebirth. You are changing. It is remarkable."

"We have some great volunteers, Living Yoga, the Dharma Rain Zen Center, Alida at City Bible Church, and a new breathing class that originated in India, 'The Art of Living.' I am a sponge. I am glad to see it's showing."

"It's like you are on retreat." Gerry slapped her knee and leaned forward. "I could do this, I could commit a crime and come in here." She mocked like she was serious.

"You'd never make it in here. The prison diet would kill you."

"Yeah, you're right." Gerry nodded.

"Once in a while, one of the girls from my meal table shares her *Martha Stewart Living* magazine or the food section of the *Oregonian*. We groan over the ingredients in miserable ecstasy. One of the girls calls it 'prison porn for celibates.' We sit around as she turns the pages. 'Oh no, not the soft-cooked egg broken over the grilled avocado BLT on swirled rye!' I actually bought a folder from canteen and have begun saving recipes that I want to make when I parole."

"What would you have first?"

"Duh. Avocados and fresh cracked pepper. Oh, and a mango and a hot, fresh Grand Central Bakery Como loaf with cold butter and salt shavings. Those things would be enough for the rest of my life."

"I shall have it on the day you get out." Gerry gathered up her clear Ziploc bag of quarters, car keys, and her driver's license. She rose to go.

"Hey," I called to her as she started for the door, "go stroke the rump of an eggplant for me." She nodded and walked her brisk East Coast walk to the door. *Eat, snuggle with the cats, wear cashmere. Love you, my friend. Thanks for coming. I wouldn't blame you if you never came back, but I know you will.*

It was late fall, but there was still sun. I was issued a sling for Tulip and we walked the circles or sat on the blacktop on a postage stamp-sized towel. Canteen sold sunscreen. A woman on J Unit who was doing life-without quipped, "Sunscreen? What's the worst that could happen? I'd die?"

One day while walking laps, I was listening to my radio. Tom Petty was singing "Running Down a Dream." I was in his convertible, I could smell the ocean, my eyes were slits.

I was walking toward a cement picnic table about twenty feet away. A group of women was sitting and talking, sharing some sort of smashed-up Little Debbie candy-cake. One woman was standing behind another's head, braiding cornrows. The woman receiving the braids was slumped, eyes half-closed, enjoying and safe, allowed the sensation of touch.

I was rousted by a quick blur. Out of nowhere a thick-armed woman appeared and began smashing the face of the braider with a full half-gallon-sized water pitcher. *Move!* My long legs felt tangled, like a nightmare when you can't get away. I hugged Tulip to my chest. The fighter swung with about three or four quick punishing blows and was gone, just like the Enforcer of Intake. The braider's face was bleeding profusely. I do not remember if the cops came or not. It slides into the inventory of fights I've witnessed. This one borne on a day of final sun and boredom. "I forgot where I was, Tulip. I let my guard down." I tucked her in properly and moved the sling to the outside, away from the fight.

Rainy and I were night and day. Not only was I an optimist, but I was a morning person. On the weekends, I couldn't wait to get up and write.

"Most of the people of the world like to sleep in a little bit on the weekends," mumbled Rainy. "The sound of your pen on the metal table is waking me up."

"Sorry." When you have no padding, upholstery, or carpet, the cell is an echo chamber. I crept around gathering my things and put Tulip in her sling.

"Now you're waking me up by trying to be quiet," she said. I left the cell on the next line movement. We told the morning exercise group that we still liked each other but maybe shouldn't be cellmates.

"I can see that, Karen," said Wise Owl. "You could step in shit and say, 'Oh! There must be ponies nearby!'"

"Yeah," said Blue Eyes. "You tend to paint your shit pink, Karen. Someday you will discover that it's really brown."

Maybe Rainy was braver than me. She actually looked at her sadness. I filled the void with busyness instead of feeling the void.

Celly number eight found me. No secrets in the slammer; she knew I was looking. Sinful was the woman who humorously told me to stop sucking my thumb in the Zen service. Sinful and I both worked at the DMV. One day as we were commuting home, she strutted up to me and said, "I think we are both looking for a roommate."

Me? She couldn't be serious. She was formidable. Sinful had the strut of a Viking, cool and slow. She had long brown hair that was turning gray at the temples. It swung like a metronome and spun like a curtain when she changed directions. Sinful was a Lifer. I did not know the details of her crime but I had heard somebody died. Her intense brown eyes were waiting for my answer.

"Yeah, um, I kinda am." *She'd eat me alive. Think, think. Speak up, you coward!*

"You seem like you can stay out of the drama and you survived living with Top Dog. She said you were OK."

"Ha. Really," I said dryly.

"If we turn in the paperwork, maybe we could find out this week."

"OK." *What did I just say? Did I say yes?*

"Done. I'm a few cells down from where you are now, a little closer to the window." She spun away and I followed behind.

What have I done? Oh holy hell. At line movement in, I looked down the tier and she smiled and gave a little salute. I waved back, a nervous tangle of elbows. She looked like she was stifling a giggle, or maybe she was wondering what the hell have *I* done?

So far, I had lived with a daughter of a gang chief, an exotic dancer, a dope cook, two alphas, and Rainy. In their way, each celly had taught me how to do my time. None of them would be people with whom I would have been friends in my former life. And yet, we all got along. I felt empathy for all of them and learned to love Celly and Mittens. Now I was about to step yet again into another person's life. I would listen to her sleep, I would turn away when she peed, I would try to read her moods and understand when to speak and when to shut up, I would learn how to honor her story and protect her privacy.

The move request was granted; without ceremony, I packed up my bags, put Tulip in the sling, and moved to 213B with Sinful. I expected Mitten's rules of the house speech but she seemed unconcerned. I wondered how many cellies had come and gone.

"My friends from the streets call me Sinful." She smirked. "I earned it. You're in for a felony drunk driving, right?" *Straight to the point.* "There are a lot of you guys in here. That's Measure 11 for you." She was speaking of the mandatory minimum sentencing in Oregon. "I'm not saying that you don't deserve to be here, but you could be doing something else, like work release or drunk driving education."

"I honestly wish I could, I'd work my tail off. It would make more sense."

"Your neighbors in the United States are not there yet. They want punishment. The politicians want to be reelected. They support Measure 11 because they don't want to be seen as soft on crime." She started to strut in the cell, her hair swinging side to side. "Now all you guys with car accidents or identity theft, anyone with an out date, have taken all the money in the budget for programs." She stopped at the front of the cell, turned toward me with a thousand-yard stare. "Lifers get squat, we're warehoused with more on the way. We used to be able to take classes but now they figure we may never get out and why spend money on us? *And!*" She stopped and circled her hand in a small salute. "What good does it do? You guys get out and come back! Recidivism is a least forty percent. People come back to prison because they still like the game. They haven't fallen all the way." She paused and went to the window. "Give *me* that chance."

As expected, she told the story of her crime starting with the bare details of a wild and free lifestyle. She hung out with badass motorcycle boys but still fought for human rights on the state capitol steps. Drug addiction nearly killed her twice. "I made a drug counselor relapse just listening to my story," she said with a smirk.

Sinful told me she was doing life, a minimum of thirty years, no out date. Yet. She finished her story and stood with her legs apart, hands on her hips, and looked out the window at the women sitting in the dayroom.

"I can't count how many women are here for being in the wrong place at the wrong time. The one sitting by the microwave was just sitting in the car waiting for her man to make a drug deal."

I walked over and looked out the window.

"The deal went bad and someone got shot. She got twenty-five years for sittin' in a car." She pointed at another woman with her chin. "The one with the long curly hair was in the room when a teenager was killed."

"I recognize her, she works in the clothing room. She was nice to me."

"Somebody in the kid's family was a major gang leader. They want her dead. She's scared that after parole, some gangsters will be waiting to kill her. So far, no one has committed a crime to get in here to do the job."

"Wait a minute," I said. "You mean someone would commit a crime, on purpose, just to get inside to kill her?"

"Yeah, it happens in men's prisons all over the county. Most of them are hired hit men and commit just enough of a crime to make it inside to the right level of custody. They do the hit, finish some time, and go back to the gang."

We moved away from the window, I retreated onto my bunk. I picked up Tulip for comfort. The reality of a life sentence was dawning on me. How would you fill your days and years? Would their family eventually fade away? Would life be worth living?

She began her slow-motion pace. "I will get out of here. I'll get my out date. I'll be in my sixties." Then she grinned. "I told the guy

I am writing, don't worry, I'll still be a decent piece of ass."
Sinful laughed and I joined her.

She told me details of her battle for an out date. For years she
had been writing lawyers, politicians, and prison reform groups. She
did the work herself because the rest of the world had thrown her on
the scrap pile.

Every evening after count, we waited for the mail. Sinful got a
letter from a male pen pal who was serving a stretch of time but had
an out date. They were old friends from her prior life. She read me part
of her letter. It was racy. We laughed at the innuendos.

"Oh! Listen to this! Keith Richards fell out of a tree. Cracked
his skull."

"Oh no! He can't die!" I cried. "I thought he was indestructible."
It bothered me more than I could explain.

"All the good Christian folk say he sold his soul to the devil."
Sinful waved her hands hallelujah style then put one hand on a jut-
ted-out hip. "He just had his blood swapped and cleaned like another
rich drug addict."

"If he doesn't make it, there's no hope for any of us," I mourned.
The Rolling Stones were a symbol of my time. When I was fourteen, I
bought my first album, *Exile on Main Street*, with leaf raking money.
Then came *Black and Blue*, *Some Girls*, and everything else. As a teen,
when my mom was out for the evening, I cranked the hi-fi stereo and,
in front of the pressed mirror tiles in the living room, I flapped my
long limbs just like Mick. "I just have to see them again, Sinful."

"C'mon, Keith!" she shouted in agreement. Sinful waved the letter from her friend. "One day, me 'n' him were hanging out in a bar in

the middle of the day. This guy walks in dressed in some sort of Indian costume with all this black makeup on his face." She circled her hand in front of her face. "I went over to the bar and sat next to him. He was fucked up, but still, a cool dude." She waved the letter again. "My friend here whispers to me, 'Do you know who that is? It's one of the guys from the Red Hot Chili Peppers!' There I was, babbling away to a real live rock star."

She paused and shook her head, that mane making "S" waves. "I met Lynyrd Skynyrd too! I was about thirteen!" She laughed at her accomplishment. "Lynyrd Skynyrd was in Oregon for a concert. My girlfriend and I knew which hotel they were staying in so we roamed around the hallways, looking for the party. We rode the elevator to the top floor and the doors opened and there he was, Ronnie Van Zant. He says, 'That's right, ladies, a genuine rock star.' We giggled—my god, I was thirteen!—and got off the elevator. There was a party goin' on."

"Did you go?" I rasped.

"What do you think? Of course! We hung out with some of the other guys in the band and the crew. My friend got wasted." She heaved a big sigh. "I was wild, but those were wild times."

The cop circled back, he missed a letter for me.

"Baker!" The letter hissed into the cell. It was from Loretta. I tucked deep into my bunk to read and Sinful climbed up on her upper bunk to finish the letter from her guy. I could hear her snicker from time to time and I snickered at her snickering, imagining the rest of the postal foreplay.

Loretta had written a note on a paper napkin from my favorite Portland Creole restaurant, Le Bistro Montage. Somehow, stains and all, the napkin made it in. I held the napkin and tried to smell the stain that she had circled. Beside it, she had written: "blackened scallops and bleu cheese."

I closed my eyes and imagined I could hear the din of conversation and the yowl of *"One oyster!"* The Montage was tucked into the armpit of the Morrison Bridge. The former riverside warehouse's new owner's peeled-back historic grime, laid black and white tile and set family-style tables with thick white linens and silver. The waiters hollering *"Oyster!"* wore white dinner jackets, the sleeves pushed up to reveal gloves of tattoos and black leather strap bracelets. They looked dangerous and therefore alluring. Back then I knew nothing of real danger.

Montage was hip, swank, and open until four a.m. Crawfish jambalaya and pot de crème were stirred with an eclectic crowd. Loretta and I used to go and people-watch, imagining we were part of the scene.

The crumpled napkin from Loretta was the hidden scroll of happier days. On the other side of the napkin, she wrote, "Stopped by after an errand downtown. Sitting here by myself. Miss you. Scallops are still in the ocean, avocados still grow on trees. It is all waiting for you."

I met Loretta on my first day working as a waitress. I was in my thirties, still married to my daughters' father. The marriage was difficult and reaching its end. The dissolution left me cowering.

"Look at you," she said to me, no-nonsense. "You're all slumped over like you've given up. I'll give you two weeks to whine and I will listen. But then you got to do something about it." *What a woman,* I thought. It was the same feeling I had when I met Sinful.

"Good letter?" Sinful asked

"A time capsule of better times." I waved the napkin. "My cohort Loretta sent this in. You two are a lot alike—strong women."

"What other choice do we have in here?"

"Count's clear!" the overhead speaker barked, followed by the sound of the heavy stainless-steel carts rolling down the corridor into the unit. As the food carts rolled into J Unit, the top tier doors slammed open. Sinful sauntered down the tier and I tried to match her pace and insouciance. Things in 213 were off to a good start.

One night, after lights dimmed, we had a fire drill. I was groggy but Sinful was wide awake.

"Fire drill! Get up, it's a fire drill!" The cell doors of the unit clanged open. She was pulling on her coat and spearing her feet into her shoes, moving like her life depended on it. "We gotta get out there. Hurry!"

"Are we in danger?" I asked, panic rising as I slipped on my shoes. She spun around in the cell door, her hair whirling around her waist. Her eyes were wild. "The stars! The moon! Oh, I hope it's not cloudy!" I hustled into my jacket, put Tulip in the pocket, and we charged down the tier. We stepped out into a cold night, the yard lights bright against the building.

How long had it been since I had stood under the moon? I couldn't remember. My only view of a night sky since January was a partial view through a skinny window, across a lit dayroom, through another set of windows, above a lighted night yard.

"Line up by cell and bunk. No talking!" shouted the night guard. We were directed to the far end of the yard. Sinful and the rest of the Lifers were long gone. I fell in with a crowd of newer inmates shuffling forward, hunched over, grumbling and unmoored by a shift in routine. As I walked toward the back fence, the lights receded. The sky was clear. I found Sinful and my place in line behind her. At the end of the yard, the sky was black velvet and filled with a waxing moon and winking stars.

"The moon!" Sinful moaned. She was mesmerized: her face soft and vulnerable up to the night sky, her body slack. She swayed like the saved women in church. The Lifers around us were pointing discreetly to the sky, smiling and whispering. The woman across from me moved her lips as in prayer: *Big Dipper, Orion, Pleiades.* I saw these women every day on the unit, but under the stars I did not recognize them. They were heavenly beings.

I imagined Nikki and Haley looking at the same moon, united. I reached for Tulip in my pocket. Under that night sky, we stood in collective grief over all we were missing. The piercing beauty of that moment was breathtaking.

"Count's clear!" shouted the corporal and we shuffled back inside. And I realized how lucky I was. One day I would walk through the fence lines. There would be a lifetime of moon and stars. I would see the night sky over cities and countryside. I would see the reflection of a full moon above the ocean. I would be able to stretch out a blanket on a warm summer night, lie on my back and stare up at the night sky naming constellations. *I am still here.* Tom and the woman in the accident were gone, Sinful did not have an out date. *I will look for all of you, I promise.*

The first time I got angry in prison was about eleven months into my sentence. We were at a Bible study meeting, and a woman—the most annoying woman I'd ever met, and I mean *ever*—was droning on and on.

"But *whhhhhy*," she would whine at every church service, in-service, you name it. That evening, she was at it again. My jaw was tight and I rolled my eyes so hard I nearly turned my eyelids inside out and had to press on them to relieve a cramp.

The volunteer was near tears as the tension in the group was about to ignite. I thought of a scene from the movie *Airplane.* The pilot is talking on and on to a passenger who was bored to the point of dousing himself in gasoline, poised and ready to strike a match.

I shifted in my seat, making a big show of leaning forward, and gave the blabbermouth the death stare to no avail. She just droned on in that nasal whine, "Whhhy would I do that? I always do it my way."

Finally I couldn't take it anymore. *"Enough!"* I shouted. "You have been talking nonstop for forty-five minutes! Maybe someone else has a question, did you ever think of that?" I glanced at the volunteer. We'd never see her again. That church lady was going to drive home as fast as she could and make herself a stiff drink. All my compressed anger was bubbling to the surface and I let it go. "How dare you take this time away from the rest of us?" I gestured like a madwoman, swinging an ape arm toward the circle. "Everyone in here is suffering." I turned away from her. "I'm sorry," I said to the rest of the group. "I just have to go." It was the first time I got angry since I fell. It felt good, I felt normal. I stood up and walked out.

A week or so later, that same annoying woman, who was apparently incredibly stupid as well, electrocuted herself when she plugged in a blow dryer as a love probe while seated on a metal toilet filled with water. It couldn't have happened to a more annoying person. The event itself was witnessed accidentally, just after the jolt. An officer was walking the cell line making a routine visual inspection.

"I heard this shout," he told me the next day at yard. "I was just a couple steps away from her window. She was naked from the waist down, spread-eagle on the floor, half off the toilet. The blow dryer was on the floor, plugged in. She was hurt and it was clear to me how it happened and what she was doing. I called Medical for backup. God! My eyes! I'll never get over it." I was shocked that he shared the story with me, but he had been traumatized and needed to talk to someone, even if it was an inmate.

The woman hobbled the hallway in a walker for days. We were sated with gossip. A group of us gathered in the dayroom to debrief. "She's not allowed to go to that Bible study again," Blondie said, laughing. "How bad do ya gotta be to get banned from a save-a-ho Bible study?"

"It's too bad the DIY electroshock treatment didn't allow for a more friendly mutation," said Wise Owl. "She'll be lookin' for a shop vac and a hurricane when she gets out." We roared.

"I heard her whining about her walker, 'Why can't I have one with *wheeeels*?'" I made a face and imitated her cruelly. "She is beyond what I can handle, I have to just ignore her now. I can't even look." I felt a tiny bit bad about making that face. But I liked the fact that I could rustle up a little anger, that I wasn't defeated.

Later, before lights dimmed, I asked Sinful for advice. "Now that I have met the most exasperating human in here, what about the most dangerous? Are there any women in this unit that I should avoid?"

"We all have the potential to be dangerous." Sinful turned and stared at me, leaning forward. "Even you."

I settled against the wall on my bunk.

"Where you just came from, G Unit? There's a lot of drug crimes, theft, assault. Those women act like they still have something to prove. They're mad and still swingin'. They swagger around like they're still a big player from the streets, but they're just punks." I thought of my chin swipe.

"It's different in this unit. About seventy-five percent of the women doing time on J are the victims of domestic violence." She looked at me as if she was sizing me up: Would I be worthy of her efforts to explain? Could I handle the truth? I kept quiet and waited. Her voice dropped an octave,

"These women have been abused and damaged by the closest people in their lives—family, boyfriends, husbands, brothers, mostly men. They got a right to be angry. They might stray into drugs or theft, but it started with violence." She paused again to let that sink in. "That's why they become addicts, to numb the pain from abuse."

I was silent. I wondered about the violence in her past.

"Most people think that all criminals are scary and deserve to be locked up. Women in here have suffered within an inch of their lives, then they finally defend themselves only to be locked away for surviving."

I had always thought of crimes as a single event; they committed *a* murder.

"If you are not incarcerated due to a history of domestic violence, you're here because you are mentally ill," Sinful continued. "You can't separate the two. Some women just aren't right, you know? They killed their kids. They hurt them first, burned them, beat them. They deserve to be here and *never* get out."

Just when you see humanity under the stars, you understand you still must maintain a healthy fear and give some women a lot of space.

"The woman next door? The gray hair? She gives a new meaning to the Christmas fruitcake."

I couldn't help but laugh, then I realized, our door was open and our neighbor's door was open. Sinful's voice was like a jackhammer. If she was in her cell, she heard everything.

"Sinful!" I hissed, my eyes wild. "The door. It's open! She heard you!"

She looked at the door, put her hands on her hips, and laughed. "Well," circle salute, "there ya go. What's she gonna do? Chop me up with a nail file? Stab me with a spork?" She shook her head, her long hair swinging.

"I've learned to pick my battles and survive in here," she continued. "I plan on getting out. The quality of my day-to-day existence and what remains of my life *when* I earn parole depends on how I do my *time*. And that takes *time* to learn." She paused for effect, "Same for you."

"How do you stay so strong?" I asked.

"Our highs and lows are shaved off. We just look for the little things: soup that is actually warm, a fire drill at night."

Both Sinful and I were accepted in the Write Around Portland class that Good Cop recommended. Of approximately a thousand women in the Medium/Maximum side, only twenty were accepted. The class was facilitated by a woman named Karen. In my other life, I would have been her friend or colleague. She wore long brown boots, a thick ribbed turtleneck, and jeans that were my urban uniform. I wanted that life again.

Karen began the class with a lead-in sentence and we wrote for five minutes without editing. I understood that this was common in writing classes but this wasn't a typical writing class. Inmates did not trust easily. Writing from the heart would be a tough assignment. But I was wrong. The writing freed them. I learned of their childhoods and the places they went to feel safe. I heard stories of self-loathing and loneliness and the desire to be loved. I would have never imagined that a woman who could commit murder had the same fears and desires as me.

The parenting class held a late fall graduation party and Nikki and Haley would take Tulip home with them. It was a quick trip to the prison for Haley. She came from California for Thanksgiving to see Sam, Christine, and the rest of the family.

The girls arrived at the graduation party and we took our seats at the long tables filled with arts and crafts. I was nervous. Was my duty, as a parent, to make mistakes and fail so that my children would choose go another direction? I blabbered on to fill the awkward silences. Perhaps I didn't want to know the extent of their suffering. What could I do about it?

When the graduation party was over, I gave Tulip one last hard hug and handed her to Nikki.

"Nate is waiting in the car," said Nikki. "We'll take some pictures of Tulip's drive to freedom." Nikki and Haley looked back at me from the sally port with survivor's guilt smiles plastered on their faces. Nikki made Tulip wave and then they were gone.

In a few weeks, a package arrived from Nikki with the photos of the graduation. "Tulip howls in her sleep for you," Nikki wrote. There was a photo of Haley, young and glorious, still growing at five-foot-nine, draped on my lap. Next, Tulip, Nikki, Haley, and I, moments before Tulip paroled. We have big smiles in all the photos. But when I look at them now, years later, I am overcome with grief by the forced gaiety.

I flipped to the next photo and saw Tulip, liberated. Nate was holding Tulip out the window like a real dog. Haley, in the backseat with the camera, captured Tulip in the side-view mirror. The background scenery is a blur of green. In the wind, Tulip's irregular smile twisted perfectly. This is where she belonged all along. The final photograph was Christine holding Tulip at the Thanksgiving family gathering. Tulip, my surrogate daughter, was home.

While I awaited sentencing, I took my daughters to New York City. Before I was shut away from them, I wanted to teach them how to navigate the big city. The way I saw it was, like Frank Sinatra sang, *If they can make it there, they'll make it anywhere.* I went through their wardrobe and selected solid colors, mostly black, and bought them cross-strap purses. Oh, how they protested. They were fourteen and seventeen, and they wanted their logo sweatshirts and bright leggings. "Trust me," was all I could say.

I laid out a map of Manhattan. "It's easy. It's a long thin island." I pointed to Central Park: "Uptown." I pointed to the tip: "Downtown." I marched them up and down my apartment hallway, giving terse instructions on how to walk in New York: fast pace, eyes straight ahead, never look up at the buildings, or down at a map. Jaywalk.

They were good students. The girls ate up the city with their long legs. On our way from Times Square to Central Park, we passed a family waiting for the crosswalk in garish Pendleton sweaters, aqua parkas, orange tennis shoes, and Hello Kitty backpacks. As we passed the psychedelic family, Nikki kept her eyes straight ahead but said to me, "I get it." *Check.*

We let ourselves have the time of our lives. I took the girls to a Broadway theater to see Bernadette Peters in *Gypsy*. We went to the Metropolitan Museum of Art and found a Mary Cassatt painting that looked just like them. In Tribeca, the girls were "discovered" by a photographer who took them for photos at the Ford modeling agency. We dined at the top of Beekman Tower at twilight and watched as zippers of lights illuminated Manhattan. It was as if that magnificent city opened its doors and let us escape our fate and worries, if only for four days.

Near the end of our trip, we were coming up from the subway. We were headed uptown to our hotel. Haley emerged first and took off like a native New Yorker. She turned her head backward toward Nikki and me, "Uptown." She turned back and strutted away, confident that we would follow her anywhere. The baby? She can't possibly... Without stopping, Haley looked back and saw us trying to peek at the map in the top of our pockets.

"*Ppfft*, Uptown!" She added a New York *duh?* hand in the air and turned around and just kept going. Nikki and I were stunned for about one long second, then I jammed the corner of my map deep in my pocket and followed my youngest child. *My job is done. Double-check. I can go to prison now.*

Thanksgiving passed. DOC made a surprising attempt at a holiday meal. For lunch, we had real chicken on the bone, stuffing, and good old instant mashed potatoes. Best of all, we were given ten extra minutes to eat. At tray up, I saw a woman make a ball of her stuffing and mashed potatoes and stuff it up her sweatshirt sleeve. She put a chicken leg up the other, grabbed her cuffs and scurried to her cell. I felt far away from home.

Around this time, the prison offered two special events in the chapel. One was a Christmas choir concert and the other was a visit from a speaker named Bo Lozoff.

"We have invited Bo to the prison," said Getshushin at our Zen service. "He's a writer and humanitarian. He started the Human Kindness Foundation, which serves as a connection to incarcerated people through writing forums and books. I encourage you to go." Of course, we did. Special events were a social event as much as a pilgrimage.

Walking into the chapel that night, I felt a new breath of energy. Women were giggling and sitting like ladies. Male energy? Bo Lozoff sat in the lotus position at the front of the chapel. He wore Johnny Cash black and was tuning a guitar.. He was smiling and talking to Getshushin and Keisei but also looking out onto the room with warmth and curiosity. The presentation began with a song and stories. He offered a message about coping, compassion, and forgiveness. He told us about the mistakes he had made and how similar we all are in nature, both good and bad. He read from a book that I later checked out of the chapel library. "Life, like any other exciting story, is bound to have scary parts, boring and depressing parts, but it's a brilliant story and it's up to us how it will work out in the end."

Bo talked about meditation and stillness despite our surroundings. "You don't have to become a holy person to feel something. It's not that complicated. The greatest people who have ever lived have also been the most loving people, so I'm moving in that direction."

He looked across a room filled with women in prison blues. "I bet some of you are sick and tired of wearing blue."

A laugh ripped through the pews and he waited until we simmered down. "You could associate the color blue with a positive change. When you leave here, I dare you to buy a blue shirt and say, 'Blue wasn't my problem.'" *He was right, blue wasn't my problem at all.*

The second event in the chapel was a Christmas choir performed by the volunteers of Prison Fellowship. Rainy told me she went last year and she never got over it. "I about lost it. Bring some TP. You're gonna need it."

Blizzard or freezing rain, the Prison Fellowship choir had never missed a Christmas concert. They began the holiday season performing in *The Singing Christmas Tree* at a downtown auditorium in Portland. Once the run was finished, they came to the prison. Festooned in Christmas sweaters and silver bell earrings, each singer put their heart into it. It was tender and bright, right up until "I'll Be Home for Christmas." The lyrics were bad enough, but the line "you can plan on me" was devastating. That was our collective problem. You couldn't plan on any of us. We let you down. Rainy was right. The women inmates trembled and sobbed.

Each of us tortured ourselves with Christmas memories. I had a vision of Haley at six years old with a Dutch boy haircut and chubby cheeks and Nikki at nine with coltish legs. I lamented the days when I was still a "good" mom, not a going-to-prison mom. I was homesick and ashamed, tearing my tissue. I limped back to the cell, my heart pierced with splinters, and threw myself on the bunk. Then, I reached for something, anything. I opened the Bible, read through my Zen notes, and opened *The Sun* magazine, where I found the philosopher Simone Weil: "To be rooted and home is perhaps the most important and least recognized need of the human soul." Haley, Nikki, and I were all uprooted and now it was the holidays.

Guilt sent me to the phone kiosk the very next day. I called the girls to see how they were managing. Did they have plans for Christmas dinner, did they have a tree?

"Auntie Christine, Grandpa Sam, and Audrey are stepping in as much as possible," Nikki said. "I am sane because of them. I do everything I can to match their efforts, in some ways I take your place and try to fill your absence. Those are some pretty big shoes, Mom."

I laughed a little, grasping at levity.

"That's because I have ridiculously long feet."

She just sighed. "What about you?"

I told her about the Christmas choir, omitting the wallowing. "We have a little fake tree on top of the microwave. It's trimmed with clumps of glued puzzle pieces hanging from dental floss. It's pretty pitiful but, hey, at least the DOC acknowledges the season. Where will you be Christmas morning?"

"I'm not sure. I'll probably go to Nate's dad's house. He likes to make prime rib."

She was quiet. Then, "It's hard to be completely happy anywhere. A piece of my heart is always broken. I feel guilty for having fun and mad at the same time. Not at you but at the prison system."

"Oh, Nik."

"Maybe you were a little too good at celebrating the holidays, Mom." It was the saddest compliment I have ever heard.

The women in the prison were anxious as Christmas drew nearer. At any time, anything could happen: nervous breakdowns, fighting, compulsive eating and vomiting, a few women cut themselves. The medical segregation unit of the Hole was full, a number of women on suicide watch.

For the first time since I moved to J Unit, the lineup at the microwave had to be regulated. We were not allowed to congregate so two women waited in line while the rest sat at the closest table, jockeying for position. Passing through the dayroom I heard one woman threaten another for attempting to cut in line.

"Bitch, don't even think about it unless you want to rumble in the broom closet."

"Yeah? Bring it, you old hag. Any day, I'll be here waitin' on you. 'Sides, you don't need more ramen with that fat ass."

I decided to cell-in. Wrong place wrong time was not the way I wanted to get hurt.

"Whew. It's nuts out there," I said as I entered the cell. Sinful moved to the doorway while it was open, scanning the tables.

"Your childhood keggers have more class than these fools," she said, her hands on her hips, staring down. "In terms of graceful living, it ranks between a bingo hall and a tractor pull"—she turned to me—"sprinkled with nut jobs."

Our Christmas canteen offered some very scary room-temperature cheese and other once-a-year offerings of questionable food. Sinful and I consoled ourselves with a few of the canteen specials and created a holiday spa night. I cleaned out the plastic trash bucket and we soaked our feet in warm shampoo water and created a homemade oatmeal mask for our faces. Sinful turned on her small television mounted on our wall. She was flipping through the channels and settled on a sappy Hallmark Christmas movie.

"Oh no! Not the puppies and the grandmas!" We laughed and blubbered our way through the days leading up to Christmas. We trusted each other, carefully.

I had the most magical visit any prison inmate could dream of. The day before Christmas, my devoted sister dug through the storage tub I had saved of the girls' childhood toys and baby clothes. She was looking for something sentimental and found their Christmas stockings. We had raised our kids together and she knew what belonged in the stocking. First the orange, then the chocolate, then the underwear, something silly and something wonderful. She had filled them just so and met the girls in the prison parking lot. Nikki and Haley opened their stockings and came immediately into the prison. The girls were genuinely happy. Christine was beaming. We were filled with gratitude for Christine. She placed our suffering on hold for a night.

Sated with my visit, I muddled through Christmas Day. Two Christmas miracles came in the form of food. First was fresh spinach for lunch. I went nuts like Popeye. I was so excited I called Nikki after lunch to tell her the good news.

"Oh no!" she cried. "There was a city-wide *E. coli* outbreak from spinach, I bet that's where it ended up. Remember when you first went into prison and you were eating all that expired food?"

"Well, I ate it all. Real greens might have been worth the risk."

For dinner, the second Christmas miracle. It was an apple. I shuffled through the serving line toward the fruit crate and spied a very different sort of apple. It was not the usual mealy Red Delicious. It was bright red with a golden collar. As I approached I could see it was firm and shiny; the tag read "Jonagold." I picked it up with two hands and cradled it to my chest. I brought my prize back to my cell and placed it on my pillow and waited for the evening. Eight o'clock was fruit time. It signaled the close of the day. I no longer had to invent activities for the time to pass. I could rationalize an early bedtime, read myself to sleep. All efforts at surviving and trying to be brave could cease, Christmas would be over. I reached toward my pillow for the Jonagold apple. It smelled of fall and baking. I closed my eyes and brought it to my mouth.

The best day in any prison, anywhere in the world, was New Year's Eve: not just another day down but another year down. Even the grumpiest of us took a shower and crawled out of our cell for the evening. There was a movie after dinner in the dayroom, and at midnight, a cart of popcorn was wheeled around to the cells. We were allowed to whoop a little and celebrate another year closer to freedom. Even though Sinful didn't have an out date, she celebrated and shouted. She was determined to be free and New Year's Eve was a recommitment to her efforts. She just kept working, learning, and taking the steps.

Over time, I asked Sinful about the women doing life sentences. "Tell me about Judy. She's very silly. Smiles all the time. Whenever I practice yoga in front of the windows, she stands in her cell and teases me. I can't do a forward fold or lift my leg without her blowing on her arm, making fart noises."

"Judy fell when she was fifteen, Karen." Sinful held out her hands in helplessness. "That's her maturity level. She grew older in here but she never grew up. Look around, who's gonna teach her how to be an adult? The cops? There are no programs to teach her those things. She has no experience managing money or a home. She never drove a car or had a checkbook. If she passes the parole board, how's she gonna make out there?" It was a rhetorical question but I answered in my head, *She will suffer but better to give her a chance. We cannot keep throwing these people away.*

"Hey, Sinful, look who's moving in." I was standing at the window of the cell, watching a girl drag her plastic bags to a cell on Front Street. She had been in the Hole for the pruno bust.

Sinful looked over my shoulder and smiled. "Miss Clever. She's something else, must have been a handful to raise, but it's hard not to like her."

"I met her in the kitchen. She's like a puppy, always into something, and looking too cute to scold," I said.

"Well, she ran out of charm, didn't she, Karen? Look where she is."

I had a chance to talk to Miss Clever a few days later. "Hey, welcome to J."

"Good to be off G. It's off the chain over there. New faces every day, butting heads in the pecking order." She smiled at me. She had dewy skin, white teeth, and the shiny brown hair of good breeding, a thoroughbred in a prison of nags.

"After the pruno bust, I saw you outside, locked in the Seg cage. You looked like a ghost, so pale," I said.

"The twenty-four-hour fluorescent lights and lack of sunlight really takes a toll on your skin. I could see my veins." She looked down at her arms. "Going out in the sunlight made me feel like a vampire. The sun burned my eyes but I went out for my one hour a week, even if it was freezing rain. We got four months in the Hole. I had a lot of time to decide if it was worth it." She grinned.

"What's the Hole like?" I asked.

"The first place you start is the holding cell. They chain you to the wall until the adrenaline of fucking, fighting, or in our case, getting wasted right under their noses, wears off." We both chuckled. "There is an overhead camera in the holding cell and the cop behind it waits and watches. Once they see you are subdued, you get strip-searched and dressed down to a chain-gang orange jumpsuit and plastic sandals. God," she said, slapping the table, "I hate those sandals."

"Yeah, who needs ankle chains," I added.

"Next comes the walk to your cell. It's like the movies. All the cell doors face a single hallway; you do the walk, and there is a face in each window, yelling and screaming through the door. The echo is like a brain aneurysm. If you're back there for fighting, and you walk past the person you had the issue with, she yells all kinds of threats." Miss Clever made a crazy mad face and was waving her arms, acting out a scene, "'Bitch, this ain't over, ya hear me? I'm gonna finish this first chance I get.' Some girls spend most of their time back there. They just cycle in and out. They can't stop the bad behavior."

She paused, I looked up from my pen and paper. She was looking at me steadily. "I've been back there before."

"Yeah, I know, I was on Intake when you whacked that red-headed girl with a tray."

Miss Clever sat up straight. "Bitch was a snitch. She knows how it works in here."

"Did they ever get her eye back in the socket?" I asked.

Miss Clever shrugged like she couldn't care less. "I almost got new charges over that."

I thought of Celly's progressive discipline speech.

"My family would disown me," she said, her face was grim. "They're good people, they're educated and have normal lives. I'm the black sheep."

"*Baaaaa*," I bleated. "Me too." That broke any of the ice. We both laughed and relaxed a little bit. "Tell me about that first day."

"The cop puts you in a cell. He gives you a bendable toothbrush, baking soda, and five sheets of paper."

"Just like Intake," I said.

"Yep, back at the bottom. Once the cop goes away, the women in Seg start shouting at once. They wanted to know the details of the pruno bust and what was going on in the prison."

"Worse than G Unit?" I asked.

"Fuckin' G times ten. Gossip is all they got."

As she told her story, I noticed her gaze was restless. She fidgeted on the stool. Yet, when she spoke she was poised. The rough language didn't suit her. It was like she was acting the part of an inmate.

"Once you are back there, you can't work, so you have no money for shampoo and stuff. Some girls try to share what they can and offer to kick you down some toothpaste or something."

"How do you get supplies from each other?" I asked.

"Fishing." Miss Clever bent her neck and hovered her ear over the table. "It's like billiards under the doors. It's physics and geometry." She tore a piece of my paper, wadded it up, lined up a shot, and flicked it off the table. "Bingo! I got calluses on my knees from fishing. We sent notes, nasty drawings, all kinds of stuff."

"What else did you do all day?" I asked.

"Waited for mail." She stared at me directly. "Mail and meals. It is the only good part of the day but more than that, it's the clock."

"I remember. I hoped that oatmeal meant morning. My days got mixed up right away." I shuddered at the memories.

"Night never comes. We set our bodies to the sound of keys, meals, and mail. I know who is on duty before they reach my cell. I can smell them, especially the men and their god-awful cologne. All day long the noise is deafening. During meals and mail is the only time it's quiet. It only lasts about ten minutes and then the noise starts up again, starting from the cells that received mail or meals first. My head pounded."

"Even at night?" I asked.

"When's night?" Miss Clever asked ruefully. "The cops back there, they look like a SWAT team, all dressed in black."

"Do they need special training to work back there?" I asked.

"Ha! They think so." She started laughing. "Have you met Sarge? You might have seen him, he walks with a limp and laughs all the time?"

"Oh yeah, he relieved Grim one day. He seems all right, he didn't treat me like I was contagious," I said.

"He is great. He's one of the few. I asked him if he liked working back there and he said, '

Any goof can pull a Seg rotation. I spend most of my day running bitch for maxi-pads and toilet paper. Not my proudest moment.' He just laughed and shook his head and said, 'I go where they send me. I'll be here long after you leave, collecting my retirement. I am just doing time like you are.'"

"So, four months for the pruno bust?"

"Four mouths, then six months back on G Unit. Long enough to lose about fifteen pounds. Even my eyesight got weird. My ears echoed for months. I heard strange noises from the vent, I hallucinated. Some women swear they hear music or experience hot and cold phenomenon in the room, it's called 'Seg sickness.' We were all one step away from the vest, ya know?"

"I saw a woman wearing a straitjacket—two cops were taking her to Medical?" I said.

"They keep 'em in the vest to keep them from killing themselves. Medical Seg is where most of the suicides are attempted. One woman tried to swallow a spork."

I just gaped at her.

"The worst and yet most efficient way to off yourself is to sit in front of the toilet, tie a sheet around your neck, toss the end in the toilet, and flush. Those toilets could take your head off."

"Oh my god." I couldn't get the picture out of my mind.

"Seg also has protective custody for an inmate who commits a crime against a child. There are women in here who had no problem beating a child to death. Fuckin' Chomos. It's prison justice." Miss Clever's lips pressed together, her eyes got dark, and she balled up her fists. I looked through my notes and changed the subject.

"It looks like you're getting your swagger back, you look fit again, Miss Clever."

Instantly, the lightheartedness returned, she started laughing. "Wanna know my Seg beauty secrets?" she asked.

"Oh yeah," I said, relieved to be back on higher ground.

"I used to spread fake butter on my face and hands because your skin gets so dry back there. My lips were beyond help. They were cracked and bleeding. I told the nurse that came on rounds that I had hemorrhoids so she ordered me a tube of Preparation H. I put it on my lips." She started laughing hard and paused to catch her breath. She then formed her lips into a small "o." "I could whistle, but I couldn't sing!"

We laughed again.

A group of young women started laughing at the next table and she stood up. She was ready for the next thing. "We done?" she asked.

I tapped my notes. "I got you right here. Thank you."

Miss Clever beamed and spun away, waving her arms at the next table. "What's goin' on, ladies?"

Miss Clever was an enigma. All that potential and here she was, in prison. She must have broken her parents' hearts. She was mischievous, but not dangerous. Or was that what I wanted to think?

The chapel volunteers arrived dressed and pressed and would often line up at the door to greet us. They remembered our names and gave us allowed hugs. They performed all kinds of outreach. I observed one volunteer who looked a lot like me in my former life. She was consoling an Intake woman who had given birth to a baby girl just hours before. The young mother was weeping: "I could only hold her for a few minutes. Then I had to hand her over to a social worker." The volunteer held the woman as she wept.

Our prison chaplain, Chappie, was all heart. She was strong, a bear-hug of a woman with tousled brown curls and a big smile. She went through the DOC-required training for her job, but was a civilian and treated us as equal human beings. Every faith was welcome in her chapel. She didn't care if we got it right, she just wanted us to come. Somehow, she kept up with the formidable spiritual demands of a women's prison and still enjoyed her post.

Chappie was the one who bore the chore of delivering bad news: grave illness, family emergencies, or death. One of the worst sounds in prison was, "Jones! You're wanted in the chapel." The woman began to cry immediately. For the rest of us, we felt the cold breath on our necks as we watched a summoned woman leave the unit like she was walking to the guillotine. I was called down once while housed on J. The walk down was a blur. *Who? I bargained with God: not my kids! Just let my dad live until I get out!* I remember turning into the chapel and there was Chappie, all grins. *Not death?*

"Hey, Baker, I think we just got a book that would help you." I fell into a seat and wept.

"Everything's OK." She sighed. "I wish I had a button that said that." I looked up and she was smiling a very sad smile. "I get that look of sheer panic on a woman's face, 'Oh please, not me!'"

"That is exactly what I thought," I said, my heart settling down. "What's it like for you to do this job? It must be hard."

"That part is never easy but I love this work. Day after day, I see women reaching for the goodness inside them that they didn't know they had. I see revelation, I see the moment of surrender. I see peace. I witness women make the initial connection to wonder and purpose.

They find something that makes life worth living. I see women in the Native American services connect with their ancestry and find family. I learn so much about the world by learning about different faiths. It's like traveling outside these walls."

"Are you from the Midwest?" I had to ask.

She threw back her head and laughed. "Yeah," the accent growing, "Minnesooota."

"Oh shoooot, me tooooo then." We had a bond. I stayed in the chapel with Chappie and we talked about how to make sense of all the faiths and traditions. "I feel like I am doing something wrong by studying the Eight-Fold Path in my Zen group and going to a Christian church service."

"Baker, God loves a seeker. This might help." She smiled and handed me a book, *Christian Zen* by William Johnston. "This priest writes about some of your questions. He believes in the quiet mind of meditation, he can hear the voice of God instead of his own. See what you think."

I took the book and flipped through a few pages. I felt hopeful.

"There's a woman on your unit who might help. She's called Angel," she said. "She's a seeker and earns her name because there is a Light about her. She had a long hard climb to get to where she is, but she'd be a good person on your unit for questions."

"I know who you're talking about. I watch her draw; she seems so peaceful." I paused, then: "Are people with religion happier?"

Chappie laughed in a yuck-yuck Minnesota way. "They say they are."

I went back to my unit. Hippie Chick rushed at me, asking if I was OK, then bluntly, who died. Her eyes were filled with tears.

Blondie came over and risked a hand on my forearm. I was so touched. "It was just a book!" I waved it in the air. Blondie and I laughed. Hippie Chick went ahead and cried a little bit more, then squeegeed her eyes. Though I would never know who was truly dangerous in the prison, I knew that with these two I was safe.

My incarciversary came and went. I would no longer mark the date on the day I fell but on the day I would be free. It would be April Fool's day.

It was Valentine's Day, a day I had planned on compartmental-izing, but I couldn't help thinking of Tom. I pictured him on the day we met. He was dazzling and I was love-struck. What would he say to me if he could? At yard time, I listened for his chuckle in the breeze, but he was quiet. The last time I held him in my hands, he was ashes.

Tom's ashes were scattered in three places: first, Zermatt, Switzerland, home of the Matterhorn where Tom's twin lived until his death by heart attack not long after Tom died. Their ashes were placed together in the church cemetery. Tom's ski buddies, his young-est brother, and I took the second portion of Tom's ashes to Alta, Utah, and scattered them at his favorite ski resort.

The final portion of Tom's ashes were scattered at Dodge Park, where he put in weekly to the Sandy River. Nikki, Haley, and I chose a day and set out for the park. The sky was ominous, sympathetic to our heavy hearts. Nikki drove the twisting road to the park as scattered droplets began to fall.

"Well, ladies," I said looking at the clouds, "Tom went boating rain or shine so I guess this fits."

We parked and walked toward the river's edge, where we took off our shoes and waded in slowly around the rocks. By the time we were at midcalf, it began to rain harder.

"Follow me!" I shouted. "Let's head for the bridge!" The bridge was only twenty feet away but the raindrops began to pound the water and hid the rocks underfoot. We sloshed our way over, trying not to stub our toes or fall in. All three of us made it just as the sky opened up. Our shouts and laughter echoed under the bridge.

"He planned this!" I shouted over the hammering of the rain on the metal bridge. "One last prank." My words reverberated off the green patina of the bridge above. Light bounced up from the water, casting our faces in hues of green and gold. The rain fell in curtains over the edge of the bridge, obscuring the river beyond. Nikki, Haley, and I were cocooned together in a sacred moment of remembrance.

I took out Tom and opened the canister. The mood was light-hearted, made to order for Tom. We tried to hug one another. Our bodies leaned toward each other in odd shapes over the rocks underneath. We each made our tender speeches and sprinkled him into the water. He joined the sand and the water at our feet in curious chunks of bone, grains, and dust. He circled in the eddy around us, caught the current, and made his final launch. He bobbed along toward the curtain of rain and we watched the last of his ashes go through the veil, beyond what we could see.

"The Sandy River will carry him to the Columbia River," I told the girls, "out to the Pacific and become rain, then fall to earth, reforming him into endless possibilities."

Godspeed, my love. In the rain on the bridge and the current and bubbles around our ankles, I could hear him laughing.

I planned to watch a sappy movie in the dayroom with Hippie Chick on Valentine's night. Instead, I got a visit. I couldn't imagine who would sacrifice Valentine's date night to come to a dungeon. Curious, I hustled down the corridor to join the lineup for the visiting room. Some of the younger girls had painted on an extra layer of baby blue eye shadow and done up their hair like a real date. It would be hard to be young and locked up with raging hormones and know that the clock was ticking.

There was a woman in front of me in the pat-in line with a crime similar to mine. She had a prince for a husband. He was faithful. He and their two boys moved to a school district nearby just to be close to the prison. Her mother moved in next door to help raise their two boys. Between her mother and her husband, her visits were like clockwork. She was committed to remaining a primary parent, even behind bars. In all the years I was incarcerated, that family was the exception. I asked her if the boys were coming for Valentine's Day and she smiled. "Nope, just my husband."

When I stepped through the door, I scanned the room. It was always a little mind-blowing to see all the colors—pink, red, polka dots. I saw a small hand rise up, covered with bracelets and rings. It was Loretta and her new husband, Robin. *Of all people, the newlyweds.*

"What are you doing here?" I said, hugging them quick and hard. "It's Valentine's Day! You should be home rubbing feet under the table. My goodness, you two look great, you class the place up."

"It was all a part of the plan," Loretta said conspiratorially. Robin beamed.

I reached out for a quick touch of Loretta's sweater. "Cashmere," I said, worshipful. I took a look at Robin's suit—midnight navy blue with a tiny white pinstripe. Under it he was wearing a crisp white shirt with gold cuff links, and a red tie with a subtle navy-blue stripe.

"Well," she began, looking around the lifeless room and making a small wave above her head, just like Sinful. "This was not in the plans. I was home, getting ready for a romantic evening, just the two of us. I had dinner prepped, put on my Paris face, and did my hair." She ran her hand through her short, reddish-blond hair. She looked down. "I had on something black. I was lying in wait." She turned to Robin, taking in his smile and his clean-cut dark hair. "And then"—she gestured toward him with another hand twirl—"he walked in looking like this."

Robin blushed fiercely.

"I give a lunch for my senior women clients on Valentine's Day," he said, ducking his head as if to avoid praise. "Most of them are widows, dontcha know." Another Minnesotan.

"He was happy to see me dressed for our date at home," Loretta said. They looked at each other and sparks flew. I was so happy for her. "But he was just so elegant." She laughed, still looking at him. "He was just bringing up his hand to loosen his tie, and I said, 'Stop right there.'" She put her hand out toward Robin's neck. "Keep that suit on, honey. I know it's Valentine's Day, but we're going to the prison. Karen needs to see a sharp-looking man." They glowed. How long had it been since I had been in the company of a loving, functional couple?

"And look at you!" I cried, reaching back to her sleeve for another quick touch of her cashmere sweater. "Oh, you temptress—and are these suede boots?"

Loretta slowly drew up her foot. "I know you're tactilely deprived."

"You're saints, that's what you are," I said, giggling. I could have bubbled over.

"I'll wear my new shoes next time," Loretta cooed.

We chatted and ate candy and I felt full of their love. They were the kind of people who put others first. They donated, fostered, and volunteered. *This is how it looks to live honorably.* I was humbled to be their friend.

Sam and Audrey couldn't visit often because the journey was over five hours one way. And Sam had had one surgery after another, joint by joint. But they came during a break between joint replacements. Sam must have got the memo from Loretta to wear soft, touchable clothing because he showed up in a black cashmere sweater. Audrey, who was not born in Minnesota, wore coral and turquoise accented by bracelets that she'd made in her studio. She was a feast for the eyes. But Sam, despite his natty attire, looked diminished. He stood only on his second attempt and I hugged gristle and bones. There was more space around the edge of his collar. He smiled with tears. Sam needed me to survive, much as I needed him to live until I was free. *Please God, let him be alive when I get out.*

Sam had not given up on me. Together, Sam and Audrey found a writing teacher who would read my work. Sam continued to research prison reform and consult attorneys. Between the accident and my injuries, my legal battle, my incarceration, Haley's move, and Nicolette's emancipation, he never gave up. But he couldn't fix any of it.

Audrey's eyes followed Sam when he briefly left the table. "A heaviness has entered our lives," she said. "I can see it physically in his body. He's feeling immeasurable agony." She turned to me, her light eyes somber. "In your father I've witnessed the resilience of the human soul. But I have the tiniest notion that your father's bulbs will never come back to full glow."

Her words stung but it was the truth. She wanted me to understand what was happening in day-to-day life, beyond the bravery in the visiting room. He felt my incarceration and the futility of his efforts, a drip line of poison that slowly aged his vessels and invaded his cells. *Remorse: to bite again, and again.*

Sinful's and my life in 213 was a paradox of wanting to be close to someone, a genuine connection, and yet at the same time, I still didn't want to have anything in common with any women inmates. I could not picture how these relationships would translate into the real world.

"There are no friends in prison," she bluntly told me. "You come in alone and you leave alone." The ugly truth was that I was relieved she felt that way. As much as I liked her, I didn't want to bring former inmates around my kids. I wanted to create space away from it all.

My test of a prison friendship that continued after parole was a friend you would trust to pick up your daughter at the airport. A recidivist was the first person I would scratch off the list. At the top of the recidivist list were the drug addicts. I thought of Hippie Chick. She was kindhearted, but her underbelly of addiction made it hard for me to imagine our friendship continuing after parole. A part of me remained detached from the women; I was afraid of complications that a commitment to friendship might bring.

Just when I thought I was figuring out prison life, I let my guard down, got in trouble, and was almost sent to the Hole. It was spring and the weather was warm. Out on the yard, I started my usual laps, trying to dull the whirring in my mind.

By the time I made my tenth lap, my thoughts began to settle and my breath took over. I stayed out as long as the yard was open. Most of the women had gone back inside. Finally, the yard felt safe enough so that I could read and walk. I stayed close to the fence as I circled. That way, I just had my left side to worry about. I was a chapter or so into the book I was reading when I looked ahead and saw the yard cop walking slowly toward me, looking the other direction. I kept my eyes up, ready to move around him. Quite suddenly he turned and ran into me. The look on his face was sheer repugnance. He yanked himself backward, horrified he had touched an inmate.

"Up against the fence!" he screamed. I flattened myself against the chain-link. "Watch where you are going!" he shouted into my ear, his breath pungent from Doritos. "I could send you to the Hole for touching an officer!" He continued to scream his horror, making a scene. "You shouldn't be reading and walking at the same time!" He called for backup. "Stay on that fence!"

I didn't say a word. I just leaned into the fence and turned my face, pressing my cheek to the chain-link. The hot metal and shame seared my cheek. *What if he sends me to the Hole?* As he continued to yell at me, I felt the stirrings of justifiable anger. *I have had enough life experience to know how to walk and read. You ran into me! But clearly, that doesn't matter.*

His back up arrived. "You touched him?" the new cop shouted at me. He turned to the cop who ran into me and shuddered in commiseration. Then together, they browbeat me until they ran out of steam.

I remained silent. *Live to fight another day.* I would see them both tomorrow and we would continue the role of cops and robbers, parallel lives, working and living side by side without integration.

Finally they let me go. I was shaking as I left the yard, and I was still rattled that evening. By that time, I was indignant instead of scared. I mentioned it at check-in at the Zen group.

"You may have been right, but they will always be righter," said Blue Eyes. "As an inmate, no matter your stage of development or intelligence, YOU WILL *OBEY*. It is like fundamentalist religion; you are required to suspend your intelligence."

"The new guy shows up in stiff boots and a shiny badge," Sinful said. "He is totally self-conscious. He won't even look at us until he learns to how to glare. Sarge told me that when he first started, he was so nervous, he was afraid to look at any of us. He said he felt like he was walking into someone's home. I told him, 'Ah, Sarge. You *are* walking into someone's home—mine.'"

"Do you have real conversations with the guards?" I asked, breaking the rule of no cross talk.

"I try not to." Sinful looked around the circle at the women from J Unit, who were nodding in agreement. "There's a couple who are OK, but never forget which side they are on. Here's what they want: no fucking, no fighting, no paperwork. Nothing that keeps them here one minute longer. Most have given up on the idea of corrections."

"I've seen both sides," said Lifer from J Unit. "Some of the women are just as bad. There's a girl on our unit who plays the vamp and grinds at the podium with blow-up doll eyes and a blow job mouth. Most of the cops are terrified. All a woman has got to do is say he made a pass at her and the guy is toast."

That night on my bunk, I replayed the scene in the yard. I thought about what Sinful and Blue Eyes said about the DOC staff. How many times would it take for an officer to give an inmate a chance, trust just a little bit, stick their neck out, only to get lied to or burned in some way? How many times would it take before it hardened them? What if their best coping strategy was mistrust and cynicism?

I knew I needed to do something to shake off the incident with the officer on the yard—something that would take my mind off where I was, something helpful. I had been hearing about how awful the medical care was in prison, and I'd seen it for myself. And I was also surrounded by women who had given up on healthy living. What if I could create a booklet that could help?

I went through the triage nurse "bouncer" and was allowed to meet with the nurse practitioner. I told her that the women inmates were disgruntled with the medical services but it was clear that many didn't know the basics of self-care.

She grunted an affirmation.

"Simple things like diet and exercise," I said. "They eat white bread and hot dogs on the food tray. They eat canteen reconstituted beans and ramen. They think Slim Jims are a meat source."

She leaned forward. "It's a sedentary lifestyle."

"I want to make a book about some of the simple things an inmate can do to take care of herself." I had her attention now. "Would you be willing to coach me on the content?"

She agreed and we discussed the basics. I went back to the unit with a fresh feeling. It was familiar—I felt *helpful*. A few days later, I walked into the dayroom and saw Angel, the inmate that Chappie recommended I speak with regarding questions of faith. I had sat next to her in the chapel groups and listened to her comments, which clearly came from deep thinking. As Chappie said, she had a light about her.

As I approached Angel's table, her dark curls bent over a drawing, she looked up with her blue eyes and luminous skin that was somehow untouched by the fluorescent lighting. If I were to guess, I would say she had Celtic blood. She was trim and committed to fitness. She would be perfect for a wellness project. "I'd like to talk to you about a health project. I think it could do some of these ladies some good, but I need your help."

"Oh? Like what?" She smiled.

I gave her a quick briefing and asked if she would be interested in the artwork. "After all, no one likes a book without pictures."

Next, I approached Pearl, from Five Alive, who had access to one of the unit's computers, and she also agreed. I met a few times with the nurse practitioner, with whom I developed an easy relationship. At one point I asked her why she chose to work here.

She answered quickly: "This is where the work needs to be done."

It seemed like she could see the possibilities of bridges between staff and inmates.

Pearl, Angel, and I worked together for a few weeks, and the finished product was a fitness book providing information for proactive health. It contained a diet section with a calorie chart of DOC and canteen food, a body mass index, and a calorie-burning chart. The exercise section included strength, stretching, posture, and body mechanics for lifting. The stress management section covered breathing techniques and meditation. Pearl designed a clean layout with large print and we featured Angel's illustrations on nearly every page.

The book was met with only moderate enthusiasm, but that was fine with me. It was available for women who sought it. The nurse practitioner was pleased with the results and kept copies in her office.

I sent the book home to my father. Sam was happier over that humble pamphlet than any of my prior professional achievements. On the phone he told me through tears that it gave him hope. "You haven't given up. Your daughters will know you've still got what it takes to pick up your life again and be successful."

I had to be successful for my girls. I was determined to. They had survived so far and seemed willing to ride out the years until their mother was free. But I worried about them constantly. Nikki withdrew from friendships and drew closer to Nate, her constant, her confidant.

Haley had made new friends in her new life at the opposite end of the West Coast, but during a phone call in May, she told me she'd cried in the bathroom before her prom pictures. "Everyone else had their mom to help them get ready and make a mother-daughter memory."

I pictured her alone in the bathroom, wishing I were there to do her hair or take a stitch to smooth her dress. Instead, she was motherless at another milestone.

"I used the experience as my high school project. I told the story with words and photography. I hope you're OK with that."

"Of course, honey."

She told me how she'd recreated that scene using a friend as the model. Later, she sent the images and words so I could see it.

"This was the way my new friends learned about you and my story," Haley said on the phone. "I wasn't ashamed. I wanted to be able to talk about you, be sad about you, not have to lie when I took a phone call." Haley told me that it had a powerful effect on her classmates. They respected her bravery. "It helped me cope."

I was proud and grief-stricken.

Remorse: to bite again, and again and again.

One evening, a woman at the phone kiosk began wailing, "No, no, Mom, no!" She was folded forward, her chest on her lap, her head in one hand, the receiver in the other. She wept raggedly.

I wanted to turn my head, but I couldn't tear my eyes away.

"Yes, I do." She sat up and leaned as far into the kiosk as she could. "Jacob, it's me, Sara. I'm right here. I love you, Jakey. I'll always love you. You were the best brother I could ever have. I love you so much." Her free hand was over her eyes. Her mouth was open but no sound came out. Then she slumped over again. "Oh, Mama, I'm so sorry. I should be there. I hate myself." She went completely limp. "Love you, Mom." She hung up and wept.

The dayroom was grief-stricken, silent. Some women were in tears, others did what we had all learned to do: shut down. The officer at the podium spoke quietly into his radio and soon Good Cop walked into the unit. She stopped at the podium, then went to the woman at the phone kiosk, leaned over and spoke to her quietly. The woman sat up and nodded, her face raw and blotchy. In the free world, this would be the time to help. We would hold her and console her and weep alongside her. But we were not allowed.

Good Cop walked her out of the unit. Ten minutes later, I left the unit for a call-out in the chapel. When I turned into the corridor, I saw Good Cop and the woman sitting on a bench. The woman cried faintly. "I can't get to him. I need to be there." Good Cop was leaning forward, elbows on knees, her face was solemn.

We were lucky to have Good Cop. She touched a lot of lives. Whenever her name was mentioned, people added their own Good Cop experience. When I saw her in the hallway I would smile and stand tall. She really saw us, and that made our experience in prison a little more bearable.

My sentence passed slowly. I was aware of every day on the calendar, marking the countdown. Most of the faces on the Honor Unit stayed the same; routines, the way of life.

A visit shook me out of the dull ordered routine of prison and reminded me that life on the outside ran concurrently.

My friend Jack was one of my regular visitors. I'd met Jack and his wife, Liberty, the same time I'd met Gerry and Loretta, at the restaurant where Loretta and I waited tables.

Jack's middle son, Sean, and his girlfriend, Sara, were ski buddies of Tom and me. Sean, Sara, and the adorable Rasta-dreaded Sunshine were on that final run with me the day of the accident. Sean and Sara, then Sunshine, drove past the accident that night, not realizing the car on its side, on fire, was Tom and me. Sean, Sara, and Sunshine were the ones haunted with those memories, while mine remained blank. After the accident, Sean, Sara, and Sunshine were at the hospital day after day pacing the waiting room to learn of my condition and collectively grieving for Tom.

Two years before the accident, Sean was the officiant at our wedding. Tom and I held the celebration on the mountain where we met, and Haley, Nikki, and I walked "the aisle" under two lines of ski poles. Two days before the wedding, Jack's spirited wife, Liberty suffered critical, congestive heart failure. Jack, Sara, and Sean attended our ceremony and then met up with Jack's other two sons at the hospital to discuss taking Liberty off life support. She died two days later.

After I was released from the hospital, Jack and I formed a two-member Widow's Club. Jack and I would go out, enjoying a safe, uncomplicated dinner where we could talk at length about navigating the unexpected new life we were both facing. Some nights we would weep and other nights we would dance. We were both in limbo. At the courthouse, on the day of my sentencing, when I took the final glance back to the handful of family and friends, Jack was there.

On Jack's most recent visit, he brought in three photos, which is all that visitors were allowed.

"This is my new girlfriend," he said about the first picture. She was close to my age but looked far younger. She had lustrous skin and a carefree smile.

"Jack! She's beautiful! Good for you."

He looked smitten and proud. "I'm trying. These are the dishes I want to use when I make her dinner." He handed me the second and third photos. "Liberty and I got them in Italy. I showed these photos to the florist and she's going to make a centerpiece in the same color scheme."

"You're such a romantic. She must be pretty special, Jack."

His smile faded.

"I'm lonely; I'm a couples kind of guy." He fell silent and I waited. "I really miss Liberty," he finally said, letting his tears flow.

"I miss her too. Her tiny frame was packed with a light and energy. She was the one and only Liberty. "

"At least I have Le Paws." Jack was referring to his miniature schnauzer. "He's exasperating with his 'schnauzerness' but he's my only link with 'the life that was.' When I think hard about that and I'm alone, I start to cry. We owe our companionship to one another—him because I feed him, I suppose, and me because of the memories he brings me."

As always, I was humbled by Jack's vulnerability and big heart. I smiled. "And now you have someone new. I'm glad that this new lady is tall and looks different."

We both chuckled and Jack wiped his tears.

"Thanks, kid."

"You know where I am. A tank of gas is cheaper than a shrink."

Some visits were not from friends, but acquaintances or friends of friends who came to the prison with their errant teens for a "scared straight" speech. A society matron arranged an approved single visit for her and her errant son. I entered the visiting room and found the society matron with the same sleek blond bob I recalled from my days living with Gerry. Next to her was her pimply teenage son. He had bleached hair that fell across one eye and was dressed in black. I stepped forward to the table.

"This is Karen," said the mother. On closer inspection, I could see she looked exhausted. I remember locking eyes with her, *I got this.* I sat down slowly. I set my jaw, tilted my head, and stared at this child with his pout and crossed arms. I didn't speak. I waited until he became uncomfortable. He sat up straight, tossed his hair out of his eyes, stole a glance at me, then his mother.

I continued to stare at him. Nervously, his eyes began to dart around the room, checking out the women inmates from under his brows. I followed his gaze as it stopped on a slinky young woman with tattoos on her neck and hands.

"She's here because she was in the wrong place at the wrong time. She didn't take the money or pull the trigger, but she was there. Now, she'll be here until she is as old as me." The boy's neck pulsed under his pale white skin. "Most of these women are here because they've had rotten childhoods. They never learned how to think things through." He looked at his mother with eyes that said, *Please, can we go now?*

"There's another group of inmates in here." Now it was my turn to sit back with my arms crossed. "See that woman over there?" I pointed with my chin to a gray-haired woman with a dainty face like a logo on a cookie package. "She killed a family member." I leaned forward and placed both my hands on my knees. "Stabbed them over and over, then burnt the body. Her only mistake was, it didn't burn all the way. The cops found body parts in the fire pit." I shrugged and sat back, imitating Top Dog picking lint off my sweatshirt. "She's on my unit with the rest of the Lifers. 'Lifer' means somebody died. I see five more just in this room." The kid froze. "It's not like the crimes on TV," I chuckled. "It's a lot messier."

The visit ended shortly thereafter. I might have pushed it just a little too far. I imagined them driving away, shaken. I was OK with my role. And if I could keep one young person on the straight and narrow and out of prison, I'd do it.

One afternoon Hippie Chick and I walked together on yard. "I need to work," she said. "I can't just sit around; time goes too slow. I want as many job experiences as I can get. If I don't get a job when I get out, I may not stay clean. It scares me. I'm never coming back."

We walked in silence for a while, and I thought of what work awaited me when I paroled. Could I get my old job back? Even though the Oregon Board of Physical Therapy allowed me to keep my license, I had little faith that anyone would hire me. How would I pass a background check and work with a vulnerable population?

"I'm going to stay clear conduct, and apply for the hair design program," she said.

I flashed back to my Intake trip to the salon for a lice check.

"If I could cut hair when I get out, I feel like I could make it. It would be a great job."

A ripple ran through me. "It *would* be a great job! It's creative and the hours are flexible. The salon I went to charged a hefty fee. It would be a good living." I was gaining traction on the idea.

The Cosmetology program included three licenses: hair, nails, and esthetician. The esthetician license had a real draw, as I had spent years working on the face and neck in physical therapy. In the following days, I spoke to some of the students and they raved about the program and the instructor. I, too, needed the security that a cosmetology licensure would provide. Hippie Chick and I applied and we both got in.

The salon was a simple setup but included all the basics: mirrors, styling chairs, hairdryers, shampoo bowls. What set it apart was the atmosphere. There was modern music and the mood was light. The students wore dark green scrubs, the color of money and progress.

They took pride in their appearance, styling their hair and using the canteen makeup with skill.

Tammy, the cosmetology instructor, was a civilian. She had clear bright eyes, long auburn hair, and luminous skin. She laughed easily. My favorite image of her was her morning entrance: she entered at the far end of the drab beige, gray, and mint-green corridor and there was no mistaking her jewel tones, auburn hair, and smiling white, white teeth. Most days she carried a colorful bag of cosmetics, hair products, décor, or flowers. She was a bird of paradise, and my heart filled with possibilities.

On my first day in the program, I was assigned my booth. We were allowed to put up a photo or two and individualize our area. The teacher explained, "I want this salon to be like a real salon in the great big world. You guys are gonna have enough trouble when you release. You'll need the confidence."

The salon customers were both staff and inmates. As an inmate, you could kite for an appointment and use your wages for haircuts, pedicures, manicures, facials, and waxing. As a student, we worked on each other. It felt like a miracle. I wrote my sister a letter about the news: "Do you know what this means? Job security, financial security, I won't be a drain on anyone. I can live anywhere the family needs me." I dared to dream, just a little bit.

The first assignment was to complete a set of skills on a manikin. I named her "Ruby," after the alter ego I invented in my previous life. Ruby was a little naughty and much more fun than Karen. Whenever I made a dinner reservation, I used the name, Ruby. "Ruuuby?" the host would say, "Nice." I preened appropriately. Ruby always got special service and better tables.

Ruby the manikin was to have curlers, perm rods, color, relaxers, and finally a haircut before I could work on a live human. One day, as I practiced a shampoo set with pin curlers and bobby pins, the manikin head blurred and, like a mirage, became my mother. I swear I could smell her scent.

An early memory came to me. I was a young girl, sitting in the backseat of the station wagon. My mother was sitting up front in the passenger seat, pinning her hair into pin curls using bobby pins, just like I was with my manikin. I tried to hide my tears. *Stay with me, Mom.* I imagined her singing *Camelot* and cleaning out the cedar closet with Fuller brushes and wearing a scarf on her head. I thought of her getting dressed to go out for dinner. As a little girl, I would sit on her white satin bedspread and watch her pick out her clothing and shoes. First, I would pack her evening bag. She explained which shade of lipstick would go with her tweed skirt and asked me to make sure the purse contained tissue. The final part of the ritual was picking out her necklace and clip earrings. I brought the light blue jewelry box back to the bed. I twisted a key and it played "Let Me Call You Sweetheart." Then I opened the lid that contained the plunder. As a teen, I learned the difference between cut crystal and glass beads but it never made the pageantry less magical.

My mother and father bought a house with the GI Bill. They joined the Honeywell Country Club and took our family on vacations. My mother's job in the 1960s was to be a wife and mother. She supported my father's vision. These were my formative years. I was raised to become a proper wife, not to create my own identity. I dreamed of supporting a man's vision of the future, not the other way around. "Don't rock the boat" was a way of life for many women back then.

In 1969 and into the '70s, the order began to shift. My father caught the wave. He began wearing bell-bottoms and a Chinese thinking cap. He said phrases like, "Think for yourself" or "I can relate." My father was no longer interested in a traditional life or a traditional wife. My parents divorced. My mother was never the same. She lost her purpose and her lifestyle. Then my mother went off the rails.

She attended Parents Without Partners meetings, which became a gateway for dating and drinking. Christine had left for college and I was alone most evenings of the week. One December when I was sixteen, I drove to a Christmas tree lot, picked out a tree, and brought it home. I set it up in our picture window that went floor to ceiling. It would be the first thing my mother would see when she came home. I sat in the living room as evening fell, but still she was not home.

I don't remember feeling sorry for myself. Instead, I put on Arthur Fiedler and the Boston Pops Christmas album and began to decorate the tree, first lights, then garlands, then ornaments. My mother would be so delighted to see the lights waiting for her when she drove up! When I finished, I lay on my stomach under the tree, facing the window, waiting for the car lights in the driveway. She would be so excited.

I was awakened by the sound of the front door. *Darn it, I fell asleep!* I missed her surprised reaction. The door swung open and my mother entered weeping. I was confused. *What had happened?*

"Oh, Karen," she cried. "I should have been here. You shouldn't have had to do this all alone!" Her face was in agony. It dawned on me that she was ashamed of herself. I wish I could say that it got better and our home life improved after that, but it did not. Looking back, I imagine she suffered depression and was on her way to becoming an alcoholic.

I was unsupervised most of high school. I used to go to Patty's house in the evening just so her mother would tell me that it was time to go home to get ready for school the next day. One night my mother did not come home. I woke up at two a.m. and still she was not there. At seven-thirty, I got up and began getting ready for school. My mother's bedroom door opened. I didn't favor her with a glance. Then she stepped into the bathroom and our faces met in the mirror.

My mother's face was dark purple. Her forehead was enormous and curved out grotesquely. I was horrified. I just stared at her. I couldn't move or speak.

"I was in an accident last night. I totaled the car. I fell asleep," she said absently, looking at herself in the mirror. I stared at her eyes in the mirror but nothing else resembled my mother. I made a step to hold her but I was afraid I would cause her pain. But I knew she'd been drinking and I was angry. She was not my mother anymore. I was sick of mowing the lawn, shoveling the snow, cooking for myself. I was scared, probably more scared than angry; I could have lost her. Why was I so stubborn? Why didn't I hold her and let her cry?

I know now that my mother was reeling after losing her identity. She did the best she could, and I missed her so much. I kept my head down, allowing my hair to cover my tears. If I could, I would tell her that she was a wonderful mother and that her grandchildren missed her. I would thank her for teaching me show tunes and taking me to art museums. I would make sure she knew the poor choices I made were mine alone. I clung tight to her images, trying to keep her in my world. *Stay, Mom.* But like a spirit, she faded away. I worked more lovingly on Ruby's pin curls as blow dryers and voices overpowered my memories.

That night in the cell, I wrote about my mother, a mad scrawl of fragments: carsick, bristle rollers in a pink box. She laughs and I see cheese and crackers in her mouth. I am throwing up and she is rubbing my back. Barf on black patent-leather shoes. I pummeled the memory and writing experience into a piece titled "Ruby." Inspired by the Write Around Portland teacher, I submitted it to a women's anthology publication called *VoiceCatcher*, my first publication.

Haley wrote me a letter of congratulations. "You have held up your spirit and let it grow—you're published!" Nikki read "Ruby" at the book release party. She stood alone before an audience and read about her mother, an inmate in prison. The audience embraced her. On her next visit, she filled in all the details: the setting, attendance, other readers. I beamed, thinking of my daughters, my mother, and me in all our states of existence, threaded together. Blue Eyes took a photo of Nikki and me on that visit. We both look real-world happy.

My best and perhaps only decent haircut in the Cosmetology program was for a woman named Tommy. We both were housed on J Unit. She was serving life without parole for, I was told, a bungled murder of a dwarf. We all knew each other's crimes, but the details spread by gossip, never the inmate herself. Because I was "the woman who wrote," I had several women come tell me their stories. Perhaps they felt it was their chance to have their history recorded by an unbiased recorder.

By this point, I had been incarcerated for over two years and I stayed off the radar. But I was still intimidated by some of the Lifers. One day, I was assigned to cut Tommy's hair. I panicked. I was not a natural like so many other girls.

That day, I waggled my scissors in the air, wild-eyed, and signaled for help. The inmate tutor came over and did not seem intimidated by Tommy at all. She ran her fingers through Tommy's hair, rat-a-tatted instructions, and left me to the wolf. I stalled by placing and replacing the cape over her, readjusting the neck, and smoothing it over the arms of the chair. I looked around at the other students, eyes pleading, but everyone suddenly looked purposeful. The tutor's expression was, *Get over it*. Tommy was staring at me.

"Cut it short and spiky."

"OK," I said and nervously ran my fingers through her hair like the tutor.

"Don't worry about it. It's just hair. It'll grow back." She paused and our eyes met in the mirror. "Of course," she said, "our hair is all we really have in here."

My heart was racing as I took Tommy to the shampoo bowl. She rested her neck in the cradle and closed her eyes. I reminded myself of my manual skills, and shampooed and conditioned until I gained some confidence. The muscles on her face relaxed, her breathing became slow and steady.

The shampoo provided rare human touch for both of us. The muscles on her face relaxed, she sighed contentedly, giving herself over to my touch. Her vulnerability was all it took. *She trusts me.* I began to feel a nurturing tenderness toward this woman, this legend. She moaned quietly when I turned off the water.

"That felt so good, the human touch." She opened her eyes and sighed. "Allowed touch."

Tommy settled into the chair and I went to work. Her calm allowed me to focus and not let my nerves carry me away. When I was done, I put a little gel on the top for a spike and we both smiled into the mirror. The haircut wasn't horrible!

"I love it. This might be one of the best cuts I have had," she said.

"Ah," I flapped my wrist and took off the cape.

"I'll be back again in about a month or so, it grows fast."

The funny thing was, I never nailed that cut again. But she forgave me for it. I would see her on the unit and say hi or share a table with her while we waited for call-outs. One morning after breakfast, she asked if we could have a word, alone.

I felt a shiver of danger but pushed it away. I was no longer intimidated by the inmate before me. I was intimidated by the woman she had been when she committed her crime.

"How about at first line movement after lunch?"

What did she want, a favor? To borrow something? We met later that day at a table at the end of the room.

"You seem like a nice lady," she said to the tabletop. "You've probably heard the stories about my crime." She looked up and I fidgeted. I had no idea that this was coming.

"Hard to keep a secret in here," I said, nervous about what she would say. Did I want to hear this?

"Our crimes are all a matter of public record," she said. "But that doesn't really tell the whole story for any of us, does it?"

"There's always more to the story," I offered. *Here we go.*

"It matters to me that good people, like you seem to be, really know what happened in my crime." She looked up at me. "I'm not the evil monster Joe Public thinks I am."

In a way, I was flattered that she thought I was worthy of an explanation and that she could trust me.

She told her story from start to finish. On paper in a criminal file, it was a heinous public crime. Her explanation of the plummeting events ended up being yet another story of drugs and jealousy that led to one stupid blunder after another, culminating with a botched disposal of the body. She never denied that someone died and she took her time with the details.

"Our mistake was that we came back to the scene. We weren't sure if the guy was dead. There were witnesses." The woman shook her head, not frustrated but resigned.

We sat in a fitting silence for a while. Then I asked the mother of all questions to a Lifer, "How do you do it? You have life without parole. What is it like to know you will never be free and this"—I waved to the beige room of tables, podium, lines of cells—"this unit will be the last place you live?"

"I will die in here. Over the years, I have collected enough meds from med line and stashed them in my mattress. It's just weird to pick a day. For now, I'm working on a quilt, so it won't be this week."

I sat with that quietly, not knowing that Tommy would die from cancer in 2019, eight years after I was released.

One evening, I noticed that I had a call-out for the Medical Unit. I didn't recognize the abbreviations on the list and asked Sinful what it meant.

"Oh!" She made a rare, overt display of joy, waving her hands and crouching with a thigh slap. "You're gonna get a mammogram!"

"And so?" I didn't get it. It wasn't the usual response to mammograms!

"You get to go out! They take you outta here to an imaging center in the real world."

I looked around the unit and out the windows to the lifeless yard. "*Out?* I am going out?" I was stunned, it was too good to be true.

"You go out the same way you came in. You leave in the same van you rode in on." For me, that would be the van from jail, with Tizzy, Buzzcut, and Silver. The same van that played Mexican polka music and had windows that fogged up and separated me from the free world. I felt my stomach drop remembering that sad day, and yet, that van was going to take me *out* to the free world.

"I would go if they gave me a root canal," I said incredulously.

Sinful and I talked into the night; poor woman, I was wired. She told me about her mammogram the previous year.

"Everything out there looks alive. You can see the whole sky. Once we hit the main roads, I kept my eye out for men on motorcycles. The bad boys can tell it's a van from DOC and they always give a wave."

"I'll look for them." I flashed to a memory of a ride with Tom. I was up against his strong back, holding on, my head tilted back toward the sun.

"I remember how green it was—the grass, the trees. The traffic was slow, thank god, and we were inching along a freeway underpass. Compared to that"—she gestured with a flamboyant wave toward the yard—"even the underpass was beautiful. I remember thinking, *Hey, this would be a nice place to camp.*"

"That's so sad!" I laughed.

"The nurse at the mammogram center will give you chocolate. A whole big bar of the good stuff." Sinful climbed up on her bunk. She was quiet. Then I heard, "The only thing worse than prison is getting sick and dying in prison."

I was devastated for her and the other lifers. I stared at the underside of Sinful's bunk for long hours into the night as I listened to her slow breathing. Out. Would it still look the same? Would it be a place I could slip into and just watch the cars pass and the trees go by the window?

The next day, I presented myself at the appointed time in the Medical Unit. I was ordered to sit in the corridor and wait on the bench where we lined up for visits. A male officer I had not seen before approached.

"Baker?"

"Yes."

"Let's go," he snapped. Without looking me in the eyes, he set off down the hall and I followed him out the door of the Medium/Maximum facility. He stopped and I preceded him, not because I was a lady but because he didn't want to get attacked by an unknown felon. We walked behind fence lines toward the receiving unit that processed inmates in and out. When we entered the receiving door, I was blindsided by the memories of my first, horrible day in prison. I walked past the showers where I was stripped nude and ordered to wash in lye soap. We passed the stacks of Intake scrubs and plastic sandals and shelves of wool blankets and worn sheets. At the end of the hall was the holding tank I shared with Tizzy, Silver, and Buzzcut. Passing by the large open door of the holding tank, I felt a damp cold, like a poltergeist. I had hit rock bottom that day, and yet, I remembered my pitiful courage. I had to place my hand on my heart in tenderness for that Karen.

Steps forward and to the door. At the end of the hallway, he opened the heavy outer door, gave me the once-over, saw I was properly submissive, and out the door we went. The day was clear unlike the fog on the day I came in. My feet made the same crunch of gravel as I was led to the sliding door of the white van. I stepped in, remembering the cage that separated the inmates from the driver. I sat in the same window seat that I did the day I entered prison. I shivered. *I am not that Karen anymore.* I got up and moved to the other side of the van.

I sat in the back row so I would have a 360-degree view. I wanted to see every possible sight—flora, fauna, people, new cars, new buildings, and Sinful's motorcycle boys. We backed out of the gate and turned toward the exit. We drove across a large parking lot. This was the lot where my friends and family parked. On the other side of the parking lot was a set of single-story buildings behind a single fence with barbed wire.

"Is that the Minimum facility?" I asked the driver.

He glanced toward the buildings. "Yep. How soon are you goin' over, Baker?" He glanced in the rearview mirror, his eyes impassive but not cruel.

"Five months, after the Hair Design graduation in August." Five months. It was hard to believe I'd already been here for three years.

"It's better over there."

I'm counting on it.

I turned around to get a better look at the prison block. It was a bunker, low and dark. I wondered what it would be like for Sinful to leave the prison walls on a trip like this knowing she would go back to the dark block and stay there, no end in sight. No move date on the calendar for the Minimum facility.

We left the driveway and turned toward civilization. The first glimpses were a few scattered homes and other cars on the road. The cars hadn't changed that much. We drove into thicker traffic and I turned my attention to the passengers in the cars. I saw suburban moms with kids strapped in the back. One mom-car buzzed past with a wailing toddler. I watched the toddler throw her sippy cup on the floor and smiled, remembering. There were several cars of sloppy twenty-year-olds not watching the road. We pulled up at a stoplight. Next to us was a mammoth RV. Behind the wheel was a big burly dude with a little dog sitting on his lap. I expected to see clothing like *The Jetsons* or *Star Trek*. But it was suits, sweats, and ball caps—same as before. I was hopeful; maybe I could somehow catch up to the life I was missing. The light changed and the cars raced ahead. Everyone seemed like they were in a hurry. *Oh, people, slow down, you might miss the beauty of Sinful's underpass!* The houses grew more clustered and then gave way to buildings and businesses.

All too soon, we arrived at the imaging center. It was a modern upscale building. We drove around the back and entered the building through a rear door, away from the good people in the waiting room. I was taken to a small changing room by a pretty young woman in hospital scrubs. She was holding a chart. "Tell me your name, please."

"Karen Baker." It felt good to use my full name.

"Good, that's what I have in your chart, we have to check. Welcome, Karen."

"Thank you," I managed, afraid I would cry at her kindness. *Karen.* She was trim and fit with a head of freshly dyed blond hair and bleached white teeth, a Disneyland princess. She showed me into the booth. "I will be right back."

"Oh please, don't hurry!"

She giggled at that.

The booth was painted in soothing tones of blue and gold, *not* mint green. The seat was padded, softer than a cloud. I took off my clothes. I realized it was the first time in three years I had changed clothes without a camera or a window. I draped myself in soft cotton that was pink and purple. I was wickedly free, no brassiere. I looked down at my breasts under the fabric and wondered if they had changed. I no longer had the year-round sun freckles on my chest and my arms. My arms were thinner and my middle was softer. I folded my prison scrubs into a neat pile as if to display civility, then I sat back and rested on the wall of the booth. I listened to the sounds in the clinic, the soft doors, a phone chirping, soft rubber-soled footsteps in the hall, murmurs of polite instruction. It was the sound of meaningful bustle and productivity.

"Karen? Are you ready?"

"Yes," I peeped.

I wondered on some level if she was afraid of me. I acted submissive and was overly helpful during the procedure. When she walked me back to the booth, she drew a handful of chocolate bars out of her deep pocket. They were the good stuff all right. I chose a bar of dark mint chocolate. I ripped open the paper and placed a square in my mouth as quickly as I could, like a Dickens character.

I slowly dressed as I let the dark velvety chocolate melt in my mouth. I didn't want to chomp it up, untasted. I'd rather eat less and savor it. I tried not to moan. I knew I couldn't help myself. I finally emerged after dressing and eating about three large squares. I was languid, woozy from kindness and oral sensuality.

I walked toward the rear exit where the officer was waiting. "Gotta leave the chocolate here," he said.

The technician was standing by a trash can. She looked down at her shoes. I gently dropped the rest of the dark mint chocolate bar into the trash, feeling sick with the waste. "Thank you so much."

"You're welcome," she whispered.

The officer stepped back and I walked through the door. The technician had seemed genuinely kind but perhaps I was fooling myself. Would she run to the sink to wash her hands and change her clothing? Would she go home and tell her family about the convict who came in for a mammogram and how they aren't paying her enough?

The mammogram trip let me know that the world had not changed all that much. I was at the halfway mark of my time. If I kept myself not just busy but engaged, perhaps the world that was passing me by in the cars on the freeway was not that far out of reach.

By the halfway mark of my sentence, the expanding Five Alive group had started to move across the street to Minimum. Tizzy was the first to go. Teddy Bear would be next, then Pearl and me. The second batch of Five Alive followed with Rainy, Wise Owl, and Blue Eyes. Hippie Chick would be the last one over. All of us had learned to do our time in the Big House by staying off the radar of DOC and giving the rest of the women inmates a lot of space.

Hippie Chick, Blue Eyes, Sinful, and I went to the Zen service every week. We were studying the Ten Essential Precepts, a set of vows of ethical conduct. The series finished with a ceremony called "Jukai," led by our Zen priests, Getshushin and Keisei. At the end of the ceremony, we were given a written lineage of the venerable teachers from our line. Our names were added to the bottom. We were a part of something worldwide and everlasting. The teacher placed a long black loop of cloth to wear around our necks that we could keep and wear at our services. It reminded us that we were committed to right living. I was still a little confused about how to make peace among traditions. *Jesus, don't be mad, OK? I need all of this.*

Hippie Chick and I were cramming for the state examination for Cosmetology. We walked circles on yard with homemade flashcards. Hippie Chick was nervous about passing the test. One part of her childhood was spent living in a cave in Hawaii. She went to school in bare feet. Her attendance was hit or miss based on her migrating parents. But Hippie Chick wanted this. She had done her homework. I quizzed her on the yard, and she yowled and waved her hands in the air like a game show contestant as she answered every question correctly. She was going to pass. We both would be at the graduation ceremony at the end of summer.

I wasn't the only one graduating. Nikki had one year of college to go. It felt like a miracle that she was making it through, not because she wasn't smart—she had more than her share of academic intelligence—but for her to survive on her own and not lose heart revealed her emotional intelligence and just plain grit.

Haley, too, was full of grit and was getting ready to graduate from high school. She had visited the prison that spring and we had a chance to talk about college. In twisted luck, the fact that I was penniless allowed both girls access to grants and scholarships for college.

Haley chose the University of Santa Cruz, which was halfway between Southern California and Oregon. She chose to be a banana slug at UCSC so she could get to each family.

I threw myself into advising Haley on majors and minors. But me assuming the role of a college counselor only caused confusion and heated conversations.

"I mean well. I want to help her," I said to Blondie one day.

"We got nothin', baby. I start to talk to my boys about what they should do and I'm back to parenting a jet airplane, remember? You need to go ..."

"I remember," I said.

"The best thing going for me and my boys is my sweet mama. She's raising my boys," said Blondie. "Chin up, we're the lucky ones."

My role, like Blondie said, had shifted. I was lucky to have the girls' loyalty and owed a debt of gratitude to the village that helped raise my precious daughters.

Against all odds, I had a surprise visit from my stepfather, Marshall. Marshall was legally blind when I met him at age fifteen. Now, thirty-five years later, Christine told me he was on the brink of complete blindness due to macular degeneration. He had beautiful tall posture and would walk straight into a street lamp. He managed to get around by turning his head to access his peripheral vision. This gave the appearance of vigilance and protection, always on the lookout. At least that was the way he made me feel: safe. Marshall lived in Minneapolis, Minnesota, and he navigated airports and taxis to see me, arriving in the same red windbreaker my mother bought him years ago. It was a little worse for wear but he couldn't see that the elbows were worn thin. Perhaps he wore it as a mighty cape from his guardian angel. We chatted easily. He was nonplussed about my environment.

"You came so far. I know it wasn't easy," I said.

He shrugged like it was. "I just had to check on you, make sure the food isn't as bad as they say." He laughed. For my mother, Christine and me, and all our children, he was a rock of stability to Sam's free spirit. I was lucky to have it both ways.

That spring, Angel was given the project of painting the walls of the visiting room. She created sea themes in the baby and toddler room, Oregon landscapes in the main room, and wall frames for photo opportunities. Our visitors were allowed to approach her and talk about her work. This meant that my daughters had a chance to speak with an inmate besides their mother.

My daughters were protective and worried about their mom, locked up with criminals. When I told them about Celly, Mittens, Five Alive, Blondie, and Sinful, I described them as sensational, hilarious, misguided, and abused. But I spoke of Angel differently. Angel's characteristics had nothing to do with being an inmate. She was honest, gentle, and merry, like the fairies she drew. I told my daughters how she walked the walk of faith and held her own feet to the fire when she slipped. In the entire prison, she was the best person in any room she occupied. I was proud to introduce her to my children.

"What did she do?" asked Nikki.

"She got mixed up with drugs, bad ones. They made her violent and she had a break with reality." Nikki looked over at Angel, sitting cross-legged on the floor absorbed in a flower. Nikki considered this for a while, looking at her.

"This meth stuff and all the combinations of synthetics are creating a New Age Dr. Jekyll and Mr. Hyde. Here they are." I gestured to the room. "Just stay away from those drugs."

Nikki looked at me, world-weary for her age, and didn't bother to respond.

"I'm not glad she's here," said Haley. "But, I'm glad she's here for you. It just seems to me that there have to be better ways to punish people. She could be put to better use. She has so much to offer and she's not doing the world any good from in here."

I was proud that they were not afraid. By getting to know Angel, they deduced on their own that there might be a better way. It was the stirring of restorative justice that first must come from the lesson of learning to love the unlovable. It would one day be to their credit, and I hoped to the credit of their generation.

Nikki, Christine, Sam, and Audrey went to Haley's high school graduation that June. A few weeks later, I received a packet of photos. There were photos of the ceremony on the football field, Haley in the crowd, Haley doing the happy dance with her diploma. There were photos of her with both her dad's family and mine. She wore a green robe and a lei of orchids around her neck. Here was my baby surrounded by people wishing her well, most of whom I did not know.

I called Haley after I got the package, photos in hand. I wanted to learn some of the names of the people who mattered to her, such as her boyfriend, Trent, and her friends. The photos of Nikki and Haley were so beautiful. Sam and Christine looked healthy and tanned. "What a beautiful day. It looks like it was a very happy event."

"It almost wasn't a happy event," said Haley.

"Nikki said she couldn't come to my graduation and I felt my heart break. Sam and Auntie Christine got into town. It was good to have family there but I still missed Nikki. Auntie Christine and I went boogie boarding and hung out at Moonlight Beach while Gramps and

Audrey ran errands. Christine asked if I wanted a snack. I said sure, and we walked up to the snack bar by the volleyball courts. As we approached, I saw a familiar face and I thought I was hallucinating. It was Nikki."

"Oh Haley," I said.

"It was like a cheesy scene from a movie, we ran to each other, hugging and crying. It was the best surprise of my life. It was a magic moment."

"This picture of you and Nikki, with your cap and gown on the school track, you're just beaming."

"It ended up being a great day, I missed you, but having Nikki there enabled me to enjoy my graduation. Before she got there I thought the day would come and go like any other day."

Nikki stepped in to be there for Haley Rose but it wasn't the first time. She had been doing so since Haley was a baby. She chose her middle name at age three: "She's my Rose girl. *My* baby." As children, they played and quarreled, but no one else could come between them. As young women, they lived apart but remained a lifeline to each other, trying to make sense of the past and navigate the future. They were closer to each other than to me. I was relieved.

The Cosmetology graduation was in August. Of the few job training programs in U.S. prisons, this program had the best track record for turning out successful citizens. The teacher kept track of the graduates and invited one of the success stories to come back as a speaker. Planning the ceremony took weeks. The teacher went all out. The theme was "New York City." Angel was the project designer and created buildings, lights, and Central Park that transformed the visiting room. I have a photo of Christine, Nikki, and me standing on a mock street corner. I am smiling in my green scrubs with a gold loop of fabric around my neck.

The ceremony was, as expected, a little schmaltzy, but it was filled with heart and promise. The room was filled to capacity. I peeked out the door and could see that my family invited Angel to sit with them. Waiting behind the door, we brushed lint off each other's scrubs. Each graduate brought a guest inmate whom we had styled, to demonstrate our skill. I chose a young, pretty woman whose brown hair held a curl. In the final moments before our promenade in, we kept busy fluffing our styles. It was all happiness and light.

The music started, some country anthem about a butterfly, and one by one, we entered the room to rows upon rows of faces. The audience was dressed in their best. Angel's decorations transformed the beige walls into beautiful street scenes. I felt pretty for perhaps the first time in three years, but more than that, I was proud. My family had proof that I could take care of myself.

My name was called and I walked toward the center aisle like a bride. I found my family near the back. Christine had a worried brow, like she was trying to tell me something. Nikki sat next to her, flattened in her seat. *What happened?* I locked eyes on my daughter and she turned her head to the image projected on the screen at the front of the room. It was me. My mug shot, my worst self.

It was worse than walking past the holding tank on the day I went for my mammogram. It was the ultimate before and after. I tried not to stumble, keeping a smile plastered on my face. I walked, head held high toward that four-foot image of my pitiful, ravaged face. *That is you, Karen, no matter how far you run. That mug shot will always be there, lurking, capable of sending you and your family into a spiral.*

In the bright lights, I masked over and found my way to my seat. Sounds vanished and I hovered in a soundless bubble. I stole a glance at the row where Nikki and Christine were sitting. I knew that if I could muster a little humor, I might be able to rescue them. I made some sort of goofy disapproving face, one that my father had taught me at his best irreverent self. It seemed to reset the nosedive for our group. *I am going to have to be the one who takes leadership in these moments. It's my responsibility.*

"How'd it go?" asked Sinful that night.

"It was mostly good," I said and flopped onto my bunk. "I got to see my family, actually hug them for more than a second and take pictures with them. Angel sat with my sister and daughter. That meant a lot to me, my worlds coming together," I said. "The bad part was my damned mug shot. When we walked in, there it was, on a big four-foot screen. Look how far you've come!" I felt the sting in the retelling to Sinful. "I looked over at Nikki and she looked like she was going to cry."

"Damn," she spat. "I heard the room looked great."

"The room was packed. The cops were on their best behavior, laughing and talking to our families. I was glad to see they possessed those emotions, but it felt phony. I had never seen the lieutenant laugh. I had never seen his teeth before—he's got a full set of teeth!" I paused then asked her, "What's worse? Knowing they have a sense of humor and empathy and don't show it, or believing that they don't have those emotions at all?"

"They laugh *at* us, Karen. It's a mean sense of humor. As much as they smile for your family, they don't like you. Don't ever forget that." Sinful paced to the window and looked out at the activity on J Unit while I changed into my prison blues.

"They usually take you across the street right after graduation," she said.

I looked up at her and she was looking as she always did, calm and matter-of-fact. The fact of my leaving didn't seem to bother her.

I had an acute attack of survivor's guilt. I couldn't say, *You'll be right behind me.* I had inhaled her exhales. I knew her sounds as she woke. I could read her moods. How could I reconcile leaving her behind? Would I ever visit her? Would she agree to see me? I didn't dare promise, didn't know if I could do it.

In the following days, I sought as much alone time as one could muster in a crowded prison. I began to break alliances with those I would never see again and concentrated on quality time with Angel and Sinful. Angel and I spent time together on yard. There was freedom of movement and fewer cameras. I asked Angel questions about her life before prison: *What is your favorite flavor of birthday cake? What were you like as a child? How long have you been drawing?* I wanted to create within me an enduring imprint of this precious soul. I wanted to talk about her with my children so she would live on in young women who might shape the world differently by knowing her.

Some of those days on the yard, we sat together in silence. Angel would draw and I would write. Everything felt futile, especially words. What went through my mind on a loop wasn't poignant or profound. It was the scene from the 1972 movie, *The Poseidon Adventure.* The surviving cast made it to the hull of the overturned ship and was trying to let the world know they were alive. Angel and Sinful were trapped underwater. *There are people down here!*

Pastor Alida's ministry did not come to Minimum. She invited me to come to her church when I paroled and told me she would be waiting for me at the door, just as she did in prison. I'd ride buses and walk miles to meet her.

Alida didn't pass judgment on my questions about faith. She was my beacon, waiting in the headlights while I bounced over the ruts, jagged into the darkness, and swerved forward in and out of the light. She told me that love and peace and joy were possible. I just had to allow it to happen. In my midnight heart, I knew that if I wanted to break free, I would have to open a very black door.

At my final service, I waited my turn as Alida hugged the women goodbye as they exited the chapel.

"This might be my last service until I see you at City Bible Church in Portland."

Alida took my hands, her gaze ministerial. "How are you feeling?" she asked.

"I'm trying to be a better human and less of a burden to my family," I said heartily. "I finished cosmetology school, I finished the health book, my kids visit…"

Alida squeezed my hands. "I didn't ask you how you are *doing*, Karen. I asked how are you *feeling*? What is in your heart?"

The pain was so sudden, the room tilted. My knees fought for balance as my emotions tumbled and crashed together. I looked toward her through tears. I found her face. "I don't know. I don't dare look at my feelings—they're too dark. Prison is not a safe place to lose it."

"May I pray for you?"

"Yes." It felt right.

She placed her hands on my shoulders. Alida closed her eyes tight and began taking long even breaths. "Abba Father, here is Karen, she is frightened to reach out for help. You know her heart. We ask for your healing so she can open her heart completely."

I matched her slow breathing and the room seemed to right itself. I closed my eyes.

I felt Alida sway.

"Oh, God. There is so much pain. There is guilt and regret." Alida hummed and muttered prayers. Then she stopped. She deepened her grip on my shoulders. "I see a garden. It is overgrown with weeds." Alida tilted her head back, her eyes were still closed. She had one hand in the air, the other still on my shoulder. "You must clear the weeds, Karen. You will have to dig and work with your bare hands. Clear out it out! Clear out the guilt, the shame! Plant the seeds of God's grace and mercy. Nourish it, and tend it. I see a new garden, I see a place of beauty." Alida's voice grew louder, commanding.

I began to tremble, my heart overflowing. I was weak and strong at the same time. I was hopeful. Alida lifted both arms to the chapel rafters. "Father, help Karen believe that grace and mercy are hers. Guide her as she uses the wisdom of her story to heal others."

Alida snapped her eyes open, refocusing on me. Her eyes blazed. She again reached for my shoulders with both hands. "You must write. You must write, Karen." She was breathing in huffs, as if she'd run miles. "You are meant for powerful things. You will help." Then she said softly, "You will heal."

The words dredged my stubborn heart and I released the tears I had been harboring for so many years. Alida pulled me into her arms.

"Only Christ was meant to carry the cross." She pulled back, looking softly into my eyes. "He did it so you don't have to. You are forgiven."

The emotions that tumbled and crashed together disentangled. I felt unburdened. My tears still flowed, but they were from hope.

"Forgive yourself, Karen. Pull the weeds, tend your garden. Write your story."

I hung on to the cleansing of that day. After several days of introspection and journaling, I pushed on the black door. I heard a few hinges creak. Tom was behind the door. I dug into the back of my homemade folder, underneath saved letters, where my photos of Tom were. *There you are.* He was alive in the pictures. He was a merry prankster, an athlete, a son, a brother. He was a husband and stepfather who tried, in his way, to gain acceptance with my daughters. He was a beautiful, big-hearted man. I felt a deep yawning wave of grief.

The next day, at morning yard, I was the sole walker. Through the fence lines, I could see the distant hillside turning green. *I am alive to see it, Tom.*

I still did not remember the accident. When I had read the accident report, it was almost too much to bear. I closed the black door so I could survive prison and created a cage of condemnation, my prison within a prison.

That morning, I pushed on the black door again and recalled the details of the accident report. What I knew was this:

Tom did not die instantly. He was shouting for help. He was worried about me.

"I'm crushing her! She can't breathe."

Was he aware of the extent of his injuries? Was he lucid in his final moments? Did the first responders comfort him? Was he afraid? Did he know he was dying? My gut tells me he would have been surprised. *What? I was only joking about using my nine lives! I have more to do!*

I allowed myself to imagine the accident. I pictured him crushed up against me, shouting for help. Then, the rescue Jaws of Life. Were his final moments lying on the gurney? The ground? I imagined his face as he succumbed and the pose of a body that no longer inhabits his spirit. *My fault.* The cage was calling.

The prison yard swirled in tears. Suddenly, in a supernatural flash, I saw Tom. He was standing before me, in his purple shirt, his ski pass around his neck. He was staring intently, leaning his head toward mine.

"What are you doing?" His expression was a little teasing and impatient. I didn't deny what was happening. It was real. I felt him, I heard his voice.

You're not mad at me?

He huffed a laugh. "Don't waste a day! I wouldn't. Be happy."

I laughed out loud. I felt a warm breeze and he was gone. The sun was shining, the breeze was light. I felt absurdly happy and unburdened. I could grieve now.

The black door of the cage was open.

In no time at all, the call was shouted across the dayroom.

"Baker, roll up!" A large blue bin rolled into the unit. When Pearl and Teddy Bear left, they scooped up their property on their shelves and in their tank drawers. They shoved their belongings into clear plastic bags, dragged them across the dayroom, and tossed them into a big blue bin. They. Were. Outta there. When Blondie moved across the street, she lingered and cried a little bit, waving in the arch of the exit. She was still waving as the women turned back to their soap operas.

I hustled down to the podium, picked up four plastic bags. Since the day I met Celly on G Unit, I had doubled up my bags, After over three years, I had extra shoes, books, and hygiene staples. They were the bags of a woman inmate who has done some time.

Sinful was pacing in the cell, ready to help. We made short work of it, all business. I wondered how many cellmates she had packed up before? Was today just another cellmate moving on? I dragged my bags outside the cell and turned to her.

"Woman," she said, "you got drive, you got enough to fly outta here and never come back. I see these dumb shits coming back over and over. Give me that chance. Just go. Don't expect me to write. The best thing you can do for me is to never come back." Her eyes were blazing with instruction, and more intense than I had ever seen them.

"I won't," I said. I stood outside the cell looking in at her until the door rolled shut. Then there was nowhere to go but down the stairs and out of the unit. I tossed my bags in the blue bin. I looked for Angel but she was not there. The tables held Top Dog, Judy, and Tommy. Hippie Chick came forward, crying across the dayroom.

"You're right behind me," I said.

"I know." She cried anyway.

I shouted a goodbye to the dayroom, gave a quick Richard Nixon impeachment salute, and walked out of the unit. I was moving to a set of buildings that had one set of fence lines and an exit gate. My kids could mark this day on the calendar. I would be going home in three years. None of my elders had died, yet. My kids were still making it. I had a way to earn money. I still had a handful of loyal friends in the outside world. It was all too beautiful. Angel, Sinful, and others had trusted me with their stories. Those stories were in me and those stories would make it over the wire.

I was on my way.

MINIMUM

Turning out of J Unit, I faced the long, lifeless corridor of Medium/Maximum for the last time. Now that I was leaving, I allowed myself to feel the crushing weight of being trapped and the utter exhaustion from the daily effort it took to survive. I could call the block by its true name: the Tomb.

I stopped not to linger but to gather my strength. My breath slowed. I began the steps toward the open air, the earth, the sky.

Like an ecstatic experience, Chappie stepped out from the chapel and into the corridor, humming and grinning. She stopped dead in her tracks when she saw me walking alongside the blue bin that held my plastic bags of belongings. This sight was familiar to anyone in the Medium/Maximum facility. It was a sign of upward progress.

"Baker!" Then more tenderly, "Karen, is this what I think it is?" She walked toward me, beaming. "Are you headed across the street?" Her molecules of Mama Bear hit me before the hug. If I had a tail I would have wagged. Instead, I whimpered a little bit and fell into her arms.

"Oh! Good fer you, now," she whispered in Minnesotan. She pulled back and saw the tears in my eyes.

It took a moment for me to speak.

"I'm leaving them behind. Sinful. Angel. Watch over them, please?"

"That's what I do," she said. "But you, you're on your way!"

And so I was.

I was instructed to wait on the bench. A guard approached. "Let's go Baker." As the mystics say, the only way out was through, and that meant out the exit door at the end of the corridor. I did not turn around for one last look. Instead, I stepped forward on a new path.

We walked through the six sets of fence lines toward the visiting room and entered the receiving unit for the Medium/Maximum facility. I walked past the lye soap showers, the shelves with stacks of Intake scrubs and bedding, and finally, past the Tank. I walked out the receiving door into the driveway cage, the final and seventh fence line. The gate opened and I stepped into the public parking lot. For the first time in three and a half years, I was outside the prison, unshackled.

I had read about people who escaped custody, running away from Minimum time. What fools. How could anyone run and risk everything all over again when they had such a limited time left?

I walked—no, I floated—toward the simple buildings I had seen from the van on my way to the mammogram. They were constructed in a bunker style, light tan, arranged behind one fence line. The guard opened the door of the Minimum receiving unit and we stepped inside. There was no Tank, no lye soap showers, no shelves of bedding, just a short hallway that led to a desk. I was greeted by Barney Fife, the same corporal who gave the speech about the importance of establishing a workday routine to the unruly women of G Unit.

"Baker, you made it over." He spoke with a clipped voice but without malice.

"Finally."

"It will be better over here. You'll have more time outside." His face softened, his dark eyes held mine. Then he tucked his thumbs into his belt and was all business. "Minimum is set up like a campus, Baker." His nostrils flared and he went on. "There is the main housing building, an education/medical building, a maintenance building, and a chow hall."

"You'll like the dining hall," said an inmate clerk I'd never seen, "the food is actually warm sometimes."

The corporal gave me my housing assignment and pointed me to the door.

"I just go there by myself?" I asked.

"The housing unit is the only building on the left, your unit is toward the back." The corporal went back to his desk and, without looking at me, said, "You'll figure it out, Baker. There's still a fence on the perimeter." He shuffled some papers then realized I was still standing in place. He looked up. "There's only so many places you could go." *True. But there is an exit here somewhere.* I grabbed my bags, hissed across the floor, and opened the door to the Minimum facility.

From a palette of black and white, the Minimum door opened to the Technicolor of Oz. The campus was bathed in light, with multihued green grass, rich brown dirt, and blue sky. I stepped forward onto a blazing white cement sidewalk and the door closed behind me. I inhaled the scent of late summer on a breeze that rippled the dark hairs on my pale arms. I knew I should go directly to my unit but the earth called to me. I looked around for the guards and saw one standing under a roofline looking out onto the yard. Women were out, walking the sidewalk, but no one was looking at me. I dropped my bags and pushed one foot into the grass. It yielded. I placed my second foot on the earth. *Alive.*

I lingered as long as I felt safe then stepped back to my bags. The layout of the campus was rectangular, with buildings on three sides. At the back of the quadrant were an exercise area and cement picnic tables. In between the buildings were sidewalks, cement benches, and grass. Above it all was a 360-degree view of the sky. I could see the trees and the parking lot.

I did not want to attract attention, so I reached down for my bags and began to drag them to the housing building. The sidewalks were bustling. I felt like I stepped off the curb into fast-paced foot traffic. I hugged the familiar and ordered right side of the walk. Inmates, cops, civilians stood in place, comingling in discussion clusters. I eavesdropped on them as I passed. *Smith, you're wanted in the treatment building. Where do I send a kite to mail out my stuff for parole?*

The yard area was busy, but I didn't see one familiar face. How was that possible? Who were all these women? I kept my eyes out for Five Alive.

"Hey! Karen!" It was Teddy Bear. I turned and saw her profile, tummy forward, arms back, beaming like a brown-haired Winnie-the-Pooh. "You made it! Now it's just Hippie Chick and we're Five Alive again."

I wanted to hug her, but of course we could not. We stood and beamed instead. She looked at my bags and nodded her head toward the housing building. "It's all dorm style over here. The units are kind of a madhouse—talk, talk, talk. What's your bunk assignment?"

I told her and she laughed sympathetically. "You got bunked with the Newbies from Intake. All pockmarked and sucked up from drugs. They're still mad and crying—clueless."

"Great," I said dryly.

"You have clear conduct. Kite today and they'll move you to a better street."

"Street?"

"Yeah, the dorms are arranged in a square, cop at the front; toilets, laundry, and showers at the back, dayroom in the center. Bunks line up on all four walls, like streets. Your street is for the new girls, another is for the rough girls." She named a few from the pruno bust. I remembered them lined up on the wall, drunk and ashamed.

"The other streets are for the rest of us who have done some time. I am kiting to the far wall." She leaned in to let me in on a little secret. "It gets a little dimmer at night and is further away from the noise." Someone across the yard called her name. She grinned at me, paused in the Pooh Bear stance, and was done with her orientation.

By the time I found my unit at the back of the building, I had seen some familiar faces but none from J Unit. I stepped into my unit and my senses were assaulted. Instead of the granite-hard tomb with slamming cell doors, Minimum was a shit storm of voices. The air was heavy from the mixture of sweat, ramen soup, cheap women's deodorant, and hair oil burned on a curling iron. Teddy Bear described the setup well. It was one room with absolutely no privacy except four shower curtains and six kindergarten-size toilet stall doors. I looked up and saw the cameras covering every angle. At the far wall of the room, I could see a woman changing her shirt. *I'm living in a fishbowl.*

I schlepped my bags over to the desk and was greeted in a businesslike manner from a sturdy female officer. "Looks like you got the lower bunk over there," and pointed to the left "street" about twenty-five yards away from the podium. "Good luck fitting all that stuff into a single tank box and a half locker."

I dragged my bags to my new bunk. The women in the bunk area watched me pass. They weren't looking at me, they were looking at my bags. Most were young girls dressed in Nobody status jeans and wrung-out State-issued tennis shoes. I knew they had not worked long enough to buy the basics and did not have the money on their books for coffee, shampoo, or tennis shoes.

Feeling the eyes of my neighbors upon me, I thought of Mittens. I imagined her standing before me with her arms crossed, and her chin jutting out at an angle: "Don't be a chump, Ka-a-ren. They comin' after yo' stuff." I pulled my scratchy wool blanket out of my plastic bag and covered my property bag. Then I set about making the bed and putting away my clothes into a single tank box. It was tight, but it all went in. My blanket still on top, I pulled my property bag over to my locker. The vultures were gathered, waiting to move in.

"Looks like you got a lot of stuff." I turned to see a slender young woman with dazzling teeth and dark skin. She looked friendly and hungry.

"Just the essential crap from canteen," I said, opening the locker.

"How long you been down?" she asked, still smiling.

"Three and a half years. Got three more to go." I turned to look at her. "You?"

"Got two and a half." Her smile faded. I knew that feeling of disgrace. I changed the subject.

"Got any ideas on how to get this stuff in here?" I asked. Her pretty smile returned. She opened a locker next to mine and gestured for me to look inside. I could see she had all the space in the world. She had a cup, a spoon, a plastic bag of oatmeal and some shampoo.

"Not a problem in here." Pretty Smile put her face in her locker. "Hello? Hello? Damn." Her voice echoed and she laughed, eyeing my bag again.

I knew Pretty Smile was giving me a soft hustle, but I learned from Celly the value of a powerful ally. As if on cue, she turned to the onlookers of the zombie nation. "Ain't y'all got something else to do?" She shooed them off with both arms. "Go on now. Some of you look like you need to get outside. There's a big ball in the sky, it's called the sun."

"I'm a janitor on the unit," she continued while I unpacked. "When I see the Old Timers like you, they use big flat books like shelves." *Me? An Old Timer? You don't know what an Old Timer is.* She turned to my bag, tilted her head. "Looks like you got one right there."

I followed her gaze and saw the side of my plastic bag, peeking out from under the blanket. There was indeed a book. It was my Jan Brett Christmas book sent in from my children. I didn't want her or anyone to touch it. I put it under my pillow.

"Tell you what, Miss Pretty Smile, you give me some help with this locker and I will see to it that you will have some coffee for that cup."

"You askin' the right person."

Pretty Smile was good to her word. We set up my shelves, I slipped her some coffee and powdered creamer. "Here are some frosted Mini Spooners. Now go and get a plastic bag for peanut butter and you'll have the basic setup."

While she scampered off, a zombie girl who remained behind slithered out from her bunk, sidled over, and smiled with a big black tooth, "Hi, nice lady, got a cup of coffee for me too?"

"You didn't help unpack, little sister. Pretty Smile got the job ahead of you." I sounded like a different person from the Karen I used to be.

By that time Miss Pretty Smile was back, she could see the moocher was in her territory. Pretty Smile had some other faces that were not so pretty. I assured her with an eyeball roll and whispered, "I told her. Not just no, but *hell* no."

"Glad you're smart. They all gonna be after your stuff when I'm not around."

"Ya know what?" I said. "I can't wait to just leave it all behind and walk out the gate."

I locked up my tank box and locker and went outside to find someone I knew from the other side. The hallway leading outdoors was jammed. The noise was worse than the dorm. I burst out the exit to the fresh air and was greeted once more by living earth and sky. I stood looking right and left, and there at the far end of the yard, walking slowly, was Blondie. My feet had wings.

Blondie swished toward me, ignored the rules, and gave me a gushing hug. "Ah, baby, you made it."

"Wow, look at this!" We stood on a blacktop track that circled a caged weight pile. Tucked around the side of the housing building was a field of thick green grass. Blondie and I stood side by side looking at the field. Women were in the grass, talking, reading, listening to music on their headphones, or just lying back, soaking up the sun with their eyes closed.

"Yeah, huh? It's called 'the beach.'" She giggled, her shoulders shaking. I had missed her. "Wanna walk and talk?"

"Oh yes, please," I said.

"Where's your bunk?" I told her and she said not to worry. "You can move. People leave every day."

"That's hard for me to fathom. Who are all these people? They look like they're straight off Intake," I said.

"Short-timers. After thirty days of Intake, they're tossed over here. They pace the dorms, waiting to get into treatment. That's the treatment building over there." She pointed at the building at the back of the quad that I'd seen when I first entered the yard earlier that morning.

"I'll never see that building. No treatment or good time for me," I said.

"Most of 'em come back anyway. I've seen a girl walk out the door, and about a month and a half later she's back again. I'll bet half the women on this side are recidivists."

"I guess treatment doesn't work?"

"It might if these girls had somewhere to go or a job. But, Karen, the drugs are powerful, it's hard to beat the craving." I remembered the burns covering Chrystie.

We walked and I gawked. "Oh, Blondie, it feels different over here. The sky is great but these torn-up girls, I feel like I got kicked back down to Intake again." I laughed. "According to a young girl on my street, I'm an Old Timer."

"Yeah." She laughed. "She doesn't know, huh. But guess what?" She turned to me, twinkling, "We're just plain old." We both laughed.

"Hey," she said in all seriousness, "you gotta find a job, quick, or they'll throw you back into the kitchen."

"What?" I asked, horrified. "We get no credit for doing our time right and staying out of trouble?"

"Fuck no, baby. You know the saying—ya got nothin' comin'."

"I hate that one. How soon do they come after you?"

"Maybe today. But don't worry." Blondie waggled a finger at me. "I'll go out to the maintenance shed and see if I can get you a gig. Walk me to the end of the sidewalk."

At the end of the sidewalk, Blondie turned to me. Her face was resigned. She tilted her chin at the women walking the yard. "Look at 'em. These girls are still mad and craving. They haven't fallen all the way."

She turned and I watched her walk to the maintenance building. Like me, she had gotten banged up in her car accident and walked with a slow swish and swivel. She took five or six steps and turned. Then she said something I'd never forget. "We can do this," she said, leaning forward, her eyes brilliant blue. "We're in the driveway." It kept me going for the rest of my time.

I returned to my dorm, stopped by the officer's podium, and asked for a stack of kites. Pretty Smile was inventing things to do around her bunk such as opening her locker and checking on her new stash of coffee, hanging a towel on the end of her bunk. "Whatcha gonna do with all those kites?"

"I'm gonna get my life in order." She stepped over, curious. "First, kite anyone and everyone for a job, anything but the kitchen. I got a lead on a maintenance job but I can't take any chances. Second, I'm going to sign up for everything—yoga, church. Third, I'm going request a bunk move—no offense"—I laughed—"to the Old Timer section."

"I've never done yoga before. It looks lame," she said, wrinkling her nose.

"It's a challenge. You'd be surprised. I do some form of it every day. I dare you to try. Here, take a kite."

"OK, ma'am. I see your challenge, but if I think it's too easy, you owe me a jar of peanut butter."

"Done." I sat on my bunk on Newbie street and looked around at all the defeated young faces. I thought of the young girls that had crossed my path on the other side. I pictured Mittens lying on her bunk with her little tiny toes in the air. She would have been out for three years by now. She was meant for so much more than taking off her clothes in a dark, dirty bar. Would anyone remind her she had potential and that if she put her mind to it, she could do anything?

That evening at the four-thirty p.m. count time, I met the young woman who was assigned to the upper bunk. She was young but old beyond her years. Her eyes were red, her nose blotchy.

"Hi, I'm Karen."

She nodded, her bottom lip quivered, and she climbed up on the bunk, trying to avoid a meltdown. She cried softly all during count. Perhaps if she could just have a decent cry somewhere in private, maybe she wouldn't leak for hours on end.

Count cleared and it was time for dinner. The room went from dead silence to turbulence. Over the voices, I heard the officer at the podium shout, "Baker." A shift change had occurred and the relieving officer was the ubiquitous DOC copper: a man about my age with short gray hair and a paunch. Standing beside him was a big, burly man dressed in a maintenance uniform. *Be still my beating heart.* I approached.

"Baker," said the maintenance supervisor, Big Buck, as a confirmation, not a question.

"Yes, sir."

"Heard you're looking for a job. A little birdie suggested I talk to you." The corner of his mouth twitched like he was holding back a smirk.

"I'm very interested," I said eagerly.

He stared long and hard, not at my entire form, just my eyes. "I'll come by tomorrow and we'll talk."

"Oh yes, please."

He bared a sly smile and grunted. There was an awkward pause, then he raised his eyebrows and looked at me as if to say, *You can go away now.* He did it humorously, not cruelly. It was good old-fashioned banter and it made me feel worthy of the effort. Back at my bunk, I observed Big Buck at the podium, leaning on his elbows, side by side with the officer. They were talking and laughing companionably. Then he stood to his full height, squared his massive shoulders, and thudded off in enormous black boots.

We were called by unit to the dining hall. We lined the wall and made our way to a serving line behind plexiglass. I could see the stainless-steel pans were sitting in a warming unit. Steam rose from the pans. Would my food really be warm?

Along the walls of the dining hall, the line passed a set of windows. When I reached them, I could see that they looked across and down to the Medium/Maximum unit. I had heard the prison was built on marshland. The Tomb sat low on the horizon like it was built at the bottom of an old lake. No wonder we never saw the sky. I saw the seven fence lines and beyond them, the outside length of the building that I knew so well from the inside. There was no sign of life, just steel and concrete. The people I met—Angel, Sinful—were suspended in time like ghosts walking up and down the corridor.

Looking out the window, I saw my reflection. I entered prison with a firm neck and brown hair. In the glass, I saw a stranger, now white at the front, and gray at the back. *My god, I have a geriatric mullet.*

"Move along," a guard snapped. I shook myself back to the room and made my way to the serving line. I watched as the woman in front of me actually chose her food. The hair-netted woman handing out a beige disk of meat was asking, "Do you want it or not?" I saw this as a huge improvement. I would be able to avoid the white bread and instant potatoes that I often nibbled absentmindedly. That night I chose canned corn and the meat patty. I passed on the potato chips and treated myself to frosted cake. Tray in hand, I looked across the room of four-top tables and chairs and found a spot that was vacated. Women stood and left when they were done. What a simple, wonderful privilege. I took a bite of the meat disk and canned corn, and it *was* warm.

"Tray up!" Now I could see why the women rushed to the dining hall. I ate what I could and continued to eat sporksful as I walked to the dish drop. A few warm bites were far better than a tray full of congealed food by-products.

Exiting the building, the cops performed a random pat-down. I guessed they were checking for smuggled bags of potato chips. To my surprise, a girl who looked about eighteen with unusually clear skin and a good haircut was caught with a piece of frosted cake up her sleeve. I stood behind and saw the cake falling out in messy white chunks. What a spectacle. I couldn't help myself and honked out a laugh.

"That's a four-hour cell-in," barked the gloved cop. The girl pouted and rolled her eyes. "Give me your ID," the cop demanded. The girl passed it to her impatiently, like she had somewhere to go. "Hope you're not in a program. You'll lose it, you know. All for a piece of prison cake." The cop was disgusted.

The girl turned white.

"You'll lose your good time and you'll have to do your full sentence."

The girl began to cry. "No please, please. I didn't know."

"Yeah? Then why put it up your sleeve?" The cop hammered on. "You think this is my first day?"

"I'm sorry. I'm so sorry," the girl whimpered.

"If treatment is in your court order and you lose it in here, you'll have to pay for it yourself. On the outside." The girl was crying, begging, and apologizing. My heart broke for her. I looked at the ground and waited my turn in silent solidarity. The cop was not done.

"Think of this time as trying *not* to break the law, OK? You wanna come back here?"

The girl shook her head in defeat.

"Cake?" The cop looked down at the crumbs, the frosting was smeared on the girl's sweatshirt cuff. "It's just cake! There will always be cake. One day, you can eat as much as you want." The cop paused, zooming in. "Lesson of the day: it's called delayed gratification. Next!"

The girl moved on, grief-stricken. I took cautious steps forward and stood in the star position for the pat-out. The cop was muttering, "Now I gotta stay after and do paperwork. Stupid girl."

I stayed quiet and moved on. I felt sorry for the cop too. What a job. How did she do it, day after day, supervising incarcerated women who were supposed to be learning a lesson, only to see them make colossal mistakes over and over again? If that girl was in a program and she lost it, what would she tell her family? *Sorry, Mom. I have to do another year because I stole cake from the chow hall.* As Sinful said, "Give me that chance." Minimum was a new land, with new forms of punishment and misery.

After dinner when the call-outs went up, I made the dreaded walk over to see if I had been recruited for kitchen duty. Nothing yet. For the rest of the evening, I read on my bunk, peeking at the women over the top of my book. Each woman seemed to recite her monologue about her innocence or her bad break that ended with a raw deal. Not one of them listened to the other.

Finally, at nine p.m., the lights dimmed. The woman on the bunk above me climbed up without a word. In the rare quiet, I could hear the sounds of breathing, snuffling, and coughing. The new sounds kept me on guard. As the minutes then an hour passed, I heard dream-state shouts and whimpers. The sound came from all directions, like a zoo at night. Finally, my eyes grew heavy. My final sensation was the slight vibration of the bunk from the girl crying above me.

Routines were similar in the Minimum facility: sanitation, breakfast, work. It was a privilege to leave the housing unit and walk outside, early in the morning. The summer air was fresh and warm.

After breakfast, the officer called me to the podium. "Baker, you're moving to bunk twenty-six. It's a good one." He pointed to a corner single bunk with the Old Timers. I saw a few familiar faces moving around their bunks getting ready for work. "You tell the Newbies," he circled his pen in the direction of my current double bunk, "if they stay clear conduct, their time goes by a little easier."

I made short work of emptying my locker and tank box and stripping my bunk. Most of the zombie nation must have gone to work in the kitchen. One girl was loitering at the end of her bunk. I stopped as I passed with my bags. She glanced at me with wet eyes and a hang-dog look.

"Look," I said shaking my head. "This is *their* house. As far as I'm concerned, they can have it. Do as they say, stay off the radar, and get the hell out of here." She nodded and wiped her eyes.

Bunk 26 was at the end of my new street. It sat in a corner with a wall on two sides. There was no upper bunk. Most of my neighbors were working. After I made my bed, I took out my writing folder, sat on my bunk, and leaned against the wall. It was the first time in three and a half years I could sit up tall on my bunk, without hunkering like a gargoyle.

Eventually, the neighbors on my street came home from work to eat lunch. I recognized or knew most of them. There were some I had known from Intake, some I had met working at the DMV. I laughed to myself when I saw Scarlett O'Hara, who was assigned a corner bunk in the next section. *That woman used to scare the hell out of me.*

Teddy Bear and Pearl walked in and welcomed me. "Score on the bunk, Karen," said Teddy Bear.

"Hey, welcome," said Pearl. "We're right over there." They were near Scarlett O Hara. "If you want to join us, we exercise in the morning, just like J Unit. Have you kited to stay out of the kitchen?"

"I carpet-bombed every department," I said.

"Can you believe the yard? Grass, real grass," said Pearl. "Just wait until you get on an evening call-out. When you walk to the education building, you get to see the stars and the moon."

After a late afternoon walk, I returned to my bunk. A woman named Glory was sitting on the bunk next to mine. I'd met her on J Unit and she struck me as a person who avoided drama and kept good company.

"Hey!" I was relieved.

"Hey yourself," she said slowly. Pretty Smile had nothing on this woman. Her smile was bright and genuine. She had dark almond eyes and a lavish black 'fro, held back with an elastic headband. "Did you just come over today?" she asked enunciating every syllable.

"No, I spent last night with the Newbies, in the corner. This bunk was a quick move for DOC," I said.

"They probably need the space over there for the girls on the turnstile." She chuckled. "Thank glorious God that we lived through those early days."

I flashed back to the early days of Intake—the deep, interior chill that pervaded my body. I looked back at my new bunkie's glorious smile and I couldn't help but smile back. Glory reached into her tank box and pulled out a drawing tablet and colored pencils. She was working on a sea turtle. She was layering the colors of a wise-faced turtle, starting with light yellow and green. *Sea turtles.*

For our honeymoon, Tom and I went to Hawaii. On the Big Island we spent days of idyll beside the ocean. We hiked rugged paths to secluded lagoons or lazed at our hotel, giggling as we rolled off our lounge chairs into the green and blue water. Every time Tom and I swam in the ocean, we saw a turtle. It felt like we were granted a sacred blessing from wise, ancient creatures. We were happy then, tanned and smiling, in the prime of our lives. I couldn't have seen the path of danger, death, and prison that lay ahead. Hawaii and turtles were from another lifetime. As I looked at Glory's steady hand by the turtle's bill, heaviness settled in my gut.

Count cleared and our unit was called to the dining hall. This time I didn't tarry. As I passed the windows, I thought of Sinful and Angel. *Stay strong, survive.* I moved ahead in the line and chose food that was warm.

When I went back to the unit, Glory was putting on work boots and looking like she had somewhere to go. "Do you work at night?" I asked.

"I have to move the sprinkler in the garden."

"Garden?" I gasped.

"Yeah, I'm the gardener. We have a garden over by the mainte-nance building. You want to go see?"

"Am I allowed?"

"Yeah." She shrugged. We walked out of the unit as women took over the dayroom, some sitting on large vinyl couches watching TV, others talking, writing letters, or using the phone kiosk. Glory and I walked out of the unit.

"You must have the best job in the prison," I said.

"The Lord has blessed me." She began humming a hymn. She led the way and I trotted along. We turned into a fenced area between the maintenance building and the housing unit. The sun was setting. The sky was streaked in hues of pink and lemon yellow. Jet trails lined the sky, their origin dissolving like teased cotton, their path a clear white line.

We turned at the end of the sidewalk and passed through a simple fence line into the garden. I paused to catch my breath. I stood before rows of vegetables and flowers. My hands instinctively reached out for the plants. I stroked the leaves and cradled the blossoms. They were still warm from the sun. I inhaled the scent of flowering rosemary, ripe tomatoes, and the loamy compost pile. I swayed and caught my balance by looking at the ground. I could see for the first time in years that I had rich black soil on my shoe. I laughed and cried at the sight. I reached my arms out and stood as tall as I could to allow the ripple of the moist air to permeate my parchment skin and chalk bones. I inhaled deep into withered lungs and absorbed the pungency of living earth.

"I am alive!" I shouted to Glory. Heart to heart across the rows of living things, Glory smiled and understood.

"Help me move the sprinkler!" she shouted. Glory held the sprinkler and I fed the hose. The hose was cool and wet. Dirt covered my hands and dribbled onto my jeans.

"The faucet is on the side of the building." Glory pointed to the maintenance building. I walked between rows of cherry tomatoes that smelled like summer salads. I found the faucet and turned the handle.

The water began to cover the rosemary that grew against the housing unit. The scent blew across the garden. Glory walked back toward me, inspecting the plants. She plucked a yellow cherry tomato and popped it in her mouth, twisting her lips to contain the juice.

"May I?" I called out, pointing to the tomatoes.

"Of course!" she said, reaching for another.

I picked a ripe red cherry tomato and rolled it in my hand, feeling its weight and warmth. It smelled as I remembered. The smell catapulted me back to my kitchen, sliced tomatoes on my Franciscan Apple plate, drizzled with olive oil and coarse salt. I put the cherry tomato into my mouth and crushed it in an explosion of warm, sweet, tangy. I groaned out loud. I walked along the row, trying not to be greedy, looking for another winning candidate. At the end of the row, I found the State Fair tomato. It was near the ground, soaking up the nutrition. It hardly qualified as a cherry tomato, it was so large and heavy. In the next row was a line of herbs. I could see thyme, oregano, mint, rosemary, and basil. *Is this really happening?* I looked up to see Glory watching me. I gestured to her with my tomato in my open palm, then I reached for a large basil leaf. I paired them together and held them high above the earth's altar. I popped them into my mouth. *Luscious. Just as good in a prison garden as anywhere in the world.*

"Come on over, listen to this," said Glory. I walked to the back of the garden, we sat on the hay bales. "Listen." I heard the sound of the sprinkler falling on leaves and dirt. I heard a bird. I heard the breeze in the leaves. It was quiet. We sat in silence for a while, then Glory began to hum, then sang a hymn. In profile, she was angelic.

We lingered on the hay bales. The sky turned the color of dark cherries and gold. We heard "Yard in!" and strolled back to the housing unit. I held my face to the sky, drinking in the colors, zigzagging along the sidewalk. "Thank you, Glory." *Thank you, God.*

The following day Big Buck came stomping into the unit. I held my breath.

"Baker," called the officer at the podium. I walked up and met the frank stare of my potential boss.

"Baker," said Big Buck. "Let's talk." We sat at a table in the day-room that was not made of metal. The chair was plastic. No more metal stools and faded circles on jeans. My bones appreciated it.

"I checked out your conduct record. It looks clean." He leaned forward on his forearms and folded his hands. "You work this job, that's the way it has to stay, no exceptions."

"Understood."

"You have a lot of so-called freedom with this job. You will have access to tools, sharp pointy ones." He wiggled his fingers. "And buildings all over Minimum. There may be times that you do not have a supervising maintenance crew member with you. I have to be able to depend on my crew. It's my ass on the line, capisce?"

"Capisce."

"We start tomorrow at eight a.m. Come out to the maintenance building. I got a couple of plumbers, a painter, I'm going to put you on the general duty crew. You'll need work boots, we'll get those tomorrow."

I was in! I tried to keep my composure until our brief interview was over and he clomped out of the unit. I swanned back to my bunk area and twirled with my hands in the air. Glory saw the entire exchange.

"Looks like we'll be coworkers. My gardening job is in the maintenance division."

"I report to the building right next to the garden, right?" I asked.

"Yep, you might even help me out, Blondie does." She laughed, a little wicked but good-naturedly. "I need help turning the compost pile."

"Oh, I don't care!" I said innocently.

"You will."

I am sure you've guessed by now that sustained happiness and prison do not go together. That same night, there was an ugly, disturbing fight just down the row from Glory and me. We were sitting on our bunks when we heard a woman's voice escalating. It began with shouts and insults from a white girl toward a middle-age black woman.

"You dumb monkey, you fuckin' smell like the jungle!"

This got our attention. Trailer Park Girl was about twenty-five. She had box-dyed blond hair with black roots, and bad skin. Trailer Park was hovering over the black woman. The black woman was sitting on her bunk. She turned her face away from the girl, not rising to the bait. "There's a word for people like you. Wanna know what that is?" Trailer Park's eyes were slits and her frown revealed missing teeth. We all knew that word. The black woman still did not look up but her shoulders rose and she sat up straight and muttered something like a low warning. The entire street was completely still. No one so much as turned the page of a book.

Trailer Park wound up her hand and shouted, "Nigger!" followed with a hard slap right across the black woman's ear and cheek. That was all it took. The black woman rose up swinging and assumed a boxer's stance and methodically punched and ducked the girl's wind-mill swings.

The cop was forty feet away. The DOC bubble, with all the supervising brass, was right outside the door. In about ten seconds, the cops jangled in and the women were hauled off in cuffs. Then I had a mini freak-out.

"What the hell was that?" I stammered.

"Hatred," said Glory. "Ignorance and hatred."

"I know we have skinheads in here but I just don't understand it."

"The DOC did that on purpose," said Glory. "They picked a lady who was a mother, a little older and black, and put her next to a skin-head. DOC uses us like chess pieces. This is their idea of corrections. Before we parole, DOC wants to see if we can learn to get along. You can only take so much, that mean white girl made the black woman mean. We all have that in our nature."

"That's appalling. The DOC put that black woman in a danger-ous position," I said hotly.

"DOC doesn't care about her," said a woman across from us. "For that matter, DOC doesn't care about any of us. DOC is here for the taxpayer. They purposely house us together to work things out, so they don't have to. They call it 'corrections.'" She waggled her fingers. "I've heard 'em talk at the podium, 'Got an Odd Couple on bunk 122A and B, a cutter and a germaphobe.' They think it's funny."

Something occurred to me. "I was used like that on G Unit with Celly. I was housed with her to keep her out of trouble. It didn't last but for a few weeks, but while we were together, she watched my back and I was her sounding board." I paused thinking of Celly, her sweet voice, her rugged past.

Perhaps as a result of the emotional high of the garden and low crash from the fight, I felt fragile. "I came to love Celly and another girl, Mittens, like daughters. I got to be a mother again." I felt the prickle of tears. "I let my own daughters down. I turned their world upside down. How will I ever make this up to them?" I had to put my hand on my heart to keep it from breaking.

Glory stood, rising to her full posture. "*Trust in the Lord with all your heart, lean not on your own understanding. Recognize him in all ways and He will direct your path.*" She paused to let it sink in. "If you learn anything in prison, Karen, it is that."

We held eyes, "Say it again, please."

She did, slowly, enunciating each word. "Proverbs 3:5." She did not move; she just stood and waited.

"I have a habit of going to God as a last resort," I said and wrote the verse in my journal.

He will direct your path. I had always been in charge. I had been the head of my household, a career woman, a volunteer, a wife, and a mother. Now I was an inmate wondering what the hell *is* my path? If I dared to turn over my life to the Lord as Glory did, would things fall into place? Could I give up my logic, as Blue Eyes said, suspend my intelligence to believe the Bible is the very word of God? Could I avoid leaning on my own understanding? Could I, in doubtless faith, believe the story of Noah's Ark and creationism and forget about fossil records? How do I combine the resonating truth I find in Zen with the feeling of redemption and surrender I feel in Christianity? Is there a Tank in the afterworld where you are deloused in lye soap before you gain enlightenment or enter the gates of heaven?

That night, sleep came slowly. I tried to read, but after the fifth time on the same sentence, I gave up, closed the book, and lay under the weight of the day's events: true joy in the garden, a job, an ugly fight born from ignorance, a safe bunk with a teacher. I fell asleep to the sounds of collective breathing.

The next morning, I put on my game face and began my new job. Glory and I walked out to the maintenance building. Blondie joined us outside her unit.

"Hey, you did it, Blondie! I got the job," I bubbled.

"Oh, baby, that's great." She came over and squeezed my hand. "You're gonna love it—well, as much as you can love a job in a prison."

The maintenance building was bigger than I remembered. I walked inside a garage door and entered Man Land. There were tools for every trade, each having its place. There were plumbing tools, garden and landscape tools. Building and painting tools, ladders, wheelbarrows, and shovels, all stored properly and in excellent condition. It was like stepping into a hardware store.

My father would have loved it. It brought a lump in my throat remembering our days before the divorce when he still lived at home. He showed me how to use saws and sanders and insisted that every tool had its place. Midway through our building tasks, he would make an excuse to go to the hardware store. We climbed in his red bubble-back Volvo and made a meandering trip to the hardware store, stopping off for an ice cream cone or to watch mallards land in the lake. He taught me how to sand and paint and build. I developed confidence and curiosity, side by side with my dear dad. The maintenance building felt like a home away from home.

Big Buck and another maintenance supervisor stepped out of the office. The second man had a brown head of hair like the pelt of a bear. Big Buck was holding a clipboard, all business. "Good morning, Miss Baker," said Bear. It was the first time a DOC staff member called me "Miss." I glowed.

The rest of the inmate crew shuffled in. Besides Glory and Blondie, I was delighted to see Tizzy. She was finally out of the kitchen. Two others joined us. There was T.W., Turd Wrangler, who worked as a plumber, and Kalikimaka, a woman I met in the Cosmetology program. Her real name rhymed with Mele Kalikimaka, which means Merry Christmas in Hawaiian. I used to sing Jimmy Buffett's rendition to her and it morphed into other nicknames: Kalik and The Kalikster. What we had in common was rare in the prison setting: stable child-hoods and a love for show tunes.

The inmate crew gathered around a large table for a morning meeting. Big Buck led the proceedings. "How is everybody today?" He sat upright with his thick arms on the table, hands crossed, and scanned our faces. There were morning murmurs, stretches, and yawns. The women seemed comfortable. It was not the usual shuck and jive. "Is there anything that happened over the weekend that I should know? Anyone get in trouble?" He peered at us above his glasses, watching for a flinch or averted guilty eyes. He gave us time. "I don't want to be caught unaware."

"No, Big Buck," said Tizzy. Glory motioned to Bear to unlock the gardening tools. The two went to a cage, Glory picked a few tools and went outside to work.

"I take it you all know Baker, here?" Nods all around. "She's gonna help out wherever we need an extra hand, right, Baker?"

"You bet!" said the eager beaver to the sleepyheads.

Big Buck checked in with the women on several projects: plumbing in the treatment building and appliance repair. We split up into groups. T.W. and Tizzy went with Big Buck. Blondie, Kalik, and I went with Bear to check on the dryers in the housing unit. Bear gathered extension cords and power tools and loaded them on a wheeled cart. We were each given a thick leather tool belt with buckles and pockets. We walked out of the maintenance building like a crew set on a mission. Slo-mo cowboy posse, jangling into town, thumbs in the tool belt. *Step aside, we mean business, ma'am. Gonna take a look at them dryers.* Bear led us across the yard, Blondie babbled on contentedly, Kalik pushed the cart.

Bear showed us how to remove lint from the dryers. I had never done this at home in my life. I didn't realize you should. I liked using the tools. It felt good to do something useful. Bear was easy to work with. Both men had manners. They used "please" and "thank you." It inspired our crew to behave in a way that was worthy of respect. I wondered how many of the women inmates had been exposed to authority figures who spoke to them with kindness.

After dinner that evening, I called my friends and family to tell them the news that I was over the halfway mark and had moved to Minimum. I told them that the visiting room was on the other side of the compound and they would have to find me. I rhapsodized to my daughters about the garden and the sky. They were relieved and I hoped they would worry about me less.

The girls were busy and gave me a brief update: Haley was getting ready for her freshman year at UC Santa Cruz. She wrote out her class schedule and drew a walking tour of the campus that included a seal statue, one our family's sentimental animals. The planning and packing fell on her shoulders. She had been working and saving for the move. She sent *me* fifty dollars. I wondered if she got used to being motherless. I missed her so much.

Nikki would soon be graduating from college. She sent me photos and copies of her projects and poetry. In a senior project poem, she described the other side of a visit to the prison. Nikki mailed me the poem, which was intensely personal and stark. Nikki's project featured a photo of me, at about age ten, wearing red rubber boots, a black-and-white snow parka, twirling my grandmother's Japanese umbrella. I stared at the picture and cried for that young, pure version of me. What happened to her?

Nikki spared me her financial worries and told me how she had figured out how to buy toothpaste from using points at the university student center. Nate was steadfast. He was her home, both literally and figuratively. Nikki told me that Nate's band, Mimicking Birds, was taking off. They were touring and selling CDs. The band was playing regularly in the most popular clubs in Portland, Seattle, and other places on the West Coast. They were so good together. I was grateful to him. Nikki was looking forward to seeing me in my new location, relieved things were going forward. She said she would bring Nate. She told me that Tulip still howled for me in her sleep.

I was still connected to my daughters, but not in the way I had been, not in the way I wanted to be. I could hear my eagerness on the phone, grasping for connection as I made unskillful attempts, commenting about their lives, not calling their friends by the correct names or using out-of-date descriptions. I wondered if I really fit into their lives. Was I still the mother who swam with Nikki in the ocean on the day a seal joined us in the waves?

Gerry told me she would come that weekend, and when my name was called, I walked buoyantly out the door. I was looking forward to Gerry's impressions of the Minimum facility.

The dining hall held about a hundred people and doubled as the event and visiting room. At lunch or dinnertime, we could look out the window toward the parking lot and see our families lining up outside in the elements. The system was first-come, first-serve. Visitors stood in line, waiting through our entire meal service, rain or shine. I wondered what happened in the winter?

Gerry was sitting at one of the tables when I walked in. She waved her bags of quarters. "Fuck the Cheetos," she said. "There's coffee! Real coffee with dairy products!" The room smelled of freshly brewed coffee, not the acrid scent of Folgers instant, but espresso and foamy hot milk. The Minimum side had set up a coffee cart manned by inmate baristas. Coffee shops were on every street corner and mini-mall in the State of Oregon, so potential employment opportunities were everywhere.

"What would you like? Have anything! This is your first real coffee in over three years," said Gerry.

I was giddy with possibilities. "A latte," I said. "I don't want any vanilla syrup or hot chocolate to muddle up the taste of espresso and real milk. Just fresh ground coffee beans and a dairy product that comes from an udder." Gerry went to the line and returned with the cups, setting my latte in front of me with a flourish. I held the cup with both hands, just smelling at first. It was bitter and earthy. I closed my eyes to the visiting room and was back at Starbucks, among purposeful people dressed in hip clothing and money to spare. I took a sip and tasted the roasted coffee beans and the sweet scalded milk. "This tastes like my old life." My hands remained clamped on the cup for over an hour. I bent over the cup inhaling the aroma before every sip.

Meanwhile, Gerry took in her new surroundings. There were two sets of windows in the dining room, now a visiting room. One set was the view west, toward the Medium/Maximum facility. The other set of windows faced the east and looked directly into the Minimum campus. Sitting at the tables, Gerry and I could see the housing unit, the treatment building, and the center sidewalk loop with green grass in the middle.

"Wow. The difference is remarkable," said Gerry.

"How was the visiting process on this side?" I asked.

"Standing in line outside is stupid. There's nowhere to sit, and you are right in the sun. Kids were running all over the place and the parents were yelling at them. There was an elderly couple, the guy had a walker, and they just had to stand there. What are they thinking? Does DOC want to punish us too?" Gerry looked up and frowned at one of the DOC officers patrolling the room.

"I'm so sorry. Please, you don't have to do this. I'm worried about winter."

"I'll be fine." She flapped an arm. "This is much better for you. It's progress. Look, you have grass!"

"There is grass and the sky, I can breathe again, my lungs feel rehydrated," I said.

"Now that you're over on this side, your freedom is within your reach. Your dad and stepdad are still alive, your kids are in college or on their way. They're doing good because you're doing your best. You haven't fallen apart."

"Ha. Yet."

"It seems better over here," said Gerry as she looked out on the yard.

"It's still prison. I am away from my people."

"Where are you in the grieving process? How do you feel when you think about Tom?"

"Something has shifted." I leaned forward to protect our conversation. "I had a strange experience, like a visitation. I saw him on the yard. I saw Tom."

Gerry held my gaze.

"I've been running from my grief since the accident. I didn't dare grieve. In prison I was afraid I would fall apart and be seen as weak. But more than that, I couldn't bring myself to think about the accident." Images of Tom and the innocent woman dying on the highway overtook me. I put my head in my hands. Gerry was silent, giving me time to collect myself.

"Before I came over here to Minimum, a very powerful woman prayed over me. It felt right and I trusted her. It gave me the bravery to open what I call the black door of my past."

Gerry continued to listen without judgment or interruption. Instead of the Great Pondering Pose, her hands were folded before her on the table and her face was open, so I continued. It had been the first time I talked about Tom since that day in the chapel.

"After the experience in the chapel, I opened that scary black door and allowed myself to recall the details of the accident report. I tried to imagine his last moments alive. Where was he? Was he on the ground, or a gurney? Was he alone? I did the same for the woman in the other car. It was rough. I took a lot of walks on the yard to clear my head. Then one day at the far turn, suddenly, there he was, in his ski clothes."

"Of course he was!" said Gerry, shaking her head.

"I can't explain it. But I *felt* him, I heard his voice." I was relieved to talk about the visitation with a dear friend who knew him.

"What did he say?" asked Gerry, sitting back in her chair, crossing her arms.

I imitated him leaning forward, confused: "He said, 'What are you doing?' He was half smiling and half irritated. 'Don't waste a day!' he said. 'I wouldn't.' Then I felt a rush of warm air and he was gone."

"That sounds just like him. He would rather be skiing or motorcycling than brooding over his mistakes."

"Gerry, it freed me. It was like the cage door opened."

"Good." She slapped the table. "Time to move on, so the rest of us can too."

I stared at her and took that in. *So the rest of us can.* It was the truth and it hurt, in a good way.

"Grief is tricky," she said. "It catches you by surprise."

"It does. It brings you to your knees. I never had the chance to grieve after the accident. I was too busy healing or releasing my daughters to the big wide world and getting ready for prison. I denied that Tom was dead. He was larger than life. It just couldn't be true."

Gerry was nodding.

"I kept his Grateful Dead T-shirt, a jean jacket, and his Hawaiian shirt in the closet. I used to go into the closet and surround myself in his clothes, pressing them around my head and breathing in his scent." I leaned toward Gerry. "This sounds crazy but I was afraid when he came back, he would get mad at me. 'What happened to my stuff? Where are my skis and my boats? Where's my motorcycle?' My god, when I trailered his motorcycle and watched it roll down the street—"

I sighed and shook my head. "It took me years to believe he was never coming back."

We both were quiet. I held my coffee cup for warmth and comfort. Gerry put the side of her face in her hand.

"You were brave and you were devastated. You never gave up getting back your strength but you were so focused on it you didn't acknowledge your pain. Maybe you couldn't, maybe it was just too much to take in." She sat up straight and placed her hands on the table. "You've always been high energy, you're driven. But sometimes that energy was misplaced with men or dangerous sports."

"True," I grunted.

"I see you using this time as a turnaround. You're writing. You're published. You're going to services and exploring things like Buddhism. You still have intensity, but you're calmer, you think things through. You are transforming. I see it."

"Your coming here week after week has a lot to do with it."

Of course, that embarrassed her; she flapped her wrist and changed the subject. We continued to talk about books and cooking while I nursed my coffee drink. Finally, I took off the top and ran my finger around the cup for the final foamy swirl. "Ahhh."

Gerry said goodbye and I watched her walk briskly to the exit. *My trusted friend.*

That night I was on the yoga call-out. It was still light out when I crossed the yard and went into the education building. I found a spot in the back of a classroom near Blue Eyes, Wise Owl, and Pearl. The familiar movements began and the breath took over. Halfway into the class, my thoughts quieted and I was just a human being in a half-moon pose like thousands before me, throughout time, all over the world. In the final balance pose, I fell out of tree pose and took a step onto Blue Eyes' mat. Rolling up our mats, I apologized.

"Hope I didn't take away from your practice. The balancing poses are a real challenge for me."

"Ah," she said nodding like a mischievous sage. "The tyranny of perfection and the ecstasy of good enough."

"Ha, that's brilliant. Freeing."

When we walked out of the education building, it was dark and there were stars. I looked to the right and the moon was rising. I thought of Sinful and that first fire drill. We both stared silently.

"Life as an inmate is filled with unknown deprivation. The average person has no idea," she said passionately. "To deny a person the sun or the night sky is cruel and inhumane punishment."

"I will never look at the night sky again without remembering when I could not." We fell silent and moved slowly across the yard, drinking in the night sky after years of deprivation. *Sinful, the moon! Angel, there are so many stars.*

"Hey, let's go," hollered the cop inches behind us. We both jumped. "Yard's closed."

He shouted in our ears. I could feel his breath on my neck.

Blue Eyes sighed angrily and we both walked away. "Just because he's in the driver's seat, doesn't mean he has to run people down," she said.

Before we went inside, I turned to look back at the moon and the yard cop crossed his arms across his chest. But I had already seen it. The moon was turning silver, high in the sky. *Beautiful.* I hummed a little Frank Sinatra, *You can't take that away from me.*

Not long after my move to Minimum, I got punked by my new protector. Pretty Smile approached as I sat at a table in the dayroom and asked if she could set some canteen items at my table.

"Why don't you just put them on your bunk? Nobody will take them," I said.

"I'm late, please?" She smiled like a child, wanting candy. She had already set them down and seemed to be in a great hurry.

"Go." I waved my royal hand. Not long after she left the unit, a commotion occurred near my old bunk on Newbie street. Someone was angry and looking for the very items that were sitting in front of me. Ice went through my veins. I was backed into a corner. The cops would bust me and I could lose everything. DOC justice would brand me a thief or, if I told the cops the truth, inmate justice would brand me a snitch.

Quickly and smoothly, I moved to the chair at the end of the table, away from the loot. Then I counted to sixty. I made sure no one was looking my way before I slithered out from the table. I went directly to the toilet and closed the door. I watched the table through a slit in the door. I waited for about five minutes, long enough to be absolved. Then I went to the sink, washed my hands, went to my bunk, and stayed there.

The woman missing the loot and a few others took up a search and eventually discovered her stuff on the dayroom table. I overheard her say, "I didn't leave this here. Someone took them and got scared."

I was the scared one, but now I was mad. I had been so desperate to mother that girl I let my heart get in the way of my judgment. I was played. I sat on my bunk, arms crossed, fuming. I kept repeating in my head: *I could have lost my job, my bunk in the honor area. I could*

*have lost my reputation as a woman who knows how to stay off the radar
and do her time. Worst of all, I would have been branded a thief.*

The short wall between me and the dayroom had a twelve-inch
mirror and a shelf on the other side. Women could pull up a chair and
do their hair, or sit and talk. That day two women were doing their
hair. One was flat-ironing the kinks out of her black hair and the other
girl was working on some sort of Latina hairdo with a teased bump in
the front. I eavesdropped on their easy slang.

"I wonder who jacked that girl's stuff," said the beautiful black
girl I had seen on the other side. She carried herself with elegance and
steely composure, like a ruler. *Cleopatra.*

"Whoever did it is gonna do it again." The other girl laughed. I
had heard her talking to other women in the unit, calling the younger
ones "mi'ja"—little daughter—like Celly did, and calling the older
ones "Auntie."

"I know that's true. She'll get caught," said Cleopatra. "Karma
always wins. The more chaotic and dangerous the environment, the
quicker karma comes back. We live on top of each other in here so we
see the spanking right before our eyes."

Mi'ja liked that; her laugh tinkled approval.

I was glad to have heard their conversation. I felt validated for
my anger and sense of betrayal. What the hell was I gonna say to that
girl? *That's a time-out, young lady?* I sucked at discipline. I grounded
Nikki, once, for staying out late and not calling. It ended up being a
punishment for both of us, the righteous mother and the surly teen.
I decided to release Nikki from her grounding if she wrote an essay
entitled "My Responsibilities as a Sixteen-Year-Old." She wrote a brief
paragraph that went something like this: "My responsibilities as a sixteen-year-old are to push the boundaries as far as I can. I should stay

in contact, within reason. But had I been given a cell phone, all of this could have all been avoided." *The cheek!* I kept that essay on my desk at work to remind me of the fact that I was barely in charge of a young woman who was far more intelligent than I ever would be. I had to admit I loved the essay and thrust it before the noses of young mothers who thought the upcoming teen years would be a nonissue in their vegan baby food, homeschooled households.

I wondered what these two girls at the mirrors would have said to Pretty Smile. *Hell no, bitch, walk yourself back to your bunk with your shit, I ain't your mama. Or, Do I look like a chump to you, bitch?* They would have known all along that it was stolen.

Finally, Pretty Smile strolled in, looked for me at my table, and saw me sitting on my bunk. She walked over, still smiling. "Hey, I'm back. You got my stuff?" asked Pretty Smile.

Cleopatra and Mi'ja swiveled in my direction on full alert. I stood up and talked over the wall, "You tried to set me up. That wasn't your canteen. I could have gotten a D.R." Cleo and Mi'ja looked at each other.

Mi'ja snuffled a laugh.

"Oh no. That was mine," Pretty Smile said with a sleazy grin.

"Get away from me," I hissed. I was embarrassed to be so vulnerable, just when I thought I was getting it.

"Ah, Karen, C'mon," she tried.

"I mean it. You're trouble. Just go, *now.*" My pulse was still racing from the close brush with disaster. I remembered the shame of cuffs and arrest. That would *never* happen to me again.

She shrugged. "You're crazy," she said and walked away shaking her head.

The two girls quickly turned back to the mirror, looking purposeful with their hairdos.

"Hey," I said to them. They peeked up slowly, caught in the act of eavesdropping. "I got punked, didn't I?" They laughed out loud, holding nothing back. "You most certainly did," said the black woman. She smiled with one corner of her mouth and shook her head.

Still unsettled from the incident, I said, "I thought I knew how to get along in here, but apparently I am still way out of my element."

Mi'ja smiled at me. I walked around the wall and sat down.

I told them how I had stayed one night over in Newbie-land and Pretty Smile was nice to me. "I was aware she was giving me a soft hustle and I gave her some coffee to keep the other parasites away, but I didn't think she was treacherous. I could have lost my job. My kids would disown me if I showed up in the visiting room in lime green. Do I look like a patsy?"

"Patsy?" Mi'ja giggled. "You look like a mom."

"You look like a nice lady from the suburbs," said Cleopatra. She lifted her chin toward me, sizing me up, probably wondering, *What hell did you do to get locked up in here?* She was fascinating. She had the lingo and the swagger one moment and a polished speech and regal posture the next. I wanted to be like her. Mi'ja was just as hip but that laugh—she had a sweetness to her.

"How much more time do you have, lady?" asked Cleo.

"My name is Karen, and I got a little less than three years."

"Ha!" She laughed. Then her face got very serious, like a scolding. "How did you make it this far without getting punked?"

"Oh, I got punked all right, in my first few days in G Unit. Someone stole, well, jacked my jammies." Mi'ja started giggling at my "jacked" and then tried to stop. She pulled in her lips, her face turned beet red.

"My first celly on G was Celly." They nodded sagely, acknowledging her elevated status. "Let's just say, she took care of the situation, and no one bothered me again. That is, until she went to the Hole. My next cellmates, Mittens and Sinful, were every bit the teacher she was. Nobody messed with them either. You'd think with all that wisdom, I would have learned how to avoid getting punked."

"You've been taken care of by those girls but you ain't learnin' your own damned lessons," said Cleo, switching easily into street slang.

"Oh yeah, das right," Mi'ja said with a giggle.

"Show me your mean mug," demanded Cleo, jutting out her chin and crossing her muscled arms.

"Yeah." Mi'ja scowled, she crouched down and frowned, turning into a completely different person. She was frightening.

"Mean mug, OK, I know what that is," I said. I thought about it like an actor, conjuring up the recent incident with Pretty Smile. The girls both crouched forward, waiting and staring, Cleo rolled her jaw to one side. I took a breath, squinched my eyes, wrinkled my nose, and jutted my lips out, in a pucker. The girls burst out in laughter.

"Do it again," Cleo commanded. I shrugged, confused. *Really? OK.* I tried to remember what I did and struck the pose. They simply fell apart. Cleo put her head on the table, her shoulders shook. Mi'ja lay backward on her chair, mouth open, no sound. They came back to the room in fits and starts, Mi'ja had to use her hands to press her cheeks down. Cleo looked like she had just done a loop on a roller coaster.

Cleopatra leaned toward me, as serious as a heart attack. "Don't ever do that again. You look like a chimpanzee."

"Oh no, and I hate monkeys." I hung my head.

"That was really, really, *really* bad," said Mi'ja, still trying to recover. She put both hands over her face and shook her head back and forth, like an Etch A Sketch, trying to erase the memory.

"You still got three years to do! How you gonna make in here?" asked Cleo. "That face, uh-uh. You ain't takin' a crap, Mama. Lord, you need help."

"You sho nuff do, Auntie," said Mi'ja.

"Am I beyond help?"

Cleo tilted her head and stared at me. Her eyes moved over me, taking in the gray hair, the billowing prison blues, the big feet, the skinny wrists. I smiled nervously. I wanted her approval.

"Maybe there is something we could do," she said, steepling her fingers. Looking at Mi'ja, she said, "Maybe she should go to Mean Mug School, what do you think? Teach her *the look?*"

"I could do her hair and makeup," said Mi'ja, clapping her hands. "We'll take photos, before and after!"

"I'm in!" I cried.

Photo day came and I started with Mi'ja in the dayroom mirror. She teased the front of my hair straight up and combed it away from my face. Then she straightened the back and made a flip at the ends. Next came the makeup. I brought out a few pieces of my canteen makeup that I used for visits: under-eye concealer, mascara, and blush.

"This all you got?" Mi'ja asked.

"No, I've got a bunch of crap that just was too garish for me."

"Garish," she mocked, "perfect." She leaned toward me wickedly. "Go get it."

She had a steady hand and applied a thick coat of eyeshadow and black eyeliner. My lips were hot pink and glossy. She wore a similar palette and looked like a sex kitten. I looked like an old hooker on a back street.

We walked outside, I felt conspicuous. Blue Eyes was on duty with the camera taking pictures of all the other girls posing with painted faces. If anyone could take a decent picture of this old floozy, it was Blue Eyes.

Cleo began the lesson:

"Sit over here on the bench, act like you're just minding your own business. Now, I come over." She swaggered toward me looking like she was about to settle a score. "Hey, bitch," she enunciated slow and sinister. "Think to yourself," said Mi'ja, "'Are you talkin' to me?' Do it Robert De Niro style."

"Yes. Think, *You're about to learn a lesson*," coached Cleo, narrowing her eyes.

I squinted.

"Lesson two: put your left hand over your right fist, like you can't control it. Like it's just waiting to connect with someone's jaw."

I copied her gesture.

"Yeah, that's right, now open your elbows to the side."

"Scoot to the edge of the bench," said Mi'ja. I scooted a little, they both kept looking. I guessed it wasn't enough, so I scooted a couple more times. It was hard with my hands together in a fist.

"You ain't some dog humpin' the bench. Lord help this woman." Cleo looked skyward.

"Do it in one smooth move," commanded Mi'ja, scowling and pumping her hand in her fist.

"Act like you could leap up any moment," said Cleo. I sat closer to the edge of the bench and struck the pose. "Better. Do it again."

We practiced a few more times. "You gonna need to do some homework on your mean mug, but you're gettin' it."

Blue Eyes came over and saw me with the girls, smiling at my getup.

"I went to Mean Mug School," I said, sparkly.

"That explains it," she said, her eyes teasing.

The three of us posed, badass, sitting, and standing. Then we took a picture, smiling naturally. Blue Eyes let us gather around the camera and look at the photos.

"Your daughters are gonna wonder who you have been hangin' out with," Cleo said. They both laughed. I looked again at the picture with us smiling naturally and thought, *These are kind, smart, beautiful women.*

I was a good student and practiced my lessons. When no one was looking, I would look in the mirror, lift my chin, and say in my head, *Are you talkin' to me? You want a piece of this?* And *Don't make me come up off this bench.* I balled my fist, elbows out.

When the pictures were delivered, I sent one home to the girls. They thought it was great. That surprised me a little. I wrote in the letter that I hoped I would never have to use my lessons from Mean Mug School, but if I did, I knew how to De Niro.

Glory and I talked about my brush with a misconduct report. "I have to practice my mean mug until it feels natural." I tried my pose on her, the half-cheek sneak on the bunk, right hand in left palm, the sneer.

"Lord, Lord, help this poor woman!" Glory laughed, lifting her eyes.

"Pretty Smile put me in danger, but I walked right into it," I said.

"There's danger everywhere," she said, "especially when we get outta here. It's a new world out there—computers, Facebook. The drugs are worse, look at the way the girls keep coming back. We don't have the answers, God does."

Glory stood up. "Think of the Exodus. The Jews fled from Egypt." She opened her arms, wide. "The Pharaoh and his entire army were chasing after them with weapons, horses, and chariots. They had nowhere to go." Glory pulled her hands into her chest and looked over her shoulder. "They were trapped, their backs to the Red Sea. Do you think they cried out, 'Oh please, Lord, part the water'?"

"No!" I shouted, captivated. Glory stood tall, inspirited. "God is so much bigger than our mortal imagination. We just need to walk in faith until we have eyes to see."

I understood her message. In a way, putting all your faith in God would be simple. But it would not be easy. I admired her faith.

"Thank you, Glory." We held eyes. She would have seen that I was moved.

There was ease and honesty between us. During our time on the bunks, we fell into a comfortable silence, side by side. I was learning how to create personal and emotional space without cell walls in the dorm setting. Glory took up her pencils and I reached for a book. When Glory finished her drawing, she held it up for me to see.

"Your colors are wonderful. It looks three dimensional," I said.

"Thank you." She tilted her head and moved the paper around for better lighting.

"I started doodling back on J," I said. "I drew a cell, our fence line, even our crappy plastic sandals. I wanted to capture the images for my writing."

"Show me." I took out my sketches and passed them to her. "Pretty good. You need to work on definition. See here"—she pointed to the sandal's edge—"that needs to be darker."

I grabbed my pencil and drew over the line.

"Not enough. Black, black, black," she enunciated with her shapely lips.

"Hmm." I tried again, using the side of the pencil for a darker line.

"May I?" she asked.

"By all means, please." I handed her my drawing, and with a few economical strokes, she made the sandal come alive.

"It looks like you could pick it up, right off the page."

"Now, try it in color." She looked through her colored pencil box and handed me a black, a light and dark umber and cream. "Start with a very light pencil sketch then layer your colors light to dark."

I started in and completely lost track of time.

"Yes!" she cried. "Work in layers, don't be afraid of the dark colors."

I finished the sandal. It was an improvement. I wanted to try another drawing on a fresh page. I started with a cell door and a bunk from the Medium/Maximum side. Then I worked on new pictures of tomatoes and basil leaves. Glory loaned a pencil or two and helped me order the basics from the canteen list. When I drew, the minutes turned to hours.

That night I lay in my bunk listening to sounds of the animals bedding down for the night. I noticed Glory reading her Bible. She closed the book, closed her eyes, and went right to sleep. *I want your peace.*

At my next Zen service, I asked how to be more skillful at my meditation practice. "I need help. I wish I had a practice that was a little easier to drop into. I try to picture my bunk as the eye of a hurricane. It takes a great deal of discipline to remain quiet. My mind keeps wandering into the conversations and the noise."

"Yes. Life is like a hurricane. We cannot push it away," said Getshushin. "It also is like the ocean. You are a wave, others are a wave, and life keeps coming at you. But you are also the whole ocean. Drop down under the waves, Karen."

I found a CD recording of the ocean from the chapel library and checked it out. The sound of the waves absorbed the voices of the dorm. I focused on the image of dropping down to the sea bottom while the waves tumbled above me. After I returned the ocean CD, I began to use my breath as my waves. I wasn't always good at it, but I stopped fighting and gained little pockets of freedom. *A trip to the ocean is on my bucket list when I am free.*

Our maintenance crew was ordered to do some repairs in the treatment building. Bear was organizing tools. "Miss Baker, we'll need both vacuums today and, Miss Smith, could you please grab a box of plastic bags?" Bear led our crew to the treatment building at the back of the compound. We entered noisily, our rattling cart and cowgirl tool belts announcing our arrival.

The women in treatment were sequestered, like a nunnery, creating a total immersion into "getting clean." The girls in the program were hard at work creating construction paper butterflies that said *Soar, Believe, Commit.* They were supervised by well-dressed civilian counselors.

"Yep, we'll see all these girls back here in about a year," said Tizzy, not bothering to whisper. The rehab counselors looked over and frowned. Bear giggled nervously.

"Shhh," he said, "you'll get us all in trouble." Bear hustled our crew back into the bathrooms. Tizzy wasn't done. Still in hearing range Tizzy said backward over her shoulder, "What they need is computer training so they can apply for a job."

We settled into our roles cleaning overhead light fixtures. Blondie wandered over to a set of posters on the wall. "Hey, look at this. This is your brain on drugs."

I walked over and looked. The posters were horrifying. Each displayed two brains, before and after drugs. The photos showed the damage of methamphetamines, crack, and heroin. In all three "after" pictures, the brain was shrunken and had gaping holes. The methamphetamine poster was the most appalling.

"My god," I gasped. "This stuff is pure evil. No wonder the users can't think right anymore." The whole crew came over to look, even Bear.

"This is the one that got to me," said Blondie, staring at the heroin brain. Compared to the smooth ridges of a normal brain, the heroin brain was one-third the size and was full of holes like a sea sponge. "If God has something better, He's keepin' it for Himself." She smiled a little and shrugged her shoulders. *Oh Blondie, please stay clean.*

We turned away from the grim images and set to work, performing our tasks with integrity, no slackers in the group. Finished, our crew walked back to the maintenance building.

"Have a seat," ordered Big Buck. Bear continued to work, locking up the tools behind metal grates while the rest of us gathered around the table.

"How'd it go?" asked Big Buck, focusing on each one of us in turn.

"Got to see our brains on drugs in the treatment building," spouted Blondie. "They had before and after pictures, it ain't pretty. Looks like your brain turns into a rotten orange."

"Any of you ever been to treatment?" asked Big Buck. There was a lot of muttering. "Is there anyone here who doesn't have a substance abuse problem?" He looked around at us. Dead silence. How could I say no? If it weren't for the alcohol, I wouldn't be in prison. Drinking less than Tom was still drinking. *I have a drinking problem.* Everyone but Kalik was looking down at the table, studying the grains of wood. "I–I don't," said Kalik, shyly. She glanced around the table, looking as though she did not want to offend the rest of us.

"I believe that," Big Buck said. "You might be the only one in Minimum."

"Something's wrong with the treatment programs," said Tizzy. "First, you have to fight your way into a treatment program, then, once you get in, you sit around making mobiles with paper butterflies that spell out 'Soar, Believe, Dream' and they don't give you the tools to fill out a job application." She was on a roll. "They have their graduation ceremony"—she fluttered her hands around her curly gray hair—"and they wear paper tiaras. Their family comes and hopes that *this* time, she'll stay clean. Then, they walk their 'I' statements out the door to the drug dealer and come right back into the revolving doors of prison. Instead of a one-way gate to a productive life, it's a fuckin' merry-go-round. It's ridiculous!"

"So, what's the answer?" asked Big Buck.

He looked at Tizzy first, then went around the table, with a bullet stare. "Huh? Who's got a plan?"

Silence.

"Well, first we need a home or place to parole to," said T.W. "You can't stay clean if you're living on the street."

"When I was on Intake, I remember this tiny little lady," I said. "She got up in front of the church and asked us to pray for her because she was leaving in the morning and had nowhere to go. It was the first time I had learned that when people parole, DOC doesn't place you in some sort of housing."

"Phhht," said T.W.

"Poor thing just stood by the altar and wept," I said. "DOC told her to go knock on church doors."

"Who *doesn't* have a plan?" asked Big Buck, looking around the table. We were all quiet. I knew my family would take me in, but I didn't know exactly who would get stuck with me.

"Never too soon to start thinking about it." Big Buck stood. "We're done for today."

We walked out of the building a pensive group. One thought was clear. I was *thinking*. Big Buck asked questions instead of telling us what to do. It was the first time since I fell that a staff member of DOC looked us in the eye and offered true corrections. Not just rote formulas from the orientation book, but questions that inspired reflection and, ultimately, intent.

Over the first few months in Minimum, I continued to hold vigil. At every meal, I looked west from the dining room windows that entombed Angel and Sinful. I was hoping to catch a glimpse of live beings. Looking out the east windows, I could see the women out walking and going to class. The tomatoes in the garden were done, fall was just around the corner. *I am in the driveway. I can do this.*

Nikki had graduated from college. She sent me pictures of the happy day. She had her hair tucked up under a traditional black cap and gown. Christine must have snapped a picture as she made the walk to the podium. She was all ages at once: my toddler with blond curls—and a poised young woman. The family celebrated graduation for both Nikki and Christine's oldest son, Travis. It was a sunny day, Sam was waving a cane in triumph for the graduates of college and his hip replacement. Audrey and Christine filled in as proud mothers.

Life went on for all of us. The girls were growing up, as they should. They were making important life decisions such as subjects of study that would lead to careers. They informed me of their choices, wanting my blessing more than my advice. I was grateful for the chance to be included.

During Haley's first visit to Minimum, I asked about the wait outside. "It's Oregon. We had to stand in line, in sideways sheets of rain and wind. My umbrella could only protect so much." The girls were dressed in modern clothes and earrings, but upon closer examination, I could see they were damp.   "We tried to get there early but the guards yell at you to go back to your car: 'It's too early!'" Haley imitated a frowning guard. "As soon as we saw one person heading over to the line and not get turned away, all our car doors opened and we speed-walked, trying to look like we weren't racing each other to get *into* a prison."

"There's no sympathy from the guards," said Nikki.

"They judge us just like they judge the inmates," said Haley. "But they are the people who see you, day in and day out. So I am respectful and I laugh at their horrible jokes. I do it in hopes they will be nicer to you." I reached out and touched their cold hands.

"We have to wear wireless bras and no tight clothing. I wouldn't anyway. I hate the way they look me over," said Nikki.

"You're being punished too. I want people to know about the damage incarceration inflicts on the families. There has got to be a better way." I looked around the room at the tables filled with inmate mothers and their kids. "What a horrible way for children to spend a Saturday afternoon. I know the inmate mothers at the other tables. Most of these kids are in foster homes. They'll become the next wave of incarcerated men and women."

Haley told me that before she graduated from high school, "I wrote a letter to Senator Ron Wyden opposing Measure Eleven. I wrote as your daughter and described the accident and pointed out the cost of your incarceration. Maybe the fact that I talk about your situation allowed me to win 'Maverick of the Year in the Strength of Character' category." She should have been beaming and proud. Instead, she looked determined, a victory won from tragedy. I was so proud of her, my youngest.

"Haley, that is admirable and valuable, especially to me." Haley was finding her way and not afraid to use her voice.

"Are you still writing?" she asked.

"Oh, yes," I said.

"If you're writing, I feel like something good is going to come of this," said Haley. "When I'm sad, I think to myself, *She's writing a book about this.* Somehow it makes Christmas and graduation a little less depressing."

"I need you to write it," said Nikki. "I don't talk about it like Haley does. The book will explain my anger." *There. She said it. She had a right to be angry as hell.*

Visitors were allowed to bring in five photos. I was able to see pictures of the UCSC campus and Haley's dorm. She was proud to have decided on her own. Nikki brought a picture of the two of them with the caption: *This is how you make s'mores.*

"We went camping," said Nikki. "We are whittling a green stick." I looked at the photo. The girls were sitting on a log by a campfire dressed in hats, boots, and flannel. Haley was removing the bark from a stick, the knife blade moving away from her. Nikki was smiling at her progress. *That should have been my job, but thank you, Nikki.* They looked happy. The photo was proof that a person can go away, even a mother, and life goes on. I wondered if I would still have opportunities to teach them things of life, or will I have missed that window of opportunity?

The last day of visiting was the hardest for Haley. She never knew when she could afford to come up and see me again and she couldn't stop crying. Nikki, her protector, had made Haley some CDs and drawing books to take her mind off leaving me.

It was Nikki, the daughter in town, who visited on holidays instead of going to other gatherings. I had asked her about plans. "Nate and I thought about Seattle, but I can't leave you." I suspected she was duty bound and remained in town. But I didn't know for sure until that day that she chose to stay near me.

"I love it that you come to see me, Nikki," I said, tears stinging in my eyes. "But please, live your life, don't hold back. I did the same thing to my mom. I was all set to move west from Minnesota and I couldn't leave her." I laughed at the memory of my mother's face when she found out. "She told me to go, to not let her hold me back."

"There was no one like her. I was her special Loon," said Nikki.

"What I wouldn't do to have one more day, one more hour with her."

We fell silent after that. Our throats were tight, our hearts burned. We each wanted to comfort the other. If I apologized, they would be obliged to bolster support. A weight settled into their spines, tears gathered in storm clouds around their eyes, nose, and mouth. The visiting room sergeant called time. My last sight of them was behind the sally port glass, their shoulders touching, and Haley's tears streaming down her face.

The girls' next letters were bittersweet. Haley had written, *One of the hardest parts about having you in prison was exactly that. You are in a place I want so badly to take you out of. I am helpless. I miss you, Mama. I will never love you more. I will never love you less, and I will never give up on you.* She sent me a drawing of her traced hand with words of love on the fingers, and a kiss imprint in the center. Nikki sent a beautiful short note, and signed off with, *"Love you more than puppas, mashed potatoes, and my right hand. You are my Best, Nikki.*

That next weekend, Gerry came to visit. I blubbered about the visits with Nikki and Haley. "I want to use this time to get things right, so they can go on with their lives and not worry about me."

"That's an appropriate response, Karen. You need to live a purposeful life, even in here. Do you still have the Viktor Frankl book, *Man's Search for Meaning*? I sent it in a long time ago when you were at the bottom."

"Yes, it's on my shelf."

"Look up the passage about people who wait for someone locked up."

I went back to the dorm after our visit and found the passage in which Frankl states that if a man becomes conscious of those who wait for him he won't be able to throw away his life. "He knows the 'why' for his existence and will be able to bear almost any 'how.'"

I closed the book and looked out onto the dayroom. It was business as usual. One woman was hollering, "Get your shit out of the dryer, now!" Another was crying at the phone kiosk. Most were just trying to find a way to fill the time: talking, watching TV, gossiping, or simply sitting and staring into space. My daughters gave me purpose. If I kept writing, they believed that something good would come from this experience of a mother in prison. I opened my tank box and took out my journal.

Winter was approaching. Blue Eyes, Wise Owl, Pearl, and I walked to dinner under a dusting of snow from a heavy sky. The flakes were too few to gather on our coats but by the time we finished eating, they began to fall in earnest. I noticed Big Buck and Bear leaning on the walls in the dining room. It was after hours for them.

"Baker," called Big Buck, "eat up, we're on snow patrol."

Our crew ate quickly and hustled back to the dorm to grab our jackets, beanies, work boots, and wool gloves. It felt magical to be outside in the snow, but it felt even better to have a special purpose. We split up the sidewalks into groups, each assigned to a maintenance crew worker or another cop. I was assigned to work with the Captain. There were three or four captains who rotated through during my incarceration. The captains ran the prison, just under the superintendent. The

Captain with me was rumored to be fair. That was a high compliment coming from the incarcerated. He and I worked side by side, shoveling a path from the dining room to the dorm. He worked with a hearty attitude, making congenial comments, and never once looked over his shoulder to see if I was going to brain him with the shovel.

We fell into a rhythm of scoop and toss. When he stopped to check our progress he said, "Nice work, Baker."

"I grew up in Minnesota, Captain."

"Ah, you're made of sturdy stuff." We went back to work, increasing our pace, trying to keep up with the snowfall that was getting heavy. "You have a good job. They don't hand this one out to just anybody. You gotta earn it. Good for you."

"I had good jobs before this. I had a real life with responsibilities. I'm a mom."

"I have a good job too." He paused and looked me in the eye, the snow falling all over his bare head and jacket, but he was in no hurry. "You know, Baker, I gotta follow rules too, just like you. I gotta drive fifty-five, I gotta pay taxes. I don't like to follow the rules all the time. But that's just life. I decided that's what I gotta do and I do it every day." He went back to shoveling. I paused to watch the snow gather on his cold head. He was humming. I took up the shovel and dug in alongside. He was right; it was just that simple. He made peace with the laws of the land.

We worked for another thirty minutes or so, two people working together to make the sidewalks safe. He made encouraging comments but didn't patronize me like other DOC officers. When we finished, he shook my hand.

"Good job, thanks for your help. I'm gonna go home and take a hot shower."

I watched him walk away, a working man who happened to be wearing a uniform. He didn't need to crack a whip to enforce the law, he lived the law. I took the shovels back to the maintenance building. When I was released, I knew wouldn't have an issue over a badge.

Christmastime was a forced march. I kept telling myself, *It's a day like any other.*

With Glory's tutelage, I threw myself into drawing. The drawings weren't very good, but I felt at peace, even happy, creating a scene. Unable to buy my friends and family gifts, I drew pictures that represented our connection, and thought of them while I worked away the hours. I drew a snow scene of the Northern Lights for my sister and thought of our childhood Christmases. For Gerry, I drew the food we cooked together. For my father, I drew a fantasy lunch with Pema Chodron, the yoga guru Rodney Yee, Garrison Keillor, and Martha Stewart. I had the most fun drawing my daughters with rock stars: Haley and Trent with Mick Jagger, Nikki and Nate with Prince. I drew Nate from a childhood photo. The camera caught him bent over a child's guitar, hair wild as he rocked the strings. Prophetic. I had been listening to his band on NPR. They would feature it on a morning show and the women around the bunk area put on their headphones and turned on their radios. If one mother had good news, we all had good news, especially at Christmastime.

I mailed out the drawings and hoped they would forgive my humble work. It was Christmas, and I had to do something. I missed giving a gift. I missed cooking for someone. I missed my girls in pajamas on Christmas morning. Then, Christmas sent me a gift.

"Dude!" It was Hippie Chick. I race-walked over to the podium where she stood with her sets of bags. A prison hug was standing close to one another, letting the atoms join between the physical bodies.

"You're here, you made it over," I said. It was good to see her.

"It's nuts over here. It's like an anthill."

"Yeah, red ants," I said.

Hippie Chick landed a good bunk. I wasn't surprised, she was making an effort to work hard and stay out of trouble. Our Five Alive was back together and we celebrated Hippie Chick's arrival at the next canteen day, eating Ben and Jerry's ice cream like deprived addicts. Hippie Chick did her Chunky Monkey dance on her chair with her famous laugh. Looking around our reunited group, I thought of each woman and what they had contributed to the women around them. Teddy Bear brought people to God, not with shame or a set of rules but with talking and listening to girls with questions. Pearl believed in the equality of all that lives and treated people with tolerance. Hippie Chick lived full throttle; she wasn't an approval seeker, like me. She had more freedom than any of us.

I received several pen pal letters over the years, intended for any number of the Karen Bakers in the prison system. The letters were pure smut and a great source of entertainment. Hippie Chick was the best audience, a one-woman crowd. "I got a pen pal letter. I don't know this guy. Wanna hear?"

"Hell yes!" She laughed. We found a table in the dayroom, away from the podium.

"You gotta sit right next to me, the writing and spelling is part of the fun," I said. "I gotta warn you, it's pretty disgusting."

"Awesome!" Hippie Chick leaned in.

Karen hi sweetie my name is mike I got your number from a friend of mine who no's a friend of yours, Well I would like to be your Pin pall's and maybe more I don't no how much time you have To do, I have Too years for driving a car that dident belong To me iTs a long sTory. Well Im 5'foot 7"inches light brown hair, brown eyes, people say I look a loT younger Then my age. I am 52 year's old verry liTTle gray hair and a liTTle moscular Karen I like your name, I like the way iT rolls off the tip of my Tounge Karen. Wow Just thinking of that is sTarTing To maKe my head starT to pulssaTing That's driveing me crazy thinking abouT you. Well I like all types of music The beetles and the rolling sTone's and I like Hot Rod car's and Hot looking women. I am a Journeyman Painter and a MachinisT, I would sure like to bor-out your block and polish you pup's Karen, so sTop the grinning and drop the linnen, I donT mean to sound so forward but I thoughT ThaT mighT puT a smile on your prettie face good night Karen

P.S.

WriTe back

Sincerely MiKe

Hippie Chick giggled and shook her head from the start. By the time we got to tips of "tounges" she was laughing and slapping the table. I looked up at the overhead camera and waved.

"He's gonna bor-out your block, Karen, yee ha!" Then she sat up straight in mock seriousness, "What's a pup? Are your titties your pups? Is he gonna polish 'em up?" She quickly circled her nipples with her palms, then looked around to see if she was in trouble for touching herself in public.

"He creeps me out," I said, looking at the letter.

"That's what pen pals are all about, dude. Writin' smut." We looked at the letter, picking out the mixed-up words. "At least he likes The Stones." She laughed.

"Doesn't everybody like The Stones? I don't trust people who don't like The Stones."

"That was hoo-larious." She paused and playfully bobbed side to side, "So, you gonna write him back?"

When I moved to Minimum, Glory was down to months before she paroled. Soon it would be days. The women from our church services were gathering a box of clothing and toiletries.

"Where will you go?" I asked.

"I have a little money saved." She shrugged. "I put it all in the Lord's hands."

But I was worried about her. The world was harsh. Would she find work with a felony? It was the question we all asked ourselves.

Meanwhile, I was throwing myself into another form of art. I was accepted into a quilting program, taught by a group of volunteers. The class met in the dining room. My tutor, Margery, was both an angel and an artist. Her quilts were landscapes and had international renown.

I learned to sew with my Gram. I knew my way around a Simplicity pattern, so after my first learner's block quilt, I asked if we could accelerate the education and go right into her world of landscape. Lucky for me, she agreed.

"What kind of landscape do you want? If you could stand before a scene anywhere in the world, where would it be?"

I didn't have to think. "The Caribbean. I have not floated in the water for years or sat on the sand. I want to work with color—pink, purple, bright orange, anything but navy blue."

I went home and sketched a few beach scenes. Glory helped with the composition. I brought my drawings to Margery at our next meeting. She flipped through my sketches and landed on a curving beach scene, at sunset, with low mountains in the distance and an empty chair, meant for me.

"Let's add some interest," said Margery. She was petite and barely had to lean over the table. "How about some palm trees and vegetation?" She swirled lightly, creating a suggestion of bushes and flowers on the shore. "It needs more color here in the foreground, to balance the sunset. How about a couple of boats here, bright and colorful?"

"Great!"

"Sketch those in, you do the work." We had a plan.

I shared a table with a black woman my age. I had seen this woman at my church services. I sat behind her and listened as she would call out to the pastors with her hand raised, "Yes, Lord. Hallelujah," or "That's right." For her quilt, Margery had collected African fabric in golds and black from the quilting guild's storehouse and arranged them before her.

"Oh, sweet Jesus. Look at this." Church Lady ran her hands over the fabric reverently. "My family will be so proud."

Church Lady sang and hummed as she worked. I was consumed with laying out strips of colored fabric, creating a sunset. We rarely looked out the window during class. But one day, a woman was set to parole and a woman at the table closest to the window was keeping watch.

"Oh, I see some cars pulling up," she said. A white van emptied its passengers and among them was a young boy, dressed and pressed. "It must be her family."

The child was impatient with the wait and bounced off the edge of the curb, bumped his shoulder into the fence, was reprimanded, and continued to fidget and squirm.

"I think she's coming," said our lookout. Inmates and teachers alike rushed to the window. There she was, a tall brown woman with short curly hair, no longer in prison blues but in capri pants and a colorful top, pushing a cart of belongings. She stopped pushing and ran to the little boy. Soundlessly we saw her cry out and drop to her knees. She held out her arms, and the boy fell into her embrace. Weeping, she pulled back, put her hands and forehead on the sidewalk, worshiping the ground. She sat back on her heels and held her hands to the sky. I choked out a sob then plastered my hands over my mouth. There wasn't a dry eye in the house, the inmates and quilting teachers side by side were caught in the spectacle of this woman's newfound freedom. *That will be me one day.* The newly released, free woman stood up still clutching the boy's hand. She embraced the others on the sidewalk, one at a time. *This will all be over one day.*

"Praise you, Lord. Praise you," said Church Lady, who was rocking and holding her hands on her heart.

"We're going out that same door." I smiled at her.

"That's right." She turned to me wet-faced and glowing. "I better get this quilt done!"

Glory left soon after, with less pageantry. She would be leaving early in the morning. The night before, she had passed the peace, "God be with you." The DOC turned a blind eye as Glory gave hugs. When

I woke up the next morning, she was gone. My beautiful teacher. The women from church service were waiting for her with a box of clothes and start-up toiletries. They arranged a place for her to stay.

A month later, Glory sent me a letter that I passed around. She had taken a bike ride from the top of a long hill. *"It was the first time I had gone faster than a trot in seven years. I was wearing a dress and my dress and hair were flying in the wind! Wheeeeee!"*

The image still brings me joy. She must have been glorious indeed.

I continued to work hard as part of the maintenance crew. The flower beds around the Minimum buildings were fallow, so Kalikimaka, Blondie, and I approached Big Buck and Bear about new landscaping. They were a great support, and the whole crew got involved. We worked in the spring rain, wearing Gorton Fisherman slickers, and under the hot sun in the summer. As thrifty MacGyvers, we collected the seeds of flowers from the pods in the fall. In winter, the whole crew gathered around the table, harvesting the seeds of hollyhocks, columbine, snapdragons, and marigolds. Come spring again, we'd plant the seeds, filling the yard with color.

Kalik, Blondie, and I still cleaned the dryers and did other odd jobs. Even wrangling turds became a positive task. It mattered because it was a service to others. Once in a while, I had a small job that many women appreciated. Every few months, the bullet hard shower nozzle, Brawny, our Resident Stud, was ordered to a mist by unsympathetic cops overhearing the raunchy gossip about date night in the shower. The male maintenance crew complied as ordered with red faces. But after a few days, I grabbed the tool from the cage, winked at the women on the unit, and dialed the nozzle back up.

One morning, Kalik, Blondie, and I arrived at the maintenance building. Big Buck and Bear were loading carts with power tools. "New orders, ladies," said Big Buck. "We're doubling all the single bunks."

"That means me," I said. I wasn't surprised. Glory's bunk had been filled just hours after she left. Like my first bunkie on Newbie street, my new bunkie cried all day and night. Then, she slept like she was no longer breathing. I remember learning about drug withdrawal in jail from Tizzy, Silver, and Buzz Cut. Melancholy Baby acted the same. Sleep, eat, cry.

Big Buck just grunted and kept loading tools. "The place is designed to triple the bunks if we have to." It was a sobering thought. Were women committing more crimes or did the prison population expand because there were more beds?

Each day, we added eight to ten bunks. Insult to injury, I doubled my own. Soon a

bunk came open below T.W., back in the honor area where Teddy Bear moved. It was quiet. My request was honored and I began packing my clothes and books.

"Do you want this?" I asked Melancholy Baby. "It is the parenting course book." Melancholy Baby lifted the wool blanket from her head and peered over the edge to look at the book. I knew she had a nine-year-old daughter who lived with her mom.

"I could really use it," she said. "But I can't take it with me when I go. Where would I put it?" She flipped onto her back and I caught a rare glimpse of her face. Her vacancy scared me, as if she was not long for this earth. "I'll probably be living under a tarp."

I thought of the old woman back on G Unit, who committed a crime every winter so she could have a warm place to sleep. Once you knew the drill of recidivism, maybe prison or jail was easier than trying to live on the outside. *Melancholy Baby will be dead in three years, tops.*

A new "girl" entered our dorm and was given a bunk in the honor area with the rest of us Old Timers. That caught my attention. She had an athletic body, chestnut-colored hair, and a high-end salon haircut. We were close in age. She spoke in clear sentences that included please, thank you, and excuse me. She reminded me of how I behaved in my early days of incarceration when I was dazed and afraid.

I introduced myself, but she just nodded, teary, and offered no explanation of her crime. She kept to herself for a few weeks but slowly began to talk. Her voice was so soft I had to lean in to hear her. I didn't ask her about her crime. The shocking stories used to be titillating; now it didn't matter to me anymore. I just wanted to finish my time and go home.

"Do you want a cup of coffee?" the new woman asked me one day. "I have all these tickets for the coffee cart." It was the first time I saw her sweet smile.

"I'd love one, I'll buy next time, Sweetie Pie." We walked outside and I told her how to buy two coffees. "You can't share, you know. DOC is afraid we'll make it into a Mafia situation. God forbid we should develop the traits of generosity or charity. Go get one, walk it back here. Wait a minute or two, then go back and ask for another. The inmate at the coffee cart won't give you any trouble."

Sweetie Pie completed her mission with a sigh and an eyeball roll. "Let's walk." We had many things in common: children in school, careers, a supportive family. We both had traveled the world and had seen The Rolling Stones. It was the first time since I was incarcerated that I felt such a kinship. Compared to my other prison relationships, we were more like a Venn diagram than bumper cars.

"Circle up, ladies," said Big Buck the next day at work. He sat with his hands folded on the table, he was grim.

"Are we tripling the bunks?" I asked. He didn't answer. He waited a few moments. "You might notice that we are one short today."

I looked around the circle. *Tizzy.* My first thought was, Tizzy screwed up and lost her job. Worse, Tizzy was in the Hole.

"Your coworker is sick," said Big Buck. "She's gonna need a little time off." There was audible relief around the table, thinking the Hole was the worst scenario. Big Buck stayed put and stared at his hands on the table.

"Is it serious?" I asked.

"I'll let her tell you." He turned to Blondie. "You two are in the same dorm. Why don't you go back and see how she's doing?" Blondie left immediately. I caught up with her at lunch.

"She's got cancer."

"Cancer? Oh no, not in here!" I thought of what Sinful said. *There are worse things than prison. You can get sick and die in here.* "Will they let her go early?"

"Oh, hell no. She's gonna go through chemo, right on her bunk."

I thought of a childhood friend whose mother was our Campfire leader. She fought through chemo and surgeries, withered to bones, and died. But in prison? I couldn't imagine it.

In less than two weeks, Sweetie Pie was next. "Hi, Sweetie Pie. Wanna go for a walk?" She shook her head. She was trying to tell me something. I could see her lips moving, but I couldn't hear her. I leaned in and peeked up under her hair curtain.

"I got some bad news today." *Not your kids.*

"I went to the medical unit today. I found a lump in my breast." Her face was fallen. We were silent for a while. "They put me on some sort of a list to go out for a biopsy. It still has to be approved. I don't know when that will be."

I simply stood by her bunk, helpless to offer aid. But I realized I needed to tell the worst part about it, so she would be prepared. "Nothing happens fast in here. Even medical issues such as this. Have you told your family?"

Sweetie Pie nodded and lay down, facing the wall. She

spent most of her time on her bunk. Occasionally, I'd see her at the phone kiosk. I checked on her throughout the day and we commiserated at the lack of progress. I couldn't feed her broth or bring her warm socks.

Our crew had a repair job in Tizzy's unit. She was awake and dressed, resting on her bunk. "I'm just exhausted," she said. Her eyes were hollow and all her brassiness was gone. I wondered how it felt to be at death's door, in public, surrounded by strangers.

Tizzy was given a course of chemotherapy; now time simply had to pass. The more dire her situation, the calmer Tizzy became. One day our crew came to her unit and she was lying on her back. There was no extra pillow or blanket, no TV tray table with broth and saltines. She told us how she spent the hours of the day.

"I have to be efficient when I get up. I do all that I need on that trip because I may not have the energy later."

She lay down and closed her eyes. It scared me to see this mighty warrior diminished and vulnerable.

Blondie was in Tizzy's unit and kept a close watch. "Big Buck and Bear drop by the unit every day," she said. "Mostly they stay at the podium, checking in with the guard. They can't do any more than we can. It's like looking at a sick tiger through the glass at the zoo."

I walked into the dorm and headed straight for Sweetie Pie's upper bunk in the back of the dorm. Her answer had come; a plan was in place. She was sitting up, writing on little pieces of paper. "It's confirmed. They're going to do a mastectomy." The tears rolled down her face. She wiped them with an open palm under her chin. "DOC is going to do it," she whispered. She looked up at me. Her face was distraught, perhaps even angry. "My brother is a *doctor*, I can afford to pay for a plastic surgeon, but I have to use a DOC surgeon for my mastectomy."

Against the rules, I simply put my forehead on her bunk and cried for her misery, Tizzy's misery, all the misery in prison. I thought of Tommy, who had hidden enough pills to end her life, *I'm working on a quilt so it won't be this week.*

Sweetie Pie touched my head, a touch by a braver woman than me. I couldn't stay there. I didn't want to put her in danger so I stepped back.

"When, how long?" I asked. She just shrugged.

"How will you get through this?" I asked.

Sweetie Pie looked at me glassy-eyed. "I have to survive, I have grandkids. Gotta focus on what I can control and let go of what I can't."

It was an admirable approach, but I was afraid. I was afraid Tizzy and Sweetie Pie would die in here. All I could do was to look at the calendar and cross my fingers.

Meanwhile, Sweetie Pie's hair needed tending, so she made an appointment in the Minimum salon. Graduates like me had an opportunity to keep our skills fresh. So that next Saturday, I gave Sweetie Pie an A-line cut made famous in the Vidal Sassoon era. It was layered in the back and longer in the front, making it look fuller. It turned out great. But like Tommy's haircut, the next cut didn't go so well. I go too fancy creating "texture," which meant slicing into the longer portions to give it lift. I wanted to cut that damned cancer out. The more I cut, the worse it became. Sweetie Pie reached out from under her cape and squeezed my hand.

"I'm sorry." The tears that blurred my eyes didn't help. "I have a way to make it up to you, tonight, after dinner. It's a surprise." Sweetie Pie gave me a tired smile. There was nothing I could give her to make up for the fact that she had cancer in prison and would have a DOC butcher cut it out.

But by Glory's God, I was gonna try.

After dinner, Sweetie Pie and I went out to yard. It was late summer. The garden, the grass, and the flower beds had bloomed and faded. "Come with me, Sweetie Pie. There is a flower bed near the maintenance building. I have to turn the water off." I winked.

She tried walking at a regular pace but slowed down. *Perfect.* It was almost sunset and I wanted the timing to be right. The view of the sky from the yard was a big improvement over the Medium/Maximum yard but it did not show the actual horizon line as it did in the garden. We stepped through the garden gate.

"Look," I said.

"The sunset!" she whispered. "I haven't seen one in so long." She began to cry. The narrow view was a slope beyond the prison land. I coiled the hose slowly while Sweetie Pie took in the colors as the sun hovered just above the horizon.

"It's the only place on this side where you can see it drop below the hills," I said. "Funny, isn't it? I will never be able to afford a view like this."

She stood and watched as the sun went from a bright orange ball to a crescent, just peeking over the hillside. The colors of the sky turned powder blue, and when I traced it straight up, it was a deep blue velvet. A single bright star made an appearance. We watched until the last rays of sun dropped below the hillside.

"Yard in!"

"Ah, my *friend*," she said, "thank you."

I had been in prison nearly four years when Barack Obama was elected president of the United States. I watched the election results and the acceptance speech sitting in the dayroom of my unit in a women's prison. The crowd was a cross-section of races, ages, and backgrounds. Together we watched as a father, a husband, a trustworthy leader promised change.

"While we breathe, we have hope… We cannot turn back… Yes, we can."

We sat out of order: black, Latino, white, Native American. We were a commonality of inmates, oppressed Americans, looking for change and redemption. Church Lady sat with her hands over her face, tears streaming down.

"This is a new day. Never did I think, in my time." She held up her hand. "Here is your beacon, Lord, praise you, praise you."

I looked over at the skinhead section. They were leaning over the short wall, glaring at the celebration. My heart was so full, I blessed them. *Touch them, God.* The officer on duty was a gay woman, near my age. She stood behind us in an official at-ease position for the cameras but did not hide the tears as they streamed down her cheeks.

Not long after the election, I was walking to my dorm and was told to stand against the wall. Two women were being escorted out of my unit in cuffs. The light from the yard obscured their faces. I could see the profiles of the guards and heard the sound of radios squawking as they led the two cuffed women toward the exit. As they came closer, I was shocked to see one of them was Church Lady. The other was a young white girl who had trouble walking and was bleeding profusely from her forehead and nose. She clearly lost the fight.

The unit was upended in gossip. I went straight to the source.

"Teddy Bear, what happened? They took Church Lady!"

"You missed it. Church Lady and some new, young Nobody got hauled off to the Hole. They got into a fight over the microwave. Church Lady turned into the Devil himself. She had the bitch by the ponytail and smashed her face into the *faucet* at least three times. Pretty sure her nose was broken. The bathroom is closed, there's blood all over the sinks."

"She was just right there." I looked at the blue vinyl couches in front of the television. "She was praying and sobbing for Obama. I sat right next to her." I was crushed. All that prayer and calling out to the Lord lost in an instant of anger. If she can't do it, how can these other women with anger problems stay out of trouble?

November gave way, and as the holidays approached, the day-to-day drama mounted. Hokey prison crafts were coping mechanisms for depression and separation from family. Beading, drawing, and crochet were the favorites. "Crocheting is prison valium. It saves my life, makes me want to wake up in the morning," said a young woman, fresh from Medium/Maximum. She held up a pair of baby booties. "These are for my daughter." She went back to working the crochet hook. "She's in foster care." Crafts were a distraction for the deep heartache we rarely talked about in prison. It was too intimate and personal. The holidays just amplified the collective wretchedness. I didn't share the details of my children. I didn't expect another inmate to understand the grief between my girls and me. Each of the other women were coping with their own. And I didn't feel safe discussing my children that way. I wouldn't feel like I was protecting them.

The girls spent the holidays in a different way every year. Sometimes they were with my family, but most of the time they were with their father. As years passed, friends and boyfriends and boyfriends' families wove into a "normal" Christmas. None of us were "home for the holidays."

We all knew how hard our families would try to have a good time. They would put on their Christmas sweaters, bake cookies, and decorate the tree, trying their best to make merry. For the families who have a mother in prison, Christmas is a joyless endurance. So inside or out, cities or states, we put our heads down and wait for New Year's Eve and the chance put the year behind us and begin a new year.

One evening a few days before Christmas Eve, I decided to soothe myself in a holiday craft project. I made myself a cup of instant coffee, added a peppermint for that holiday twist, and I bunked myself in so as not to be disturbed.

I set about recreating a Christmas village by Martha Stewart. Martha made wooden buildings with chocolates inside. I could just imagine her saying, "Now who wouldn't want to find this at their place setting on Christmas morning?" The planning, the crafting, and the delivery filled a lonesome hole, and the spirit of giving that I missed.

The craft program didn't have balsa wood and paint or chocolates. So I bastardized Martha's holiday village by building the houses out of paper bags from canteen. But now that I was in Minimum, I was allowed to order glue instead of toothpaste and check out real scissors, instead of the fold-and-tear method. I just hoped they lasted until Christmas morning. I planned on passing them out to the women in my bunk area. I had about two and a half hours until lights dimmed. I put on my headphones and dialed a radio station that played the Christmas songs of happier times. I was impregnable. Then I realized I wasn't alone.

A woman named Billie sat down on the other side of the short wall at my bunk about two feet away. Billie was staring directly toward me, pulling on tufts of hair at her bang line. *Creepy.* I looked over my shoulder and saw that it wasn't me she was staring at but a girl she fancied.

Billie was in her late twenties, but had the paunch of menopause. She wore holey Converse tennis shoes and tugged on a mannish number-four clipper cut on her big round head. Billie lived in her own bubble of mental illness. She was an unimaginable thief and stole money to buy street drugs that quieted the voices in her head. It was her fourth tour of duty in prison. One of Billie's behaviors was holding conversations with people who were not there. Sometimes she would shout at invisible people, inches from your face, and scare you to death.

I went back to cutting and folding the gingerbread houses, *Use a ruler for a perfect line*. But even with headphones on, I could hear Billie talking to someone in her head.

"That's stupid," she shouted. "You can't say that!" Then she started grunting and rocking. I tried to ignore her. She kept on banging her back into the plastic chair, making squeaking noises on the linoleum. I looked at my bunk scattered with supplies. It would take too much time to pack it up and move. Through my lashes, I peeked up at her. She was still on point for the girl behind me. Without straightening my elbow, I knew I could reach out and touch the single hair on Billie's face that sprouted from her chin. *Go away. I am trying to have some friggin' Christmas cheer around here*. My jaw was clenched, I turned my shoulders to block out her presence. Squeak, squeak, squeak. *Ignore her.*

Then she shrieked, "That's Led Zeppelin, not Ozzy Osbourne! Everybody knows that!"

I jumped. My back hit a metal bunk pole and knocked my headphones off my head. I could hear the tinny sound of Judy Garland, *Have yourself a merry little Christmas*. I looked around for moral support. Everyone was engrossed in their own form of distraction. It was just me and Billie, and Billie had to go. I was tired of being nice. I was tired of putting on my game face day after day, year after year, biting my tongue. I didn't want to pray about it. I didn't want to follow the Zen ocean and drop down below the waves. I wanted to yell and scream. I *wanted* to be mad.

My pillow was the only thing between her and me. I watched my hand gathering the nubby cotton pillowcase and draw the pillow to my chest. I took a breath and slipped outside myself, *This is where I lose it.* I marked the distance from the pillow to her Butterball turkey head, tightened my grip, and swung like a batter! I felt the solid contact of pillow to head. The swing sent my brown paper Christmas village and peppermints flying. Billie leaped up, her chair crashing backward. She crouched, ready for a second attack from anywhere. I held my breath and she was gone. Judy was still singing, from underneath the bunk, *From now on your troubles will be out of sight.* I was triumphant.

The women in the bunk area heard the clamor and saw Billie take off toward the bathroom. *Crazy Billie.* They shook their heads and went back to their activities, never suspecting the nice lady of foul play. I took a breath, waiting for the cops watching from overhead cameras. Nothing.

My feeling of triumph evaporated. *I whacked a vulnerable person, I'd lost it.* Prison had finally got to me. It wasn't self-righteous anger that made me swing. It was the anger of being fed up with the powerlessness over my circumstances. *Breathe.* I was ashamed of myself.

I had to find Billie and apologize. I walked to the shower area and peeked under each curtain but it was empty. Then I looked for Billie's Converse sneakers under the toilet stall doors. She was at the end of the row.

"Billie." I tapped quietly on the stall door. "I'm sorry," I said.

She stood slowly, her full moon head rose above the short stall door. Her round eyes stared at me. I moved away so she could walk out of the stall. She kept her eyes straight ahead and went to the sink. She turned on the water.

"I didn't mean to hurt you." She washed her hands. "I freaked out about my space."

Billie turned to me and just stared, not speaking. The water kept running.

"I wish I could take that back. If it wouldn't get you in trouble, I'd I hand you my pillow, right now, and let you whack me with it, as hard as you want. What d'ya say?"

The right side of Billie's mouth twitched and lifted ever so slightly. I mirrored her half-smile. But then she blinked, her face went vacant. She faded back into her mind, turned, and walked away.

Over the winter months as the maintenance crew harvested seeds, we had interesting discussions that ranged from such topics as religious tolerance to the right to die. The women's depth surprised me. In our discussions, I learned that despite the variation of education levels and past experiences, the women had high ideals and values. They listened patiently to others' opinions and admitted when they did not know enough about a subject to comment. Before prison, it had not occurred to me: the depth and impressions of incarcerated women.

As each of us drew closer to our parole dates, Big Buck would toss out topics relevant to parole planning. He never pushed the issue. Instead, he would cast a word in the air and let it land on the table. Job. Saving money. Not one woman had a solid plan.

"We have no Internet to research jobs or affordable housing," said T.W. "We don't even know when the buses run. And get this, we have to *pay* for parole and transportation to the parole office."

"I have not talked with my family about where I'll live," I said. "They have already been through so much. I want to be able to take care of myself. But when I do the math, saving up for a first and last month's rent and a cleaning deposit on an inmate salary is impossible."

"Number one, two, and three on the parole plan is a place to stay," said Blondie. "A bus pass might keep you out of the rain but it's not a home. You'd have to live out of a backpack and be at the mercy of every creep or scammer on the bus."

"Dude," said Hippie Chick, "I've *got* to have a place. I need to find my daughter and give her a place to live." Hippie Chick wiped her eye with the pinky side of her hand. "I can't be on the streets. That's where all my connections are."

"I guess I'm the lucky one," said Kalikimaka. "My mom will be there for me. But I worry about women like us who have had longer sentences. We don't have updated computer skills. My daughter tells me that everything is online now. We don't even have e-mail accounts."

"We are not *allowed* access to the Internet," said Tizzy, throwing up her hands. "Too many of these women are locked up for Internet scams and ID theft."

"I'm lucky too. My Little Mama is taking me in. She already has my boys," said Blondie. "If I had to rely on the law library I'd be SOL. It's a joke. They have zero resources. They've got a little metal shelf with those orange occupational handbooks from when my parents were graduating from high school and looking for careers. There are no lists for housing or felon-friendly employers." The group was nodding in agreement. "DOC says, 'Don't come back.'" Blondie leaned in and waggled her head side to side. "'Make good choices.'" Then she sat back and tossed up her hands.

The seed harvesting table hit a wall and fell silent. No one looked at each other except Big Buck. He sat back in his chair and scanned the women's faces at the table, "So what's your plan?" Silence. "Take the rest of the day off. Go back to your units and think about it."

I dreaded asking my family this question. My daughters were busy establishing themselves as adults. My sister? I just couldn't ask. She had already sacrificed her personal life nursing me back to health and caring for my children. Sam and Audrey and my stepfather, Marshall, would need help themselves before long. There was something terribly wrong with the parole system.

The prison budget kept us fed and sheltered but ran out of money for reform. DOC's idea of character development was an action-and-consequences model. But without behavioral education, it was simply discipline and punishment. It's hard to learn concepts like integrity and honesty when an inmate is shackled, sequestered, and made to wear lime green shirts. DOC was overwhelmed with budget issues brought about by overcrowding. So DOC passed the buck for behavioral change to outside programs such as religious services, Living Yoga, and Mercy Corps Northwest. At the end of a prison sentence, the woman who strives for change will be released alongside the woman who has spent every day in the Hole. Behavior change falls on the inmate.

Tom used to say, "If ya got a problem, throw money at it." I had a big problem and would need every inmate check to fix it. I saved every cent from my inmate checks. I researched the newspaper's classifieds for rentals. I scanned the grocery prices. The statistics from an article on prison came from a 2004 study by the U.S. Department of Justice: Ten thousand inmates are released every week, 650,000 inmates release in one year. It was clear to me that the prison system could not afford to parole the people they incarcerated.

At our facility, the answer for a successful parole was the Lifelong Information for Entrepreneurs (LIFE), offered by Mercy Corps

Northwest. A group of teachers from backgrounds such as finance, medical services, training, and development came to the prison and taught financial and business planning. Eligible women within eighteen to twenty-five months to release interviewed for an opportunity to attend. Only twenty-four were accepted. The word was, if you got into this class you would make it on the outside. The interview process was no different than my prior professional career. I gave it all I had and got in. So did Hippie Chick, Lala, Blondie, Tizzy, Cleopatra, Blue Eyes, Pearl, and Wise Owl. "I need this class," Lala said. "I've never held a real job or had a bank account before."

Each week we covered a new topic, such as time management, goal planning, and creating a business plan. We were required to attend class and complete our homework. If we showed we could save money by the time we released, Mercy Corps would match us with five hundred dollars.

We prepared for class like we were going to work: LIFE folders and pencils in hand, clean clothes, and professional hair. We were on time and comported ourselves with dignity. The LIFE teachers spoke to us as colleagues in a workplace. When it was my turn to talk, I sounded like the professional I used to be, before I was an inmate. *These* are my people.

I returned from class one day and Sweetie Pie was not on her bunk at evening count. Not a good sign. I knew she wasn't taken to the Hole because her bunk was still made. If she were in trouble, which I could not imagine, the cops would have rolled her up. We sat in silence while count cleared. Meanwhile, mail was delivered.

"Baker!" The cop tossed the latest Martha Stewart on my bunk. She continued on around the bunk area. When she came to Sweetie Pie's bunk she called her name.

"Medical came and got her," said her bunkie. "Said she might be gone for a day or two."

Sweetie Pie did not come back the next day. I was not the only one praying for her. I saw a woman walk up to her bunk and place her hand on her bed then place that hand on her heart. Teddy Bear and her Christian circle prayed together in the dayroom. Our yoga group dedicated our day's practice to her. *Oh God, protect her.* I prayed with all my heart. I prayed like Alida. I prayed like Glory. I felt emboldened and expectant. God was not my last resort, he was my first response. *She is in Your hands.*

Gerry came for a visit the next day. "So, what's the countdown? A year and two months?"

"And six hours." I smiled. "I have a lot of planning to do. I have been saving my pennies, literally, but I will need to have a heart-to-heart with my family about where I will land. I'm going to need a couple of months to get on my feet."

Gerry leaned forward and placed her hands on the table. "Live with me."

"Oh, Ger." I was stunned. "You've already done so much."

"I would miss our talks."

"Me too, but still."

"Your room is still there," she said.

I felt all the air go out of me, and I had to squeeze my eyes shut to control my tears. I knew she meant it. I put my head on the table and wept. Before the surveillance cameras picked up my behavior, I raised my head.

"We could cook?" I asked hopefully.

"We could cook." She nodded slowly, as though she knew it all along.

I sat back in my plastic chair looking around the prison chow hall. I closed my eyes and envisioned the day-to-day life of my future. I saw the bed where I would sleep and the cupboards and refrigerator where I would store food, the plates from which I would eat. I saw the neighborhood and the walking route to the bus stop that went to Nikki's neighborhood. Facing the other direction was a bank that held a hundred dollars in a checking account. Beside it was a bagel shop, a park, and a bike path. If I were looking for Gerry, I would find her and her cats moving around in the kitchen. I would take my seat at the tall stool on the opposite side of the counter and chat about the day as I watched her pickling beets or stirring something on the stove. It was too beautiful. I opened my eyes and saw my best friend.

"I have a home to go to."

"Yes!" Gerry said, slapping the table. My greatest stumbling block to a successful parole was solved.

All that night and into the next day, I kept to myself. I didn't dare make eye contact. I wouldn't have been able to hide my bliss. Good news in prison is best kept to yourself. Prison is deeply competitive. The schadenfreude environment where one experiences pleasure at another's failure is a way of life. The opposite is true and more dangerous. Bitter jealousy and harsh retaliation are issued for those who have success. My *home* was too precious to risk talking about.

I called the girls, Christine, Sam, and Audrey and told them the news midday, when the dayroom wasn't busy. Then I wrote letters about the details of paroling to Gerry's house. I felt the weight of uncertainty lift off my shoulders. I would not have to put my family through another sacrifice for my benefit. I wanted to begin thinking about making my own way. Although they didn't say so, I knew they were relieved. After all, who would I be at release?

Gerry had come to the prison two to four times a month. When I asked her why, she told me, "I couldn't bear to see you fall into despair." Now she was invested in my successful parole. She had witnessed the arc of change that occurred during my incarceration. She might have a better idea than me of who I would be when I walked out of prison.

Two days later, I walked out to the yard and there was Sweetie Pie, post-mastectomy, shuffle-jogging around the blacktop track.

"You're back! Look at you, jogging. You're tough as nails," I said.

"It's easier now." She looked down at her chest. She looked drained and dazed. I fell in and shuffled beside her. Her focus was down toward the track. "I'm gonna buy a perfect set when I get out." *Gritty.*

I eased up and let her go because I was uncomfortable and had no words to offer comfort. She circled on. She never looked up, she just ran and ran, like it would solve something for her.

I worked out on the weight pile for a while, then feeling ashamed of myself for ditching my friend after her ordeal, I joined her on the track. "You must have run before coming in. You're fast," I panted.

"Yeah, marathons," she said. "I run to keep my mind quiet."

"This is the fastest I've moved in over five years." I laughed. "The black top is blurry. I feel a breeze on my skin from my own locomotion."

"Yeah," she huffed. "Along with everything else, we're deprived of speed."

"I got a letter from my former bunkmate, Glory, describing a bike ride," I panted. "It was the fastest she had gone in years." As we moved along the sidewalk, I imagined Glory's huge smile and halo of hair. "Go on," I gasped. Sweetie Pie continued one more lap, running full tilt. Her chestnut hair streamed back from her determined face. She trotted her last steps and we stretched at a picnic table.

"You OK?" I asked, trying to keep my eyes at her face and not her chest. I was worried she had ripped the stitches and there would be blood.

"Mmmm." She sighed and folded her body forward to stretch her legs.

I thought again about Glory. I saw the bike going faster and faster. My heart fluttered in a flash of fear. Then I saw me on the bike, out of control picking up speed. All at once, I am in a pale blue car with large windows. It is unlike any car I have been in. I am riding in the passenger seat. We are going faster, too fast. I feel my throat close, *dread*. There is an impact. The car is flying through the air, twisting to my side. I am about to land. I snapped out of the vision. My knees buckled and I sat abruptly on the bench. Sweetie Pie was looking at me, concerned.

"Sorry," I gasped. "I was in a car. No, first I started on Glory's bike. Then I was in a car. It wasn't my car. It was like an old Chevy. I don't know who the driver was. But we hit something and we were flying and twisting above the street."

I put my head on the concrete table. I was afraid to close my eyes for what else I might see. I welcomed the cool and nubby stone that brought me back to the present. Sweetie Pie sat down next to me.

"Are the memories coming back?" she asked.

"Maybe it was part memory and part warning," I said. "Before I came in, friends and family used to drive me around. Some drove so fast, or maybe they didn't. Maybe it was me, overreacting." I sat up and shook myself. "Oh god, I'm sorry," I groaned. "This is not *my* day to have a breakdown. Here you are, jogging fer Christ-sakes. After a mastectomy."

"Naw, naw." She looked at me with dark circles under her soft brown eyes. "It's good. It feels better to help, get my mind off it."

"I am terrified to ride in a car," I realized. "Absolutely terrified. What am I gonna do?" Then it dawned on me. I held my cheeks in both hands. "I haven't ridden with Haley. She learned to drive in Southern California." We both laughed. Suddenly I felt light and theatric. I waved my wingspan toward the fence. "I'll probably freak out on the ride out of here. Can you just see me hanging out of the car that is literally driving me to freedom and waving my arms, hollering for help?" We stood and walked slowly back to the dorm.

"You still don't remember the accident?" she asked.

"No. But every time, whenever I rode in a car, my body remembered." We walked in silence. Two women in miserable surroundings, in bodies that betrayed us.

Next Monday, the maintenance crew circled up for the weekend report. Big Buck waited for us to self-report about any transgressions or updates on Tizzy.

"That woman is made of boot leather," Blondie said. "You know she just wants to sit on the floor of the toilet and puke but it ain't her home." Blondie looked around the table, spinning tragedy into folklore. "She's got people checking on her all the time." She shrugged. "I hate that she suffers but it's good for some of these women to worry about someone else besides themselves. She's a great role model for the young miscreants."

We went around the table giving Big Buck the weekend update. When it was my turn, I talked about my terror of riding in a car again.

"Sounds like you need to get back on the horse," said Big Buck.

I nodded but couldn't imagine it.

The next day, Kalik and I were landscaping at the back of the compound, pulling hoses and creating drainage troughs, when the female crew boss approached. She was about my age but looked a whole lot better. She was fit and tan. She wore her silver hair short and stylish. Kalik and I stopped working and turned toward her. As she approached, we could see that her blue eyes were dancing with mischief.

"I heard that a part of your rehabilitation might be preparing to ride in a car again."

"Who told you that?" I laughed.

"A little bird."

"How about a ride in one of our carts?" She poked her thumb over her shoulder at a golf cart with a shovel in the back.

"Look at that, Kalik"—I nodded to the cart—"wheels and speed." I walked over to the cart and looked at the saggy driver's seat and the well-worn pedals. I took a step back and looked at the golf cart from the side. The beast might have been tamed but my stomach said *Whiplash!*

"I dunno. I'm scared, ma'am."

She looked at The Kalikster.

"Do you want to drive?"

"Oh sure!" said Kalik, the cowgirl. She hitched up her jeans from the yard work, turned to me and said, "Let's ride!"

Crew Boss smiled, tickled with herself. I looked at her wide-eyed.

"Go on." She gestured with a wave of her arm. "Give it a spin." The yard was closed and the sloping hill and "beach" of grass were ours. We climbed in.

I drew a breath. Not at all sure, I grabbed the sidebar and the dash.

"OK." Kalik nodded her head, all business, and we lurched away toward the wide-open prairie. My tender bones rattled with the bumps. Kalik drove like a cowgirl. I whooped and hung on. The wind was in my face, my hair plastered back. I smiled so hard, my lips stuck to my teeth. Kalik went as fast as she could, just shy of ripping up the sparse lawn. I dared to look around at the scenery. I forgot to be afraid.

Then she stopped. "Your turn."

I looked back at Crew Boss and motioned *May I?* She nodded and held up her hands, as in, *That's the whole idea.*

Respectfully, I tested the brakes. I wiggled the steering wheel left and right. *Inhale, exhale.* I looked over at The Kalikster, who was red-cheeked and pleased.

"When all this is settled," I told her, "one day, I'll have to drive. I will have to get myself to work and get to my family. I don't want people to have to drive me around. I *need* to do this." I stepped on the peddle. We lurched and stalled, our necks snapped back.

"Sorry, nervous, I guess."

Kalik wrapped her hands around the back of her neck. "Let 'er buck!"

We turtled along, feeling every bump. Then I stepped on the gas and we moved on to a trot. The peddle was only halfway down but I felt safe and in control.

I pulled up to the sidewalk like a driver's ed student.

"Mission accomplished." I was smiling, not shaking. We walked over to Crew Boss, who was smiling with laugh lines around her blue, blue eyes.

I fought back tears of gratitude. I didn't want to embarrass her. "You did a grand thing today, ma'am. Thank you so much." I stood up and patted the hood of the cart. The gesture was more than corrections. It was a restoration. Another piece of the release puzzle was in place.

With less than a year to go, one by one Five Alive began to parole. Teddy Bear went first. We gathered around her at five-thirty in the morning while she brushed her hair and put on makeup. We peppered her with questions such as, What is the first thing you are going to eat? Who is picking you up? Before we knew it, they called her name and she was gone.

Pearl followed. Ever practical, she decided to walk out the gate in the State-issued gray sweats. As a LIFE graduate, she rationalized that she would have to buy them anyway. "I will need them for yoga." Pearl wrote Wise Owl right away. Pearl's first outing was the Living

Yoga studio. They welcomed her with open arms. They gave her a mat. She took a class. After making herself useful, sweeping and cleaning, they gave her a job. She said she was back to wearing flowing skirts and beads and had kissed a man.

Tizzy made it out alive. She finished her chemo and was working her way back to sassy. In my prison survival tool kit, Tizzy had been the duct tape. She did it all. She was my teacher from the first miserable days in jail and my guide for staying under the radar in prison. She handed out the Samuel L. Jackson slap when I needed the wake-up call. But it was Tizzy's courage and determination in her battle with cancer, under dire conditions, that remains my deepest lesson. When I needed inspiration, I watched her walk of life.

Blondie was next. I was really going to miss her. No one else had the wit and insight to look good-naturedly at the human condition. She was going home to her Little Mama's house and would live with both her sons. In her final days before parole, I wanted every minute she could spare. I wanted an infusion of her magic, in hopes that it would sustain me until I could be with my family. We walked slow, deliberate circles on the yard. We talked about what kind of clothes she would wear: flowing skirts. What she would eat: food that was hot. We walked past a row of fall dahlias we planted last spring. "Wow, baby, them are nice." *Them are nice, where have I heard that before?* It was the shower, on Intake. A woman had said that about my breasts. Then it dawned on me.

"It was *you.*"

"What?" She smiled innocently.

"A long time ago, when I was new to prison, I was taking a shower. And the woman in the next stall looked over"—I gestured to my chest—"at my rack and said, 'Them are nice.' It was you!"

Blondie shrugged and giggled.

"Come 'ere." She crooked her finger and led a fast-paced swivel-walk into the maintenance building. "Show me one more time," she said, grinning ear to ear.

I lifted my T-shirt and bra in one fell swoop, paused as long as I dared, and pulled it back down.

"Them are still nice." She laughed.

I wondered about Blondie's observation. Was it true? How would I know? Living literally on top of each other we saw each other as-is. We were aging ungracefully under stress and fluorescent lighting. We were semi-sedentary and had poor nutrition. Our only beauty tool was cheap skin lotion. Maybe the lack of mirrors was actually a godsend.

One morning I joined Blue Eyes as she was braiding her hair before the mirror. "These mirrors are cruel." She leaned in and leaned out. "They're set at a very bad angle. Who wants to look at themselves from the neck up?" Blue Eyes had finished braiding and was now just sitting and staring at her reflection. I pulled up a chair and sat next to her, noticing how old I looked from that angle.

"I look like Willie Nelson," she said flatly. I looked at her reflection. *Oh-oh, she does.* Then I looked back at mine.

"At least Willie's cute. I look like Keith Richards." We both laughed.

"Oh god." I had his wild gray hair, indoor skin, and chiseled face. "You know, love," I growled in my best Keith imitation, "we all got a little rock star in us." We looked around the dorm and found a

Rod Stewart with spiky hair and a Snoop Dogg at a braiding station. Then, the stout cop waddled into the unit.

"Easy," said Blue Eyes as she stood to leave. "Meat Loaf."

I wondered how I compared to a woman my age in the free world who has access to gyms, hair color, and spinach salads. My gray hair made me invisible, which wasn't a bad thing in prison, it kept me off the radar. But did I want that in the real world? Would I want to be seen? Would I want to date again? Would anyone even want me?

The average age in my dorm was about thirty-two or thirty-three. The younger they were, the more they talked about sex. By the time they were ready to parole, they were chomping at the bit. "Pass me the parole condoms, I'm about to pop this cherry of prison virginity."

If I were to ever resume a sex life, I would need to know what I had to offer. Nighttime provided the cover for shy body surveys: the side-lying potbelly droop, the "pork chop" handful at the inner thigh, or the supine breast migration toward the armpit. The shower provided a place for the lift-and-drop bootie check or the bingo-arm waggle. But standing up naked? I felt too frail to know the truth about my body. I had lived through my sentence, treating my naked body like a stranger, something that needed covering up.

It wasn't just my skin that needed a lube job, my mind needed to prepare for speaking to a potential employer. I decided to enter a contest provided by the local Rotary Club. We were to write an essay for their code of ethics, The Four-Way Test. We would be asked to read our essays to a group of Rotary members in the visiting room. I had been asked to speak to previous organizations from the community. One was a news piece, "Day in the Life of a Female Inmate."

It felt contrived of course—Meet a Live Inmate! But keeping in touch with the public was a way for me to test whether or not I would be accepted back into society. DOC chose me for two reasons: One, I owned up to my crime. And two, I was predictable and mature. I had been declawed.

During a question and answer period with the Rotary Club in the visiting/dining room, I asked to use the restroom. The door was unlocked for me and I went in. I was in a walled room all by myself, no curtains, no cameras. There was a toilet and a paper toilet seat cover, what a treat. There were a sink and paper towels. What a treat! I had been air-drying my hands for my entire sentence. On the wall was a full-length mirror. It was a fabulous and frightful opportunity.

I locked the door, peed first to rid myself of even a teaspoon of liquid pooch, and stood before the mirror. Without sucking in, I hoisted my State brassiere and dropped trou. I turned north, south, east, and west. I saw a pale, curvy body. This stranger's body was not young, but it was not old. Maybe even a little cute? I zipped up and washed my hands, looking at myself in a mirror that was flat on the wall, not neck up. I was grinning triumphantly. I swung open the restroom door and walked out like a swaggering macho dude. I was Tina Turner. Everything felt different.

The closer a woman got to the gate, the more gentle she became. I noticed the shift in me too. Instead of placing all my energy into watching my back, adjusting to a new officer in the DOC shift rotation, gathering nutrition on trays, inventing ways to stay relevant to my family, and biting my tongue, I turned my thoughts to the other women doing their time. I now had the patience to be sympathetic to the new girls who I knew were scared. At night, when the Old Timers in my bunk area made their zoo sounds, I imagined them as sleeping children, innocent. Instead of studying compassion, I began to feel compassionate. What a marvelous step forward to be moved by the suffering of someone other than myself!

I became more gentle with the cops, as well. After all, I was leaving. Sarge told me out on yard one day, "I'll be here long after you leave."

"How much longer until you can retire and get the hell outta here?" I asked.

"I gotta do two years and four months, Baker," he said, still framing it as we did.

"How do you not get hard like so many of your coworkers?"

"I try to find the humor in the situation. Take the lying—I like to hear a new spin on an old story." He chuckled, looking skyward. He must have heard some whoppers. "I got a good gig this rotation. I take the work crew to the Silver Falls State Park for trail work. We have a good time. It's no fun being an asshole."

"Eats you up," I agreed.

"It's a balancing act, Baker. Sometimes you got to lead with a carrot and sometimes you gotta lead with a club."

"You were good, you were fair. Thanks, Sarge, for showing me a little humanity once in a while."

"Go and never look back." He looked around the yard and turned back to me. "The things you have in common with these women are the things you'll want to forget."

I had three months and change to April Fool's Day, 2011, the day I paroled. I wrote my last Christmas letter to thank people for their loyalty. I thanked them for the letters, the books, and money for life-saving tennis shoes, Martha Stewart magazines, and craft supplies that allowed me to make crocheted hats for Christmas presents. Loretta wrote back: *"I am so glad this is your last Christmas letter. I dreaded that envelope. It was so depressing. Made me feel guilty about my crab puffs and prime rib."* I created a different form for the last Christmas letter:

Things I Learned in The Clink

1. Possessions are wonderful. Even John Lennon had shoes, a refrigerator, and carpet.

2. There is dignity in simple work.

3. I fear technology and will not remember that I am carrying a purse.

4. It is a human right to share and provide human touch.

5. Asking for help is difficult, receiving help is an art form.

6. Things to love: darkness, silence, going fast, nudity, warm socks, the ocean, spontaneity, and freedom.

7. The people you fear might be your best teachers.

8. As long as we draw breath, we have a chance to be better people.

Goodbye to dark foggy days and slick sidewalks. Hello to budding leaves and moist musky air. Parole approached for both Kalik and me, and we threw ourselves into grooming the landscaping that would be passed along. We passed the days singing show tunes. For *The Sound of Music*, Kalikimaka sang the part of Maria and I sang the part for the goats, *Lady-who-da-lady-who-da-la-de-hoo.*

"We live on top of each other, literally, Kalik. We share tables and toilets but for most of these women, when I say goodbye, I'll mean it."

"I'll keep in contact with a few," she said, "but I'm not taking anyone home with me. I see women, usually the young ones, make all these promises to stay friends. Some of those women would be extra baggage."

"You're going back to the country life, right?" I asked.

"Yep. I look forward to the mountains and the prairie. I'll live with my mom and get a job doing hair." I watched her plant seeds in the flower beds for the next set of landscapers. She was in harmony with the earth. "I'm also gonna grow my plants, have my own garden," she said.

I thought of the superintendent who started the Minimum gardening project because he wanted to leave the "campsite" better than he'd found it.

"Do you think we left our campsite better than we found it, Kalikimaka?"

She leaned on her rake and looked around.

"This was all dry dirt when we started. Do you remember the officials who were walking around last fall? They complimented us on the columbine. We told them we propagated the seeds, and sowed them the following year. We didn't have money in the budget for seeds, so we collected them ourselves," said Kalik.

"Crew Boss loved that, so did Big Buck. Made them look good," I said. "The truth was, you and I would rather be out in the wind and rain, creating things to do, than be locked up inside wrangling turds."

"Who am I gonna sing with after you go?" asked Kalik.

"Good luck, you better shine up your hip-hop. We're a dying breed. I tried to use some ghetto slang the other day, and some whippersnapper laughed at me and said I sounded like her mom. I told her, good, I guess I served my purpose," I said.

"Are you all ready to go?" she asked. "What are you going to wear out the gate?"

"Black and turquoise," I said definitively. "They are my superpower colors!"

Gerry came for her last visit. We laid plans for my release day. "What do you want to do? Do you want to go out somewhere?"

"All I want to do is sit on the couch with the people I love and hug them for as long as I like, no cameras, no cops to tell me to stop. I can't wait to rub my feet on the carpet and have heat."

"What do you want to eat?" she asked.

"Easy. Ripe avocado with a Triscuit and black pepper." The same thing I had the morning I was sentenced. My Zen teacher who was teaching me about greed and grasping energy told me, "The idea, Karen, is to enjoy the Triscuit." *Not Release Day, Master.* I was ready for a little sin. I wanted it all together in a luscious bite.

"Cheese?" Gerry arched a brow.

"Oh hell, yes! And Grand Central Como loaf—and mangoes!"

"What to drink?" she asked slowly, sitting back in her chair.

"Diet Snapple!" I cried. Gerry looked freed from a doubt. I recognized that. "Don't worry," I said seriously.

"Good." She said and slapped the table.

Before we paroled, we met with a DOC "counselor," who, as I learned on Intake, did not offer counseling. The counselors were shepherds. They herded you into a cell or bunk for your time and gave you a sparse checklist out the door. Their number one instruction was, go directly to your parole office. The priority question was, how are you exiting the facility? Will someone pick you up or will you be riding the bus? The day you paroled, once off the property, an inmate was no longer DOC's responsibility.

Christine went shopping for my parole outfit and mailed it into the prison. I called her the night before I was to walk out the door. She told me that wondrous things awaited in the receiving unit: underwear, new socks, and clothes that were not navy blue.

I requested my medical records and mailed them out with all my books and photos. I had one chapter left in a book in case I could not sleep and kept a simple set of toiletries to take out. No, to take *home*.

Release Day was tomorrow. In my mind, I planned the move a thousand times. I would be up and out before the unit came alive. It hurt my heart to say goodbye to Hippie Chick. I worried about her. That night I told her, "You can do this. You got the tools to stay clean."

She was already soaked in tears.

"You really applied yourself in here," I told her. "Go home and find your daughter."

"I will," she said, wiping her tears with the heels of her hands.

"No one has ever made me laugh like you do." I made one last reckless attempt at human contact and dug my hand into her thick muscular wrist. "You have kept me going. I needed you and you were here for me. Don't let this world get you down."

"I'm scared, Karen." We both cried, worried about the unknown of the coming struggles. Then we hugged goodbye. The lights grew dim. I settled into my worn cotton sheets and my scratchy wool blanket for the last time and tried to sleep. And, because I didn't understand how much work I still had to do, I thought, *It's over. It's over. I will be free tomorrow.*

RELEASE

April Fool's Day, 2011, was my release day after serving seventy-five months in prison. No joke. It was Friday and the next day would be Saturday. From that day forward, my days would be marked by the Roman calendar of the free world, not five more Christmases or halfway marks. The daily fantasies of food, fleece, and family were within my grasp.

I was allowed to get up and shower at 5:30 a.m. I washed in tepid water and dried off with my postage stamp towel for the last time. I wanted to be sitting by the podium when the officer got the call. I put on my prison blues for the last time. I put on my worst pieces and dumped the seasoned felon wear on the Con Marché bin. Then, I sat by the door, waiting, bobbing my knee. The unit was still dim and the women were still asleep.

The cop on duty looked at me. "Leavin' today?"

"I sure hope so. I won't believe it until I am out that gate," I answered.

"Don't worry, DOC doesn't want to pay the cost of housing you another day." She tilted her head to her radio. "Receiving, you ready for Baker? Anyone here to pick her up? Copy that, ma'am." She looked at me with a small smile. "Your people are here, you can go."

They're here. I knew they would come, they were the kind of people who made a commitment and showed up. My mind played tricks with me the night before. I wondered if they might change their minds. But in the light of day, I knew they would show up. They were here to take me *home.* I stood up and pushed my cart with my two boxes out of the unit. I didn't look back. I hit the fresh morning air and crossed the yard toward the receiving unit that had the door with an exit to the other side. I stepped into receiving and was greeted by War Horse. There would be no fun and frivolity today.

"Wait here," she snapped. "I'll go get your parole clothes."

"It's a black outfit, with a turquoise scarf," I bubbled.

She trudged away.

"And a real brassiere!" I called out.

I heard another voice and clunking boots. "Where is she?" It was Big Buck. *Ah, he's come to say goodbye to his loyal crew member.* They both walked toward me with grim expressions.

"We got a problem, Baker." His face was serious. War Horse crossed her arms. "Found this tool in your property," He waggled a screwdriver. "We're gonna have to keep you. That's theft." I kept smiling; they had to be joking. Three long seconds passed. They weren't joking. Big Buck couldn't look at me. He shook his head in disappointment. I started to panic.

"Oh, c'mon, a screwdriver?" I pleaded. "You think I would blow my release, my future, for a screwdriver?" Those few seconds seemed unreal, like the backward collapse of falling again. "You can't be serious, my family is outside!" I looked back and forth between them, my heart pounding. Big Buck was the first to break. One side of his face started to twitch and his shoulders began to shake.

"Oh you guys."

War Horse made a stern face and crossed her arms. But I could see she was purposely overacting. They laughed, smug with themselves, and War Horse looked completely different with a smile on her face. I realized it was over.

"April Fool's!" Big Buck laughed. He paused and looked at me with his signature death stare over the glasses. "Good luck out there, Baker." His voice was concerned. He tightened his smile like he was girding for battle. Then he grunted out a laugh and the three of us all laughed together. Big Buck clumped toward the door, turned back one more time, standing up tall and loose, smiling a wide uncomplicated smile. He was happy to see me go.

It's hard to explain why their joke didn't make me angry. First, they teased me like a normal human being who was worthy of a prank. They did it with humor and softness in their laughter. It was a safe way of giving an inmate a special send-off that wouldn't get them in trouble for favoring anyone. I felt seen. The second reason I didn't get angry was because I was not a law-breaker, my heart was free and clear. My family was out there waiting for me and I'd never be back.

"Let's see you in these clothes, Baker," War Horse said, handing me a hanger with my ensemble.

A hanger! I am going to be overwhelmed today. I pulled back the curtain to a changing room and stepped inside. There was a small midsize mirror and a chair on which to place my beautiful new clothing. I put on each piece like a bride. First, black underwear with a lace muffin-top band, and an underwire bra. I looked ten years younger. I went from a dust-bowl woman to Roxy Rack. The black top and pants came next, a perfect fit. The ensemble included a pair of new black shoes, soft black socks. I sat down and put them on, luxuriating in the padding of the sole. Last, the turquoise scarf. It was soft and long, with different hues of turquoise and a stripe of black. I stood up to look in the mirror. Except for the gray hair, I looked like myself again—Karen. I made a loose knot in the scarf and leaned into the mirror, noticing my pierced-ear holes had closed. I mentally put that on the to-do list. *A safe prick and thrust will be my version of losing my prison virginity.* I started laughing to myself, hugging my ribs, and rolling my neck in the scarf.

"What's goin' on in there, what's with all the noise?" grumped War Horse.

"I think it's texture overload." I flung the curtain aside and stepped out. War Horse stood, fists on hips, looked me over, and nodded her approval.

"Here's your bus pass, your fifty-dollar food stamp voucher, the money from your savings, and your parole condoms." She looked down at the condoms and sighed, world-weary. "You got a group of people waiting for you outside. Make 'em proud."

It was time to go. But I couldn't leave without pausing to remember Tom and the woman who died alongside him that day. *Please, God...* I didn't know what to pray.

"Six years will never bring them back," I said to War Horse, trying not to cry. "I'll think about them for the rest of my life."

"You should," she said soberly. She sighed and shook her head quickly to clear it. "Get out there, Baker, your family is waiting and they've suffered too."

I moved from the receiving unit toward the gate. I stood at the final door, looking out a window to the parking lot. I could see my friends and family and a mixture of well-wishers from DOC. Crew Boss was talking to Gerry. They were laughing; Crew Boss might be warning Gerry about my driving. Christine and Shane were there talking and laughing with Sam and Audrey. There was Haley, she made it. She promised to graduate a semester early, just to be there. Nikki stood alone, dressed in black, with a black beret. Her hands were folded in front of her, her eyes toward the ground.

I still had one more set of doors before I could leave for good. Frosty, the ice-cold cop from Intake, was manning the outside final door. Full circle. At last, DOC gave an officer the perfect post. Frosty was the ultimate poster-cop to reduce recidivism. *You wanna be a criminal? If you come back, this is the guy you're gonna have to deal with, day after day, year after year.* He used to be so handsome, now he was balding and paunchy. What was that Cleopatra said about karma? In prison, it was fast, and occurred before our eyes. He avoided my eyes, stepped outside, and held the door open.

It's happening.

I stepped across the threshold. My friends and family turned toward me and I walked toward them. I was free.

I fell into the arms of my children. They smelled like the outdoors. We held and hugged. Teary-eyed, I made the circle, hugging Christine, who cried crocodile tears, then Gerry, sniffing and patting my back. Sam broke down and sobbed. His shoulders were so narrow. Audrey held us both. Shane beamed. When I hugged him, I realized he was man-size now.

Crew Boss looked me in the eyes, her blue eyes twinkling, and she hugged me. "Good luck. You'll be all right. You have a nice family."

I looked around at my loyal loving family. "I do." Suddenly, I wanted to go. My family was already loading into cars.

"Let's get the hell outta here!" Sam joked. Car doors slammed. My family had enough of waiting lines and fences, of darkness and heartbreak. I nestled into the back of Christine's car between my daughters. Christine backed up the car slowly, and changed gears into drive. She swiveled her head backward toward us, grinned wickedly, and peeled out.

Our first stop was a café with fresh food, real dairy, and room for a rowdy crowd. Christine's other son, Travis, joined us. It was another hug from a grown child. I sat on a padded chair, in the middle of a smiling table. I placed a snowy white cloth napkin across my lap and petted it like a cat. The waitress looked me in the eyes and asked, please, if she could take my order, then thanked me for doing so. I ordered greens of arugula, chard, and spinach topped with rich bleu cheese dressing. It arrived looking like a garden, tangy and soft. Each bite tasted like a vitamin injection. I ate tomato basil bisque soup that was hot and hung on the spoon, then coated my mouth. I could feel its warmth clear down into my innards.

Our group was noisy, animated with nervous energy. I was released from prison and they were released from waiting for me to get out. Gerry announced that we would be gathering at her house later that day.

"First stop is the parole office," I said. "Then let the festivities begin!"

Most of my family went on to Gerry's. Sam, my daughters, and I drove into Portland. I was required to check in with my parole officer to receive my orders of conduct. These were the requirements of my law-abiding parole: I must live at the address I provided and be prepared for inspection day or night. I must seek employment, never carry a weapon, and obtain written consent to travel. We drove along the right street and I noticed a cluster of ne'er-do-wells loitering around the outside of a building with a grimy entrance in the middle of the block.

"That's gotta be it," I said. "Wait here. This is mine to do." I walked into the building, found the proper office, and checked in at the desk. The clerk was seated behind plexiglass, I assumed for protection from harm more so than germs. "Baker," I said and gave my SID number. Baker was the call to submission. *Baker had to go, sorry, Tom.*

I turned away from the desk and surveyed the crowded lobby. It was mostly men and one woman. It was the first time in years that I stood with a group of men in a small area who were not the staff of DOC. They were a rough bunch. They reminded me of pen pal photos. One man was dressed in State-issued sweats and State-issued gray socks. He was a fresh one, just like me. Would I ever be able to look at gray socks the same way again? The woman was more accurately a teenage girl. She was barely in charge of two very young children and looked like she was ready to give birth to her third. She sat on a plastic chair and hissed at her kids, who were playing on the filthy floor.

The lobby talk was all street slang. Men called women "all kinds of bitches" and talked about their "crew." "Girl," said a man limping toward me, "you can't be waitin' on a PO. You jes' too fine for that." He had lank blond hair and one prominent gold tooth poking out from a sleazy smile. I could smell his breath from four feet away. "You got a place to live, Mama? Where are you from?"

It raised my hackles. I wanted nothing to do with this man or the crushing pain in that room. I couldn't help them. I was still adjusting to wearing an underwire bra and riding in an elevator.

"Karen Baker?" I was saved by a woman holding a folder, who called me by my first and last name.

"Here." I stood in my best posture, wanting to make a good first impression. I had my paperwork and was ready to take notes. I had practiced my introduction speech in my head for days. First, take responsibility...I understand that I must...

But it was just another day and I was just another inmate for her. It was a one-way conversation, her to me. She rattled off the same requirements I had been given in prison before I paroled: remain at the provided address, do not leave the state without permission, and keep all post-prison supervision appointments. Within a few brief minutes, the parole officer (the PO) signed the conduct order and I was released to go for the second time that day. I passed through the lobby with my eyes straight ahead and fled the building. It was time to go home. *Thank you, Gerry.*

When we arrived at Gerry's house, I went straight for the couch and patted either side for my daughters. The weight and the heat of my daughters' bodies tipped slightly toward me. I hugged them again and again. I luxuriated in textures: my daughters' clothing, their hair, the nap of the couch. I raked my toes through the thick rug underfoot and stroked the fur of Gerry's friendly cat, Parsifal.

We nibbled on the planned menu of all the food I missed and I dreamed of while in prison. I sliced a mango with a sharp knife. No one took me to the Hole. I shared food with my family and did not get celled in.

"This is for my sisters inside." I held up a slice of freshly baked bread, slathered it with cold butter using a heavy silver knife, and bit into it like a cave woman. The crisp crust was a battle. I scraped the roof of my mouth on the way to the tender, soft inside. "And this too." I held up a cloth napkin and wiped my lips and took a sip of sparkling water, on ice.

I took my time eating. I could set the food down, talk or hug, and come back to it. If I chose, I could reheat it or save it for later. I thought of Blondie. *What do I miss? The fridge, just standing in front of the fridge.*

The day continued at a relaxed pace, the mood one of relief. We had all made it safely over the finish line. I was radiant, gazing over my family gathered in the room. Everyone was smiling. I noticed Audrey holding and fussing over Nikki and Haley. I could tell they had established a bond in my absence. I was grateful. Shane and Sam talked tools, Travis told jokes. tine flitted about between groups bussing dishes as Gerry ruled the kitchen. The next family get-together would be Haley's graduation from college. The plan had been in place for months. The entire Campbell Clan would attend.

At the end of the day, my family left for their own homes and I would remain in mine. In the morning they would go back to the routines they had been following for the past six years and I would begin a new one. I tenderly hugged my precious daughters goodbye and watched the two of them walk down the sidewalk. It was the first time I could watch them leave and get into the car and drive away instead of being forced to stay seated and wave to them behind the glass of the sally port. They didn't cry this time.

Sam and Audrey were the last to leave. I walked my dad to the door. He looked exhausted, but he still twinkled. "This felt more like a celebration than a release," he said. "It a was positive experience today. I had no thought about justice or wasted time." He shrugged.

"It happened. It could have happened to any of us." As he leaned in to hug me, he felt shorter and more brittle. He stood up and found his posture. "Your release is not just another chapter, Karen; it's a whole new book."

I took that in, memorizing his determined face. *It was a whole new book.* Nothing about my first day of freedom felt anything like a continuation of my prison sentence. It was a privilege to be alive and relish the details of the senses restored. Tomorrow I would have the freedom of choice to create a new purposeful routine. I thought of Tom and the woman in the other car. *I can't bring you back, but I will do right by you.*

One delicacy remained on my first day of freedom—a bath. The guest bathroom designated for me was spacious. The large oval spa tub had armrests and a golden faucet. I turned on the water and opened the tops of the bath bubbles and scents that Gerry had laid out for me. I chose lavender, hoping it would mellow me out so I could sleep. Gerry rapped on the door.

"Wait!" she said and scampered off, shouting from down the hall, "I got you a brand-new, great, big, *mumfy* towel." She came back triumphantly and handed me a light blue cloud. I hugged it to my chest and rubbed my cheeks on the softness.

"We did it," I told her tenderly. She waved a victory fist and walked back downstairs to straighten up the kitchen.

I hung up the towel, turned off the water, and slid out of a robe Gerry had left for me. I sat on the edge of the tub and stirred the warm water, sending the bubbles to the other end of the tub. Then I dipped my legs into the warm water. *Ahhhh.* I looked down at my fifty-three-year-old body. The scars were less angry and my parts still worked, no complaints. I slid into the warm, scented water, sinking until the bubbles crackled in my ears. The tub was long enough for most of me to float. I submerged my head underwater, blocking out the sounds of the house. I heard my pulse low and quiet. *Yes, this is real.* I sat up and rested my head back on the edge of the rim. I did not think about prison that night or compare experiences. The mind was quiet and the senses ruled.

I stayed in the tub until my head was hot from the warm water and steam. The only bubbles that remained were huddling by the faucet. I dipped underneath the water one last time for a fresh finish and stood. I was woozy. I held on to the tiled wall and stepped over the rim of the tub like a fragile elder. The cool spacious room revived me. I reached for my "mumfy" towel and wrapped it around my back and held it with arms crossed in front. I lingered there, with my head lowered in the light blue cloud.

I dried off with my cloud, stood in the nude, and brushed my teeth, put on the robe, and crossed the hallway to *my* bedroom. The bed awaited. I climbed up the impressive wooden bed frame onto a sumptuous queen-size mattress with an obscene number of pillows. I lay on the bed in the star position. I stretched out my arms and legs and still did not hang over the side. I rolled over without having to do it in a tight spin of twenty-seven inches. I stuffed pillows all around me and under my knees. Then I pulled up the freshly laundered sheet, smoothed out the satin comforter, and settled in. *Gratitude.*

The next morning I woke to the smell of freshly brewed coffee and the sound of Gerry puttering in the kitchen and talking to the cats, Parsifal and Gawain, her knights in furry armor. Out the window was a view of the morning sky, still coming into its colors. I laughed, I cried, I praised. *I made it.*

It was my first full day of freedom, and I hit the ground running. My sister had brought a box of my personal documents and a stored tub of essential clothing. I held my breath and peeked inside, hoping she tossed out the black travel wear I wore at the sentencing. *Gone.* I gathered my notes from my LIFE class for post-prison planning and headed downstairs.

"What's your plan today?" she asked.

"I got pages of plans," I said. I laid out the timeline I had crafted before I released, starting from Release Day to four months out.

"Wow. Impressive."

"Not really, I had the time. Kept my feet on the ground," I said as we looked over the list.

"Color hair," Gerry stabbed at the list. "Already booked it for you. You talked about it while you were still in prison. It's a good idea, it's a fresh start."

She was right.

"You have an appointment at noon."

"Thank you," I said, beyond grateful.

A few hours later, I sat in the styling chair, this time as a client while the cape was draped around my neck. The background sounds were similar to the prison salon: music, laughter, and the conversations between women. My stylist was quick and efficient. Some people are better at this than others, and certainly better at it than I was. While the color was processing, I picked up a current fashion magazine. It was intact instead of torn up for collages. I turned a stiff page and there was a Prada perfume sample. The time I celled with Top Dog came rushing back. I could see her ripping through a new magazine, ripping out the girly perfumes and tossing them on my bunk while I sat hunched over, wanting so badly to pet the dog. I felt my heart close in. I was scared that the slightest trigger from the past would set me off and I wouldn't be able to control how I felt. Just then the stylist came by to check on the color and asked could she bring me a cup of tea?

"That would be lovely," I said. *Stay present, Karen. Here is a wonderful chance to use your Zen practice.* Top Dog was a memory.

When the stylist was done, she spun me around toward Gerry.

"Remarkable," said Gerry about my new look. "There's the Karen I know." The stylist covered my white-brown hair by weaving in blond and brown. She cut three inches off the length for a more youthful look. I smiled in the mirror at myself. I was spunky.

As we walked to Gerry's car, I was still buoyant, but Gerry was pensive. "Yesterday when you were processing through," she said, "I was scared for you to come out. When I saw you in your regular clothes, I worried about you. I worried that you might have trouble adjusting, and to what cost? I wondered if you would lose your verve and your joie de vivre, and perhaps be a totally different person."

I responded: "I had a vivid memory of prison today in the salon. I coached myself using my Zen practice so I wouldn't spiral into some dark corner. It worked, Gerry. The Zen practice, church, and all I studied is right here." I patted my heart. Then it dawned on me. "The searching wasn't just a distraction to pass the time. I was seeking something that existed outside prison and all over the world." I stopped walking and looked up at the sky. "I have been connected to the outside world in that way for years." I chuckled. "And today when I needed it, it worked! Ha, one in a row."

Gerry nodded slowly, not ready to let go of her concern. "It will be a process, Karen. Think of what you have been through. After the accident, the medicine made you so sick. You looked like you walked out of Auschwitz. You aged ten years. The doctors told us you would never be the same. You would never ski, or dance. Look at you now. It's a miracle. You are still blooming. If anyone can make something out of this, it is you. But you have your work cut out for you."

Busy is good. It was the mantra that had got me through six years of prison. In the weeks that followed my parole, I woke in the morning and I worked on my release plan. Looking back, I see it as a frenzy of activity, scratching off items on the to-do list, trying to prove to others but mostly to myself that I was still a productive person in society, that I would not be a drain on my family.

I gathered my personal documents and went back to the bank that held my one hundred dollars and reactivated it. I bought a planner and vitamins. I went to Dress for Success, a nonprofit that provides clothing, shoes, and accessories for women who are in transition, and selected an interview outfit. I bought my maiden name back again. It cost over three hundred dollars and was worth every cent. Goodbye, Baker. I was a Campbell again.

I rode a bus to Living Yoga. Pearl was there, dressed in the clothing of a yogini and looking settled into a new lifestyle. She walked with confidence as we toured the facility and took pride in the simple work she was assigned. I was invited to stay for a class. The teacher was one of the instructors who had come to the prison. I fell easily into the poses alongside the women and men who attended the class. Just like prison, that day I was just a woman in a triangle pose, like the hundreds of women who have been practicing yoga for thousands of years. After class, as promised, I was given a mat. After all the years of living in granite-hard surroundings, I chose a soft pink mat with extra padding.

An important part of my release plan was to follow up with the Mercy Corps LIFE class contacts. I made an appointment with a non-profit health clinic for a checkup. I rode a bus to the Mercy Corps reentry center and checked out the suggestions for employment. I was directed to go to the unemployment office. I found the buses that would take me there, and once inside I realized this would be a long day of going through the hoops. Waiting and being told where to go and what to do was old hat for a felon. All of the employment options required computer skills just to apply. Finally directed to the right desk in the right department, I learned that access for jobs information was on computers. My skills were pathetic. It took all day for me just to enter myself in the database.

Later that evening I told Gerry that I needed to bump up my computer skills if I wanted to get a job.

"Have a seat, see if you can fumble around on my laptop and I'll cook," she said. She showed me how to find the Internet icon and search. I Googled all kinds of things: golden retrievers, fashion, and ocean beaches. I peeked up at her from time to time to see if she was chopping or stirring. She looked happy having someone to cook for.

"Oh, I gotta check on the boys!" I told her. "Here they are, The Rolling Stones."

"They're all still alive. It's remarkable," said Gerry.

"Hey, they might tour this year! Listen to this. Keith Richards says, 'Who said it should stop, and who said when? Only we will know when it comes to an end, with a crashing halt.'" The article went on to say that there had been persistent reports that the sexagenarians were going to pack it in. "'Not so,' Richards explained: 'We're looking forward to working.' Whoopie!" I cried.

Gerry stood in place with her hand on her hip, looking at me with a droll expression. "People say they look old but I say they've looked old for a very long time."

I was so glad they were still alive. "I'm comin' to see you, Keith! You guys stay healthy. I need to start a bucket list, Gerry."

"You are hard at work," she said. "You never take a day off."

"I don't feel like I can. It's not just to let my family off the hook. I want to do right by Tom and the other woman in the accident."

Gerry struck the pondering pose. "Maybe the hypervigilant plan is the way you can be in control after so many years without any control at all."

"I want to move away from the identity of an ex-con. Truth is, I feel like I'm walking around with an ex-con stamp on my forehead and everyone I meet on the street and in doctors' offices or the grocery store can tell I am fresh out of the joint. Sometimes I worry that it could all be a joke, an illusion, and I will wake up back in prison."

"Do you ever think about the guards?" Gerry asked.

"I try not to. I met a few who were human beings and treated me as a person with potential. Sarge made me laugh, and Big Buck and Bear. They were the only ones who asked us questions about our lives after parole and whether we were prepared."

"What about Good Cop?" she asked.

"Oh my god. She cried along with us when Haley visited." I pictured her on the bench in the corridor, listening to the woman who just lost her brother. "Those types of DOC workers made me feel like myself again, like a contributing member of society, a person of worth.

I tried to repay them by being worthy of their trust. I wanted them to believe that I owned my crime and was willing to work to make amends." I shook my head. "Still, and maybe I'm just too fresh out of prison, but I never want to see them again. If I did, I would be Baker again."

The heaviness returned in an instant. I buried my face in my hands and went into a tunnel. I felt the ball and chain again. *Baker.* Then a shaft of light. I thought of Bear calling me "Miss Baker." I remember how dignified it made me feel. He was a decent man. Perhaps one day, when I was reestablished and my confidence had returned, I would run into Big Buck. I pictured his eyes staring over his glasses. I would like to ask him an opinion of a current event. First, he would grunt out a laugh before he said anything. Then, "What do *you* think? What would you do about it?" And Good Cop. She had been the one who encouraged me to write. She showed compassion for my daughters.

Gerry had been quiet while I was chained to my memories of prison.

"I would love to see Good Cop."

"I still think about them," she muttered shaking her head. She suffered too. For her and all my other visitors, they had their own traumatic memories of prison. *There just has got to be a better way for justice to be served without dragging people, their families, friends, and community down into the abyss.*

"I brought this up because I ran across something that might help." Gerry was leaning on the counter with both hands. She looked concerned. "I put it up in your room." That night, I found she had left something written by Bill Clinton and published in *Mandela: The Authorized Portrait.* Clinton asked Mandela why he'd invited his jailers to his inauguration and whether he was still angry with them. Mandela responded that he realized if he continued to be angry, they would still be keeping him prisoner. He smiled at Clinton and said, "But I wanted to be free, and so I let it go."

It was easier to let go of my prison experience when surrounded by good friends and family. The Campbell Clan gathered together to attend Haley's graduation. It was the first post-prison experience on my bucket list, which had four entries:

1. Attend Haley's college graduation with my family.
2. Go the beach and call out the names of the women still inside.
3. See The Rolling Stones before they die.
4. Get a golden retriever of my own.

Haley had graduated early to be in Oregon for my release but would "walk" that June. I was granted permission from my parole officer to attend. It was the first truly happy gathering for our whole extended family. Both my daughters committed to college-earned scholarships and loans, and finished their degrees without my presence or financial help. The whole Campbell Clan, plus Haley and Nikki's father, Nate, and Trent and Trent's mother, sat in a long row on a cliff overlooking the ocean. These were Nikki and Haley's primary people. Their father was their primary parent. Christine and Audrey were their mother figures. Sam provided the wisdom and magic. I was their mother. There was no doubt about that, but I functioned more like a guest to the ordered routines of the rest of the group.

The sky was blue with wisps of clouds and double halos around the sun. I closed my eyes and thought of the mothers inside and outside prison walls. I thanked God for my privilege to be in that seat on that day. When I opened my eyes, I saw Haley take the stage and prance back to her seat. *The future is in good hands, certainly better hands.*

After Haley's graduation, while still in Santa Cruz, I asked Christine if we could go to the beach and see the ocean. "It would take care of bucket list, number two. I promised the Lifers." Christine agreed easily.

I had promised the women in Coffee Creek that I would go to the beach on the Oregon coast, stand in the ocean, and call out their names to the surf. Originally, I made the promise to the Lifers but I was moved to include my young teachers Celly and Mittens, Five Alive, Blondie, and Sweetie Pie. While I was incarcerated and the subject of the beach came up, the women's voices grew soft, their bodies relaxed and their breathing slowed. They stared out into space and sighed when they said the words "waves," "sand," "tide," "sun," "seagulls," and "wind."

"Go stand in the surf for me," said Sinful.

"I promise."

"When you remember all you have been through, remember to forgive yourself." Sinful's face was serious. "Go write your book. You are no help to others when you are powerless."

Christine understood my desire to speak to the waves. She and I discovered that when we stood by the ocean, we both called out to our mother. "Every time I find a whole sand dollar, I pretend she is sending it to me," I told her.

tine's eyes filled with tears. "She loved looking for shells."

"You never outgrow missing your mother." We both sank into our memories for a while.

Haley suggested we go to Davenport Beach, just north of Santa Cruz. The beach was at the bottom of a high cliff. The path led to a white, curving beach. A stream formed from a former railroad tunnel and ran to the shore. The cliff walls were white and covered in green moss. We walked together for a few minutes and took some pictures, then I set off on my mission to speak to the waves.

Before and after prison, like a pilgrim, I sought the ocean for truth. Heartache or joy, the ocean takes you in and sends waves in ceaseless cleansing. Acceptance and Angel's peace. I took off my shoes and stood in the cool blue, green, and gold water. I closed my eyes and listened to the surf and the birds for Sinful. I soaked up the sun. I thought of the women on J Unit. I started on the bottom tier and went through the unit. I thanked Mittens and Celly. *You helped me when I was so scared.* I thought of Tizzy and Sweetie Pie's victories over cancer.

Then my thoughts turned to my mother. *Mama, I miss you, you died too soon. You would be so proud of your grandchildren.* I called out the name of the woman who died in the car accident. I called out to my daughters. I pictured the girls, trapped in their mother's nightmare, tumbling, falling. *My actions threw you both out into the world. I caused unimaginable pain. I failed to protect you. It was you who had to protect me. You never really told me about how much you suffered. You were afraid I wouldn't survive: first in the hospital and then in prison. I will do everything I can to live a good life and earn your trust. Take your time. I can wait.*

The emotional work would have been crippling in any other setting but the ocean washed me clean and encouraged me to take another step into the waves.

Tom. I stood there a long time before I could begin to think. The emotions swirled, overpowering. I felt loneliness and futility, but not self-pity or condemnation. *You wouldn't have it, would you?* Then, I heard him laugh, at first out over the breakers then all around me. I was illuminated. It was as if suddenly I understood everything. I understood the sand and the sky. I understood how Tom's atoms moved apart and reformed from the river into ocean waves, sunlight, and a laughing seagull and the mist above. Tom was the excitement and brilliance of the green flash and would shine forever, laughing. *You forgive me.* I stood before the unceasing, loving waves until I was all cried out. I stood there until I was at peace for Tom.

Bucket list numbers one and two accomplished, it was time to find a job, save money, and move into my own place. I started with my old job, a national medical company. My former boss was thrilled to have me back. She was heartbroken for me after the accident. Years ago, when she put me back on the schedule after the accident, I looked like the worst physical therapist assistant in the world. I was the last person from whom you would seek advice about your physical well-being. I was bone-thin, peaked, and had a cast on my arm. When I introduced myself to my patients, they would look at me, confused and repulsed.

I was scheduled to begin orientation to return to work, but then my former boss called me with bad news. I would not be eligible for rehire. "We use a national human resources company and you could not pass their background check. I am so sorry. Most of the big companies are doing this now. You might run into this on your next attempt."

She wished me luck and I threw myself into finding a job. She was right, background checks were the norm. Formerly, background checks were for agencies researching senators and police chiefs, but now background checks were for landscapers and housecleaners. It was the same routine every time: "You have excellent skills and references, you seem eager. We would love to offer you a position."

Then I would say, "I would love to work for your company but I need to be completely honest with you about something that happened in my past." They would look at me like they'd heard it all. What could you have done? "You look like my mom," one woman laughed. Then I'd lower the boom and tell them a frank version of my history without adornment. I watched the smile slide off their face. They'd stare at their desk or concentrate on rolling a pen between their fingers.

A typical response to my crime was, "That could have been me! I have driven home after drinking." I knew people were shaken. They looked at me and I could see them watching their lives flash by their eyes. Maybe it was my role to shake up some of these people, make them think twice about ladies' night and margaritas.

But regardless of their shock, sympathies, or apologies, a criminal record closes the door on job placement. Finding a job was daunting and humiliating. No wonder so many parolees went back to the corner to sell their bodies or drugs.

I was determined to keep trying, though, and about one month after I released from prison, I got lucky. The private owner of a premier physical therapy clinic in Portland gave me a chance. The employer who hired me was a humanitarian. She made it her mission to volunteer and lift up struggling people from all over the world. She was a volunteer for Doctors Without Borders and Habitat for Humanity. Her physical therapy staff were volunteers for the dancers of the Oregon

Ballet Theatre. She was esteemed in her community, and sin
Mercy Corps Northwest people.

Once I had laid out my story in the interview, she ans
with a tragedy of her own. While I was still in prison, she had hir
bookkeeper who embezzled from her business. She was sentenced to
Coffee Creek. I had seen this woman in Minimum. Angel Boss wanted
to hire me anyway. She was a wonder. How could her heart not be
bitter or punishing? How did she turn the other cheek and give me a
chance? With all the choices and applicants, why me?

But Angel Boss's lawyer, who led the criminal investigation of
the bookkeeper, advised against offering me the job. She pushed back.
The lawyer insisted she practice due diligence and investigate me fully.
First, I had to dig into my plastic tubs and reread the accident report
and my hospital records. Then I had to pass this on, giving her a full
disclosure and gruesome details of my accident. I had to talk frankly
about the presence of alcohol in my past. I had to provide additional
character references and voluntarily attend a substance abuse program. I followed every order. I wanted her to feel confident about her
decision to hire me.

The application process had taken weeks to complete. My children were involved as references. It was an emotional walk backward.
The details were revived, not in our chosen narratives but the stark
dreadful details that we were trying to put behind us.

Finally, the application process was over and Angel Boss officially offered me the job. The lawyer advised her to remain vigilant.
She had nothing to worry about. I committed to becoming the best
employee she had ever hired. It was the least I could do.

From the application and job seeking process, the history of the
accident and its consequences became current again. It required my

daughters and me to pull off the scabs that we had formed. There was tension between us. I was singularly focused on the job, wanting to establish myself and win back their trust. I clung to the idea that if I had a job and an apartment of my own, I would be myself again and have something to offer. It was a grave error.

I should have made more time for them instead of focusing on my agenda. Nikki and Haley had been waiting for their mom to be free. They wanted to show me who they had become, both in the grand scheme of things and in the small details. They wanted me to spend time and get to know their boyfriends. By then, they had been together for six or seven years. They wanted to show me where they worked and what was their favorite restaurant. In my absence, they had created a family of friends, and I hardly knew any of them. My focus on reestablishing myself was the beginning of a second tragedy between my daughters and me.

Blind to a well-rounded approach of reentering society, I continued to build my platform to reestablish myself. My new job was in downtown Portland and would be an hour-long MAX train ride each way. I needed to find an apartment close by, just on the other side of the river in an affordable neighborhood. I was a single bus ride away from Nikki and Nate.

The search for a new dwelling brought back the vicious cycle of background checks. I was denied three times. Then I found an exception. I found an apartment that was owned by an elderly woman. The application looked like it was printed on a mimeograph. It did not ask *the* question: Have you ever been convicted of a criminal offense? My job as a parolee was to jump through hoops, find the lucky loopholes, and hold on gratefully to the opportunities that came my way. I got the apartment.

The apartment was a one bedroom in an older building in a renovated neighborhood. I could walk to a cluster of shops, restaurants, and a Whole Foods store. Using the money I had saved in prison, I bought a long couch where Haley could sleep if she came for a visit.

Gerry cooked our last meal together. "You got out on April Fool's Day and in three months you have a job, an apartment, and a lifestyle," said Gerry. "I am overwhelmed with respect."

I smiled at my friend. "I know this all affected you deeply," I said.

"It affected all of us. I talked about your accident in my writing classes when it was relevant," she said. "I noticed the change when I visited you in prison. You have a lot more depth. You take life more seriously now. You have spent a great deal of time reflecting on what happened." Gerry leaned over the counter where I sat on the stool. "Time to move on. What about dating?"

"Ugh!" I groaned. "Dating terrifies me. It's a strange mix. On one hand, I don't feel worthy and on the other hand, with all the change I've gone through, I doubt they'd be worthy of me."

"Go for a mate with a little maturity next time, will ya?" Gerry slapped the counter and grinned, then went back to stirring her famous Hungarian mushroom soup.

"I still believe in love," I said quietly, rubbing behind Parsifal's ears.

I packed up my tubs and moved to the apartment thirty-one blocks away from the river. On my daily commute to my new job, I rode the bus across the neighborhoods on the east side of Portland, crossing the Willamette River on the Burnside Bridge, which was three blocks long and, at the time, was the epicenter of homelessness. The bridge emptied into the roughest part of Portland. This was where the Salvation Army emergency shelter was located. It stood alongside soup kitchens, Catholic outreach, and Mercy Corps Northwest headquarters. The neighborhood to the right had the worst gang activity. About three blocks into the city was a large building that provided housing, rehab, and basic medical services. I learned about it while still in prison. As a parolee, if you were lucky enough to be placed, this is where you would start over again.

Each morning as I rode the bus across the bridge, I would see people rolling up their blankets and gathering their bags, tarps, or scraps of cardboard and loading them into shopping carts or backpacks. And every morning I would see the face of a woman I'd known in prison. Some were almost unrecognizable. They looked worse as a free people living on the streets than as prison inmates.

One morning, I sat in a window seat on the bus on the lookout for women who made it out the gate. As we crossed the bridge, I saw the same woman I saw the day before, rolling up her blue tarp. She looked exhausted. We began the ride up the hill to the more affluent neighborhoods and stopped in front of the rehab building. Standing on the corner was a tall woman. *It's the Enforcer!* She stood on the corner looking confused, as though she didn't know which direction to go. I couldn't take my eyes off her. She had been a mighty warrior with long golden curls who walked with poise and purpose. Her hair was shorn, as if she'd cut it all off herself. She was pale and thin and stood with stooped shoulders, crossing her arms as if for warmth. My bus began to move, but she remained on the corner, just standing, with nowhere to go.

Our family spent Thanksgiving together at Sam's house in Talent, Oregon. Audrey went east to her biological family's house, which was for the best. We had dogs and people everywhere. I asked Sam if there was a music store in Talent. I told him about the moving phone call I had received while working at the DMV.

"That closed several years ago," Sam said. "I used to wander in there just to poke around, nice guy." I wondered if he moved to New Orleans.

My girls were cautious around me, watching me. I craved their touch and wanted the connection we used to have on our trips to New York and San Francisco. I wanted them to fight over me a little and seek me out. But everything was off. I powered on through the weekend unskillfully. I entertained with stories of the Clink or reentry, trying not to be nervous. But in my desire for connection, I carried on more like Auntie Mame than their mother.

I noticed that they sought out each other first. They joked with Gramps and giggled and hugged Christine. I felt like I had walked on in the wrong scene. I wanted the deep connection we used to have and I wanted it right away. But I had to step back. They had made it through. We all survived. *Let them be.*

In between full-time work, and trying to be present with family and friends, I kept in contact with Blondie and Sweetie Pie through Facebook or the occasional phone call. They both seemed to be doing well, and though I never thought I'd want to maintain friendships with the women from prison, I realized that I did.

Blondie and I arranged a lunch date for four former inmates. It would be Blondie, Blondie's longtime friend who had served time, Hippie Chick, and me. The day came, and Blondie, her friend, and

I gathered at the Olive Garden, something nice enough but not too expensive. Hippie Chick was late.

We waited and watched out the window. Nearly an hour later, we had gone ahead and ordered. During the Endless Salad course, I saw a woman in a peacock-colored dress and five-inch neon green platform shoes running across the lawn to the entrance of the restaurant. *She's here.* Hippie Chick's black hair fanned behind her, like a wild child in the wind.

She stomped in fearlessly on those Elton Johns, panting and apologetic. "Dudes!" she cried and yanked back her chair. She dove into the salad, and in between bites, she roared and laughed her way through what sounded like a made-up story about being lost. At the end of the meal, we walked out the front door, and Hippie Chick's ride was outside. Behind the wheel of a souped-up muscle car was a steamy-looking man. As they roared off, Blondie's friend huffed out a laugh. "Do you think she was high?"

Blondie and I didn't answer, though I'd wondered the same thing. *Please let me be wrong.* I hoped she was just the free-spirited Hippie Chick I knew. Maybe the costume gave her power. *Dude, I've missed you.* That's when I realized I had not laughed, really hard, since I laughed with her in a damned prison.

On my way to work, I would still keep watch for paroled women on the bridge and read the paper, trying to update myself with current affairs. In the lifestyle section, I learned that the Stones were coming back to the United States on tour.

Bucket list number three: See the Rolling Stones. I made it out in time. All four of them were still alive and they were touring. They were scheduled to play a single concert in San Diego because some fat cat hired them for a private party, so they added a concert. My cousin Drew was a huge fan, as well, and we agreed to go together. We flew down to San Diego and walked into that huge venue. The set list included all the favorites. Mick strutted around the stage like he was in his twenties. Keith's first cords and Charlie Watts's cowbell in "Honky Tonk Woman" had the crowd leaping to its feet singing "Ya, ya, ya, WHOO!" It was as if no time had passed at all. I don't know what I was worried about. The way they performed, those boys will never die.

The concert was a quick trip that gave me a chance to see Haley. After graduation from college, she moved back to San Diego, which made sense. This is where she finished growing up. Her boyfriend and friends were there. Her dad was close by. Trent, Haley, Drew, and I went out for fresh seafood near the beach. Haley and Trent brought their English cream golden retriever along, and the three of them looked like a postcard of Southern California living. She was a California girl now, not an Oregonian.

I had been out of prison for about a year and a half. Sometimes I would go without thinking back on the days of incarceration for two days in a row. Other times it was a matter of hours. I was beginning to lose the shuck and jive of an over-apologetic felon. The Ex Con stamp on my head was fading. In a simple human encounter with a waitress, she looked me in the eye and said thank you. I stammered out a rusty you're welcome. There were many small things about reentry that awaken memories purposely forgotten and buried. One day at Rite Aid, I saw the plastic sandals I wore in prison. In a flashback, I heard the echo slap in the tomb-like corridor and felt my callused pinched toes gripping slick plastic. The shame and dread are written on the body.

"Excuse me." A woman's voice resuscitated me in the shoe section of Rite Aid. She was smiling at me apologetically, trying to pass with a full moon, pregnant belly.

"Oh!" I turned toward the shelves of miserable sandals. But life pulled me forward.

"Thank you," she said, smiling as she passed.

"You're welcome!" I nearly shouted as I bubbled back to the present day.

Early on in my incarceration, I didn't think I would return to Coffee Creek, not even as a visitor, not ever. But Tammy asked me to be a guest speaker at the Cosmetology graduation in the Medium/Maximum facility visiting room, and I heard myself say yes. And when Tammy told me Angel was doing the decorations, I figured that alone was worth a panic attack.

I went back and, like my visitors, I had to be approved on paper and pass through the fence lines and metal detectors. I stood in the same waiting area where my daughters were ogled. *This is where they stood, this is what they did for me.*

Tammy greeted me with a hug. I was to wait outside the visiting room as a surprise guest speaker. While I waited with the DOC staff, they grilled me with questions.

"Are you staying out of trouble?"

"Yes!" I was indignant.

"We've seen too many come back, Baker," said an officer, shaking her head. The other officer on duty nodded and puffed out his cheeks and blew out hot air in a long noisy exhale. I could understand their mistrust. I had seen the women in the relativistic turnstile just as they had.

"It's Campbell now," I corrected gently. "I went back to my maiden name. I don't want to be Baker ever again." I tugged at my black skirt and adjusted my fitted top. I dressed up in a simple black Calvin Klein dress and had my hair touched up, not to show off, but to show hope. Then the door swung open and I was introduced.

The speech told the truth about the struggles on the other side. I told them to stop consoling themselves with Little Debbie snack cakes because even with a career in cosmetology, they would need every penny. I told them that if they had never prayed or meditated, it was time to start. "Clean up your act and clear the way for a fresh start. You will need to hit the ground running with a plan A, a plan B—maybe the whole alphabet."

I finished the speech, giving credit to Tammy and the program. "Tammy reminded us of our worth and created a program of excellence and job security. The program and the skills are rock solid. The question is, are you? Have you done the inner work? It's easy to make proclamations about your intentions when you're locked up in here. Do yourself and the program justice."

While giving the speech I scanned the audience and found Angel in the back row. She had transformed the visiting room to Paris in springtime. She wrapped pillars to look like the Eiffel Tower and gardens.

I went to her immediately after the speech. I was now a visitor, not an inmate. Because of that, I was allowed to hug her. It was the first time I did so. She felt solid and slim. It was so good to see her blue eyes smiling back at me. We toured her artwork, then the women inmates tugged on her for attention. I had been worried about her.

Was she lonely? Was she keeping up her spirit? But I could see from the attention in the room that she was beloved, as I had found her to be. We were allowed one more hug and a brief cry before I left. This time it was me behind the sally port waving goodbye. I walked out through the metal detector, out the doors, and through the fences lines. *I didn't fall apart.* I recalled one of Keisei's Zen teachings: *Be curious. Sometimes our most dreaded emotions come out with a poof instead of a bang.*

There was no denying the tension between my daughters and me; we were unnatural around each other. Emotions began leaking out all over the family. Holidays meant expectations and disappointments. I had become accustomed to saying what sounded less offensive, but I constantly worried that I would offend someone.

The girls were relaxed with Sam and Christine. They chatted happily in conversations they had been having for years. Sam would ask about new developments in Haley's job or Nikki's jewelry business. Christine would ask about Nate's latest music release.

I remember standing in the room like an outsider, trying to interject comments about which I knew nothing. Then Christine would sense my anxiety and try to include me. The conversation became awkward. It ended when one of us escaped to another part of the house. The girls and I were frail and unhappy, and I didn't know how to fix us. Could we be fixed? Would we ever have the loving, easy relationships we had before I fell?

I thought of Sinful often and I knew I needed to see her. I had been paroled seven years when I went back to Coffee Creek to see her. I stood outside the prison waiting my turn to be buzzed into the gates.

Meanwhile, I watched the officers as the morning shift exchanged duties with evening shift. I kept a running count of how many I knew and how many were fresh faces. The count was one to ten, nine new staff members. Was it because the prison was that crowded? Or because the job was soul robbing? No one recognized me. Why would they? Baker wore prison blues and had salt and pepper hair. As they walked in and out of the gate, I watched their expressions. Most looked straight ahead, faces impassive. One said hello to other guards leaving their shift and joked to the visitors, "At least it's not raining."

Once admitted into the waiting room, I thought about the lines of Nikki's poem "The Visit":

> I do not talk to anyone unless it is to tell them how
> to use the lockers,
>
> because those sons of bitches steal your money
>
> faster than any criminal is physically capable
>
> and I know that at least 95 percent of visitors are
> living in poverty
>
> so lost quarters are worth talking for.

I imagined her and Haley and all my other visitors enduring this unseen part of the visits. That they came again and again was a testament not of who I was but who they were. I placed those damned quarters into the locker and assisted a confused woman fumbling with the keypad. She was elderly and primly dressed. She startled when I spoke.

I made sure I had worn a sports bra that had no snaps or metal, I had taken off my shoes, and was prepared to place my plastic bag of quarters and State ID into the bowl. Then I saw Chappie exiting from her morning shift.

"Chappie," I called, moving toward her. She smiled at me, kindly, but her face said, *Do I know this person?* Then, *Yes, I do. I know her, I like her, who is she?* Then, the light went on.

"Baker!"

We walked toward each other with huge grins on our faces.

"It's Campbell now, took my maiden name back."

"Oh, fer God sakes. You're here to see someone! Who are you seeing?"

"Sinful."

"Oh good, good!" She was still smiling. Then her mouth flattened and she leaned toward me as her brows came together. "This doesn't bother you?" she whispered "Coming back? Are you OK?"

I shrugged. "I will never do *anything* to put me back inside, so I have nothing to worry about. Besides—" I looked toward the visiting room. "There are live people in there. Sinful and Angel gave me certain instructions, to do certain things for them, watch the stars and the moon, go to the ocean, It's a part of my bucket list. One by one, I intend to get them accomplished."

We said goodbye and I moved toward the visiting room. I waited in the sally port, then checked in at the desk. I wondered if the alarms would ring or, for some reason, I would be turned away, but I gave my name and was instructed to sit at an assigned table like everyone else. I waited quite a while and, meanwhile, looked around the room. I recognized a few of the women inmates and we nodded at each other. I had a genuine feeling of affection toward them but at the same time I wanted to weep. I felt the heaviness of incarceration. *Pull up, Karen. Breathe, count.* I kept my eyes on the door, waiting for my friend.

"Who are you waiting for?" I jumped to the question asked by the visiting sergeant. I told her Sinful's legal name and she returned to her desk and the phone. I could hear her say, "She's been here for about twenty minutes. OK." She hung up the phone and came over to apologize. She was embarrassed about the delay.

"It's a finite place. It's a wonder she can't be found. She's still here, isn't she? There's not some sort of tunnel or something, is there?" I asked this with all seriousness but added a touch of quirky-fidget, just to mess with her a little bit. It restored my confidence. This officer had no idea who I was. All the better.

The door swung open and there she was. She was lifting both her shoulders and grinning as she hustled toward me. I stood and we embraced in a swirl of emotions: joy, incredulity, and relief. Both of us stepped back quickly as we were programmed to do. Against all odds, she looked great. Her skin was flawless. The lack of sunshine made her look ten years younger than me. We fell into our conversation pattern easily. Sinful sat perched on the edge of her chair, gesturing and waving her arms in a ramped-up double circle salute. She told me about her volunteer position for hospice, and despite the competition for programs, she was trying to take part in anything that came her way. She remained engaged and fearless. She had connected with her family and was now a grandmother. We laughed and ate chocolate candy bars as she told me about her plans to become eligible to go before a parole board. At the end of our visit, I told her, "Never give up."

"I won't." She shook her head vigorously, shaking her Viking mane. "Go do your job, watch that moon for me."

"I think of you every time, without fail." I felt my throat swell. "When I look at the moon and the stars, I say thank you for the privilege of being alive, one more day." I looked into her deep brown eyes thinking she may be incarcerated but she still added value to the world and would always be a mentor to me. I felt my throat swell but I didn't want to burden her with my tears of frustration over her being locked up. She was the one looking at me with courage. "I think of you every time I watch Forrest Gump."

"Peas and carrots, Jenny."

After working for Angel Boss and living in Portland for two years my stepfather, Marshall, passed away. Before he died, Christine went back to Minnesota for a visit and busted him out of the nursing home for one more rally with his coffee gang. Marshall's condominium had not been sold. Christine told me that nothing had changed since our mother was alive. Because of Marshall's poor eyesight, he kept order so he could live independently.

"I opened the kitchen drawer and sure enough, one fork, one spoon, and one knife. Peanut butter and mac and cheese in the cupboard. All Mom's things still in the same place." Christine began to cry. "It was like she could walk in the door at any minute."

He was alert until the end. But one day he was wheelchair-walking in the hallway and suddenly told the nurse, "I think I'm dying." He went back to his room and died peacefully that afternoon.

Sam, on the other hand, began having memory lapses. Audrey sent up the red warning flag, stating that some of the lapses occurred while he was driving or lighting the pellet stove.

Christine and I decided we would take a quick road trip to check on the situation. On the way down, we stopped at a rest stop in the middle of Oregon. Seated under an awning was a woman holding a cardboard sign for gas money. I knew her from prison, but I hardly recognized her. She was in her twenties but looked older than me.

Those damned drugs. I stood some distance away with my b.
and dug through my purse for food and money. When I d.
power bar and some money into her hat, I acted like a heartle.
ard. I made sure she did not see my face. I did not want to give ᵤr a
ride. I did not want to give her my jacket. I wanted distance from that
ugly past.

Christine saw me pass by the woman on the ground and give
her some money. "That was nice of you."

"I knew her from inside. She was kinda creepy." I snorted. "She
got caught smuggling a cookie in her underwear."

"Eeeew."

"She was gonna give it to her girlfriend."

Christine mocked gagged.

"Now that we're on the subject of prison, Sis, is there any unfin-
ished business between us that you would like to tell me?" I asked.
"Something I should know or understand about my incarceration?"

She was quiet, her eyes darting back and forth.

I encouraged her to speak. "I am on a damage-control patrol,
cleaning out the cobwebs. You can tell me."

She shrugged her shoulders and the tears started. "I just wanted
you to get out. I just couldn't wait."

My dear sister.

She shrugged off the sadness, smiled at me, backed out of the
rest stop, and we headed for Sam, our family defender to the end.

Christine and I saw with our own eyes that Sam was definitely
confused. Not all the time. But when he was, would it be in a life or
death situation? Christine had been the engine and the glue for the

family. She had a solid opportunity at retirement. She couldn't uproot now. If one of us should move, it should be me, for so many reasons.

I went home and told Nikki and Nate about the situation. It would have been better to seek their opinion, but I hadn't been doing that anyway, though I should have been. But the move felt like the only thing I could do for my dad and sister, who had done so much for me. No matter what, Sam needed me. I was out and free and he was still alive. I would miss my girls and I hoped they would visit, but it was time to let them focus on things that brought them joy. So often they told me that they could never truly be happy with me inside. It was time for them to lead their own lives without worrying about me. So I hired some movers, packed a POD with my humble bed frame, kitchen equipment, and my prized possession, a six-foot couch that my girls could sleep on if they visited.

I told Angel Boss and the company supervisor, Scott, the situation and that I would not be able to extend past a two-week notice. Gentle Angel Boss wished me luck. Scott hissed, "I'd *fire* someone to have you back." I needed to hear that.

Before I arrived in town, Sam drove to his physical therapist's office and asked him if he'd consider giving me an interview. The physical therapist knew my father well and saw him through hips, knees, and shoulders. When I arrived in Talent, Oregon, he told me about his conversation with the PT. Sam immediately began crying and it took a while for him to collect himself. "I told him everything," he finally said. "I discussed the accident, your injuries, the sentencing, incarceration, and ultimately your release. He's heard it all." Sam wiped his eyes and looked at me. "I'm so proud of you."

Sam hung his head and wept and so did I.

"You pulled through," he said. "There were so m
didn't think you would survive."

I rubbed circles on his back. I let him cry years of tea
tired of the fight. It was like Audrey had described in the visi   ᵧ ᵣᵤᵤₘ
at the prison. This aged him. It could not be undone.

I felt the familiar pull of guilt.

"Thank you for believing in me, Dad."

He looked up. "That will never change."

I made an appointment and met the PT at his clinic. He greeted
me like a long lost relative. I had turned in my résumé ahead of time
and we discussed it as we walked around the clinic admiring all the
bells and whistles of balance machines, whirlpool, and exercise equipment. Our meeting was less of an interview and more of an orientation. Sam got me the job. I would not have to start at the bottom again
and endure the agony of more criminal background checks. I had one
more break.

Later, Audrey drove me around the neighboring town of
Ashland, looking for an apartment. A woman was pounding a For
Rent sign into the grass at a condominium complex that was walking distance to the shops, restaurants, and theater it was famous for. I
joked with the woman as I walked up the driveway,

"I'll take it."

We went inside and toured. My heart was pounding in hope and
fear. Perhaps my selling point was that I came with my "mom." I let
Audrey's artful elegance pave the way while I filled out an application.

"Just fill out these lines." She pointed to the lines for contact,
employment, and references. "I don't care what you've done. I'm looking for people I can trust."

I practically saluted. I had a new home, a new job in a new town. After all the years of no sharing, no consoling, and "that's not your bunk area," I was going to be helpful. I would help the people who had given all they had for me and my daughters. Sam and I could work on projects again just as we did years ago when I was his pal.

In the evenings, I took walks and ate simple wonderful food. Still trying to make up for years without plant-based vitamins, my diet revolved around fresh vegetables and fruits. For a treat, I might eat a bowl of buttered noodles for dinner and have a spoonful of ice cream after breakfast, just because I could.

I did not make friends, let alone date or even make eye contact with men. The requirement of working in a medical setting meant confidentiality. Specifically, I could not talk about my past. Nor did I ask patients about theirs.

Outside of work, if an opportunity for friendship came up and I didn't tell the truth about my past, I would feel dishonest. If they found out, months or years later, they might feel betrayed. But I couldn't stand to come right out with it either. I had disappointed too many people. So instead I chose to isolate myself. It wasn't healthy but it was safe.

It was during this time that I opened the prison writing box that contained my journals, letters, scraps of the women's quotes, photos, drawings, the girls' art projects. The box contained the books of the writers that inspired me: Viktor Frankl, Garrison Keillor, Anne Lamott, Pema Chodron, Junot Díaz, and David Sedaris. At the bottom of the box was my trusty, taped-together, three-inch-thick paperback thesaurus.

It was time to do what I had promised my family and so many of the women inside: write. It was a mammoth undertaking. It would take months to organize before I could even begin. But I had a second-hand desk that sat under a second-floor window that looked out over a million-dollar view of the Rogue Valley. Ashland had four full seasons: warm days and starry skies in summer, multicolored foliage in fall, snow-peaked mountains in winter, and purple vetch on the hillsides in spring. It would be solitude, not loneliness, a chance to accept and transform the suffering and write my way out of that pit for good.

There was only one thing missing.

Bucket list number four: get a golden retriever. I had never had a dog of my own. All my life it had been everyone else's dog, including in prison. I had learned a great deal watching Top Dog train her puppies on J Unit. I wanted a gentle female that would be properly trained and would be free to go with me everywhere. My plan was to volunteer at the animal shelter and troll for my girl.

On one of my first shifts, I was asked to bring some animals to a garden/feed store, where they would be adopted out. Another woman volunteer and I loaded her car with cages and crates of kittens and small dogs. One of the dogs was a Chihuahua mix and the other was a Yorkie. The Chihuahua was a male and spent most of his time humping blankets and water bowls. The Yorkie didn't stand a chance in the same pen with that party boy, so I rescued her from the cage. She was trembling. Her bones were so delicate that even the Chihuahua could have snapped her in half. I needed a bigger dog, one I could hike with and hug on the floor.

I stood in front of the cages holding the Yorkie. Out of the corner of my eye, I saw two women from different parts of the store. Their eyes were locked on the Yorkie. The two women stock-car-raced with their shopping carts to the cages where I stood. One was an overly tanned, bleached blonde in pink slides who careened around the bags of chicken feed and ran into an aluminum tank filled with baby chicks. The tank stayed upright but the chicks were screeching. She didn't look back, just kept coming.

The other woman was a cowgirl with a kitchen haircut and roper boots. I put my money on her. I figured she knew how to cut an animal out of the herd. They were coming toward the cages from equal distances. I lowered my head like I was cuddling the dog, all the while darting my eyes left and right. This could be a fight, my first in the free world. I decided to throw the fight by side-stepping toward the wrangler, pretending I was rocking the quivering Yorkie. Pink Feet moved quicker than I expected. They both arrived at the exact same time.

The women began shouting at each other. "I was here first," pouted Pink Feet.

"Like hell you were," said Wrangler slowly and quietly. She folded her fists under her arms. The other volunteer's eyes were wide open and her mouth was in a tiny "o."

I played the part of a concerned dog handler, allowing the two to face off. But my weight was on my back foot and one of my elbows jutted out, protecting the Yorkie and my face. Gerry's son Michael would be proud.

Pink Feet's voice was escalating. She was shouting and baby dolling about how she always wanted a dog like the Yorkie. She waved one arm toward Wrangler and the other hand was on her expensive purse. She was either going to open up the purse for cash or swing it at Wrangler. Wrangler stared her down with her chin raised. Her fists remained against her ribs, under her arms. *Just like Mittens when she was holding back from taking a swing!*

"Ha!" I shouted with joy, remembering her talk, her lessons. I knew exactly what she would have said. An instant awareness came over me in that store as I faced off between the two women. I had graduated from prison. The lessons and experiences lived in my body. When they arose, they didn't have to drag me down. I had the self-confidence and power to choose what to do with the prison experiences. That day, the lesson from Mittens was a conflict resolution tool.

I assumed an expression of flat calm and kept my elbow high and my feet in a fighter's stance. I lifted a brow toward Wrangler, as if to say, *I got this. The dog is yours.* I channeled Mittens using my own dialect and turned to Pink Feet. "This isn't a showdown. You're in a feed store. What is it about this performance of yours that would make me think that you'd be a good dog mama to this little girl right here?" I lifted my bundle of shivering dog. "Woman, you don't even have the right footwear to take a dog outside to use the backyard. I couldn't trust you with the responsibility."

I turned to Wrangler. "This woman needs some anger management, for real."

I handed the Yorkie to Wrangler who untucked her ropy arms and held the Yorkie with surprising delicacy, keeping her eyes on Pink Feet.

Pink Feet pouted and seemed, at least I hoped, just a little intimidated by the badass animal shelter lady.

The other volunteer and I returned to the shelter with one of the cats and the shameless Chihuahua. I wondered if there was another dog for me in the pen area. I strolled the rows of doggie prison cells, noticing the majority were pit mixes or the ubiquitous short-haired dog that ran free on Mexican streets. They barked for attention with their faces at the bars. *I know how you feel, buddy.*

At the back of the dog area was a set of men working behind a chest-high cinder-block wall. The men were from the Jackson County work release program. I felt completely comfortable approaching the wall.

"Hey," I nodded, felon style. The men dressed in scrubs looked at each other then back at me. I casually draped an arm over the wall. "Whatcha got back there? Any golden retrievers?" I smiled hopefully.

The men looked at each other. One man looked at his feet, shuffling in the old shuck and jive. "We're not supposed to talk to anyone." He lifted his eyes, but didn't meet mine.

I snorted a laugh. "Said the rule followers." The men snickered and stole a glance up at me. I was smiling openly and it seemed to defuse the situation.

The closest man spoke. "We got a golden retriever today, just came in."

"Yeah," said the second. "Name's Thunder."

"Thunder! Whoa."

"He's due for a pee break. You wanna take him to the outside pen?"

"Hell yes, gentlemen!" I was dancing in place with excitement. The trustees went to a cage and brought forth a stunning blond-red male golden retriever. He was young, maybe two years old at the most. "He's beautiful! Why in the world would someone want to give him up?"

The men shrugged and shook their heads in agreement. As Thunder and I went through the rows of cells, the dogs went crazy. Some were desperately barking for attention, others lunged at the bars. Thunder burst through the doors and zoomed around the fenced

outdoor area, peeing and running full tilt. He was a beautiful handful. I had wanted a female, something a little less rambunctious, but I
could adjust. I returned Thunder to his keepers and asked what happened next.

"He needs to be quarantined for two weeks. Then he'll come up
for adoption."

I thanked the men and told them good luck with their parole.
Then I practically skipped to the front desk. An enormous, tired-look-
ing woman sat at a chair on the far side of the reception desk. I waited
at the counter.

"Yeah?"

"I think I found a dog!" I gushed. She sighed and chair-walked,
pulling on the counters instead of standing up to speak to me. She
took out a form, slapped it on the counter.

"Which pen number?" she asked, not looking at me adding a
pen to the counter.

"It's one of the new ones, Thunder!"

She looked up, her eyes narrowed.

"You're not supposed to be back there. Just because you're a volunteer you got nothin' comin'. You have to wait the two weeks like
everybody else." *Got nothin' comin'. Top Dog again.* I looked over her
shoulder at a pet adoption calendar.

"I'd like to confirm, that would be Tuesday, the twenty-first?"

The woman grunted and swiveled on her chair, pushing on the
counter. "Yes. Not a day earlier."

I was undaunted. "What time do you open?"

"Eleven a.m. Bring a leash."

The day came and I had arranged for Sam to come and pick me up at the PT clinic. I stressed that we needed to be there early. I had brought a leash and a pad for the car ride home. The car pulled up to the clinic. Audrey was behind the wheel, Sam was riding shotgun looking like he was on a grand adventure. Audrey subtly indicated that it was better that she drive.

We stood at the door of the shelter. I planned to be the first one in. The door was opened by a cheerful brunette, a good omen. I dashed to the dog room, found an employee, and told her I was hoping to adopt the golden retriever that was up for adoption today.

"Which one? The male or the female?" she asked.

"Female?" I gaped.

"Yeah, brother and sister. The male got her pregnant on her first heat. Sixteen puppies. I guess the husband brought them home to his pregnant wife and two-year-old son. Can you imagine?"

A female! My heart was pounding.

"She's over here." She started walking down the second row. "She's still wet, just out of the bath."

I stepped to a cell with bars on the door. At the back of the cell sat a soggy, russet-colored golden retriever. I crouched down to say hello. She walked to the bars, put her forehead in my hand, and just stood there. That was it.

"I'll take her," I said, not moving.

"Do you want to take her outside and walk around with her?"

"Does she have to go potty?"

The woman just stood there smiling at us. "Sure, she might have to go."

I shrugged. Sam and Audrey found me outside. My beautiful girl was sniffing the scents of other dogs. She jumped once on hind feet to see out the fencing then came back to me. I crouched down and she lay down on my feet, putting her head on my leg. Her coat was starting to dry and her fur rustled in the breeze. Her back was red, her sides were blond, and her belly was white. She was all the colors of the golden retriever rainbow.

"Here she is!" Sam came squirming forward, talking in a sing-song voice, greeting the new member of the family. "Oh, she's so sweet!"

"Does she have a name?" Audrey asked.

I wanted her to forget about her past life, poor thing. "Her new name is Clover, from the Etta James song, 'At Last.'" I sang, *"At last, My dog has come along, My heart is wrapped up in clover."* Clover looked up at me. "The lyrics are supposed to be *at last my love has come along* but 'dog has come along' sounds good to me. Right, Clover?" Clover dipped her nose under my hand and lifted it so it would land on her head for a pet.

Once Clover and I were settled, I enrolled Clover in Therapy Dogs International and trained her to be a therapy dog. She didn't have the skills of the Canine Companions. Her only real skill was comfort. I brought her to the clinic from time to time when I had a fearful patient. Clover distracted the knee replacement patients while I bent their knees. Clover didn't care if I had made mistakes in my past. She didn't judge my isolation from the world as I sorted scraps of quotes for the book. In fact, she thrived on it. I'd like to think she was home, at last.

In my new town, it was Clover, Sam and Audrey, and me. But then I met Emily at the clinic. Emily was a beauty inside and out and spoke with a Tennessee drawl. She was a dedicated humanitarian and volunteer. For one of her projects, a fundraiser, she posed as a senior calendar girl showing off an ageless pair of legs.

"Honey, let's meet for coffee sometime," she asked after an appointment. My heart said yes. But I knew I would have to tell her my story. I hoped she would still want to be my friend. We met at a quiet local coffee shop, and she hugged me and called me "Dew Drop" or some other pet name. I took a sip of coffee and dove into my story. She listened to the whole thing, leaning in and keeping her soft eyes on mine.

"I could tell something was goin' on." She nodded. "I understand what it's like to be the underdog. My people had to flee Egypt and have been overcoming struggle for years." She waved her bracelets.

She invited me to her temple to attend a fundraiser. "It's a benefit concert for one of our long-time members who had a massive stroke. He was a brilliant musician who had a heart for charity. His son died, he was only fifteen. It was heartbreaking. After Hurricane Katrina wiped out New Orleans, he closed his music store and brought everything down there, donating and repairing instruments."

"Oh my god," I said, recognition thrumming in my veins. "I know him." My heart pounded in the glory of kismet. "Peter."

I told her the story about the telephone encounter I had with Peter when I worked for the DMV. "How bad is the stroke, Emily?"

"It's bad but he's still in there." Emily shook her head. "He lost most of one side. You need to write to him. Tell him who you are and how much he helped you. Tell him everything." And so I did. I thanked him for rescuing me in my darkness. I told him I would be at his fundraiser.

The day came. Emily and I met at the temple. Peter was sitting in a middle pew. The stroke had been devastating. He drooped to one side, his arm in a sling. At a break in the music, I walked over to introduce myself and waited my turn among the well-wishers gathered around him.

When I stood before him, he knew immediately who I was. He struggled to stand, and I struggled to keep my emotions in check. The others around him looked at this stranger and wondered who I was. I reached down to help, taking his good hand, and he made it to his feet. I held his good hand and reached for his affected hand, unfurling it so it could be held. We spoke with our eyes. We cried tears of loss and struggle and tears of survival.

Sam never slowed down and neither did the progression of his dementia. Soon he required 24/7 supervision. I was still working full time, so Audrey hired a wonderful home aid, Louise. Christine took early retirement and moved down to the Rogue Valley as well. Together we tag-teamed as long as we could, then Sam was placed in assisted living.

But Sam kept trying to go home. The facility called him "a runner." Compared to all the degrading descriptions Americans use for our elders, like "long in the tooth" and "over the hill," "runner" still has some appeal. Sam was eventually moved to a nightmare memory facility. It broke our hearts to see him there. Louise found a note Sam had written himself before his final tragic placement: *Check out of body.*

By this time, I was driving. One day I rescued him from the memory madhouse, tucked him into the front seat of the car with a blanket and a cup of hot chocolate, and we drove through the valley to one of his favorite fishing lakes. I played Sam's favorite music: Enya,

Beethoven, and some mournful Scottish ballads. Sam fell asleep. "You can let go now, Dad," I whispered. "You could die right here with me." He came close. Still holding his cup of hot chocolate in both hands, his breathing slowed and his head dropped to his chest. But the breaths continued. I drove for two hours, reluctantly returning him to the memory care facility. By the end of the day, he suffered an undiagnosed event and the family arranged for hospice. Sam drifted in and out. He came to once and said, "Oh, sorry, sweetheart. I guess I drifted off into my thoughts."

"Your thoughts are a good place to be," I told him. "I love you, Dad."

"You have always done a good job of showing me that," he said. Those were his last words to me. I had disappointed many people. To hear that this rare, magical man knew that I loved him was one of my greatest accomplishments.

Christine sat sentry through the night on Sam's final days. The night he died, she called to tell me how he'd gone. She was buoyant. "The last time he sat up on the edge of the bed, he said, 'Jesus?'" Then he asked Christine, "Do you see him? He's right there."

"Of all people!" I said.

"He lay back down. His breathing was uneven. He gasped and that was it."

I laugh-cried.

"The men came to take him away. Sam requested to go in the nude—no surprise there." She laughed in approval. "They zipped him up and were taking him out the door, and I thought, wait a second. I reached into the top shelf of his closet and grabbed a T-shirt and laid it on top of the body bag."

"Which one was it?" I asked, bobbing along on her joy and relief.

"The one that said, 'As Is.'"

Later that summer, the family gathered to scatter Sam's ashes at Ashland's Emigrant Lake. Sam's chosen son and dear friend, Dennis, stood atop a rock outcropping beside the lake, prepared to scatter the ashes in the water. Dennis focused on his thoughts for a few moments, as we did, then tossed the ashes toward the water. A playful gust of wind swirled the ashes high above our heads in a glorious plume, then they floated in the breeze toward the lake and settled into the gentle waves—Sam's showy, wondrous goodbye.

Audrey arranged a graceful memorial with eulogies that lasted for two hours. The eulogies of his grandchildren Travis, Shane, Nikki, and Haley were the best of the bunch and a testament to his legacy.

It had been three years since release and I still hadn't written a word. It took great emotional energy to move forward. Each time I opened the box for the book, I was yanked back to slamming doors, obedience, and separation from my family. Clover was a wonderful helper. She knew just when to put her paw on top of mine and stare at me. *Let's go for a walk.*

It was my original intention to write a guidebook because I had wondered so many things before sentencing. There was so much I hadn't known. I organized piles from the scraps of paper with the women's quotes. I picked through them, and each one conjured a picture, recreating scene after scene. *She won't get in the driveway at my house. Sinful.* I knew exactly where we were sitting and with whom. I could see Sinful leaning into the table giving her speech, then sitting back with a smug look on her face, pleased with her wit.

I could see Mittens strutting up and down the cell, stopping to smooth out her hair or cross her arms to contain her fists. I recalled her leaning over my bunk, slowing down her story just so I could get every word of slang right.

What started as a survival guide shifted to being a story about all of the women I once feared. What to do with all this? I needed help. I recruited help from writing coach Kate Hopper and Michelle Smith, a brilliant writer and my father's former associate.

Kate read that first draft and called it a "beautiful mess."

"This has to be a memoir. Who are you in the book? *Where* are you in the book? Why would I trust you to tell me about this horrible, painful situation if I don't know who you are? I want to know these women. Who is Sinful? Tell me more about Gerry. How did your daughters feel about visiting you in prison?"

She hit a nerve. My daughters. As difficult as it was to go back into the stories of prison, it didn't compare to trying to unravel the complicated stress that compromised our family for so many years.

Oh God, Oh Alida's God, God of mercies that are new every morning. Help me. The Great I Am answered: "Call Blondie."

"Oh, baby, it's so good to hear from you." I could just picture her, lifting both shoulders and wiggling, even if she was sitting down. "Are you still writing the book?"

I sighed. "Yes, when I have the energy to go back in."

"You've got to do this," she said. "*Orange Is the New Black* is a start but someone has to tell the stories of the women in a full prison." She sighed. "We're the lost, baby. I don't want to say it, but we're the

Donner Party. You keep writing and let people know we are people like everyone else."

"I'm trying," I said, "but some days it rips me up. I've been writing about Sinful and Angel. I've been writing a little about the cops, too. But now I've been told by my editors that I have to write about myself." I whined, "I have to write about who I am and what I did and how it affected my family."

"Oh, baby, kill yourself now. You thought prison was bad!" Blondie chuckled.

"I have to go to my friends and family and ask, *What was it like for you and what did you go through while I was in prison?*" I paused and she waited. "They were protecting us, Blonds."

"Yeah, huh?" Blondie let out a long sigh.

"I have to ask them how they suffered, I have to say, *Tell me everything*. I asked my sister if she had anything she needed to say. She told me just wanted me out. Said she couldn't wait."

"There's one in your corner," Blondie quipped.

"I'm scared to ask them. It's like poking a hornet's nest. How did that go for you? Did you ask your sons to describe what really went on?"

"Boys do it another way," said Blondie. "I'd open my mouth, say somethin' stupid, and they'd just crush me. Like they were savin' it up. Boys keep it locked up inside. Ya never know when it's comin'. Out of nowhere, they'd *roast* me and say, 'Do you know what those years were like? Do you have any idea what we went through while you were gone? You missed so much.'"

I could picture her, confused and hurt.

"But I'm lucky. They're still with me."

I needed a little more confidence before I spoke to the girls. Gerry had been a pillar of honest reflection during the entire ordeal. I knew where I stood with her. I decided to call Loretta, as well. When she answered, she was in the car running one set of grandchildren to one event and picking up another one from school.

"Bad time?"

"It's always like this!" she said over the car speaker. "The car is a great place to talk. All these kids are buckled in place."

I could picture her driving the hills and valleys of her town, Boring, Oregon. Ironic—her life was anything but boring.

"It's about the book," I said. "The editor wants blood. I have to talk about myself and my family. So I am going around mopping up after my big mistake. Is there anything you'd like to tell me, anything I should know?"

Loretta sighed and said very slowly and softly, "I hate that you and your family suffered. But you had a chance to take a hard look at yourself and take inventory. You are a better person now." She paused and I could hear the sound of the car coming to a stop. "Bye-bye, have fun!" And then I heard the slam of the car door. "You are so hard on yourself, Karen. It makes it hard on other people."

"It's this damned book."

"Finish it," she said.

Next I called Jack. It was morning and he'd just finished listening to NPR. He immediately went into a castigation of the ignoramuses of the political world, then switched to the report of his previous evening walk around the venerable streets of northwest Portland that included a light meal at his favorite restaurant. About five minutes in, he switched his tack.

"What's going on with the book? How come it's not out yet?"

"I'm working and working on the book. The editor says it has to be a memoir. I have to write myself into the book. It's awful. All the black doors are open. I am bleeding on the page."

"Yep. That's the way to do it." He chuckled. "Life is not a fairy tale."

"Got a question," I said.

"Shoot."

"Is there anything you want to tell me?" I asked.

Jack was quiet, which was unusual.

"You've changed. You are a different, more mature, thoughtful Karen than before," said Jack. "Six years of confinement fostered a lot of introspection, brought out your literary talents, and made you sharper mentally, almost to the point of abruptness. You have lost some of your shimmer. I have to get used to a more removed Karen, but it's clear you want nothing more of either your old life or your life in the joint. Despite what you had to endure, you are better for it."

He paused, I waited.

"I miss you. I miss our dinners out as the Widow's Club."

When we said goodbye, I promised to make the time for a Widow's Club meeting at a restaurant in his neighborhood. In my desire to call up the people closest to me and ask what they thought, it helped to hear that a man as savvy as Jack thought I was mature and introspective and he trusted me to handle constructive criticism. Had I become abrupt because after living with fools in prison, I no longer suffered them? Had I lost my people skills? The thing that stuck with me and still does is that I'd lost some of my shimmer. What a terrible thing to lose.

Of the family, Audrey was the first on the list, our family truth-teller. Her command of the English language cuts to the core so elegantly that you don't even know you are bleeding. I invited Audrey to lunch at a restaurant on the creek in Ashland. After the waitress took our order, I dove in. "I need to ask you something. I would like you to tell me what you went through after the accident. I need to hear it."

At first she seemed shocked and sat very still. "Do we really have to talk about this?" she asked. Then she laid both hands on the table and faced me. "Could we *please* talk about this?" The question opened the door to a gaping black hole, a wilderness. *They have been waiting for this.*

Audrey spoke to me unaware of the tears rolling down her cheeks. "If you are going to ask us how we feel, you must understand that it will be real and raw."

I mirrored her pose, face-to-face, hands on the table. "I have to know," I said. "I thought when I got out, our troubles would be behind us. But we are suffering and it's my fault. I am willing to throw myself forward and I know it's gonna hurt. But I need to know so I can apologize, fully informed."

Audrey turned her whole body toward me, keeping her hands on the table. "The accident, your physical recovery, the legal battles, and prison took over all of our lives," she said. "We had little else left over to tend to ourselves." She paused, her eyes remained on mine. "Your father was never the same. It took a toll on him mentally and physically."

My heart sank in my chest, deep-knowing. "Every time he visited, it looked like he had aged five years," I said. "He might still be alive if all this hadn't happened." The life toll just kept coming, the accident like a poison. I pushed on, "What was it like to watch your husband age before your eyes?"

She shook her head, resigned. "He wouldn't have done it any other way."

"What about you?" I asked.

She paused and gathered her thoughts. "By some delicious accident, I was a safe harbor for the girls and their tears. And even after you got out, I get to keep helping them so they could ease back into a life that makes sense."

I knew this was true. It was evident every time the family got together. My daughters gravitated to Audrey and Christine. I watched the ease with which my daughters laughed or cuddled with them. I hated myself for envying their connection. The harder I grasped for my daughters, the further they stayed away.

"Once you were out," Audrey continued, "I wondered, am I still useful in your life? It's hard to know, you never admit to your weaknesses, you keep them to yourself." Audrey sat back in her chair, looking out at the creek. "I don't see you as tentative as you were when you first got out. I feel your gratitude and grace. But your frailty and pain override your trust that we love you *as you are*," she emphasized.

I nodded to indicate I understood the concept. But a cruel voice inside me whispered, *as you are? Worthy?* I stared down at the creek to hide my tears. I watched the water flow downstream. In that span of seconds, I heard the voice of Pastor Alida. She grabbed me by the back of the neck and shook me a little bit: "*We will neva get it roight. Isn't it maavelous? We are forgiven!*"

"Thank you for showing up for your life and asking us how we feel," said Audrey, shaking me back to the present. "Such great stuff, nothing tidy about it."

I looked at her. I knew she could see my frailty. I knew the talks like this were not over. I also knew I was on the right track.

While I was incarcerated, our family kept the communication between us on middle ground, shaving off the highs and lows. We didn't burden one another. I spared my family the unfathomable realities of prison life, as I suspected they protected me from theirs. We each wanted the other to make it to the other side. But the protection separated us from the truth of what was taking place in our lives. Each of us went about our lives hoping that things would smooth out. But they never did. We carried a heavy load and we needed to break the shell.

The girls were in town for a visit. I prepared them ahead of time and asked them to please tell me the truth about what it had been like for them. I spoke to Nikki alone first. We sat outside. In between her words, I planned to stare at the plants that grew tall just behind her. I was afraid of what she might say.

"Your accident, then your prison time was just one very difficult part," Nikki began.

I knew the pain was coming.

"But when you came out of prison, we all had to adjust again. It's another enormous phase. As you got closer to release, I grew worried. All the things I had been so angry about resurfaced and fused with new fears." Nikki was composed, my heart was pounding.

"All you could do was talk about the things you were going to do and where you were going to live. I didn't hear myself in the narrative at all. It hurt me so deeply. I had sacrificed so much for you—my time, my money, my energy, my college years. I felt I was living for you. The second you wouldn't need me, I would be cast aside."

I did not look at the plants, just watched my daughter telling her truth. This new awareness of how she suffered broke my heart. It explained why she never really laughed around me, only the tiny smile.

"You were so determined to show me that I could go back to my own life," she continued. "You wanted desperately to relieve me from taking care of you. You were ashamed of how much you affected my life."

I had been writing her words as she went. This slowed down the conversation, nothing edited out. I looked at her and then looked at the pages that contained the years of pain, effort, and disappointment. I was willing right then to stop writing the book, leave the past in the past. "Will you be OK if I write about this and how you feel?" I asked.

"I need you to write this story about our family. People said I had anger problems. This is my story of what happened and why I was so angry. I want people to know." She looked me in the eyes. "Think of the thousands of dollars you are saving on the family's therapy, letting us all say what we need to say. I wanted acknowledgment from you for everything I sacrificed and became resentful when I didn't get it."

"What would you say to someone else going through something like this?" I asked.

"Give the person in transition a lot of space," she said. "Give them a chance to show what they can do. The fewer expectations you have, the less you will be disappointed by small things that probably won't matter in the end, and pace yourself for a long transition."

"How are you now? Are you still angry?" I asked.

"I am finally in a place where I am happy. I don't expect anything from you. I don't overthink your intentions. I have examined and reassembled my identity so many times, I'm tired. I don't want to be held to some unattainable standard anymore. I hope I can allow myself and others that freedom. When you go through something like this, you know forever that the people you love and love you are the only things that matter in the world. They bring meaning to everything. They make the hard times bearable and the good times extraordinary."

There was no embrace afterward. She remained standing. I knew the people who were the only things that mattered in the world were the people who saw her through the struggle. Nate, Haley, her father. Sam, Christine, Audrey, and a few trusted friends had stepped into the role as her people. She and I were on better footing and working out her description of a long transition. She had sacrificed years of her life for me. I had never loved her more.

Haley was next. Every time I saw her we had to catch up because I missed being with her when she grew from a girl to a woman. Her life was in California. She had her father, her boyfriend, her friends, and a golden retriever of her own. A four-month gap of time was about our limit. Although we talked on the phone, it was not the same as being there. I had no idea what a typical day for her would be. I didn't know her favorite flavor of ice cream anymore. I didn't know what brought her joy or what caused her pain. The same was true for her when she thought of me.

"You've changed," said Haley. "You still have a kind and gentle spirit, but prison had a big impact on you. You are more guarded now. You had to process a lot in a very difficult and isolated place."

I listened, writing everything down.

"I learned some things too," she continued. "I learned firsthand that inmates are not the thugged-out monsters we assume. You were not the only one who was a good person and made a mistake. I would grant a second chance to someone who has changed."

"I am hoping that the book will help, but it will take upstanding family members like you to give society's undesirables a voice," I said. "That's hard work for you and you have already suffered so much."

"I told you this before; I need you to write this book. It kept me going at Christmas and all the other 'firsts' that you missed."

"The holidays were rough," I said.

"While you were in prison, I had to facilitate our family gatherings. When you got out, it changed again. You naturally went back to your role as the mom, the facilitator. But I am no longer a child and I'm not sure where I fit in sometimes. I spent years putting in the effort to see family, Auntie Christine, Drew, Gramps, and Grandma. Our relationships blossomed. I know you have felt that. They see how uncomfortable you are, so they back away. They are protecting you. I feel like I've lost that closeness with them and I feel lost as we all try to find our identity and adjust our roles."

In between writing, I stared at her. I saw the changes in her face and committed them to the updated memory of what my youngest child now looked like. I still saw the child I used to cuddle on the couch, stroking her hair and holding her feet. But she was a grown woman now and, perhaps reading my mind, she told me so.

"I've had to pick myself up and put on my pants, one leg at a time, and go to work. I am not the baby anymore." That was abundantly clear. I was so proud of her.

Those conversations were the beginning of healing, real healing. Since then, it has been years of both messy and glorious days. When the girls and I visit, it begins with a happy reunion. Then my smoldering lack of confidence creeps in and I fawn and grovel for their attention. It is exhausting for them.

Meanwhile, I continued to write the book, plugging away year after year. I'd say to myself, *I owe it to the women. My children said it kept them going.* With each bloodletting on the page, there was a notion that something was missing, something had been left out. I kept rewriting the last chapter, searching for a better ending.

Finally I set a deadline. On the morning I was revising the final pages, an emerging thought came closer and closer. The thought was dark and terrifying. I felt heavy, my eyes blurred and my stomach dropped. I had been standing and had to grab the desk or surrender to the downward pull of the words that were forming.

"I am damaged."

I began to weep, instantly. "Prison. It damaged me. I see it now, *of course*, I am damaged." I felt like I was falling again.

The faces of the women swam before my eyes. I remember asking Celly, "What kind of women do they turn out of here?" She had answered, "Fucked-up people who don't even know how to hug someone anymore."

I had learned so many of the wrong things. I learned how to swipe an extra fruit and hide it up a sweatshirt sleeve. I learned how to compartmentalize and deny my emotions. I learned how to be meek and obedient instead of using critical thinking skills. In fact, I learned my opinion didn't matter at all. I learned how to live away from society and inclusion. I learned how to go without human touch. I was watched and observed at all hours of the day and I learned that I was not to be trusted. I paroled from prison believing I was not worthy of trust, inclusion, or love.

"Prison was really, really bad," I wept out loud, doubling over. Images swam before my eyes of echoing hallways, wool blankets, and slamming doors. I saw the women inmates sitting at metal tables, staring into space, heartsick with loneliness and uselessness. We had done something horrible, something that couldn't be undone. We buried the shame of our mistakes deep in our bodies so we could focus on physical and mental survival. We didn't heal in prison. We were lucky to survive it. That's why so many women ended up back there. They hadn't healed. Drugs and old patterns that lead to crime are easier than overcoming the endless emotional work of redemption.

On my final day of writing, I looked at my desktop, scattered with notes and quotes of the women. I had been so preoccupied with their stories I neglected to write my own. Beside the desk were pictures of my family: Nikki, Haley, Christine, Sam, and Clover. They had never left my side. "They love me," I said out loud, surprised at myself. *Not, I hope they love me, or how could they love me? But, they love me.* "My family loves me," I said again. Why hadn't I been able to believe that earlier? They had always loved me, even though I made a devastating mistake, even though I was locked up, away from them all those years.

I thought of all we had been through: the accident, the recovery, the courts, lawyers, and sentencing. Then came six years of prison, missed holidays. and rites of passage. When I got ready to parole, I wondered what would I say to my family who had waited for me? I'm coming out, but I am a mess? I am emotionally scarred and changed? I couldn't do that. So I denied any damage, tamped down the emotional baggage, and pasted a smile on my face. I got out and got busy reestablishing myself, wanting desperately for them to return to their lives and not worry about me. I withdrew from the world, kept only old friends, not trusting that anyone new could handle the truth of my past. I stood at my desk and looked out the window where life was going on. *I have been locked up, still, and I did it to myself.*

I felt a swirl of warm air spiraling upward in my body. It was a feeling of levity. Just as I watched the birds circle above the prison yard, I felt I was circling with a current, climbing higher, becoming lighter. I felt weightless. Then I knew what had been holding me back. *Confidence. Self-worth.* I was so burdened with self-judgment that despite what my family told me, I was not confident that they could or even should love me. This was the damage.

My family had loved me all this time. They wanted it—prison, the book, everything—over.

"I am the one holding us back."

The crushing weight of prison just a few minutes earlier was gone. I laughed out loud, "I'm not perfect but I am included and I am worthy. They love me!" I was released. It was freedom for all of us. Only now could we really begin to put this behind us.

I will never forget Tom or the woman I killed in the accident. I will carry the weight of my crime and the damage of the prison experience for the rest of my life. It is *in* me. But it does not define me. I am Karen, a dog lover, an honest worker, a mother, and the little girl who sang to Winnie-the-Pooh, and I am good. It is that essence that continues to move ahead, clearing out the weeds and planting seeds of worthiness, self-confidence, and joy.

On days that I'm floundering, which I do, still, I go to the water's edge. I go to the place I scattered Sam's ashes and think of all those who have gone before. The creek gurgles down the valley and feeds the pear blossoms in the spring. I shout to the moon and stars for the women inmates. I say a prayer for Sam, for Marshall, for my mother, for the woman in the other car, and for Tom.

I do not feel Tom like I used to. He has moved on. So must I. I understand now that I am a part of a story of failure and redemption, but that the story will continue, will be woven with new stories—stories of hope and compassion. So I stare out at the moving water, take a deep breath, stand up straight, and take my next best step.

EPILOGUE

Land v. (landing) 1. To bring into or cause to arrive at a particular place, position, or condition; 2. To accept the status of an ex-felon but identify as a successful parolee, dedicated to restoring justice to the people he or she harmed; 3. To be accepted by family and society; 4. To look deeply at oneself, take inventory and let go of personal suffering for everyone's sake, because we are no longer broken.

I was released on April Fool's Day, 2011, and finally finished this book in 2020. The healing process for my people was like a great big ship in a little tiny harbor. Our ship turned slowly and clumsily, lurching forward and putt-putting backward, making *a-ooga* noises, bumping into things. But in steadiness and faith, the ship passed out of the port and is headed for open water.

In each retelling of this story, the weight of shame slips further away. Every April Fool's Day, I reflect, ask forgiveness, and celebrate spring. Because I've realized that I didn't survive to suffer; I survived to do something good.

Epilogue

This morning, almost a decade after I was released from prison, I walk up the stairs to my humble office with its million-dollar view. I pause before I enter the room, and unseen, observe the pair already there: Clover and the tender, steady man I have dared to love. He sits drawing, or trying to, with Clover resting her muzzle on his thigh. I watch as Clover then bumps the crook of his elbow, *Pet me, pet me.* He admonishes her with a chuckle, and I walk into the room with a smile.

GLOSSARY

Big House: Penitentiary, the Slammer, full custody prison, not some soft-time summer camp.

bubble: A glass outpost assigned to a DOC staff person for security/observation. Job requirement: stay awake and watch the same women day after day, sitting and watching TV.

the cage: A chain-link dog kennel, sides and top, human-size. It is used in Segregation for one hour of outdoor privileges, once a week.

call-out: Posted list of the inmate's daily schedule.

canteen: A source for inmates to purchase items to supplement the basic issue of bedding, prison scrubs or blues, worn-out tennis shoes, baking soda toothpaste, lye soap. The primary purchases: tennis shoes, junk food, ramen soup, and instant coffee. Tampons, shampoo, toothpaste must be purchased from inmate paychecks. Starting pay is $0.90/hr.

cell-in: The inmate is required to go her cell and stay there. It can be for security reasons, dayroom closure, or discipline. It is a prison "time-out."

cheeking: Placing medication under the tongue or tucked into the cheek for recreational use, for sale, and trade, or for storage.

Chomo, Cho: Child molester or anyone with a child-related crime. It is the lowest level of hell in prison.

Con Marché: A large blue recycle bin in each unit that contains clothing meant to be returned to the clothing room. The Con Marché is a place to trade up and improve your status. This is also against the rules and teaches an honest woman how to steal.

Cops, Po-Po, PO-lice, Badges, Guards, Pigs/Bacon, Officer: The staff of DOC. Their preferred description is similar to the military, beginning with the uniformed officer, corporal, sergeant, lieutenant, captain.

counting jiggs: Spotting for skullduggery. The primary post outside the showers while two or more women have hasty sex. Looking out for a planned fight.

crop dusting, drive-by: Anonymous and planned flatulence used as a passive-aggressive weapon against the staff of DOC.

Cutter: Person who causes self-harm with a lady shaver, or something even blunter.

Dayroom: The living room of the unit. It includes TVs, tables, laundry, telephones, the call-out bulletin board, all under the command of the officer's podium, aka "the bubble."

DOC: Department of Corrections, The Man, the power machine.

D.R.: Disciplinary Report. Progressive discipline: cell-in, loss of job, busted from the Honor Unit.

Exorcist: A head-spinning punch on the jaw.

fall: Arriving and beginning a sentence in prison. It is the day that creates a definitive line in your life and the life of your loved ones; life before prison and during prison.

fishing: The game of passing items back and forth under the cell door in Segregation.

Front Street: 1. A location across from the podium or some other obviously visible location; 2. To be personally revealed either by your own hand or someone else's betrayal.

flat back ho, top dolla' ho, golf cart ho, snow ho: Flat back: A ho who actually has to lie down to get paid instead of payment for the pleasure of her company. Top dolla' ho: Expensive call girl. A golf cart ho: A woman who works the seniors on the golf courses in a cart. A snow ho rides snowmobiles between ice houses.

ho bath/PTA: Pussy, tits, and ass cleanup in the sink.

Hole, Hole time: Living/doing time in Segregation, then resuming time at the bottom of the pecking order.

ho stro: Whore street, the corner, the turf, the beat of a prostitute's territory; swagger.

in the vest: Certifiably having a break in mental health. It is both literal and figurative. Women are placed in a restraining garment to avoid harm to self and others, mostly self.

kick-down: Share a creature comfort such as a cup of coffee to get another person over the hump.

kite, kiting: The written message system in prison.

Lifer: A person serving a prison sentence of twenty-five years or more, or to the end of her life. Life "without" means they will die locked up. The Man does not suffer fools.

Glossary

LOP: Loss of privileges. It is a prison misdemeanor and you are celled in. You are required to wear a lime green shirt, which makes observation easier for the cops and the overhead cameras.

MacGyver, MacGyvering: Based on the 1980s television secret agent who could take simple items and recycle them into weapons or survival tools.

Mean School: In-service training for DOC and volunteers for how to behave among inmates, renewing mistrust.

mean mug: A look of aggression.

Mean Mug School: tutoring in how to make a mean mug.

mug shot: Photo taken for criminal records that will follow you the rest your life.

off the hook, off the chain: Crazy/loco, not in a silly way but a disturbed, dangerous way.

on the chain: To be shackled with other women for transport/mobility.

Orders of Conduct: Conditions of Parole/Post-Prison Supervision. These are the laws a parolee must maintain to stay out of trouble. Parolees must pay for parole.

pat-down: The inmate stands in the star position, the cop slides gloved hands along sleeves, ribs, back and the Playtex cross-your-heart region, legs, socks, and a sweep at the intersection of the inner thigh and genital region.

P.C.'d up: Protective custody status. An inmate is State property and, to avoid damage to its property, the State places inmates in Segregation or a single cell. These folks are typically Chomos, snitches, or perpetrators of crimes so foul, it repulses seasoned inmates.

prison friends: Temporary, aggrandized friendships inside; most are terminated upon release.

rape-o status: Looking or behaving like such a clueless loser that you could be raped.

recidivists: Those who return to prison after release. It has to be the worst that can happen to a person, second only to the death of a child.

roll up: To pack up your meager belongings into plastic bags and move.

skins, strip search, squat and cough: A body search down to the skin, including a squat and cough.

snitch, a teller: An informant to DOC or a rival gang, resulting in outcast status. A danger to both inmates and staff alike.

stretch: A lengthy prison sentence.

tank: Intake holding cell in a jail or prison.

tossed: Cell search for contraband.

ACKNOWLEDGMENTS

I am grateful to my family, who encouraged me to write this book: my beloved daughters, Nikki and Haley; my steadfast sister, Christine; and true-blue friend, Gerry Barra. Thank you to the helpers: Audrey, Patty Zeid, Robin McGregor, Loretta McGregor, Jack Horner, and Clover.

I am grateful to my mentors and supporters: Michelle Smith, John Haines, Alida Little, Gwen Kisei Martin, Randi Getshushin Bronx, Owen Smith, Terry Noxon, and the teachers at the Living Yoga Foundation and the Art of Living.

To editor Kate Hopper and publicity production agent Cornelius Matteo, I thank you for your belief in this project. It is because of you that *Falling* came to fruition.

To my father Sam, who cried tears of pride over my simple health booklet for Coffee Creek Correctional Facility, thank you, I miss you. Here it is.

Thank you to my tenderhearted mate, Tom Giordano, who listened as I read aloud the stories. It was your laughter and tears that confirmed I had something important to tell the citizens of this country.

Standing day after day, and year after year, on hard floors, I wish good health to the staff of the Department of Corrections. I am grateful for those who extended dignified kindness to me and my family and the other inmates of Coffee Creek.

Finally, I thank the women inmates of the Coffee Creek Correctional Facility. It was your tenderness and patience that taught me how to survive six years in prison. I am honored you trusted me with your stories. I share them now with the intent to humanize not just you, but all the prison inmates in the United States. I have hope and confidence that by sharing our stories we can move prison reform toward a better way up and out.